Henry Neville
and
The Shakespeare Code

Henry Neville
and
The Shakespeare Code

Brenda James

MUSIC FOR STRINGS

Copyright © Brenda James, 2008

All rights reserved. No part of this book may be reproduced or transmitted in any form, electronic or otherwise, without written permission from the publishers.

Published by MUSIC FOR STRINGS
9 Hambledon Place, Bognor Regis, West Sussex, United Kingdom, PO21 2NE
Email for orders and enquiries: sales@musicforstrings.com
website: www.musicforstrings.com

ISBN: 978-1-905424-05-4

Contents

Acknowledgements

First of all, as always, my sincere and loving thanks go to my family, without whose patience, understanding and practical help none of this work would have been possible.

The following people have also given their kind support, and I shall here not even attempt to place them in any order of precedence:

Robin Wade, Wade and Doherty Literary Agency; Dr. John Casson (who has written such erudite and original Papers for *The Journal of Neville Studies*), Dr. Emanuela Handman and Professor James Goding, George Sayn [for his infectious and constant enthusiasm about the whole project], the late Mark Barty King, John Julius, Lord Norwich, Nicholas Prosser, Tim Cornish.

Many thanks to David Keys for pointing out to me the archaeological research which uncovered the wreck of a ship containing Gresham cannons destined for Denmark.

My special thanks go to Petros Palamidas who kindly translated the first half of the Greek inscription on the near-life-sized portrait of Sir Henry Neville, now in Audley End House. He was also able to say that the second half of the inscription was definitely a cipher, though it used some Greek letters. However, the translation Petros gave of the first half - 'Everywhere without ...' enabled me to track down the work from which the inscription was quoting. Neville and his friend, Sir Henry Savile, were Greek scholars, and both were also democrats, against any form of absolute monarchy. One of the main anti-monarchical Greek writers was Thucydides, so it did not take too long to find the whole quotation to which the unencrypted first half of the Neville inscription was alluding. It comes from Thucydides' history of the Peloponnesian Wars:

> *The whole earth is the tomb of heroic men, and their story is not graven in stones over their clay but abides **everywhere without visible symbol**, woven into the stuff of other men's lives.*

This is such an appropriate quotation for a 'concealed poet' to have placed on his portrait. Sir Henry Neville was concealing his authorship yet, by this half-encrypted quotation, at once revealing that he was a man of great humanity, and secrecy. His own invisible symbols were truly woven into the stuff of those historical characters he brought to life again in his plays. Petros' contribution to revealing the hidden sign of Sir Henry's true life cannot be over-estimated.

And finally, thank you to all the kind correspondents who have contacted me through my website, www.henryneville.com

Brenda James, 2008

William Shakespeare

This was the portrait of Shakespeare, by Martin Droeshout (1601 - 50) which appeared in the First Folio of the Plays. Below it, Ben Jonson (a member of the Mitre Club, along with Sir Henry Neville) wrote:

> This Figure, that thou here seest put,
>   It was for gentle Shakespeare cut:
> Wherein the Graver had a strife
>   With Nature to out-doo the life:
> O, could he but have drawne his wit
>   As well in brasse, as he hath hit
> His face, the Print would then surpasse
>   All, that was ever writ in brasse.
> But, since he cannot, Reader, looke
>   Not on his Picture, but his Booke.

Sir Henry Neville

Engraving by W.N. Gardiner (1766 - 1814), after the
portrait by Marcus Gheeraerts the younger (1561/2–1636).
Gheeraerts lived near to Neville in Lothbury, London, and
Sir Henry referred to him as 'my cosen, Garret'.

This book is dedicated
to James Goding and Emanuela Handman

Chapter 1

THE SHAKESPEARE MYTH AND THE NAME IN THE CODE

There are some things we tend to take for granted: Shakespeare was born in Stratford upon Avon, wrote all those erudite plays, and came to London as an actor at the Globe Theatre, where he continued to write his philosophical, poetical and witty works. These are among impressions early-inculcated and rarely questioned. Yet my own experience has proved that we should never take anything for granted: this is the story of the Shakespeare myths and how they were replaced by genuine historical research and discovery.

I was born within half an hour's journey from Stratford upon Avon, so I was not initially a Shakespeare-doubter. Post-war South Birmingham was an unglamorous, damp, dull, bomb-damaged place; Stratford represented that unreal yet ideal world of the past on which I based my hopes for the future. Even though my family warned me that I should not take everything presented there at face value, and even though my uncle wrote an article on the Shakespeare Authorship Question, it is fair to say I took little notice of them. I lived - spiritually and mentally - in a world of opera, art galleries, cinema, museums and drama, and Shakespeare and Stratford necessarily played key roles in that world.

Then, when I was fourteen years old and spending a wet summer holiday in my local library, I happened upon books dealing with Shakespeare criticism. At school, we studied the plays from the standpoint of their text and meaning, but the books I read now linked the plays' innuendos, language and incidents with the wider culture of the time. I suddenly realised that one could lead out from the texts, becoming a kind of historical detective - and my favourite novels had always been detective stories. The books I now read outlined one or two of the mysteries surrounding the creation of the Shakespeare works. But the mystery that intrigued me most was the search for the identity of 'Mr. W.H.', the otherwise unnamed dedicatee of Shakespeare's Sonnets.

I read those sonnets again and again. Without knowing their true background, they were certainly difficult to understand or to fit into any sort of pattern. One or two of the books I read at the library affirmed that the Dedication to the Sonnets was itself a code intended to hide the identity of the dedicatee. They said that if this code were cracked, then subsequent historical research would reveal the true interpretation of the Sonnets themselves.

I therefore hurried to read various theories concerning this 'code', but none of them was truly explanatory. Nevertheless, I somehow knew - betraying the usual arrogance of teenagers, I suppose - that I'd crack it one day. I reasoned that if I could positively identify Mr. W.H. then the rest of Shakespeare's secret life would be revealed. After all, Mr. W.H. must have been an influential man at the time, with important connections, otherwise the author wouldn't have bothered to hide Mr. W.H.'s real identity. If a positive link between Shakespeare and an influential circle of the time could be proven, then this would finally explain and illuminate all the inside, privileged knowledge and learning suggested in the text of the works. Tracing these connections would then indeed be like indulging in some of the most fascinating historical detective work of all time.

My family, however, were not so keen. My father persuaded me that I ought to be spending my time on more fruitful occupations. Thus, the years went by and life overran my teenage determination. The *positive* outcome of my literary experience, however, was that I eventually realised I should train as a Cultural Historian, so that's what I did. But subsequent lecturing at home and abroad, together with bringing up a family all put the Dedication Code on the back burner, with the echo of my father's edict against wasting time ringing in the back of my head whenever I opened my edition of Shakespeare's Sonnets.

But the longing to follow up the Code's trail would never leave me. I was lecturing and studying for a post-graduate in Linguistics, when I decided I could wait no longer. Administrative and teaching pressures were seriously restricting my time regarding the private research I had in mind. Having already studied Elizabethan history and philosophy as an undergraduate, and now armed with new analytical linguistic skills, I left academia and began serious independent research in

Elizabethan cryptography, politics and culture as a prelude to tackling the Dedication Code. I therefore learned the Dedication to the Sonnets off by heart, reasoning that I could go over it in my mind whenever I wished, and whenever I read a relevant work, and thus directly apply that work to the form and wording of the Code itself. This would give me the best chance of thinking of a way to solve it. And this is what I did.

Now, looking back and analysing those days, I realise that I had quite unwittingly re-created the conditions in which many 16th and 17th century readers and writers had lived. Knowing the Dedication off by heart, I could even close my eyes and go over it. Elizabethan and Jacobean readers had no electric light. They could not therefore read for such long hours as is possible for us today. We have become what is known in Linguistics as 'eye-minded'. But they were not afforded the luxurious conditions in which to develop this faculty of sight so strongly that it over-balanced the stimuli of sound and imagination. They too must have committed poems and literary passages to memory, so that they could have some kind of private diversion for their minds during long, dark hours. No wonder poetry had been so popular at the time - it is so much easier to memorise than prose, and there are so many condensed meanings in it, all of which affords endless hours of internalised entertainment in the dark. As will be demonstrated, the Dedication to the Sonnets is written in a form which invites mystification and stimulates attempts at solving its strange syntax. It is therefore highly likely that some readers of the time also learnt it off by heart, alongside learning one or two of the Sonnets themselves. It is even possible that one or two readers might even have hit on the first stage of the Code's decipherment. But this is a multi-layered code, so perhaps only a very few people - if anyone - would have untangled its final message.

Eventually, then, I began to visualise how the code might be solved. However, I realised that this initial visualisation wouldn't be nearly enough on its own. The subsequent sleuthing I had to carry out led to unexpected areas of research. The solution to the Code was so unexpected and innovatory that I could not ask outsiders for help, for fear of having my discovery - and my work - taken over. Nevertheless, this is how it all began, and but for that order of commitment, Sir Henry Neville might never have been uncovered as the author of the Shakespeare Works.

Analysing the plain text of the Dedication

From Professor Leslie Hotson's book entitled 'Mr. W.H.' I obtained the first actual facsimile of the original Sonnets' Dedication that had ever been widely available in secondary sources. Its layout was certainly stranger than any of the reproductions I had in my own editions of the Sonnets. Here, below, is a transcription of the text and layout of the Dedication:

TO . THE . ONLIE . BEGETTER . OF .
THESE . INSVING . SONNETS .
Mr .W. H .   ALL . HAPPINESSE .
AND . THAT . ETERNITIE .
PROMISED .

BY .

OVR . EVER-LIVING . POET .

WISHETH .

THE .WELL-WISHING .
ADVENTVRER . IN .
SETTING .
FORTH .

T. T.

To begin with, U and V were printed as the same letter in Shakespeare's time. Also, the letter W was written as double V - 'VV', though I didn't realise that this would eventually prove significant. Most of all it was the layout and strange wording that were so intriguing.

Who is Mr. W.H? Who is THE WELL–WISHING ADVENTURER? Why is the Dedication written completely in capital letters? Why are there full stops between each word? And what does it all really mean? There certainly are enough puzzles here to encourage everyone to start playing the decoding game. I set out to analyse the text, and then to read yet more around the subject.

On a first quick reading, we can see that there are three people mentioned here: the Begetter of the Sonnets, the Poet, and the Adventurer. A reader might assume that he knows the poet is

Shakespeare, but the only clue we are given to the *Begetter's* name is his initials. However, it seems to be the *Adventurer* who is sending his good wishes to the Begetter, not the Poet himself. Ergo, the Begetter is involved in some way with an Adventurer. This is the very best clue in the whole Dedication, because the meaning of an 'Adventurer' was very specific, at the time. An ADVENTURER was an investor. And the Investment Company which was given its Royal Charter the very same year as the publication of the Sonnets was the Virginia Company - an organisation set up for the exploration, settlement and entrepreneurial exploitation of North America.

I had first read about all this in a newspaper article by the historian, A.L. Rowse back in the 1960s, though I thought he stretched a few points when it came to his attempt at decoding the Dedication. For instance, he tried to say that the word 'Begetter' could mean simply 'obtainer', which actually does not at all accord with its true meaning, either in the 17th century or nowadays. Neither does 'beget' ever mean 'obtain' in any of the Shakespeare works. No, the BEGETTER is surely the person who first gave rise to the whole idea of writing **sonnets**, as opposed to the earlier **epic** poems which Shakespeare had written.

However, as Linguistics had been one of my studies, I was well aware that I should now research some of the words and phrases in the Code. There were obviously going to be differences between how they were used by the Jacobeans, and their present-day meaning. To begin with, ONLIE could mean 'chief', 'first' or 'principal' in the 17th century, just as easily as it carried its present day meaning of 'one and only'. This helps greatly to clarify a few things: after all, if every one the 154 sonnets had been actually begotten by and *addressed* to Mr. W.H., then how does it come about that some of the Sonnets speak to at least one woman - a dark lady with bad breath - while others betray the presence of a much more refined lady? And there is no guarantee either that the sonnets addressed to a male recipient are simply addressed to one man in particular. In other words, there could be several addressees, even if there is only one BEGETTER or principal 'inspirer'. But a complete understanding the 17th century meaning of the word 'onlie' certainly suggests that Mr. W.H. was simply **the main or first inspirer** of the sonnets, and that other addressees crept in as the writer added further sonnets over a substantial number of years.

And what about the EVER-LIVING POET? 'Ever-living' meant 'immortal' and was often used after someone had died. Yet Shakespeare - whoever he was - did not die in or before 1609, the year in which the Sonnets were published. Plays from the same hand kept appearing for six years after that time, and some of them contained very contemporary references. The wider themes and tone of the later plays also betray the surrounding context of post-1609 concerns. For instance, *The Tempest* was performed in 1611, by which time exploration and settlement of North America was under much wider discussion than in the pre-1609 years, because it was in 1609 that the first Royal Charter was granted to the Virginia Company. Moreover, the play was based partially on the experiences outlined in a secret letter written in 1610, which was seen only by members of the Virginia Company. (Things were already therefore beginning to show a pattern, even within the seemingly confused Dedication plaintext.) So EVER-LIVING had to have a metaphorical rather than literal meaning. The most probable explanation is that the Sonnets marked Shakespeare's last appearance as a *Poet*. Only *plays* appeared from his hand after this time, though his earlier epic poems had been popular enough to allow him to be called an 'ever-living' - i.e. 'immortal' - poet. The Sonnets marked the writer's death as a pure *poet*.

Shakespeare's previous poems - *Lucrece,* and *Venus and Adonis* - had been addressed to the Earl of Southampton, and it was now this same Earl who headed the Virginia Company. It was therefore becoming a logical assumption to my mind that Mr. W.H. might well be Mr. H.W. – Henry Wriothesley, Earl of Southampton. Yet there was also the point that 'Shakespeare' could have been associated with William Herbert, Earl of Pembroke, who became a patron of the First Folio of Shakespeare's works. But it must be admitted that a writer would hardly address him as plain **Mr.**, whereas the same rule did not always apply to the Earl of Southampton. Southampton was stripped of his titles when he was imprisoned in the Tower for being involved in the Essex rebellion. While in the Tower, therefore, that Earl was addressed simply as 'Mr.'

On the other hand, 'Mr' can also be a short form of 'master' which suggests a young boy. If the very first sonnets were addressed to someone the writer knew as a young boy, then this too would make sense, so on *those* grounds, the young

Master William Herbert - not yet Earl of Pembroke - may not ultimately be ruled out.

This kind of ambiguity clearly demonstrates why the Dedication has been sending everyone round in circles over the centuries - just as it was intended to do. However, the point is that only those right inside a privileged business and aristocratic circle at the time – and only the most meticulous historians ever since – would have had enough privileged information to think all this out. And one factor always remains hidden until the text is decoded: it is far from obvious in the plaintext of the Dedication that the 'ever-living poet' and the 'Adventurer' could be one and the same person. Only when the Dedication is properly decoded does this point emerge for certain. Thus, even knowledgeable readers at the time who were able to reason that Wriothesley was the most likely Dedicatee would be just as confused about the meaning of the Dedication's text as we are today, unless and until they decoded it correctly.

However, working through the puzzle itself and following up all these attendant details brought me closer to facts that were far nearer the surface of people's minds at the time the code was composed. In precisely 1609 – the date the Royal Charter was given to the Virginia Company – many courtiers and gentry would have had the names of the founding 'Adventurers' at the top of their minds for a short time, only to forget them within the year itself. Thus can connections between time and events be so quickly dissociated in anyone's mind. The historian who tries to retrieve them years later has so many events to sift through that, although he may find the individual events themselves, he or she may not necessarily perceive the inevitable connections between them that existed at the time.

But one thing the very strange wording of the Dedication inevitably encourages everyone to do - across the ages - is to think of puns and multiple meanings. Are there any possible double meanings? The last word in the whole Dedication is FORTH, so could this be a pun on FOURTH? If so, then FORTH could be pointing to a *mathematical* basis of the Code itself.

The Renaissance mind did not compartmentalise its learning. Mathematical puzzles were as intriguing as linguistic ones, and layouts commonly used for *mathematical* tables, with rows and columns containing *numbers,* could also house *letters.* This much I knew, and I must have had it subconsciously in mind, because lying there in the dark and musing on FORTH and

FOURTH, I suddenly decided to go through the whole text in my head, counting up its letters and dots. Could there be an arithmetical significance here?

By counting all the characters in the Dedication (including the full stops) I got nowhere. Then it occurred to me that the dots might be a sign that the spaces between the words should *not* be counted. Eureka! There are 144 letters in the text, not counting the dots and spaces, so this immediately suggested to me a 12 x 12 square. Perhaps I was supposed to lay out the letters of the Dedication in a grid. (The last word of the Dedication being FORTH was still at the back of my mind, though my first attempts to establish this as a clue on its own gave no meaningful results. For instance, taking every fourth letter of the text leads only to gibberish, so it soon became clear that the meaning of FORTH would have to wait a while for a solution.) So I began by setting down the first 12 x 12 layout:

	1	2	3	4	5	6	7	8	9	10	11	12
1	T	O	T	H	E	O	N	L	I	E	B	E
2	G	E	T	T	E	R	O	F	T	H	E	S
3	E	I	N	S	U	I	N	G	S	O	N	N
4	E	T	S	Mr	W	H	x	A	L	L	H	A
5	P	P	I	N	E	S	S	E	N	N	D	T
6	H	A	T	E	T	E	R	N	I	T	I	E
7	P	R	O	M	I	S	E	D	B	Y	O	U
8	R	E	V	E	R	L	I	V	I	N	G	P
9	O	E	T	W	I	S	H	E	T	H	T	H
10	E	W	E	L	L	W	I	S	H	I	N	G
11	A	D	V	E	N	T	U	R	E	R	I	N
12	S	E	T	T	I	N	G	F	O	R	T	H

[In laying the text out in any matrix at all, we are probably meant to place the 'r' of 'Mr' inside one single cell of the grid, since the r is the only lower case letter in the original Dedication. There appears to be a large space after 'Mr. W.H.', so I reasoned that this should probably represent a blank space, so that there would still be 144 squares in the matrix. This necessarily has the effect

18

of moving the letters W and H one space back, which turns out to make a little difference, as laying the letters out in the grid reveals new word clusters. The resultant matrix appears above, and the letter X has been placed in the blank space.]

Immediately, the compiler of the Code is telling us we must be on the right track, because the word TWELVE is written out in a block of letters, with TT directly below it. In the original layout of the Dedication, the letters TT can be seen to the right of it. These are the initials of Thomas Thorpe, the publisher and printer of the Code. This surely suggests we should now look for messages in similar clusters. (And, naturally, there are other possible layouts too: 16 x 9, 9 x 16, 18 x 8, etc., which will be dealt with in the course of this chapter.)

But I was finding that so many different word formations were possible. This was when I realised that perhaps Renaissance coders had some way of sorting out which word clusters were significant and which were not. Clearly, I had now to study Renaissance cryptography, if I were to progress at all. Most of what I found in the few texts I tracked down seemed to have little connection with what I had discovered, so I kept scanning the 12 x 12 setting, desperately seeking clues. I still thought my best clue lay grouped on the final line, as it contained the very word which I had always felt had a double meaning. The phrase on line 12 was SETTING FORTH, and surely the clearly-defined word TWELVE was leading me to think about the meaning of the twelfth line. As already observed, FORTH could possibly also mean FOURTH, and it was surely significant that this whole phrase was situated on the 12th line, and that there were twelve lines in the original 'setting' of the Dedication.

Then, at last, an idea occurred to me. I was supposed somehow to make **four settings** of this particular layout. But how? There must be an answer embedded in the very form of the thing, I thought. After looking through the few old books on deciphering I had been able to access, I finally hit on the solution: I was here dealing with a 'transformation code'. I had somehow to transform this 12 x 12 tableau. The essence of the system I finally used is actually detailed in the **1974** edition of the Encyclopaedia Britannica, under the heading 'Cryptology' and later editions deal with variations on this method too. [The writer of the 1974 article, (who signs himself L.D.C., which stands for Lambros de Calimahos[1]) makes the point that 'The most important and authoritative works on the subject are classified governmental publications, unavailable to the general public'. It is therefore not surprising that this code had remained unbroken for such a long time.] Having hit on the 'word square' idea, however, (such as the one laid out from the Code, above) I was now able to set out on the transformation which de Callimahos describes. The point is that a so-called 'word square' sometimes uses a **keyword** in order to transform its meaning.

The best way of understanding how a keyword works is to show one in action. Below, I have written a coded message, and even though mine is not in plaintext like the Dedication Code, it illustrates what is happening. My intention is to send this message, already coded, to a receiver who knows the keyword. The receiver also knows that she must fit the letters of the Code into a grid.

The coded message reads: DWTT ITOON AILN RGAT OLM NIKM ES GAHE TSEE RA NWOKT ONE. This message contains 44 letters, so it is easy to imagine that it would be best set out in an 11 x 4 tableau, thus:

1	2	3	4	5	6	7	8	9	10	11
D	W	T	T	I	T	O	O	N	I	A
L	N	R	G	A	T	O	L	M	N	I
K	M	E	S	G	A	H	E	T	S	E
E	R	A	N	W	O	K	T	O	N	E

Now my receiver takes the keyword which we have pre-arranged: ATTRIBUTION. She writes this word below the grid, thus:

1	2	3	4	5	6	7	8	9	10	11
D	W	T	T	I	T	O	O	N	I	A
L	N	R	G	A	T	O	L	M	N	I
K	M	E	S	G	A	H	E	T	S	E
E	R	A	N	W	O	K	T	O	N	E
A	*T*	*T*	*R*	*I*	*B*	*U*	*T*	*I*	*O*	*N*

What she must do now is turn the letters of this word into numbers, ordering them according to their appearance in the alphabet. When two of the same letters are present, then the numbering is done according to the order in which they appear in the word itself, so that the first T to appear in ATTRIBUTION is given the lower number:

A	T	T	R	I	B	U	T	I	O	N
1	8	9	7	3	2	11	10	4	6	5

We now have the numbers for the re-ordering of our columns. If we place our columns in this new order, we may read the true message, from left to right:

1	8	9	7	3	2	11	10	4	6	5
D	O	N	O	T	W	A	I	T	T	I
L	L	M	O	R	N	I	N	G	T	A
K	E	T	H	E	M	E	S	S	A	G
E	T	O	K	A	R	E	N	N	O	W

So the message reads: DO NOT WAIT TILL MORNING. TAKE THE MESSAGE TO KAREN NOW.

Column one has been left where it is, then column 8 has been moved next to it, 9 next to that, and so on, the order being dictated by the keyword. (An illustration of the complete process follows):

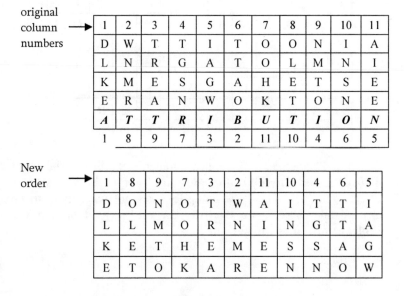

original column numbers →

1	2	3	4	5	6	7	8	9	10	11
D	W	T	T	I	T	O	O	N	I	A
L	N	R	G	A	T	O	L	M	N	I
K	M	E	S	G	A	H	E	T	S	E
E	R	A	N	W	O	K	T	O	N	E
A	*T*	*T*	*R*	*I*	*B*	*U*	*T*	*I*	*O*	*N*
1	8	9	7	3	2	11	10	4	6	5

New order →

1	8	9	7	3	2	11	10	4	6	5
D	O	N	O	T	W	A	I	T	T	I
L	L	M	O	R	N	I	N	G	T	A
K	E	T	H	E	M	E	S	S	A	G
E	T	O	K	A	R	E	N	N	O	W

If the original text is nonsense, it is possible to turn the **whole** message into complete sense, just as has been achieved in the above message. However, the Dedication Code is made up of a *sensible* text, so that only the odd significant word or the occasional phrase will appear, whatever the process to which it might be subjected.

But one thing is certain: when it comes to the Dedication Code, the keyword has to be SETTING FORTH. We can logically conclude this because the Dedication Code was meant for everyone who bought a copy of the *Sonnets*, so its compiler must have wished at least some of its recipients to work out the keyword for themselves. The **12 x 12** setting is logical because it makes a square; the **twelfth** row includes *whole* words, not just *part* of them; the word **TWELVE** appears in the first grid layout:

	1	2	3	4	5	6	7	8	9	10	11	12
1	T	O	T	H	E	O	N	L	I	E	B	E
2	G	E	T	T	E	R	O	F	T	H	E	S
3	E	I	N	S	U	I	N	G	S	O	N	N
4	E	T	S	Mr	W	H	x	A	L	L	H	A
5	P	P	I	N	E	S	S	E	N	N	D	T
6	H	A	T	E	T	E	R	N	I	T	I	E
7	P	R	O	M	I	S	E	D	B	Y	O	U
8	R	E	V	E	R	L	I	V	I	N	G	P
9	O	E	T	W	I	S	H	E	T	H	T	H
10	E	W	E	L	L	W	I	S	H	I	N	G
11	A	D	V	E	N	T	U	R	E	R	I	N
12	S	E	T	T	I	N	G	F	O	R	T	H

The letters 'TT' appear immediately below the word TWELVE', as if to tell us that 'Thomas Thorpe' the publisher, is directing affairs. Thus, the compiler does not wish there to be any mistake here: **the twelfth row of the grid setting (or tableau) provides the keyword.**

If SETTING FORTH is the keyword, then SETTING FORTH is dictating the *new* order for the original columns. We must now therefore number SETTING FORTH according to its alphabetical order:

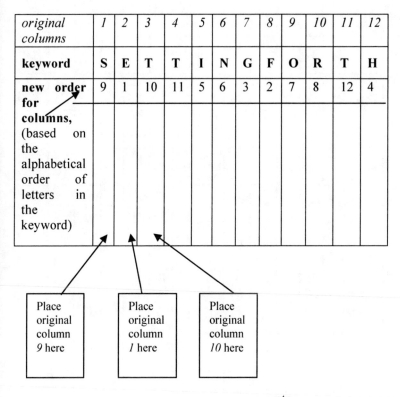

original columns	1	2	3	4	5	6	7	8	9	10	11	12
keyword	S	E	T	T	I	N	G	F	O	R	T	H
new order for columns, (based on the alphabetical order of letters in the keyword)	9	1	10	11	5	6	3	2	7	8	12	4

Place original column *9* here

Place original column *1* here

Place original column *10* here

etc.

It may be easiest to imagine each column as a separate stick, and we now have to pick up each stick separately and replace it in the order dictated by the keyword. Thus, original column 9 is re-laid in the first position, original column 1 in the second position, original column 10 is put into the third position, and so on.

The resultant transformed grid appears like this:

Original Columns	1	2	3	4	5	6	7	8	9	10	11	12
New Arrangement	9	1	10	11	5	6	3	2	7	8	12	4
1	I	T	E	B	E	O	T	O	N	L	E	H
2	T	G	H	E	E	R	T	E	O	F	S	T
3	S	E	O	N	U	I	N	I	N	G	N	S
4	L	E	L	H	W	H	S	T		A	A	Mr
5	A	P	N	D	E	S	I	P	S	E	T	N
6	I	H	T	I	T	E	T	A	R	N	E	E
7	B	P	Y	O	I	S	O	R	E	D	U	M
8	I	R	N	G	R	L	V	E	I	V	P	E
9	T	O	H	T	I	S	T	E	H	E	H	W
10	H	E	I	N	L	W	E	W	I	S	G	L
11	E	A	R	I	N	T	V	D	U	R	N	E
12	O	S	R	T	I	N	T	E	G	F	H	T
	1	2	3	4	5	6	7	8	9	10	11	12

Needless to say, I was at first somewhat disappointed that the new arrangement had not at least produced one meaningful phrase. Yet I was sure I was at the beginning of the right track. Then I got it – SETTING FORTH, was both the keyword *and* what Thorpe (or the compiler) was telling me to do: this was where the word 'FORTH' (or fourth) came into its own! I had to carry on applying the keyword to every new setting until I got to the fourth setting of this keyword progression. The grid above was the **second** setting of the tableau, so I had two more to construct before I could read a direct message.

I had therefore made a prediction; if this prediction turned out to be correct, then my decoding methodology would be confirmed as being correct also. Had I now at last found the intended algorithm for this particular transformation Code? **Would there be a definite message in the fourth setting of the Code?** Only carrying on relentlessly would reveal whether I had hit on the actual coding method used by its constructor, or not.

I renumbered my **second setting** from one to twelve (as shown on the bottom row of previous page) and then proceeded to apply my keyword again. In short, what I had to do was pick up my separate sticks once more. This is not easy to illustrate in two dimensions, so I have shaded a row below the grid in the last illustration, in order to show that this is the new order of numbers from which I would pick up the appropriate 'column sticks' and re-lay them into the prescribed order for the third setting. So I had to place grey 9 to position 1, grey 1 to position 2, and so on.

My third setting was constructed as follows:
Grey column 9 goes to position 1 in the third setting;
Grey column 1 goes to position 2 in the third setting;
Grey column 10 goes to position 3 in the third setting;
Grey column 11 goes to position 4 in the third setting;
Grey column 5 stays in position 5 in the third setting, as does grey column 6;
Grey column 3 goes to position 7 in the third setting;
Grey column 2 goes to position 8, etc.

Second Setting Order	1	2	3	4	5	6	7	8	9	10	11	12
Keyword order for third setting position	9	1	10	11	5	6	3	2	7	8	12	4
1	N	I	L	E	E	O	E	T	T	O	H	B
2	O	T	F	S	E	R	H	G	T	E	T	E
3	N	S	G	N	U	I	O	E	N	I	S	N
4	X	L	A	A	W	H	L	E	S	T	Mr	H
5	S	A	E	T	E	S	N	P	I	P	N	D
6	R	I	N	E	T	E	T	H	T	A	E	I
7	E	B	D	U	I	S	Y	P	O	R	M	O
8	I	I	V	P	R	L	N	R	V	E	E	G
9	H	T	E	H	I	S	H	O	T	E	W	T
10	I	H	S	G	L	W	I	E	E	W	L	N
1	U	E	R	N	N	T	R	A	V	D	E	I
12	G	O	F	H	I	N	R	S	T	E	T	T
	1	2	3	4	5	6	7	8	9	10	11	12

At this point I realised I was already producing significant clusters of words (such as TRAVELD STETTIN highlighted above). (These words ultimately turned out to be significant too, as the person finally named in the Code did indeed go to Poland) but I ignored them for the moment and carried on to the fourth setting, having predicted that the **main** message would be there.

The new numbers of the columns this time appear in hashed grey, overleaf:

Third setting order	1	2	3	4	5	6	7	8	9	10	11	12
Keyword order for **fourth** setting	9	1	10	11	5	6	3	2	7	8	12	4
1	T	N	O	H	E	O	L	I	E	T	B	E
2	T	O	E	T	E	R	F	T	H	G	E	S
3	N	N	I	S	U	I	G	S	O	E	N	N
4	S	X	T	Mr	W	H	A	L	L	E	H	A
5	I	S	P	N	E	S	E	A	N	P	D	T
6	T	R	A	E	T	E	N	I	T	H	I	E
7	O	E	R	M	I	S	D	B	Y	P	O	U
8	V	I	E	E	R	L	V	I	N	R	G	P
9	T	H	E	W	I	S	E	T	H	O	T	H
10	E	I	W	L	L	W	S	H	I	E	N	G
11	V	U	D	E	N	T	R	E	R	A	I	N
12	T	G	E	T	I	N	F	O	R	S	T	H

Fourth layout (or 'setting') of the code
THE WISE THORP HID THY POET

So at last we have a clear message, which could not have occurred except by design. The Wise Thorp (the publisher) had declared himself and what he had ostensibly done. He claimed to have hidden the name of the true 'poet'. Even without the benefit of a full knowledge of Renaissance coding systems, there can surely be no doubt here. THE WISE stands out in a straight line, which could not have occurred by chance. The fact that TT-Thomas Thorpe - placed his initials at the foot of the Dedication makes us aware of his presence, so our eyes are automatically guided upwards in the grid, where we immediately find his name. Once there, we are definitely looking for connected letters forming a meaningful phrase - and there it is.

So the astounding and unexpected message that stood out above all was THE WISE THORP HID THY POET. For the very first time, here is the shocking news that the poet is hidden, and therefore not 'Shakespeare' at all. This took me completely by surprise. There were more clusters to be seen within all the settings, which the compiler of the Code probably did not intend us to ignore completely. Yet his main message was surely the one concerning the identity of the poet. GET IN FOR (four) he says at the very bottom of the grid, therefore the main message certainly lies in this, the **fourth** setting.

So this code, that had purported in its plaintext version to hide Mr. W.H. – the dedicatee – had really hidden someone else too. And is there not a complementary sentence also within this setting?

1	T	N	O	H	E	O	L	I	E	T	B	E
2	T	O	E	T	E	R	F	T	H	G	E	S
3	N	N	I	S	U	I	G	S	O	E	N	N
4	S		T	Mr	W	H	A	L	L	E	H	A
5	I	S	P	N	E	S	*E*	A	N	P	D	T
6	*T*	*R*	*A*	*E*	*T*	*E*	N	*I*	*T*	H	I	E
7	O	E	R	M	I	S	D	B	Y	P	O	U
8	V	I	E	E	R	L	V	I	N	R	G	P
9	T	H	E	W	I	S	E	T	H	O	T	H
10	E	I	W	L	L	W	S	H	I	E	N	G
11	V	U	D	E	N	T	R	E	R	A	I	N
12	T	**G**	**E**	**T**	**I**	**N**	**F**	**O**	**R**	S	T	H

Fourth layout (or 'setting') of the code
PARIS TRAETEE IT IS BY POET

Paris and a Treaty - those had to be significant clues towards the poet's identification.

I was now frustrated. The compiler of the code had told me that the poet's name was hidden, but he gave no further clues on how to find that name. I looked at the Code again and again, and still the only clues were SETTING FORTH and GET IN FORS.

Then these instructions suddenly made a different kind of sense: if 12 x 12 was my **first** setting, then perhaps 13 across could be an alternative **second** setting, fourteen across a **third** setting, and fifteen across a **fourth** setting. So this time, I set out a 15 column grid:

1	2	3	4	5	6	7	8	9	10	11	12	13	14	15
T	O	T	H	E	O	N	L	I	E	B	E	G	E	T
T	E	R	O	F	T	H	E	S	E	I	N	S	U	I
N	G	S	O	N	N	E	T	S	M	R	W	H		A
L	H	A	P	P	I	N	E	S	S	E	A	N	D	T
H	A	T	E	T	E	R	N	I	T	I	E	P	R	O
M	I	S	E	D	B	Y	O	U	R	E	V	E	R	L
I	V	I	N	G	P	O	E	T	W	I	S	H	E	T
H	T	H	E	W	E	L	L	W	I	S	H	I	N	G
A	D	V	E	N	T	U	R	E	R	I	N	S	E	T
T	I	N	G	F	O	R	T	H						

HENRY appeared right down the centre! HENRY was obviously the poet's first name, and HENRY was the POET. But how was I ever to discover his second name? I stared and stared at the Code and all its settings. Then, as I stared repeatedly at all its settings so far, something strange happened. I began to see what looked like a name constantly trying to assert itself in every single setting. Yet it kept flitting in and out of focus. As I could not definitely focus in on it, I began to reason logically again. If HENRY was placed *above* the word POET, then Henry's second name was going to be clustered somewhere around POET too. Only in this way could the man's first and second names become interlinked with POET. Yet I had to bear in mind that the writer did not want to make his identification absolutely obvious, even in a Code. Otherwise, he could just as well have declared it openly on every one of his writings.

So, with this in mind, let us now look again at the 15 x 10 setting:

1	2	3	4	5	6	7	8	9	10	11	12	13	14	15
T	O	T	H	E	O	N	L	I	E	B	E	G	E	T
T	E	R	O	F	T	H	E	S	E	I	N	S	U	I
N	G	S	O	N	N	E	T	S	M	R	W	H		A
L	H	A	P	P	I	N	E	S	S	E	A	N	D	T
H	A	T	E	T	E	R	N	I	T	I	E	P	R	O
M	I	S	E	D	B	Y	O	U	R	E	V	E	R	L
I	V	I	N	G	P	O	E	T	W	I	S	H	E	T
H	T	H	E	W	E	L	L	W	I	S	H	I	N	G
A	D	V	E	N	T	U	R	E	R	I	N	S	E	T
T	I	N	G	F	O	R	T	H						

The possible names clustered around POET include WELLER, GELLER, WELLTER, TULLER, and NEWELL. Then I remembered that in old printing the W was written as two VVs, so I also reasoned that the name was most likely to be NEVVELL. In fact, NEVVELL can be read from two different starting points on the above grid, as if the compiler was trying to make sure that no one who has come this far should miss it entirely. Besides, NEVELL was the name that had begun to appear hazily in other settings too.

1	2	3	4	5	6	7	8	9	10	11	12	13	14	15
T	O	T	H	E	O	N	L	I	E	B	E	G	E	T
T	E	R	O	F	T	H	E	S	E	I	N	S	U	I
N	G	S	O	N	N	E	T	S	M	R	W	H		A
L	H	A	P	P	I	N	E	S	S	E	A	N	D	T
H	A	T	E	T	E	R	N	I	T	I	E	P	R	O
M	I	S	E	D	B	Y	O	U	R	E	V	E	R	L
I	V	I	N	G	P	O	E	T	W	I	S	H	E	T
H	T	H	E	W	E	L	L	W	I	S	H	I	N	G
A	D	V	E	N	T	U	R	E	R	I	N	S	E	T
T	I	N	G	F	O	R	T	H						

Once I began to research HENRY, POET, NEVELL [or NEVVELL], I discovered that a man called Henry Neville had been our Ambassador in France in 1599. There was a connection with PARIS! I therefore soon noticed the 'banner' held up by Henry's name in this same 15 across setting:

1	2	3	4	5	6	7	8	9	10	11	12	13	14	15
T	O	T	H	E	O	N	L	I	E	B	E	G	E	T
T	E	R	O	F	T	H	E	S	E	I	N	S	U	I
N	G	S	O	N	N	E	T	S	M	R	W	H		A
L	H	A	P	P	I	N	E	S	S	E	A	N	D	T
H	A	T	E	T	E	R	N	I	T	I	E	P	R	O
M	I	S	E	D	B	Y	O	U	R	E	V	E	R	L
I	V	I	N	G	P	O	E	T	W	I	S	H	E	T
H	T	H	E	W	E	L	L	W	I	S	H	I	N	G
A	D	V	E	N	T	U	R	E	R	I	N	S	E	T
T	I	N	G	F	O	R	T	H						

HE ONLIE BE OF THE SEIN(E) – This particular Henry Neville whom I found in the Dictionary of National Biography had worked in Paris. What's more he had almost identical birth and death dates to those of Shakespeare. Furthermore, in addition to the Seine being the river which runs through Paris, 'le sein' in French means 'the bosom' or, figuratively, the 'heart' or 'centre', as in the phrase 'le sein de la terre' - the bowels of the earth. Thus is the compiler of the Code making it clear that HENRY is literally and figuratively at the centre of this mystery, just as his name is at the centre of the Code. Underlining this meaning is the very fact that the Code itself is composed of 144 letters, because 144 was the diplomatic Code used to stand for Henri IV, King of France - the very King with whom a certain Henry Neville dealt. As if to add yet another meaning to that word FORTH, we now had a King Henry who was the fourth of that name! Yet these facts took me a long time to discover and link up with the Code. I found out Henri IV's code number only when I discovered the letters and dispatches of Sir Henry Neville - the French Ambassador named in the Code. On 28th August, 1600, the Sir Henry Neville, who must clearly have been the man named in the Code, wrote the following partially coded letter to his secretary:

> I thinke it not amisse, that upon apt occasion you should likewise let fall some speech unto *191 Resolution* [the Duke of Bouillon] and unto *27 Religion* [Mons. de Rhosny], that you are of the opinion that if *100 State* [the Queen] might have any assurance to be *6gukyoswugθnwph* [repaid her debt], were it by 300.000 Crownes yearly, she would undoubtedly resolve to continue the *sbyggubuholwΔ200* [War with Spain]; and hereupon to urge them to deal with *144* [the French King] in this seasonable time while matters are 'enbransle'.[2]

(The editor of Neville's letters had kindly inserted the decryption of his codewords!) Now, standing back and looking at the pattern made by highlighting the relevant area in the Code, it appears almost three dimensional – like a pillar, with a base and a topstone. Surely we have now discovered our poet, and on looking back at the first 12 x 12 setting, the name was again confirmed:

	1	2	3	4	5	6	7	8	9	10	11	12
1	T	O	T	H	E	O	N	L	I	E	B	E
2	G	E	T	T	E	R	O	F	T	H	E	S
3	E	I	N	S	U	I	N	G	S	O	N	N
4	E	T	S	Mr	W	H	x	A	L	L	H	A
5	P	P	I	N	E	S	S	E	N	N	D	T
6	*H*	*A*	T	E	T	E	R	N	I	T	I	E
7	P	*R*	O	M	I	S	E	D	B	Y	O	U
8	R	*E*	V	E	R	L	I	V	I	N	G	P
9	O	*E*	T	W	I	S	H	E	T	H	T	H
10	E	W	E	L	L	W	I	S	H	I	N	G
11	A	D	V	E	N	T	U	R	E	R	I	N
12	S	E	T	T	I	N	G	F	O	R	T	H

HAREE NEVELL WRITER were not words I would have seen without all the other clues, but there was no mistaking the fact that they were there – interlinked, even in the first tableau. Once I had been given the clues to what I was supposed to be looking for, they stood out quite plainly.

But where was Mr. W.H.? Perhaps nowhere. Perhaps this intentionally misleading Code was indeed intended only as a pointer to the *author himself*. However, on repeatedly reading the Sonnets themselves and studying a great many books on them, I still thought the most likely dedicatee was Henry Wriothesley, Earl of Southampton. As soon as I discovered that Southampton had been imprisoned in the Tower with Sir Henry Neville following the Essex rebellion, everything began to point even more firmly in Southampton's direction. I read that both men had been stripped of their titles at this time. That is surely why plain 'Haree Neville' appears in the Code without 'Sir' in the first setting . In this case, Southampton's name – if it appeared in the Code at all - would have reverted to plain **Mr.** Henry Wriothesley, whose initials are of course WH reversed. Moreover, the message REVERSE IT (starting at row 8 and going up diagonally through rows 6 and 7) can be clearly distinguished in the 12 x 12 setting:

1	T	O	T	H	E	O	N	L	I	E	B	E
2	G	E	T	T	E	R	O	F	T	H	E	S
3	E	I	N	S	U	I	N	G	S	O	N	N
4	E	T	S	Mr	W	H	x	A	L	L	H	A
5	P	P	I	N	E	S	S	E	N	N	D	T
6	*H*	*A*	T	E	T	E	R	N	I	T	I	E
7	P	*R*	O	M	I	*S*	*E*	D	B	Y	O	U
8	*R*	*E*	*V*	*E*	*R*	L	I	V	I	N	G	P
9	O	*E*	T	W	I	S	H	E	T	H	T	H
10	E	W	E	L	L	W	I	S	H	I	N	G
11	A	D	V	E	N	T	U	R	E	R	I	N
12	S	E	T	T	I	N	G	F	O	R	T	H

WH reversed is of course HW. The name Wriothesley is pronounced 'Risley', and when it came to spelling, Elizabethans and Jacobeans certainly cared more about the sound of a word than any written standardisation. (It was quite the usual practice for Neville himself to spell any one word in several different ways on the same page.) So now I looked to see if I could spot any cluster resembling the 'Risley'. And there it was – written out twice, with each appearance intertwining with the word 'writer', and placed above Neville's own name:

	1	2	3	4	5	6	7	8	9	10	11	12
1	T	O	T	H	E	O	N	L	I	E	B	E
2	G	E	T	T	E	R	O	F	T	H	E	S
3	E	I	N	S	U	I	N	G	S	O	N	N
4	E	T	S	Mr	W	H	x	A	L	L	H	A
5	P	P	I	N	E	S	S	E	N	N	D	T
6	*H*	*A*	T	E	T	E	R	N	I	T	I	E
7	P	*R*	O	M	*I*	*S*	*E*	D	B	Y	O	U
8	R	*E*	V	E	*R*	*L*	*I*	V	I	N	G	P
9	O	*E*	T	W	*I*	*S*	H	E	T	H	T	H
10	E	W	E	L	L	W	I	S	H	I	N	G
11	A	D	V	E	N	T	U	R	E	R	I	N
12	S	E	T	T	I	N	G	F	O	R	T	H

I was now content to see if more clues appeared in any of the other possible grid settings. What if I placed the letters in a 16 x 9 layout, for instance?

	1	2	3	4	5	6	7	8	9	10	11	12	13	14	15	16
1	T	O	T	H	E	O	N	L	I	E	B	E	G	E	T	T
2	E	R	O	F	T	*H*	E	S	E	I	N	S	V	I	N	G
3	S	O	N	N	*E*	T	S	Mr	W	H	X	A	L	L	H	A
4	P	P	I	*N*	E	S	S	E	A	N	D	T	H	A	T	E
5	T	E	*R*	N	I	T	I	E	P	R	O	M	I	S	E	D
6	B	*Y*	O	U	R	E	V	E	R	*L*	*I*	*V*	I	*N*	G	P
7	O	E	T	W	I	S	H	E	T	H	T	H	*E*	W	E	L
8	L	W	I	S	H	I	N	G	A	D	V	E	N	T	V	R
9	E	R	I	N	S	E	T	T	I	N	G	F	O	R	T	H

HENRY OF THE SEINE, NEVVEL, NEVIL SAVILL

As letter U was written as a V in those days, the name 'Neville' began to appear everywhere, in many different directions. (I was later to discover that Henry Savile – editor of the King James' Bible – was one of Neville's best friends, and a man whom a mutual friend recorded as being assisted in his writing by Neville.) And soon I knew that in discovering Sir Henry I had also discovered THE WELL-WISHING ADVENTURER, for Sir Henry Neville was an officer and 'adventurer' in the Virginia Company which had received its Royal Charter only a few months before the publication of the *Sonnets*. The POET and THE WELL-WISHING ADVENTURER were one and the same person, which makes the plaintext of the Dedication rather easier to understand.

The construction of this Code was so ingenious that I soon decided to try and construct one of my own, attempting also to make the original plaintext tie in with the messages I wished my readers to tease out. I spent about three hours in the process, and the results can be seen in the Addendum. However, mine is of course not nearly so refined and ingenious as the Dedication Code, and, additionally, Neville had to design the whole *idea* in the first place. This may suggest that Neville began to think out the construction of his Code during his incarceration in the

Tower, when he had a great deal of time on his hands and a great need to divert his tortured mind. The naming of the Earl of Southampton as plain 'Mr.' would have been relevant at this time. The Code was then probably completed (or possibly modified) after both he and Southampton knew that the Virginia Company was going to receive its Royal Charter.

Now the identity and extra clues and messages I found in the Dedication to Shakespeare's Sonnets had been confirmed by even the initial stages of my research. I was very willing to admit - when I looked back at the tableaux - that there were other perceivable words and word-blocks inside the matrices, but at the same time the plaintext of the Dedication itself substantiated the very messages I had found. And, besides, the message-blocks stating THE WISE THORP HID THY POET, and HENRY POET, could not have been there by accident and could not have been missed by *any* observer who had come this far in the decipherment. Only very little extra logical extrapolation and observation was then needed to sort out the rest of the compiler's intentions - and the name it presented proved to be the most perfect explanation of the Shakespeare mystery. No other word blocks in the tableaux referred back to the plaintext in any cohesive way at all. It must be stressed therefore, how improbable it is that such an astounding set of concurrent circumstances could exist against any other background than that of the true identification of the true writer. Moreover, I was later to find NEVILL in the Code in a straight line when the text was subjected to yet another transformation. But for the moment I had found quite enough to make me want to find out more.

Chapter 2

TO BE OR NOT TO BE SHAKESPEARE

The results of my decoding made it necessary to examine the Authorship Question. Up to the time of solving the Code, I had been principally concerned with the plays rather than their authorship, because without more definite clues than had been hitherto available, a purely blind search could lead to misconstructions of history. But refusing to tunnel my vision in any one particular direction regarding the authorship question meant that I was still open minded enough to look into whatever positive clues presented themselves. Even if the evidence provided by the Code had been in favour of William Shakespeare himself, I would still have researched things further. Viewed historically and logically, however, there are certainly many reasons against William Shakespeare of Stratford having written the plays.

To begin with, William Shakespeare is recorded as being at only two venues in England: Stratford and London. He never travelled abroad - not even to Scotland, which was a foreign country during his lifetime. Yet he set his plays in Italy at a time when no travel books on Italy had been published. Shakespeare of Stratford never possessed a passport. Had he done so, there would have been a record of this, as it was not a privilege handed out by the State as of right, in those days. A nobleman or high official had to provide letters of recommendation and permission for anyone wishing to travel abroad, so noblemen were careful to keep records of those whom they had recommended. To attempt to travel abroad without a genuine passport was a serious crime.

Moreover, the plays tell of the English Court and politics, yet Shakespeare never mixed with courtiers and politicians. He may have haunted the margins of the Court later in life when he and his father were seeking a Coat of Arms for themselves, but even then he would have had to be careful not to be 'familiar' with those above his station. Yet even the earliest plays show a knowledge of noble families and state politics.

No letters penned by him exist at all, so we have no confirmation that he was ever even interested in such matters. There was no mass media to tell him anything about the Court and politics either. Yet the writings *attributed* to 'Shakespeare' witness their author always knew about all these hierarchical English concerns. Additionally, the plays contain knowledge taught only in universities, yet William Shakespeare finished his education when he was only 12 years old. Or did he even attend school at all? He is not registered on the rolls of Stratford Grammar School.

Had William Shakespeare been a gifted and steady student at Grammar School, then he would surely have been chosen for a University Scholarship. Schoolmasters, and even great statesmen like Lord Burghley, were always keen to hear about, interview, support and find patrons for promising young men from the artisan classes.[3] Christopher Marlowe, for instance, was just such a man. He was a cobbler's son but gained a University scholarship, while even Michael Drayton's patron was known by name. (Drayton was not as talented a writer as Shakespeare, and yet we know the name of his patron!) Both he and Marlowe were born within a year of Shakespeare's birth, so there is no reason that one rule should apply to them and another to Shakespeare himself.

Then aspiring writers had to display their craft in order to gain ongoing support. The usual root for young writers seeking patronage was to pen poetry and dedicate it to at least one prospective patron. If their dedicatee approved, then his patronage of the poet became public knowledge. 'Shakespeare' dedicated *The Rape of Lucrece* and *Venus and Adonis* to the Earl of Southampton. Both epics were great literature and well received, yet it was never announced that the Earl of Southampton became Shakespeare's patron. No evidence to that effect has been discovered since, either - despite a great deal of research. Yet that same Shakespeare - whoever he may have been - did not openly dedicate further works to that Earl, or to anyone else. This is strange in itself, since a young, penniless author would either wish to continue pleasing his known patron, or else, if he had not in fact succeeded in gaining the patron at whom he originally aimed, then he would try dedicating works to someone else. In Shakespeare's case, neither of these things happened. This rather suggests that whoever really wrote the poems did not in fact do so with a view to patronage at all.

The *true* writer's financial situation was therefore such that he probably needed no patron. (This means that the true writer's reasons for dedicating his works to the Earl of Southampton were in pursuit of friendship and lasting alliances, rather than patronage.) Besides, if a patron was supporting a man for his *writing*, it is highly unlikely that that man would then change his profession and risk losing his patron's support by becoming an *actor*. Nevertheless, that is what we are expected to believe happened to Shakespeare, even though this course of events is highly improbable, and even though evidence in favour of them is missing.

Shakespeare's contemporaries must have reasoned all this out too, because fellow writers thought the unlearned William Shakespeare a ridiculous sight as he went around pretending to have written the plays. William was a vagabond when he first came to London. Unlike recognised actors of the time, he didn't even have a known patron. Under a law passed in 1572, actors who had no patron were legally classed as vagabonds. But why should a writer whose plays had already been accepted for stage performance voluntarily get himself classed as a vagrant? The true writer would have had no need to do such a thing.

Vagabond or no, however, by the time William came to London the Shakespeare **name** was already billed as the writer of learned history plays. What did his contemporary, Robert Greene, poet, traveller and university-educated man, think of that?

> There is an upstart Crow, beautified with our
> feathers, that with his Tygers hart wrapt in a
> Players hyde supposes he is as well able to
> bombast out a blank verse as the best of you;
> and being an absolute Johannes fac totum, is
> in his own conceit the only Shake-scene in a
> countrey. [4]

To the best of Greene's knowledge, Shakespeare was an odd-jobbing factotum, not a writer at all. When he first came to London, Shakespeare was found selling 'a lod of old stone'.[5] Yet he came to the capital only *after* supposedly completing those long plays on Henry VI. It is unthinkable that such a learned and already-successful author would ever have been placed in this kind of position. It is as ridiculous as if Steven Spielberg had decided to change his career and sell ice creams, *after* gaining recognition as a film director! In fact, it comes as a surprise to many that Shakespeare's name was only put on the official Stationer's Register as author of the plays years after they first appeared on the stage, and years after their very first printed editions.

But it was easier to see what was happening if you were living through the times themselves. Most educated contemporaries of Shakespeare seemed to know - or at least *suspect* - that the name 'Shakespeare' was a pseudonym, a joke. A certain unattributed 'Will-I-am' shaking a spear at anyone who wanted to come and challenge the writer's version of history. They *experienced* the sequencing of these implausible events. They knew it must have taken years to research and put together those plays, yet the Stratford pretender lived in London as a vagabond, had no books, and never even penned so much as a letter as long as he lived!

Joseph Hall, Clergyman and satirist, was one man who voiced his opinion on the plays' doubtful authorship at the early date of 1596.[6] By 1598 even the playwright John Marston had joined with the doubters, perhaps hinting in Neville's direction, as he describes his suspect as 'Rufus' meaning 'red-hued', and Neville's hair and complexion certainly matched that description[7]. Then the writer of a play performed at Cambridge University said exactly the same things about Shakespeare as Greene and Hall had written too:

> England affords those glorious vagabonds
> That carried earst their fardels on their backs
> Coursers to ride on through the gazing streets
> Loping it in their glaring satten sutes,
> And Pages to attend their maisterships
> With mouthing words that better wits have framed
> They purchase lands, and now Esquiers are made.[8]

That playwright was definitely hinting at Shakespeare when he wrote those lines, because Shakespeare was one of the richest actors. Yet Shakespeare did not even have the same stable financial background as other actors, and he had no known patron[9]. Shakespeare was the man who was suspiciously coming into more money than could be accounted for; Shakespeare was nothing short of a front man for the real author. As the passage quoted above avers, he became a jobbing actor who spoke words written by someone with wits and learning way above his own.

Even the playwright John Fletcher (who collaborated with 'Shakespeare' in later life) hints that Shakespeare, the jobbing actor, was always less than truthful. For instance, William Shakespeare and his father eventually tried to claim kin with the senior branch of the Arden family, though they had not been formerly known among that branch of the Ardens. From the following passage from *The Woman Hater*, it seems that Shakespeare - this son of a one-time glove-maker - might well have been trying to push his claim through Court, for here is the advice one of Fletcher's characters gives to a lady in the play:

> They say one shall see fine sights at the Court? I'll tell you what you shall see. You shall see many faces of man's making, for you shall find very few as God left them: and you shall see many legs too; ... another pair you shall see that were heir-apparent legs to a glover; these legs hope shortly to become honourable; when they pass by they will bow, and the mouth to these legs will seem to offer you some courtship; it will swear, but it will lie; hear it not.[10]

Fletcher and his co-author, Beaumont, almost certainly knew the truth, for they did not send their own work to be scrutinised by Shakespeare, but by our Sir Henry Neville - the very man named in the Code as thy hidden 'poet'![11]

The true writer had an encyclopaedic knowledge of the noble families of England too. Ergo, the writer must have been some sort of gentleman politician himself - a gentleman and politician who was connected with the aristocracy, and who would have been publicly debated, and then laughed to scorn if he had been known as a writer for the public stage. Hall thought that perhaps it was someone like Francis Bacon, though Hall was not so incautious as to state it was *definitely* Sir Francis. He simply suggested that that was the direction people ought to be looking in, if they wanted to find the true author.

The true author had to be someone as serious about politics as Francis was, but someone with a merry side to him too. Probably also someone a bit wealthier than Sir Francis, - someone who could *afford* to be 'merry' even in the face of known adversities during the times in which he lived, and someone who did not always have to be pleasing a master by his writing. Francis was not wealthy in his own right, and eventually showed himself willing to betray old friends in order to stay in a paid office.[12] In other words, Francis was not the sort of man to

have risked being dismissed from a job he absolutely needed -
and he would have been dismissed from the political arena, had
he been discovered as the writer of plays strung through with a
thread of criticism when it came to the office of Kingship.
Richard Simpson (1820-76) - a perceptive Shakespeare analyst -
crystallised the political leanings to be gleaned from the plays
and poems. He expressed their writer's attitude perfectly:

> ... There was a political current in Shakespeare's
> mind, which in the days of Elizabeth led him into
> opposition. If he welcomed the accession of
> James, he was soon undeceived, and when he set
> his hand to the history of Rome, the winter of his
> discontent had become gloomier than before. His
> tragedies point to the same conclusion, and show
> that the sentiments of the 66th Sonnet, and of
> Hamlet's 'To be or not to be.' were his real ones.[13]

Bacon was never an oppositionist. Unlike Sir Henry Neville, he
actually supported James I's ideas concerning the Divine Right
of Kings. His opinions are certainly not the ones expressed in the
plays.

Yet if the real writer behind Shakespeare was a
politician, then he was partly supported by public funds, and so
would have been extremely reluctant to reveal that he was
writing entertainments while serving the public in a serious,
official capacity. But that writer must also have possessed his
own means, in order to risk bringing the political system into
debate. In other words, the real writer must have had some
independent sources of finance. Even finding the time and
resources to research and write in those days was an insuperable
problem for *working* men like Shakespeare, without external
financial support. After all, there were no public libraries and no
unemployment benefits.

He had to have been someone with a lot more respect for
women too, than Sir Francis Bacon - and much fonder of women
than the misogynistic Earl of Oxford - yet another unwieldy
contender who, in any case, died years before many of the plays
were written! And even Shakespeare himself didn't think enough
of women to teach his daughters to read and write. Think of all
the strong, clever women in the plays: Queen Margaret in the
Henry VI trilogy, Portia - the lady who is able to disguise as a
barrister and shine in that profession in *The Merchant of Venice,*

Imogen in *Cymbeline*, Beatrice in *Much Ado* - and so the list continues.

Neither could the real writer have been someone who fitted into merely one classification of society. He had to be used to the world of business as well as old chivalry - the author of *The Merchant of Venice* and *The Comedy of Errors* certainly knew about international trade. Yet in spite of his ignorance of such affairs, young Shakespeare appears to have been traversing London ostensibly trying to claim the plays as his own - just as Greene says. Even the true writer himself suggests this is what is happening in a passage from *As You Like It*. Here, the true author is surely satirising William Shakespeare, characterising him as a 'clown' or peasant from the Forest of Arden. Touchstone - the jester/philosopher in the play - is questioning Will as to whether he is really a wise, learned man, or whether he is not 'the' man at all. All the time, there is the hint that Touchstone himself is the writer in question, has heard of Will's false 'flouting' and is out to teach him a lesson:

TOUCHSTONE. (meeting a certain Will of the Forest) It is meat and drink to me to see a clown. By my troth, we that have good wits have much to answer for: we shall be flouting; we cannot hold.
... WILLIAM. And good ev'n to you, sir.
TOUCHSTONE. Good ev'n, gentle friend. Cover thy head, cover thy head; nay, prithee be cover'd. How old are you, friend?
WILLIAM. Five and twenty, sir.
TOUCHSTONE. A ripe age. Is thy name William?
WILLIAM. William, sir.
TOUCHSTONE. A fair name. Wast born i' th' forest here?
WILLIAM. Ay, sir, I thank God.
TOUCHSTONE. 'Thank God.' A good answer. Art rich?
WILLIAM. Faith, sir, so so.
TOUCHSTONE. 'So so' is good, very good, very excellent good; and yet it is not; it is but so so. Art thou wise?
WILLIAM. Ay, sir, I have a pretty wit.
TOUCHSTONE. Why, thou say'st well. I do now remember a saying: 'The fool doth think he is wise, but the wise man knows himself to be a fool.' The heathen philosopher, when he had a desire to eat a grape, would open his lips when he put it into his mouth; meaning thereby that grapes were made to eat and lips to open. ...
Give me your hand. Art thou learned?

WILLIAM. No, sir.
TOUCHSTONE. Then learn this of me: to have is to have; for it is a
figure in rhetoric that drink, being pour'd out of cup into a
glass [he performs this action], by filling the one doth empty
the other; for all your writers do consent that ipse is he; **now,
you are not ipse, for I am he.**   *ACTV/SC.1*

Touchstone is the man who owns the cup; Shakespeare is the
mere vessel into which the water is poured by Touchstone. And
'Touchstone' was an aptly-named character, because a
touchstone was a piece of basalt - a stone - used to test the
difference between gold and iron pyrites. The two metals left
two distinctly different traces on the stone, after being drawn
across it. Touchstone therefore knew that simple William (who
possessed very limited, rural knowledge) left a very different
trace from that of the universal learning displayed in the plays.

It is also easy to see, however, that a politician, a
wealthy, wise, influential man - when writing such plays - might
well be wary of letting the world look in his direction and
examine his motivation. Many such men also had family secrets
to hide, and pressure from their families not to turn the
spotlight's glare onto them. Like the old Romans, they feared
the evil eye.

Wealthy, an aristocrat, a radical politician and a businessman -
the plays demonstrate that the true writer must have been all of
these things, and yet all these varied stipulations rule out the 'old
pretenders' when it comes to the authorship debate. We are so
used to simply *admiring* Shakespeare that it is easy to forget to
analyse the true writer's cultural situation. He lived in dangerous
times, when writers had their hands chopped off, or were even
sometimes executed, for saying the wrong thing. The true author
was obviously a brave, opinionated man. He portrayed the upper
classes on the public stage, showed their thought patterns by
getting them to speak soliloquies, and repeatedly characterised
the institution of Monarchy as one inherently flawed. If Queen
Elizabeth I had been able to trace the real 'Shakespeare' as an
insider - a politician and courtier - behind these writings and
these opinions, that man would surely have been silenced.

Only one *successful* King is featured in all the History
plays - Henry V - and even then the writer sees fit to add an
Epilogue to the play, saying how all King Henry's gains were
lost under the mismanagement of his son and heir. Finally, the

History plays, when viewed together, send a message which suggests some serious thought should be given towards a new solution for Society. Yet rebellious, ignorant upstarts like Jack Cade are definitely not portrayed as part of that solution. The History plays en masse are indeed designed to be thought-provoking; they inevitably initiate political discussion.

And odd-jobbing man of the Forest, William Shakespeare himself? - what would *he* know of all that? And how could he have learned the Italian and French needed to read some of the sources of the plays? Modern languages weren't on the Grammar schools' curriculum. William's definitely ruled out, for that and all the other reasons.

The most likely profile for the true writer is that he was someone who was never known as a writer at all, otherwise he probably wouldn't have bothered to invent such an elaborate, complete disguise. But trying to set out to find that writer without the clues given by the Code would be a daunting task. Over four hundred years have passed since the plays were written. Contemporary quips in the lines have lost their immediacy and innuendo. There's no one left to question on the subject who was actually alive at the time. We were seriously in need of a message from the past.

The Code had sent us the message from the age in which 'Shakespeare' wrote - it unexpectedly provided me with a definite enough clue on which to base some primary research. And make no mistake, **primary** research is the key to studying history. Unfortunately, some secondary sources have misguided us for too long. The errors of previous historical reviewers have sometimes gained credence simply by dint of repetition; but their bases still remain as unsteady as dry sand. True historical research consists of grasping existing, available threads from the past, then going back to the documents of the times in order to re-knit those threads into their original design. But in order to carry out fruitful primary research, one must know quite a lot about of the whole fabric of the time, so that one can fit research results into their historical background. I was glad that I had already studied the culture and historical background of the Shakespeare era.

Thus was I unwilling to take the Code's statement at face value. It was merely a thread, and I now had to attempt to find its place in the fabric from which it purported to come. If no supporting material could be discovered, then the thread was probably not truly a part of the Shakespeare pattern after all. Some secondary sources had at least already usefully confirmed that Henry Neville was a direct contemporary of Shakespeare and that many aspects of his life echoed the content and timing of the plays. But the primary source trail was not easy to follow, because other secondary sources had contained occasional errors which confused the issue. Yet primary sources of the Elizabethan and Jacobean era are more difficult to decipher than later documents, due to their decay, and to the fact that their handwriting styles differed from those used today. To my overwhelming surprise, however, everything I verified about the named man fitted in with the works of Shakespeare. The colour and texture of the Code's threads patched up the holes in the Shakespeare fabric. Eventually, I even discovered erstwhile unattributed documentary evidence to support the Code's claim that Sir Henry Neville was the true writer.

But I experienced tremendous problems in presenting my work. To begin with, the named man was no longer well-known. He had played a prominent role in history, but never published anything under his own name. True, he was still remembered and studied for his political vision and brilliant ambassadorial dispatches for over two hundred years after his death, but general memory of his ideas did not survive the coming of the industrial age. This is perhaps because his humane and economic policies came about quite naturally as society developed. The true writer was visionary enough to 'look into the seeds of time and say which grain will grow and which will not'. Thus did the true writer's ideas eventually become so widespread and generally-accepted that there was no longer any need to quote his original thoughts on the subject.

Without the permanent testimony of published works under his name, men forgot even that name itself, which seems to be what the true author of the *Sonnets* really wanted to happen:

> No longer mourn for me when I am dead,
> Than you shall hear the surly sullen bell
> Give warning to the world that I am fled
> From this vile world with vilest worms to dwell:
> Nay if you read this line, remember not,
> The hand that writ it,   *Sonnet 71*

and he says directly to his dedicatee:

Or I shall live your epitaph to make,
Or you survive when I in earth am rotten,
From hence your memory death cannot take,
Although in me each part will be forgotten.
Your name from hence immortal life shall have,
Though I (once gone) to all the world must die,   *Sonnet 81*

Many of these poems also imply that they were written by a man who was once in deep trouble - a man who expected to die in ignominy, and so did not wish his name to be remembered and bring disgrace on his family:

When in disgrace with Fortune and men's eyes,
I all alone beweep my outcast state,
And trouble deaf heaven with my bootless cries,
And look upon my self and curse my fate,
Wishing me like to one more rich in hope ...,*sonnet 129*

and

Do not so much as my poor name rehearse;
But let your love even with my life decay.
Lest the wise world should look into your moan,
And mock you with me after I am gone. *sonnet 71*

Once lauded and respected as a learned scholar, politician, witty after-dinner speaker, wise man and someone to whom contemporaries turned for advice on their own writing, the true writer named in the Code was indeed nevertheless a man who was once disgraced and thrown into the Tower for two years, where he feared for his life and for that of his friend, the Earl of Southampton.

Thus, for all these combined reasons, did the name in the Code pass from many annals of history. But I have at last been able to reconstruct the image behind that name in the Code - **Sir Henry Neville, the secret writer.**

....

47

The Nevilles, Sir Henry and the Shadow of Shakespeare

What kind of background did Sir Henry spring from? Where was he born? What kind of early life did he lead? First and foremost, who were the Nevilles?

The Neville family is said to have come to England with William the Conqueror. But the first truly documented Neville of note was Alan de Neville, who became Henry II's chief forester in the second half of the twelfth century. (Keeper of Forests was then a traditional role which was passed down in our Sir Henry's line of the family, and the author of *The Merry Wives of Windsor, As You Like It and A Midsummer Night's Dream* certainly knew about forests and their mysteries.) From Alan stemmed the rest of the large and powerful Neville family, some of whom married into the Plantagenet dynasty. Ralph, sixth Baron Neville of Raby, became the First Earl of Westmorland. He supported the overthrow of Richard II by Henry IV, both of which kings and their descendants were prominent in the History plays attributed to Shakespeare. John of Gaunt was also prominent in those plays, and he too was a Neville - an ancestor of Sir Henry. Sir Henry Neville had access to the Neville and related family trees. This therefore explains the true writer's knowledge of this and related family ancestry, as witnessed by the plays. Indeed, it is usually the case that when the history plays stray occasionally from the historical records, they do so in a manner which bolsters the Neville family, and our particular Sir Henry's branch of it.

By the time Sir Henry Neville was born, the family had taken part in so many fortuitous marriages and escapades that they were extremely rich and influential. Sir Henry's own father benefited from Henry VIII's seizure of monastic lands, so even though this particular branch of the family was descended from some of the *younger* sons of noblemen, its riches and influence were still great. Indeed, King James I's great grandmother was also the great aunt of our Sir Henry's father. Sir Henry's father bore the same name as his son, as did his slightly younger cousin, who inherited the title of Baron of Abergavenny, so this became yet another reason for our particular Sir Henry not wishing to use his own illustrious name on anything he wrote. That cousin's family - the Neville Barons of Abergavenny - lived in Sussex, near to where our Sir Henry also ran a house and business. But it also owned lands around Abergavenny, stretching Eastwards into Stratford upon Avon. Indeed, Neville's uncle owned the house in which Shakespeare's mother was born. Shakespeare's father attempted to get the family ennobled through the Ardens, as Shakespeare's mother was Mary Arden. The senior branch of the Arden family had intermarried with the Nevilles, and another of our Sir Henry's cousins had a mother named Barbara Arden. Yet Shakespeare's father could never finally prove any link between his wife and the senior branch of the Arden family. However, the Nevilles knew of his vociferous attempts to do so. It thus becomes quite clear that Sir Henry Neville knew of the Shakespeare family, and knew the name of 'William Shakespeare'. Besides this, a neighbour of Sir Henry's ancestral home at Waltham St. Lawrence was called William Speare, so there is little doubt that Neville always had the name in mind.[14] As will become clear too, the name 'Shakespeare' itself bore other significances for Neville, making it altogether appropriate that he should choose it as a pseudonym.

Most notably, Sir Henry Neville was the fourth cousin of Richard Neville Richard Neville was the famous Earl of Warwick, called the Kingmaker. From this man stemmed what became the traditional Neville role - that of advising (and, often, *leading*) Kings of England. Richard Neville dominates two of the *Henry VI* trilogy of plays, and his work of detection over the death of Gloucester, plus his dying speech singles out his character as cleverer, braver and more eloquent than any of the other men in those plays. His speeches and power are second only to those of Queen Margaret - and here again it is remarkable that women - Joan of Arc and Queen Margaret - are portrayed as the strongest characters. This trait is accountable, if we see Sir Henry as the author, since he was brought up alongside strong females. His own mother was an independent woman, as was his strict, learned stepmother. Henry Neville's aunt (Elizabeth Hoby) was a published translator. His female siblings wrote to him in strong terms, while Neville himself produced eleven children - six daughters and five sons. In one of his letters he says 'I would be glad of some small amenities to my younger sons, whereby I might be able to give them good education at the least, being eased of that charge, to do the more for my daughters.' Finally, as we shall see, Neville left some of his most precious and secret documents with one of his daughters on the Isle of Wight.

The specific 'Henry Neville' (1561/4 – 1615) to which the Dedication Code refers died nine months earlier than

Shakespeare, which gave William of Stratford time to 'disappear'. His 'French Connection' is not surprising. Continental settings abound in Shakespeare, while the writing of *Henry V,* with one of its scenes written wholly in French, was concluded when this ambassador was actually resident there. So even these initial findings are significant. This same Sir Henry Neville was involved in the Essex plot, and many literary analysts have noted oblique and direct references to the Earl of Essex within the plays.

It was, then, with much justification that Sir Henry Neville, owner of a large estate in Berkshire, M.P., keeper of Windsor Forest, polyglot, Ambassador to France, and a follower of the Earl of Essex's rebellion (for which crime he was eventually imprisoned in the Tower along with his patron and champion, the Earl of Southampton) became my prime suspect.

A descendant of the Earls of Westmorland, Abergavenny and Warwick, Sir Henry Neville was born the son of a father bearing the same name. This father was well-known in Court circles, and was respected as a clever linguist, soldier, wit and deviser of entertainments at the King's parties. He was directly descended from the Plantagenets, and also from the ancient Kings of Scotland. This means that King Duncan, (the monarch murdered by Macbeth), together with Edward III and John of Gaunt (the wise old statesman in *Richard II*) all figured in his wider ancestry, as did Richard Neville, Earl of Warwick who, with the Talbots (other relatives of the Nevilles) were heroicised in the *Henry VI* plays.

Henry Neville, the father, married[15] a rich and well-connected lady, Elizabeth Gresham, daughter of Sir John Gresham of Norfolk, and niece of Sir Thomas Gresham, founder of the Royal Exchange and Gresham College, London. Our Sir Henry was their first son, and thus heir to his father's and to part of the Gresham fortune. Sir Thomas Gresham died with only an illegitimate daughter as his heir, so decided to leave his Sussex land and ironworks to his great nephew, young Henry Neville. Henry's own mother died when he was nine years old, but about two years later his father married Elizabeth D'Oyly, nee Bacon, the much older step-sister of Sir Francis.

Thus was our man born to parents who were from wealthy and intelligent families – one aristocratic and the other risen from the merchant classes, both of which strata of society are prominently represented in the works of Shakespeare

Young Henry graduated from Merton College, Oxford, when only about fourteen to seventeen years old. Showing particular interest in astronomy and modern languages, the teenage Neville immediately began a four year sojourn abroad under the protection of Henry Savile, his Oxford tutor, who became a life-long friend. He is known to have stayed in Italy, Austria, Poland, France and the cities of Prague and Vienna, in all of which venues he met, and impressed, philosophers and scientists of the day. And his touring must have begun with a visit to Denmark, as will be detailed in following chapters.

On his return, Neville seems to have been fired up with political ambition. His own father had studied Law at Gray's Inn, and though it is not clear whether young Henry also attended an Inn of Court, it is probable that he did so in some capacity, as we find him later advising Parliament on legal matters and also possessing a 'bed in the Star Chamber'[16] [a court of law] as he became a judge there too. His father had built up a new and magnificent home for himself in Berkshire – Billingbear House – on land given him by Edward VI. He was also a keeper of part of the Windsor Forest and a tutor in hunting to Elizabeth I[17] – both of which occupations he passed on to his son.

But not all the sport of Windsor could keep young Henry away from politics; from the age of twenty, he sat in Parliament, becoming a member for New Windsor in 1584 and again in 1593, Sussex 1588-9, Liskeard, Cornwall (through a link with his brother in law) 1597-8, and Berkshire 1604-11, and again in 1614. At the beginning of his Parliamentary career, he was involved in manufacturing and exporting ordnance from his inherited ironworks. However, his political ambition led him to sell most of his interest in this in 1597, as he wished to rise in Court and politics.

Even thus far, however, perhaps partly because of his involvement in Sir Francis Walsingham's (secret) service[18], periods of our Sir Henry's life are clouded by confusion and mystery. Much of the confusion has been caused by his sharing the same name with his father and his younger cousin, who was also his neighbour in Sussex. For instance, some historians report that our Henry Neville was the one who accompanied the Earl of Essex on his 1596 Cadiz campaign, helping to burn the ships that the King of Spain was constructing in the hope of invading Britain once more. These same historians say that he was subsequently knighted by Essex, though others dispute that this was Sir Henry of Billingbear[19].

However, much of his life seems to confirm his identification with the Cadiz escapade, as he was a specialist in ordnance and also such an open admirer of the Earl of Essex that one of his own descendants was to write of his 'excessive attachment to that Earl.'[20]   In Elizabethan times, one owed loyalty and allegiance to the Lord who had knighted you.   What is certain, however, is that Sir Henry was put in charge of the defence arrangements for Berkshire in 1588 when the Armada threatened, so that this experience and his involvement with armaments would seem to have fitted him to work on the Cadiz campaign in some capacity, even if only travelling there as a military and munitions advisor.

But by 1599 we enter the realms of certainty once more. Sir Henry was appointed Ambassador to France, a post for which he was well qualified but which he took under protest.   For weeks, neither the Queen nor Cecil could persuade him to go willingly on this mission.   By this time he was married, had a growing family, and was just in the process of buying land from his neighbour, Sir Henry Unton, who had been the previous ambassador in France.   Unton had been impoverished through having to spend so much of his own money while abroad.   This, and the fact that poor young Unton eventually died from stomach trouble he contracted while there, probably also had much to do with Neville's resistance to the appointment he was now offered.

Throughout his life, Neville loved the possession and managing of land and people,[21] so he was afraid that the expenses involved in representing his country abroad would make him less capable of indulging in his favourite pursuits.   (With the somewhat mean Elizabeth in charge, there was never any guarantee that ambassadors would receive their full expenses. At the very least, they were expected to pay their passage out of their own pockets, and a place aboard a ship to France often amounted to an astronomical sum of money.[22])   Indeed, it was only at the request of the Earl of Essex that he finally agreed to go to France, Essex's own representative there - Sir Robert Naunton - having begged to be allowed to return to England.

Neville believed *both* his allocated tasks in France were most likely doomed to failure from the outset.   He did not think the French would readily agree to repaying their loan to Elizabeth, and he most definitely did not think anyone in the world could persuade the Spanish to sign a peace and trade treaty with the English. Supposed to remain abroad for two years, he had had more than enough after half that time, and begged to be allowed to return home for a while. So desperate was he that he declared if he could not obtain official permission then he would return secretly and live as a hermit in the Forest [of Windsor] 'and contemplate my time as a bad ambassador'[23] (surely precursing the characterisation of Jacques in *As You Like It*.) Robert Cecil (his cousin by marriage, and Secretary of State) at last managed to arrange for him to come back for a few months' break, but this turned out to be just in time for his involvement in the Earl of Essex's rebellion, with Essex naming Sir Henry as his preferred candidate to lead the country in the place of Sir Robert Cecil himself.

Neville had also been such a constant friend of the Earl of Southampton that he and that Earl were ultimately housed near to each other in the Tower, following their mutual conviction for involvement in Essex's uprising. Both constantly feared each day might be their last – only a little more hard evidence would have been needed to have forced 'a course of more severity' against them' as Robert Cecil said.[24] Surprisingly, however, Cecil remained a friend of Neville and helped to preserve his life during his incarceration. Indeed, even the hard-headed Cecil balked at harming 'that noble knight'[25], Sir Henry, his erudite friend, who was also his cousin's husband. Yet Henry remained in the Tower for two years, despite the fact that he had taken no *direct,* overt action in the rebellion. When Queen Elizabeth died, one of King James' first acts as new monarch on his way down from Scotland was to order the joint release of Neville and Southampton, which came as such a surprise and relief to Neville.

Surviving the Tower experience, Neville rose to prominence in the Popular Party under James I, and became an Officer in the Virginia Company, while also taking a prominent part in the Muscovy and East India Companies. When Cecil died he was a candidate for the office of Secretary of State. In parliament he was voted the messenger between the Commons and the Lords, which led him into the unofficial office of 'Undertaker' – a parliamentarian who undertook to negotiate between the King and Parliament in order to forward national government business. His efforts in this direction formed the basic ideas of Constitutional Monarchy.

And we have even more to thank the visionary Sir Henry for: along with his friend, Sir Hugh Middleton, he was an initiator and major shareholder in the New River Company. This project brought fresh water through Islington to homes in North London, and was just one of the social improvements Neville envisaged. He was also keen on mass education and was involved in raising funds to set up local Grammar Schools. In the field of international politics, he foresaw the creation of a secure Belgian state, and the development of the New World, projecting a time when Europe and America would be united to their mutual benefit through peace treaties based on international trade. He could thus be said to have heralded the financial might of the USA. As an officer in the Virginia Company, he helped to establish the English settlement in North America. One of his last public services was to draw up a trade route between England and India, using the Eastern European countries as a trading warehouse and thus uniting them with Western Europe. It was therefore probably his far-reaching and centuries-early concepts that made him less widely appreciated in his own day than he should have been. Even Sir Francis Bacon thought him an impossible idealist.[26] Sir Francis, though advanced in scientific philosophy, showed his lack of political foresight by continuing to support the King as a divine, independent and autocratic ruler. Only those few who were in some way approaching Neville's intellectual visionary level could truly appreciate his worth. To those true friends, however, he was known as a great philosopher and orator, whose words in Parliament had the effect of silencing all opposition and promoting deep thought.

Yet in addition to his intellectual gifts Neville, like his father and grandfather before him, enjoyed the fun of life. In his younger days he was a large, handsome man with an impressive presence, who loved disguising[27]. He could, and did, thus gain popular appeal through these gifts and through his fair-mindedness. Even though everyone worried as he grew older, heavier and less agile around Parliament, he was still the most popular candidate for the office of Secretary of State after the death of Robert Cecil. The Earl of Southampton was particularly active in his campaign, but it was, perversely, because of his very popularity that James I feared Neville, and so rejected him, scurrilously giving the post to Neville's own friend and secretary, Sir Ralph Winwood. However, mutual friends told how the two men lived near each other and worked together, Neville being the true initiator of state policies under Winwood's management. Indeed, Neville himself engineered this partnership, suspecting that the King and supporters of his autocracy would oppose Henry's personal candidature. Winwood was a less well-known figure, so had fewer focused opponents, as Neville knew well. Thus did Neville eventually emulate his famous Kingmaker ancestor - Sir Richard Neville, Earl of Warwick, whose life and political role he emphasised in his early History Plays. Like Richard, Henry at last became the true, but hidden, power behind the English throne. His own personal tragedy was, however, that he lived only one year to enjoy this position.

In addition to his life in public service, Sir Henry was a family man, being the father of eleven surviving children. In his letters he shows concern that his sons and daughters should be well educated. However, he generally kept his private life very much a close secret, and this book will reveal his very strong reasons for doing so. He married Anne Killigrew, a lady whose family was of Cornish origin, and ultimately lived for a long time in his diplomat father in law's house in Lothbury, London, along with a number of his wife's relatives, just a stone's throw from the Royal Exchange, and the London publishers' venue at St. Paul's, which was also near the London theatres. His children and later descendants became academics and writers, one of them being the original editor of Pepys' diary.[28] His wife's relatives included an early poetess and several playwrights, one of her second cousins opening a theatre with William Davenant, who was reputedly the illegitimate son of William Shakespeare. Anne Killigrew's mother was one of the Cooke girls of Gidea Hall, who were reputed to be the best educated and wittiest ladies in the land, and on whose community *Much Ado About Nothing* is often said to have been based.

Even though Neville left eleven surviving children and a large circle of friends, mystery surrounds the manner of his dying. He had been a member of a London Writers' and Philosophical society, the Mitre Club – which had links with The Mermaid - and was a well-known 'after-dinner' speaker from this group, appearing alongside Inigo Jones and John Donne[29]. However, he did not arrive at his last engagement, and only days later did the audience hear that his unexpected death on 10th July, 1615 was the cause of his absence. Greatly lauded and respected as he was in his lifetime, there was no public funeral at his passing, and a blank space still remains for the inscription which was never placed above his tomb.

Thus much is a précis of the known facts of Sir Henry Neville's life; but the language and innuendos in the letters by himself and others, the documentary and circumstantial evidence of his concern with the written and spoken word, his familiarity with ciphers, spies and secret channels of communication leave another, concealed, parallel story to be told.

Chapter 3

A VOYAGE AROUND SIR HENRY NEVILLE AS SHAKESPEARE

I was now discovering so many details of Sir Henry Neville's life connecting with the Shakespeare Works that I began to make a list of some of the major points in order to assess the evidence en masse:

- Henry Neville was named as 'thy poet' (i.e. the real Shakespeare) in a the Code which formed the Dedication to Shakespeare's Sonnets.
- Subsequent research into Neville's life proved that his background, education, knowledge and experience match those specific qualities reflected in the plays. (I was soon to discover too that Neville had even named himself [covertly] in the *Sonnets.*)
- Sir Henry's birth and death dates (1561/4 - 1615) were virtually identical to those of William Shakespeare.
- The chronology of the plays synchronised with the emergence of Neville's life events
- Sir Henry had many reasons to hide his identity - I found evidence that his political work, family inheritance, even his life, would have been endangered, had he been discovered. So Neville never published anything under his own name; yet he was sought out by his contemporaries - including Beaumont and Fletcher and King James I - for advice on their own writing. Neville must therefore have been a 'concealed' writer.
- After meticulous research and analysis, I found Neville's linguistic usage and style (in his letters and dispatches) correlated with that of Shakespeare.

These, then were huge factors in favour of Sir Henry's candidature. But there were also many *specific* points of Evidence which now needed to be at least partially listed:

1. The chances of an author named in the Code matching up with 'Shakespeare' in **every respect** when researched are very small indeed, unless Neville's identity is the true one!

2. Neville was a well-connected politician, and a close friend of Southampton (dedicatee of The Sonnets). Additionally, the Shakespeares tried to prove a connection between William's mother, Mary Arden, and the Ardens of Park Hall (Warwickshire), to whom Sir Henry was related by marriage. Neville's grandfather owned the house in which Mary Arden was born.

3. As the descendant of a great and noble family, Neville had access to restricted sources witnessed in the plays: e.g. the documents of his Plantagenet and other ancestors including John of Gaunt in *Richard II*, Warwick the King Maker in *Henry VI parts* 2 and 3, and King Duncan of Scotland in *Macbeth*. As an officer in the Virginia Company, he had access to a **private** letter which became a source for *The Tempest.*

4. Neville was multi-lingual, (some sources used for the plays were available exclusively in French/Italian/Greek/Spanish etc, which we have no reason to believe Shakespeare knew.)

5. Neville became French Ambassador at just the time the French-based *Henry V* was written.

6. 1601 marks an abrupt change in the plays from histories/comedies to the great tragedies. In 1601 Neville was in the Tower - under threat of execution for his part in the Essex Uprising, so this sudden literary transition was at last explained too.[30]

7. The character Falstaff was partly based on Neville himself. Falstaff was initially going to be called **'Oldcastle'**, an antonymic pun on Neville's ('New Town' or **'New Villa'**) name.

8. Neville was an international trader: this is reflected in *The Merchant of Venice* and *The Comedy of Errors.* He resided on the Continent (1578 - 1583). My recent research (detailed later in this chapter and elsewhere in the book) proves that he had overwhelming reasons, during those years, to visit the Jewish Ghetto in Venice, and Elsinore (Denmark - setting of *Hamlet*) in pursuit of his newly-inherited iron and ordnance business.

9. 'Steel' is mentioned 74 times in the works; 'iron' 48 times; 'cannons', and 'ordnance' 30 times. The name 'Touchstone' (*As You Like It*) is metallurgical too. Other such specialised terms - e.g. 'dross', 'unaneal'd' - are also present. Neville is the only person to combine this knowledge with all other 'Shakespearean' attributes. He was an aristocrat/merchant hybrid by ancestry: his father was a 'royal' Neville and his mother a 'merchant' Gresham. And, of course, Neville inherited and ran the Mayfield iron works.

10. Neville was the first Englishman to receive forward knowledge about the Count Orsino and his **possible** visit to the English Court. **Only he** had time to write Orsino into *Twelfth Night.*

11. Neville - unusually for his time - majored in Astronomy at Oxford. Knowledge of Astronomy is present in some of the plays. The Copernican concept of 'infinite space' (mentioned in *Hamlet*) was totally unknown outside of specialised circles in England at the time.

12. Neville and his father became lame through gout[31]. References to the author's lameness occur in the Sonnets, and painful references to gout are present in the plays.

The Documentary evidence I found included:

13. The Northumberland Manuscript, discovered in 1867, has Neville's name and 'family motto poem' at the top, plus repeated practising of William Shakespeare's signature lower down.

14. Previously 'lost' documents, include one he wrote in the Tower of London (1601-1603) - The Tower Notebook (which I discovered in the Worsley Collection in the Lincolnshire Archives). Its contents tie in with the plays, including passages later used in *Henry VIII,* **but the notes had been written by Neville eleven years before that play was performed.**

15. In 1623, the writer Ben Jonson was involved in putting Shakespeare's name on the First Folio edition of the Plays. Jonson was then employed by Gresham College - a London educational foundation instituted by Sir Thomas Gresham, Neville's great uncle and benefactor. I have now discovered an extensive document by Jonson

suggesting he knew about the 'front man' arrangement and that he helped promote the fiction of Shakespeare's authorship at the behest of the Nevilles. All this is described - *for the very first time* - in the present book.

16. An annotated edition of *Halle's Chronicles* (a known source for Shakespeare's plays) was possessed by the Worsleys.[32] Sir Richard Worsley was Neville's friend and son in law, and it was among his documents that I found the Tower Notebook (now in the Lincoln Archives). Another of the documents in the Worsley Collection was referred to in a letter by Sir Richard Brooke - another of Sir Henry's sons in law. This document was known to have been written by Sir Henry and a 'Mr. Dwne' (who may well be John Donne - who often spelt his name that way - Sir Henry's Mitre Club companion.) **All this means the documents in the 16th and 17th century 'Worsley Collection' are now evidenced as formerly belonging to Sir Henry Neville**.

17. Sir Henry Killigrew - Neville's father in law - was appointed as a reviser of *Holinshed's Chronicles*[33], another known Shakespeare source. For many years, Neville and his wife and children lived with Killigrew at his home in Lothbury[34], London, near the publishers and theatres of the day.

Looking through, and constantly adding to, this list while I was still in the process of research confirmed Neville's identity as Shakespeare for me - beyond reasonable doubt. But many of the points of evidence are so intertwined with each other and with Neville's life that the best way of getting an over-all concept of them is to discuss them in relation to one other as well as in the isolation of a bullet-point list.

Sir Henry thought of himself primarily as a politician and a political philosopher, so that is where we shall begin this voyage around his secret works.

Sir Henry's political outlook and his attitude to Kingship were rather unconventional for the Elizabethan Age, and this same unconventional outlook is reflected in the Shakespeare works. Neville and his Oxford tutor, Sir Henry Savile, were keen readers of Tacitus, the Greek republican, and so were no great fans of Monarchy in principle. Sir Henry's branch of the family was by no means at ease with inherited Kingship as an institution. After all, Sir Henry's own grandfather had been executed by King Henry VIII. This occurred after Grandfather Neville had taken part in a masquerade, in which he disguised so successfully as King Henry himself that Cardinal Wolsey was taken in. Things then went from bad to worse, as far as Neville's grandfather was concerned, with Henry VIII finally accusing him of joining plots against him. If truth were known, however, that Tudor King always feared the Neville family, for both he and they knew that the Nevilles - should they ever wish to pursue it - had a greater right to the throne than the Tudors. But our Sir Henry certainly did not wish the family to pursue any such claims: he hated the idea of civil war. Sir Henry's final solution was to suggest a constitutional monarchy, with monarchs being guided by Parliament and the needs of the country. Sir Henry was therefore just the man to have written plays about Kingship in crisis, in the same 'Shakespeare' plays which clearly deplored civil war and civil strife of any sort.

Being a Neville at once accounts for the knowledge of noble families which 'Shakespeare' demonstrates in his history plays too. It also accounts for many instances where the author heroicised or whitewashed the Nevilles' true actions. Who but a Neville would have bothered to foreground Nevilles like that? And there are so many Nevilles and closely-related families in those plays. The writer calls them by their titles - Earl of Westmorland, Old Abergavenny, for example, but it is so often the case that the men and women who possessed those titles at the time were Nevilles. The writer also carves out a persistent role for the Nevilles - he portrays them as councillors, great statesmen, the power behind the throne - the very role Sir Henry Neville sought for himself throughout his political career.

This overwhelming and early political interest of Sir Henry's is reflected in the earliest Shakespeare plays - i.e. the Henry VI trilogy. It was therefore becoming clear that I should be able to look at the plays and poems in chronological order and see Sir Henry's outlook and experience reflected in their work. This indeed turned out to be the case, and it persuaded me to begin annotating the works and referencing them back to Sir Henry's experience and knowledge. I certainly amassed too much material for one book, and that is why I eventually decided to institute The Journal of Neville Studies.

I had planned to write about each of the plays in chronological order in this chapter, examining how each of them connects with Sir Henry Neville. But analyses like that take an enormous amount of space. Besides, there are many aspects to all the Shakespeare plays; they are never *exclusively* a reflection of a particular moment in time. Moreover, though the timing of the plays is generally witnessed by records of their performance, topical allusions, and printed versions, some aspects of the ordering of the plays is occasionally a matter of discussion.

Edmond Malone (1741 - 1812) was the first scholar formally to date the plays, in line with his extensive research. But as John Dover Wilson (while editor of the New Cambridge Shakespeare in the 1930s) pointed out, there is evidence within each work of a long brewing of ideas, and of constant revision. I was able to demonstrate that Wilson was indeed correct on these points, since Henry Neville's Tower Notebook contained notes on the concerns of earlier plays, as well as notes on a play which was to appear eleven years after the Notebook was compiled. It is also true that Shakespeare-Neville's earlier plays contain many more rhyming couplets than his later ones, yet we occasionally find a passage of rhyming couplets in a later play. The logical assumption is therefore that Shakespeare-Neville made extensive notes of ideas, and versified some dramatic episodes, drawing on these later when the final compilation of a play was attempted. This is noticeable in *Timon of Athens*, for instance. The play was finally produced (though not performed) as late as 1605, and its *early* scenes bear all the hallmarks of the writer's later work - yet a later scene in the play suddenly includes rhyming couplets:

> **Alcibiades** ....And with such sober and unnoted passion
> He did behove his anger ere 'twas spent,
> As if he had but prov'd an argument. ...
>
> As you are great, be pitifully good.
> Who cannot condemn rashness in cold blood?
> To kill, I grant, is sin's extremest gust;
> But, in defence, by mercy, 'tis most just.
> To be in anger is impiety;
> But who is man that is not angry?
> *ACT3|SC5*

So my discovery of the Tower Notebook was actually substantiating what had been noticed already in the works themselves. Thus, although the chronology of the works always blends in with direct circumstances in Neville's life, there is a complex psychological working of **recall** intermingling with the moment of creative compilation.

Neville was indeed intermingling various periods of his life experience, and also intertwining various philosophies throughout the plays. He chose elements from many places and many times, so it eventually made sense to voyage around these elements rather than confining them within a mere timeline.

I discovered all the above in a frenzy of researching after my excitement on first discovering Neville's name. But in actuality, the very first thing I found was that Neville's birth and death dates matched Shakespeare's. That was quite remarkable in itself, and the chances of a name in the Code matching in such an important single respect through pure coincidence alone were already quite small. But when such a wild conglomeration of further points indicating that Neville was the writer kept flying in my direction, I simply had to sit up and take notice. I noticed very soon a precise inter-meshing of the knowledge embedded in the plays and knowledge possessed by Neville. But the question which had then to be answered was whether a vast number of Renaissance Englishmen may not have possessed the same attributes.

Further extensive research revealed that no other man's footprints matched those of Shakespeare in such a total, comprehensive way as did Sir Henry's. And with no other man did the chronology of the plays fit the chronology of their lives. Even the very sudden change from comedy, and historical themes to dark tragedies was completely explained. As I continued to look at Neville's life experience and knowledge it became clear that only he possessed absolutely every element directly echoed in the works, or otherwise implied in them. No other Authorship contender can claim all this. And the chances of this happening and Neville being named in the Code too are infinitesimally small, even on a statistical basis alone. In fact, a statistician I consulted proclaimed it to be something like two hundred and forty eight million to one against all these factors coinciding, if Neville wasn't indeed the man.

Unlike any other authorship contender, there are pointers to Neville every single way we turn in the works. It is really hard to pick holes in the theory. Even Neville's birth and early upbringing immediately connect with Theatreland. As he was of aristocratic descent, I thoroughly expected Neville would have been born in some stately home. Consequently, I waded through the baptismal records of Waltham St. Lawrence - the place where his father built his grand home of Billingbear House, near Windsor - but I couldn't find our Henry's name anywhere. Then I found out that his father had also purchased a lease on a Blackfriars property around the time Neville was born. There was our Henry's baptismal record - 10th May, 1564 at St. Anne's, Blackfriars. What's more, his father was a friend of Richard Farrant, director of the Windsor Chapel boys choir, and Richard Farrant became director of the very first Blackfriars theatre. He actually managed to do this through the good offices of Sir Henry Neville's father. I then discovered that Sir Henry senior had always been keen on entertaining and masquerading - like his father before him. In fact, Sir Henry's father devised court entertainments along with his life-long friend Henry Sidney, who was the father of Sir Philip Sidney. Our young Henry was therefore surrounded with theatre and poetry.

Sir Frank Kermode in his book on Shakespeare's language avers that even the earliest play - *King John* - shows a knowledge of the Theatre, and this is hardly surprising when we discover Neville's unexpected birthplace.

One thing just kept linking up with another. All the time I was researching I kept uncovering things which I hadn't particularly set out to find - I kept getting all the answers even before I'd formulated the questions! That only happens in research when you're on the right track. It was tremendously exciting. Not only was the young Henry surrounded with play-acting, but he also had an Italian fencing master for a neighbour.[35] There were many complaints from the good people of Blackfriars that the fencing master was practising his skills with his tutees at all hours - and overshooting his own piece of land. Residents could walk out into the courtyards and be confronted by duelling men wielding sharp steel. No wonder there are so many lively fencing scenes in the plays! And Shakespeare's are the first plays to show fencing on stage.

When the whole family is researched, one grasps the background of theatre, wit and unusual (at the time) respect for women, against which young Shakespeare-Neville was reared.

All family backgrounds are somewhat haphazard, never truly formalised. They influence the child from many different points of view, so I started looking into Henry Neville's mother and her family. They of course turned out to be important for Neville and the plays. Everything I discovered about his mother's family affirmed the knowledge that appeared in Shakespeare's works. She came from a merchant class. Her uncle was Sir Thomas Gresham - an international businessman and founder of the Royal Exchange. The Royal Exchange produced wealth which bolstered the Tudor economy, which is yet another reason why our particular Neville was feared and respected - even by monarchs. In fact the Royal Exchange which Gresham founded ultimately became the basis of the Bank of England.

The links between Sir Henry and his rich uncle were palpable and visible - which must have made any monarch a little reluctant to have too many adverse dealings with Sir Henry, together with the fact that they found his intellect and physical strength and size somewhat frightening. Sir Thomas Gresham had no legitimate children, so our Henry became his major heir. As we have seen, Thomas Gresham left Neville his Mayfield land and ironworks, and it is significant that a knowledge of iron and metal is prominent in the plays - as Touchstone's name has already testified in the extract from *As You Like It*, quoted in a previous chapter. The name 'Touchstone' was a give-away for anyone who knew Neville's secret: it must have made one or two of his close relatives smile. Even the name 'Shakespeare' has a metallurgical ring about it. A spear was the symbol of the old ironworkers. Added to all this, the theatrical manager of the time, Philip Henslowe, had connections with the Neville family. Amazingly too, the famous diary Henslowe kept when managing his theatre in London was written in a book originally begun by his brother, who had been an iron manufacturer's agent and a neighbour of Neville's in Sussex[36]. There were thus many unexpected connections between Sir Henry Neville and the theatre, revealing new aspects of theatrical history. But like all carefully laid conundrums, the Henry Neville = Shakespeare solution is obvious when you already know the answer, but impossibly complex when viewed by outsiders.

Metallurgical imagery abounds in the plays and poems. Some of it displays just as much specialist knowledge as does the name of Touchstone, as seen in this speech by the ghost of Hamlet's father, for instance:

Sleeping within my orchard,
My custom always of the afternoon,
Upon my secure hour thy uncle stole,
With juice of cursed hebona in a vial,
And in the porches of my ears did pour

> The leperous distilment; whose effect
> Holds such an enmity with blood of man
> That swift as quicksilver it courses through
> The natural gates and alleys of the body,
>   ...
> Thus was I, sleeping, by a brother's hand
> Of life, of crown, of queen, at once dispatch'd;
> Cut off even in the blossoms of my sin,
> Unhous'led, disappointed, unanel'd,
> No reckoning made, but sent to my account
> With all my imperfections on my head.

The ghost uses a few strange words about his spirit being unprepared for the afterlife, including a version of 'unannealed'. This is a metallurgical term which few who hadn't worked in the business would really appreciate - even today. And the word 'dross' appears five times throughout the works. Again, it's a word whose precise meaning only a metalworker would know. Yet the writer of the works uses it in its precise sense: 'Dross' is the name for the impurities which float to the top when metal is molten, and Shakespeare-Neville uses the word Dross when he wishes to signify impurity.

But there were inevitably intertwined tragic incidents too. Neville's mother died in 1573, and his father married Elizabeth Bacon-D'Oyly - the half-sister of Sir Francis Bacon - two years later. Characteristically respectful of women, 'Betty doth wear the breeches' was something Sir Henry's father was to write about her,[37] and she was indeed a learned, strict lady who had no children of her own but who was nevertheless keen that children generally should receive a good education. Consequently, Henry entered Merton College, Oxford, where his tutor was a distant relative - Henry Savile. The eleven/fourteen year old Henry Neville, however, chose a subject in which his step mother did not take a direct interest. His main enthusiasm was for the newly-emerging developments in astronomy, so he majored in that at Oxford. At the time, astrology was considered an aspect of astronomy, but Neville veered towards the new, scientific study of Copernican astronomy. He must always have been sceptical of astrology, since he was a life-long friend and one-time student companion of George Carlton, who wrote an early attack on Astrology and defined its separation from Astronomy. Neville and Carlton (who later married Neville's widow) were forward-looking young men. This advanced thinking is reflected in Sonnet 14:

> Not from the stars do I my fortune pluck,
> And yet methinks I have astronomy,
> But not to seek of good or evil luck...

This is an amazingly early separation of astronomy and astrology, in terms of their cultural history, so it is hard to think that anyone outside the then small circle of 'new', scientific astronomers could have written it. Alongside astronomy Henry studied mathematics, rhetoric, classics and law. But to learn about astronomy, one was expected to take on board astrology too. Yet Henry Neville, like Edmund in *King Lear*, never thought his fortune or future had anything to do with the stars:

Edmund. This is the excellent foppery of the world, that, when we are sick in fortune, often the surfeit of our own behaviour, we make guilty of our disasters the sun, the moon, and the stars; as if we were villains on necessity; fools by heavenly compulsion; knaves, thieves, and treachers by spherical pre-dominance; drunkards, liars, and adulterers by an enforc'd obedience of planetary influence; and all that we are evil in, by a divine thrusting on. An admirable evasion of whore-master man, to lay his goatish disposition to the charge of a star! My father compounded with my mother under the Dragon's Tail, and my nativity was under Ursa Major, so that it follows I am rough and   lecherous. Fut! I should have been that I am, had the   maidenliest star in the firmament   twinkled   on   my   bastardizing.
ACT1|SC2

However, Neville's famous tutor, Sir Henry Savile, was a Platonist and rather clung to the old Ptolemaic ideas of the sun going round the Earth. Henry Neville was always more of a Copernican, but he still absorbed from Savile a great enthusiasm for ancient Greek learning, together with a thorough knowledge of the old beliefs, even though he did not personally subscribe to them. A knowledge of all these varying concepts is consequently displayed in the plays, but such direct castigations of Astrology as those given above show where the true author's mind truly lay.

Neville spent his vacations back home at Billingbear House - the stately home which his father built on the edge of Windsor Forest. Here he hunted with his father, who also tutored the Queen and her maids in hunting - a scene directly reflected in *Love's Labour's Lost*.[38]

Our Henry's learned aunt, Elizabeth Hoby, lived two miles away in Bisham Abbey - the one-time home of Richard Neville, Earl of Warwick. Richard Neville's tomb is at Bisham. He is the same Earl of Warwick who plays such a large part in the *Henry VI* trilogy, so Henry would have surely visited his ancestor's tomb there, and also have met yet another strong lady - Elizabeth Hoby herself. Indeed, Neville's eventual wife was also a niece of Elizabeth, so the family connections with Bisham were extremely strong.

It was rumoured Aunt Elizabeth Hoby once beat one of her sons till the blood ran - all because he would not or could not learn his Latin. She then locked him in the attic, where he starved to death[39]. Aunt Elizabeth thereafter was seen sleepwalking and trying to wash the blood off her hands - an incident which famously appears in *Macbeth*. Neville was family: he would have known this story, though it was obviously not something which the family spoke of to strangers. Elizabeth Hoby's husband, Sir Thomas Hoby (1530 -66) translated *The Courtier* from the Italian - a book which is said to be the basis of the bantering in *Much Ado About Nothing*. Henry and other gentlemen of the day studied this book to learn about the social norms expected from men of their class. One of Elizabeth Hoby's sons was named Thomas Posthumous (1566 -1640), because he was born after his father had died. Incidents in Posthumous' life are often said to be mirrored in *Twelfth Night*,[40] while 'Posthumous' is also the name of a character in *Cymbeline*.

Then, in 1578, young Henry Neville's studies were interrupted. His great-uncle Gresham's trading ship was sunk in the Thames estuary. Its remains were discovered in 2003, together with its lost cargo. It was carrying iron rods and Gresham cannons for the King of Denmark[41], to add to his collection at Elsinore fortress.

Gresham was old and ill, and young Neville was his inheritor. Neville, Savile and Robert Sidney - Sir Philip's younger brother - therefore set sail on a prolonged continental tour which included elements designed to be useful for Neville's future business. It is known that Neville visited friends of Tycho

Brahe - the Danish astronomer - and that they travelled as far afield as France, Poland, Vienna and Prague. By 1581, Neville and Savile were at Padua University in Italy. They toured northern Italy - including Venice - where Greek and Latin books were being brought in by the shipload. Savile was on a quest to learn about St. John Chrysostom, and the pair also bought books by Barlaam of Calabria[42] - the tutor of Boccaccio and Petrarch. It is therefore no coincidence that these two Italian writers are a source for so many of the Shakespeare plays.

Neville's visit to Venice is of particular interest. At the time, the city contained the world's first Jewish ghetto, and it is the origin of the word 'ghetto' which affords a particular pointer to Sir Henry Neville's authorship of the plays. 'Ghetto' comes from the Italian 'to throw' or 'to cast', and it was so called because the area of the city known as the Ghetto was where the old bronze cannons were cast. Eventually, it became the centre for making iron cannons too, so Neville certainly had reason to visit the area. German Jewish workers were imported there because they were already skilled in all kinds of metalwork. In *The Merchant of Venice*, Shylock actually mentions his German origins:

> SHYLOCK. Why there, there, there, there!
> A diamond gone, cost me two thousand ducats in Frankfort! The curse never fell upon our nation till now; I never felt it till now. Two thousand ducats in that, and other precious, precious jewels. *ACT 3/SC.1*

It can be reasonably inferred that Henry Neville had been sent by Thomas Gresham both to apologise to the King of Denmark for the loss of his cannons, and also to research continental cannon making. Sir Thomas was ill by this time and knew his great nephew would have to take over his Sussex cannon works when he returned from his tour. In fact he died in 1579, while Henry was in Vienna, which would have made it all the more urgent for young Henry Neville to obtain all the ironworking tips he could once he went to Venice. He would not have been allowed to visit the latest Venetian arms' centre. That was the Arsenale, and forbidden to foreigners. So he would have definitely gone to seek out what memories remained of the older works, and this meant visiting the Jewish quarter of Venice. No other authorship contender had reason to do this. The combination of the Jewish and merchant-shipwreck themes in *The Merchant of Venice* were close to Neville's heart and mind, which is a subject on which I expand later in this book.

Similarly, the theme of the shipwrecked merchant repeats itself in The Comedy of Errors:

> AEGEON A league from Epidamnum had we sail'd
> Before the always-wind-obeying deep
> Gave any tragic instance of our harm:
> But longer did we not retain much hope,
> For what obscured light the heavens did grant
> Did but convey unto our fearful minds
> A doubtful warrant of immediate death ...
> The sailors sought for safety by our boat,
> And left the ship, then sinking-ripe, to us; *ACT 1/SC.1*

Even in later years, the horror of shipwreck and its consequences had not left Henry Neville. In *Hamlet, Twelfth Night, Pericles, The Winter's Tale* and *The Tempest* we have echoes of Neville's wide experience of sea travel, and especially of the time when he spent three days tossed on the sea with his family crossing to France to take up his post of Ambassador in Paris.

In 1583, Neville returned home from the continent. His father and step mother were entertaining Queen Elizabeth at one of their country houses, but there was to be no such leisure for young Henry. Neville's future father in law had been a great friend of Sir Francis Walsingham - head of Elizabeth's diplomatic and espionage services. Young Neville had been reputed book-learned, academically-prodigious and 'virtuous' by the continental scholars he met, and by the Sidneys - Walsingham's relatives by marriage. Walsingham knew too that young Henry had already met and impressed the Earl of Essex. As it happened, Walsingham had arranged a diplomatic mission - headed by the young Earl of Essex and bound for Scotland. Sir Henry went along too.

The English diplomatic missions to Scotland were lodged at Glamis castle. It can therefore no longer be counted mere coincidence, then, that *Macbeth* was later set at Glamis, even though the historical Macbeth was not associated with that castle.

On his return, young Henry married Anne Killigrew, who came of a Cornish family of pirates and strong-minded females. From this family came writers too - Anne's great niece was a tragically short-lived poetess of the same name, and her nephews and great nephews became playwrights. Indeed, Sir Thomas Killigrew was given an exclusive licence by Charles II to perform Shakespeare's plays in London - together with William Davenant, who was often reputed to be the illegitimate son of Shakespeare himself. Did Anne assist her husband in the writing of the plays? Possibly - perhaps even *probably*. Thus does coincidence pile on top of coincidence. Yet surely coincidence alone cannot be so endlessly elastic!

Soon after his marriage, Neville and his wife went to live in Mayfield, East Sussex, near the Kent border. Neville plied the trade of a cannon maker in Mayfield, a factor which at last explains why there are eight references to cannonry in King John - a play written at this very time. Anne Killigrew and Neville actually lived in Sussex for only some of the year. They were often in London too, where they stayed at Anne Killigrew's father's house in Lothbury. It is also greatly interesting and significant that father-in-law Killigrew was one of the men appointed to revise Holinshed's Chronicles - the work which informed the history plays of Shakespeare. Neville would therefore have had access to this work through Killigrew's library. Also, the man who published the new edition of Holinshed was Ralph Newbery - a neighbour of Neville's in Berkshire, and father of a man who was ultimately to become a beneficiary under Sir Henry Neville's will[43].

Meanwhile, back at Billingbear House, Neville's stepmother's maid had married Thomas Morley, the composer. Morley was allowed to come and live at Billingbear. It was he who set a famous song in *As You Like It*: 'It was a lover and his lass'. Morley was the pupil of William Byrd, and it was Byrd's music that was used for the compilation of *My Lady Nevell's Book*,[44] the Lady Nevell in question being none other than Lady Elizabeth Bacon-Doyly-Neville, our Henry's step mother. Byrd's patrons, the Pagets, were also friends of Sir Henry Neville.[45]

But all was not well with Sir Henry's ironworking. Neville turned out to be far too incorruptible a person to ply the armaments trade for very long. He always refused to pay bribes, which were traditionally charged by the authorities for turning a blind eye to certain practices, such as exporting more armaments than English law allowed, or even just for obtaining an export licence .[46]

Neville's incorruptibility was later celebrated in a 1610 epigram to Sir Henry by his friend, Ben Jonson. This same poem cryptically and covertly revealed too that Neville was a 'muse' (Jonson's term for a poet) who owned 'titles' but lent his life to someone else:

> Who now calls on thee, NEVIL, is a Muse,
> That serves nor fame, nor titles; but doth chuse
> Where vertue makes them both, and that's in thee:
> Where all is faire, beside thy pedigree.
> Thou art not one, seek'st miseries with hope,
> Wrestlest with dignities, or fain'st a scope
> Of service to the publique, when the end
> Is private gaine, which hath long guilt to friend.
> Thou rather striv'st the matter to possesse,
> And elements of honour, th[e]an the dress;
> To make thy lent life, good against the Fates:
> And first to know thine owne state, then the State's.
> To be the same in roote, thou art in height;
> And that thy soule should give thy flesh her weight.
> Go on, and doubt not, what posteritie,
> Now I have sung thee thus, shall judge of thee.
> Thy deeds, unto thy name, will prove new wombes,
> Whil'st others toyle for titles to their tombes.

(This is so cryptic a poem that I have interpreted it in *The Truth Will Out*. Jonson certainly knew Neville's life was half-concealed, in that he declares Henry is the same in 'root' as in 'height', while simple re-structuring of the punctuation gives 'Nevil is a Muse That serves nor fame nor titles...'.)

Neville soon realised that he wanted to be a courtier - in order to be at the centre of government. He had been lauded for providing cannons for the Cinque Ports during the Armada of 1588, and for being involved with national defence strategies. But he also realised that Queen Elizabeth had been getting reports that he had exported more cannons than he should have. He reasoned that she - and the public - would never trust him while he carried on this sort of trade, so he gradually sold up his interest in the business. To Queen Elizabeth, Neville was always someone of whom to be wary. Less open with her than his father, yet clever. She never seems to have felt easy in his presence.

Neville was a descendant of the Falconbridges and Longavilles, so his actual personality and social position seem to be reflected upon by the Queen and her attendants in the following scene from *Love's Labour's Lost*, for the character of Longaville (a name in the Neville pedigree)[47] may well represent an aspect of Neville himself:

PRINCESS OF FRANCE. (i.e. QUEEN ELIZABETH of
   England)
   Who are the votaries, my loving lords,
   That are vow-fellows with this virtuous duke?
FIRST LORD. Lord Longaville is one.
PRINCESS OF FRANCE. Know you the man?
MARIA. I know him, madam; at a marriage feast,
   Between Lord Perigort and the beauteous heir
   Of Jaques Falconbridge, solemnized
   In Normandy, saw I this Longaville.
   A man of sovereign parts, peerless esteem'd,
   Well fitted in arts, glorious in arms;
   Nothing becomes him ill that he would well.
   The only soil of his fair virtue's gloss,
   If virtue's gloss will stain with any soil,
   Is a sharp wit match'd with too blunt a will,
   Whose edge hath power to cut, whose will still wills
   It should none spare that come within his power.
PRINCESS OF FRANCE. Some merry mocking lord, belike;
   is't so?
MARIA. They say so most that most his humours know.
PRINCESS OF FRANCE. Such short-liv'd wits do wither as
   they grow

   (The 'Princess of France' is often termed 'Queen' in the text of the play. She is therefore probably synonymous with Queen Elizabeth herself.)

   "Well fitted in arts; glorious in arms", yet sometimes avoided by his peers because of the strength of his will and his biting wit - how well that describes Henry Neville of the time. However, despite the suspicion with which he was received at Court, it seems Neville put his knowledge of weaponry ('arms') to good use: he was most probably the Henry Neville who accompanied the Earl of Essex on his raid of Cadiz, as weapons' advisor, as mentioned earlier.

   This happened in 1596. The King of Spain had been building up his fleet again after his defeat by the English in 1588.

So Essex and his troops took pre-emptive action by burning the ships in a surprise raid on Cadiz harbour. This turned out to be one of the most clinical attacks in history. Even the King of Spain himself remarked in amazement how the Earl of Essex worked to try and ensure his men did not attack the civilian population.[48] Such behaviour doubtless impressed the humane Sir Henry Neville. Indeed, Essex appears to have knighted him after the battle, along with one of his erstwhile continental travelling companions, Arthur Throckmorton. But the Queen was so annoyed at the number of men Essex knighted on the campaign that the vulnerable Sir Henry seems to have kept very quiet about it. Elizabeth was worried because, under the old chivalric laws, one owed loyalty to the Earl who had knighted you. Even by this early date, then, it was clear that Queen Elizabeth already feared the charismatic young Essex's popularity. A descendant of Sir Henry Neville was later to write in his commonplace book of Henry's 'excessive attachment' to that Earl.[49] Yet for many years it was to be a secret attachment, which Henry would later deny in order to save his own life.

In Parliament, Henry was well connected enough to be promoted. During the reign of James I, he became the messenger between the House of Commons and the House of Lords. This was a difficult post to fill in those days, since most Lords refused to speak to commoners, even if they were Members of Parliament. Sir Henry - the hybrid - however, was of such an elevated family and had such a name for being an intellectual that both Houses were willing to listen to him. Indeed, one important point we've missed out so far was that Henry became an M.P. when he was very young - just on the verge of his twenty-first birthday. But being an M.P. didn't automatically ensure you would become a courtier. And it was being seen in court that helped gain promotion. Henry Neville's very powerful connections were able to help him in this respect. He was related to Elizabeth's chief advisor, William Cecil, Lord Burghley. Burghley's mother was actually a Neville, and Burghley's wife was Anne Killigrew's aunt, so Henry and Anne Neville were always close to the Cecils. Added to this, Henry's father had been one of Lord Burghley's greatest and most trusted friends, so the families were always together, even from young Henry's childhood. This meant that our Henry Neville and Robert Cecil - Lord Burghley's son - had been virtually brought up together.

And so it was hardly surprising that Lord Burghley himself introduced Neville at Court.

From all accounts, I suspect that young Henry had always outshone Robert academically - and physically - so it's not surprising that they were friendly rivals. I visualise Henry always being a little bitter that Robert Cecil eventually became Secretary of State, simply because he took advantage of having such an eminent father. Henry was kindly and considerate by all accounts, but he was never unsure of his own abilities. All the Nevilles had a reputation for being rather dramatic and boisterous, so it was undoubtedly an effort for Henry to hide his feeling that **he**, not Robert, would always have been a better Secretary of State. The fundamental difference between the two was that Robert was a ritualist while Henry was a visionary. Robert Cecil was content just to hold the reins of power and administer the kind of justice that would simply keep the office of Secretary itself going, and allow the monarch the public appearance of seeming to be in absolute control. Henry, on the other hand, had creative ideas about building up England's wealth and power and, above all, extending education and ensuring rights for politicians and the people[50]. Their two differing outlooks were therefore bound to come into conflict one day, though both of them did their best to pretend - in everyday life - that this conflict would never happen.

But I think old Lord Burghley owed a secret debt of gratitude to young Henry - and neither old Burghley nor Robert, his son, ever wanted this to come out. Let's go back a bit in time to the moment when the young Henry Wriothesley's father died, because that was the time when Wriothesley became the Earl of Southampton, and also the time he was given into the wardship of William Cecil, Lord Burghley. Neville later admitted that he had known the young Earl at this very time, and it can be no coincidence that this is precisely the young Earl to whom the Shakespeare Sonnets are most widely considered to have been dedicated. Indeed, 'Shakespeare' composed letters of Dedication to the Earl of Southampton which still head most editions of *The Rape of Lucrece* and *Venus and Adonis* for him.

The Cecils were always trying to ally themselves with the aristocracy through advantageous marriage arrangements, and the young Earl of Southampton seemed a perfect match for old Cecil's granddaughter. When Wriothesley became a teenager, his relatives, in collusion with Sir William Cecil, Lord Burghley, were in correspondence about the idea. The trouble was, they couldn't persuade young Wriothesley to take much interest in the girl. However, it's always seemed that the first 17 of the Shakespeare Sonnets were written in order to try and persuade a young man to marry:

> From fairest creatures we desire increase,
> That thereby beauty's rose might never die ....*sonnet 1*

> How much more praise deserved thy beauty's use,
> If thou couldst answer 'This fair child of mine
> Shall sum my count, and make my old excuse'
> Proving his beauty by succession thine.
> This were to be new made when thou art old,
> And see thy blood warm when thou feel'st it cold. etc. etc.

Wriothesley's name (usually pronounced 'Risely') was often also pronounced 'Rosely' at the time, so 'beauty's rose' in Sonnet number one seems straight away to be a reference to him. Not too much left to the imagination when it comes to persuading him to marry and produce an heir, either! My contention is that old Cecil probably asked young Henry Neville to write those Sonnets. Old Cecil knew the Nevilles. He knew how clever and learned young Henry was. The Nevilles were family too - they could be trusted not to give old Cecil's scheme away. It is, however, unthinkable that he would have asked an unknown Stratford boy to have pried into his affairs and written all those very pointed words. Besides, the division of the classes in those days was as strong as any caste system. Cecil would simply have had to have chosen a writer whom he knew personally, who was related - and probably one who was in some manner under his power. All these circumstances applied to Neville. This would explain too why the Sonnets were published only after old Cecil had died, and only after the Earl of Southampton was married and had an heir. The Earl didn't marry Cecil's granddaughter, in the end. He ran away to fight for Henri of Navarre in France, together with the Earl of Essex. And once again, coincidence piles up on top of coincidence, since Neville was already in this circle, and was later to serve as Ambassador to France, under that very Henri, after he became King of France.

But because the Sonnets weren't published for years, Sir Henry Neville was able to keep adding to them. The later sonnets apply to Sir Henry's subsequent life in a way that is both meaningful and poignant. It would take a whole book to explain all these overlapping circumstances, but as this present book proceeds I shall briefly demonstrate how the Sonnets tie in graphically with Henry's life.

At around the same time as Neville got to know young Wriothesley, he also became acquainted with a then member of the Wriothesley household - one Charles Paget, a friend and patron of William Byrd, the composer. Paget was himself known as something of a secret writer.[51] But he was also a bit of a shady character. The Earl of Southampton's father had been a Catholic, and Paget - who was also from landed gentry - was supposedly a Catholic too. Yet he was one of those 'moderate' Catholics who had no liking for Jesuits or the Spanish Inquisition. The last thing moderate Catholics like Paget wished to see was a Spanish king on the throne of England, so Paget was eventually employed by the very Protestant head of Queen Elizabeth's secret service - Sir Francis Walsingham. Walsingham was a close friend of Neville's father in law, Sir Henry Killigrew, and it is not beyond the realms of possibility that Neville and Paget had some writing projects together, because I discovered *Leycester's Commonwealth* (usually thought to have written by Paget) among some of Neville's lost documents. Neville had heavily annotated the manuscript of that work.

All this is more fully detailed in *The Truth Will Out*, but the point here is that Neville was himself well and truly in that world of diplomacy and espionage run first by Walsingham and then by the Earl of Essex, who was friendly with both Henry Neville and the Earl of Southampton. Neville would therefore have been even more careful than Paget not to reveal the fact that he was an author. After all, Neville's family was much more famous, and thereby more vulnerable, than Paget's. A spy called Thomas Morgan worked closely with Paget, and it is my contention that these two men formed the basis of the characters of Rosencrantz and Guildenstern in *Hamlet*. This seems especially feasible and especially significant when one remembers Neville's knowledge of Tycho Brahe, whose portrait had been passed round the friends of Henry Savile, Neville's Oxford tutor and companion. (Rosencrantz and Guildenstern were ancestors of Brahe, and their names and coats of arms were on the border of the Brahe portrait.)[52]

Neville was to contact Paget, the spy, again when he went to France as Ambassador. When Neville came back to England and was ultimately imprisoned in the Tower of London, Paget - the spy - would have therefore been a recent acquaintance of his, again illustrating how the chronology of the plays fits in with incidents in Neville's life.s

The position of French Ambassador had not been the job Neville was hoping for, however. He had ideas for expanding England's wealth through international trade, so he was rather hoping for an elevated position in English politics. But it was never likely that the Queen or Robert Cecil would fail to use Neville's linguistic skills - and neither would his friend, the Earl of Essex. Essex's man in France desperately wanted to return home, so Essex begged Neville to become Ambassador so that he could have a new, reliable man out there. The Queen must have been rather concerned that it was the Earl of Essex and not she herself who finally prevailed on Neville to take the French ambassadorship. But one can understand Neville's concern. After all, he had to pay for his own and family's passage over there, and with tickets to France costing an extremely substantial amount, this was going to be an expensive exercise.

When Neville reached Dover in April 1599, however, the wind was 'directlie contrarie' as he put it in a letter to Robert Cecil[53]. He and his family finally spent three weeks in a Dover inn, waiting for the wind to change direction so that they could set sail. *Henry V* is one play we know the writing date of for certain,[54] and it turns out that Neville was housed in the atmosphere of the Dover inn, while Falstaff's death in that play was staged in just such an establishment. Falstaff was one alter-ego of Neville's - the large, overfed, over-contented, over-confident, gouty English gentleman. But Neville was being forced to leave this side of his persona behind, now that he had to take up a public position in France. Thus are there immediate and timely connections between Sir John Falstaff and Sir Henry Neville. Furthermore, the Chorus in *Henry V* describes the scene at an English seaport, whereas Shakespeare of Stratford is never known to have seen the coast of England:

Play with your fancies; and in them behold
Upon the hempen tackle ship-boys climbing;
Hear the shrill whistle which doth order give
To sounds confus'd; behold the threaden sails,
Borne with th' invisible and creeping wind,
Draw the huge bottoms through the furrowed sea,
Breasting the lofty surge. O, do but think
You stand upon the rivage and behold
A city on th' inconstant billows dancing;
For so appears this fleet majestical,
Holding due course to Harfleur. Follow, follow!
Grapple your minds to sternage of this navy
And leave your England as dead midnight still,
Guarded with grandsires, babies, and old women,
Either past or not arriv'd to pith and puissance;
For who is he whose chin is but enrich'd
With one appearing hair that will not follow
These cull'd and choice-drawn cavaliers to France?
Work, work your thoughts, and therein see a siege;
Behold the ordnance on their carriages,
With fatal mouths gaping on girded Harfleur.
Suppose th' ambassador from the French comes back;
Tells Harry that the King doth offer him
Katherine his daughter, and with her to dowry
Some petty and unprofitable dukedoms.
The offer likes not; and the nimble gunner
With linstock now the devilish cannon touches,

Such scenes were fresh in Neville's experience and mind when *Henry V* was written, and one cannot mistake the immediacy of the Chorus' description. Added to the first-hand knowledge of a sea port, Neville's touch is seen in his account of the ordnance, the cannons, and the mention of the Ambassador. In no other authorship contender - and with no other Englishman of that very time and moment - is there such a thematic convergence.

Similarly, at the same time as Neville shows his concern over the Earl of Essex in Ireland by writing frequent letters to Cecil asking for news of his fate, so does the Chorus in *Henry V* talk of that Earl's hoped-for triumphant return to England, and even uses the **metallurgical** metaphor of the quick forge and working house of thought:

But now behold
In the quick forge and working-house of thought,
How London doth pour out her citizens!
The mayor and all his brethren in best sort-
Like to the senators of th' antique Rome,
With the plebeians swarming at their heels-
Go forth and fetch their conqu'ring Caesar in;
As, by a lower but loving likelihood,
Were now the General of our gracious Empress-
As in good time he may- from Ireland coming,
Bringing rebellion broached on his sword,
How many would the peaceful city quit
To welcome him!

While in France, Neville soon met up again with Charles Paget again - the spy and one-time steward of the old Earl of Southampton. Through various circumstances, Paget was a spy who had been forced to stay out in the cold[55]. But Paget had also offended Queen Elizabeth - probably because he was the secret author of *Leycester's Commonwealth* - a work accusing the Earl of Leicester of all sorts of crimes. Elizabeth famously doted on Leicester. Thus she refused to allow Paget to return to England, even for a visit, despite Neville's pleadings on his behalf. Neville, however, knew what a good intelligencer Paget really was, so he used Paget's services, despite the Queen's dislike of him.

Finally, it was probably Paget who looked after Neville during a period in which he seems to have 'disappeared' while he was abroad. Neville's eventual absence without leave came about through a number of circumstances, mostly concerned with the number of hopeless and thankless tasks the Queen had set him to do while in France. These thankless tasks culminated in his being required to progress a peace and trade treaty between the French, Spanish and English. The Spanish sent unprofessional, but noble men, who looked down on Neville's lack of aristocratic title. They also claimed they should have precedence in the negotiations and in the terms of the proposed Treaty. Their prejudiced, unjustifiable points annoyed Neville and the other English delegates greatly. To add insult to injury, however, when the negotiations broke down and the other English delegates were allowed to return home, Neville was commanded by the Queen to stay where he was - away from

Paris and his family - and wait sixty days to see if the Spanish could be persuaded to return to the negotiations.

Neville was so angry that he wrote to Cecil and told him that if the Queen would not give him a licence to return, then he would come home nevertheless and "live hermit in Ashridge or the forest, and contemplate my time as a bad Ambassador."[56]

During the following month, no one could raise any reply from Neville. Where was he? Not back in England, unless he had truly returned and lived in Ashdown forest, where he had ancestral lands, and near where his old ironworks were situated. One month later however, Neville was to write and tell his secretary that he had only just returned to England, so it is highly unlikely he had already hidden out in an English forest, and totally unlikely that he would have crossed the Channel without his family. So where could he have hidden on the continent during his AWOL (Absent Without Leave), incommunicable period? The obvious answer is that he went to stay with his friend Charles Paget at his house in the Ardennes. This seems especially likely, since Neville had been in Boulogne for the Treaty negotiations, which took him nearer to the Ardennes at that exact time. Moreover, Sir Ralph Winwood later wrote to Robert Cecil, telling him that Neville had purposed to go to Brussels once the negotiations ended.

Can it therefore be mere coincidence that *As You Like It* is set in the Ardennes, with Touchstone - the oh-so-aptly titled jester, whose name means a test stone for metals, and with Jacques, the runaway, disgruntled philosopher-courtier? Put these two characters together and you have the two sides of Sir Henry Neville. Sir Henry the wit, and travelling philosopher, and Sir Henry, the 'French' disgruntled courtier and diplomat. Confuse Ardennes with Arden and you have the testing ground for William Shakespeare, born a country bumpkin in the Forest of Arden - Will of the Forest, who has the water poured into his glass from another goblet, by a man whose name connects him with metalworking. Many of the names in the play - apart from Touchstone's and Will's - are French: Jacques, Oliver de Boys, Amiens, for instance - not names commonly found in the Warwickshire Arden.

But by the time Neville finally obtained permission to return to London, there was rumour of a foreign visitor about to enter the English Court. Neville's secretary - Ralph Winwood - wrote to tell Neville that a certain Duke Orsino was seeking refuge with Queen Elizabeth, as he had had a big argument with the Pope. Now, this was all restricted information, and it is difficult to see who else at Court would have had such forward warning of Orsino's visit. Yet, within a few weeks, Orsino appears as one of the leading characters in Twelfth Night - a drama often thought to have been written specifically to celebrate that Duke's stay in England. Scholars have hitherto tied themselves in knots trying to explain away how Shakespeare could have known about Orsino's visit in time to have included him in a play, and how any writer could have known about specific incidents in Orsino's life and adapted them for the hastily-written *Twelfth Night*. Yet all is explained once we know of Winwood's explanatory letter to Neville, written in November, 1600. This was just in time for Neville to adapt the play he had already begun for the 1601 Twelfth Night celebrations - in time for *Neville* to do so, but for no one else.

Coincidence on top of Coincidence? Unlikely - what did George Orwell say - something like, one coincidence = happenstance; two = interesting; **three** = call the secret service! And here we already have dozens of overlapping circumstances, to which we're now about to add more.

So, here was Sir Henry, back home on a short break, claiming that his hearing was impaired. This might just have been the case, for besides testing cannons, deafness existed in the Neville family. His old uncle, Baron Bergavenny, was completely deaf. Even if Neville's own claim wasn't exactly true, however, what better excuse could an errant diplomat have produced? Neville - a man born next to the theatre to a family who played in court masques, a man himself used to disguising (as he betrays in one of his letters to Cecil)[57] - could have carried it off. But nevertheless, the Queen was constantly breathing down his neck to go and complete his two year mission in France. Finally, Neville ran out of excuses to stay at home, so it came about that Sir Henry was - perhaps by chance, perhaps by conspiratorial design - more than ready to join the Earl of Essex's rebellion when specifically requested by him and the Earl of Southampton to do so.

There must always have been mutual respect between Neville and the Earl of Essex. It was only Essex who had finally persuaded him to accept the post of Ambassador in France, but now Essex offered him a much greater opportunity. If his rebellion succeeded, he told Neville, he wanted him to become the first Minister of State under his new Constitution[58]. What had Neville to lose? He felt he might die if he had to return to France - he'd suffered from something like hepatitis there, and he also felt he did not wish to take his large family into virtual exile again. He wouldn't take an active role in the uprising itself, either, so he reasoned he was unlikely to have been found out, if the rebellion failed. But if it succeeded, then he would be the top politician in the land, and he could then return to France if and when it suited him, and also be funded to do so out of the public purse, not his own.

Neville's immediate reply to Essex's proposition was later recorded by his friend, the historian William Camden. From its text, Neville clearly had his doubts from the start about Essex's actual ground plan: ''Tis mad, wild! 'Tis among the number of those things which are never praised till performed.'[59]

The same thing could be said, of course, for stage plays. And it is curious how Neville keeps using the language of the stage in his own utterances. For instance when, later in life, he was offered the position of Treasurer by King James I's favourite - another job he did not want - he used yet another 'dramatic' metaphor, (as reported by his friend, John Chamberlain), saying that he had 'not been so long upon the stage for a secretary, to accept a meaner place.' [60] The role for which Neville had by then rehearsed, and still wanted, was the position of first minister or, as it was termed then, Secretary of State.

So, back in 1600, Neville chanced his all by joining his admired friend, the Earl of Essex. But, of course, the Rebellion failed, and its main activists were rounded up by Robert Cecil. Essex himself was executed, together with some of Neville's and Savile's learned friends. Prominent amongst the activists who survived, however, was the young Earl of Southampton, who, it seems, still looked younger than he was and still proved somewhat timid. When threatened with torture to reveal all, he confessed privately to Cecil that Neville was considered by Essex to be his 'chief man'.

By this time, Neville had at last thought it best to run away, even though he knew nothing of Southampton's confession. He had long possessed the Queen's permission to travel, so he now at last made use of it. Whether he intended his family to fly with him is not certain. What is certain, however, is that the soldiers sent in pursuit of Neville discovered him at

Dover, together with his wife and family, ostensibly saying a long farewell[61].

As soon as he saw the soldiers, Neville jumped on his horse and fled, leaving his amazed family behind him. Neville was a big, heavy man - nicknamed Sir John Falstaff by the Earl of Southampton's wife - so it did not take the soldiers long to catch up with him. He now did not resist arrest but went with them quietly back to London.

At his hearing, Neville denied having any particular friendship with the Earl of Essex, and also claimed not to have seen the Earl of Southampton much 'Since he was a boy in my old Lord Treasurer's house.'[62]

Both these statements were of course untrue, and must have preyed on Sir Henry's mind, when he was finally imprisoned in the Tower for treason, along with the young Earl of Southampton. I say, must have preyed on his mind, because in *Hamlet* - the play Neville wrote while in the Tower - there is early mention of the cock crowing, as at Judas' denial of Christ, as will be discussed in a later chapter.

The haunted, glooming atmosphere which pervades *Hamlet* is altogether explained by Neville's circumstances, and by the execution of his friend, the Earl of Essex. Hamlet's character is a mixture of the Earl's and Neville's own. Hamlet is Neville, the philosopher, coupled with Essex, the derring-do, kind, progressive nobleman, but occasional emotional madman. *Leycester's Commonwealth* - the book by Paget, named on the Northumberland Manuscript, and later turning up among Neville's own documents among the Worsley Collection in the Lincoln Archives - talks of Essex's stepfather's misdeeds. These alleged misdeeds included poisoning the Earl of Essex's father in order to marry his mother, and holding a banquet at which the 'wrong' people drank from the poisoned chalice. The parallels are simply too direct to be ignored. The young Earl of Essex often claimed (the text of *Leycester's Commonwealth* reports) that his own fits of madness could have been occasioned by his mistakenly sipping from a cup his stepfather had intended for one of his banquet's victims. Just the same 'mistakes' occur at the conclusion of *Hamlet.*

Neville must have been assessing his past life, while in the Tower. This is evidenced by the fact that cannons and cannonry are mentioned more frequently in *Hamlet* than in any other play since King John. And King John was written during the time Neville was actually making his cannons in Sussex. It was now quite natural that Neville should begin wondering whether he might not have fared better to have remained in his international ironworking business, and never have bothered with the Court and politics. The disdain with which he spoke of the Court in *As You Like It* shows Neville's disenchantment had truly begun while he occupied his reluctant Ambassadorial post in France. Again and again, therefore, we see how both the tone and the themes of the plays fit hand in glove with the course of Neville's life.

The satirical, despairing, almost nihilistic *Troilus and Cressida* was also written while Neville was in the Tower. And this play also appropriately includes philosophising on the problems of attempting to change even one element on which the feudal state was based - that of seniority, status or degree:

> The heavens themselves, the planets, and this centre,
> Observe degree, priority, and place,
> Insisture, course, proportion, season, form,
> Office, and custom, in all line of order;
> And therefore is the glorious planet Sol
> In noble eminence enthron'd and spher'd
> Amidst the other, whose med'cinable eye
> Corrects the ill aspects of planets evil,
> And posts, like the commandment of a king,
> Sans check, to good and bad. But when the planets
> In evil mixture to disorder wander,
> What plagues and what portents, what mutiny,
> What raging of the sea, shaking of earth,   {ACT1|SC3 }

In addition, the writer uses astronomical imagery here - Neville's very first enthusiasm at university!

There's little doubt that the true writer, now in the Tower, was reflecting on life - and death. Many of the Sonnets show a pre-occupation with Death - that particular dark lady:

> Tired with all these for restful death I cry,
> As to behold desert a beggar born,
> And needy nothing trimmed in jollity,
> And purest faith unhappily forsworn,
> And gilded honour shamefully misplaced,
> And maiden virtue rudely strumpeted,
> And right perfection wrongfully disgraced,

And strength by limping sway disabled
And art made tongue-tied by authority,
And folly (doctor-like) controlling skill,
And simple truth miscalled simplicity,
And captive good attending captain ill.
Tired with all these, from these would I be gone,
Save that to die, I leave my love alone.   *sonnet 66*

He is clearly disgruntled with all society's ills, and with his own
'limping sway' through the gout which affected his leg. (I had
originally discovered Neville's disability when I looked through
the Neville papers in the Berkshire Record Office and read a
letter from his sister in law, commiserating with him about it.)
And who was Neville's 'love' - mentioned in the last line of the
Sonnet - whilst he was in the Tower? There's no doubt he truly
loved his wife, but he had always reserved part of his love for the
boy he had known since the old days in Lord Burghley's house -
the boy who had lost his father at nine years old, and had met
Neville and his wife before they had children of their own. That
boy was now incarcerated in the Tower with Neville - he was the
Earl of Southampton, the dedicatee of Shakespeare's Sonnets,
but also the same man who had betrayed Neville by telling
Robert Cecil just what a key man Neville had been in Essex's
rebellion. It must have been hard for Neville to forgive the Earl
for this, but if we are to believe the sentiments in the Sonnets,
Neville seems to have managed to do so:

No more be grieved at that which thou hast done,
Roses have thorns, and silver fountains mud,
Clouds and eclipses stain both moon and sun,
And loathsome canker lives in sweetest bud.
All men make faults, and even I in this,
Authorizing thy trespass with compare,
My self corrupting salving thy amiss,
Excusing thy sins more than thy sins are:
For to thy sensual fault I bring in sense,
Thy adverse party is thy advocate,
And 'gainst my self a lawful plea commence:
Such civil war is in my love and hate,
That I an accessary needs must be,
To that sweet thief which sourly robs from me.   *sonnet 35*

Then, against all expectation, Neville and Southampton are set free. Queen Elizabeth - the mortal moon [what a plethora of astronomical imagery] - has died, and James I has issued a proclamation announcing that the Earl of Southampton and Sir Henry Neville shall be released immediately. Sonnet 107 was Neville's try of Triumph:

Not mine own fears nor the prophetic soul
Of the wide world dreaming on things to come
Can yet the lease of my true love control,
Supposed as forfeit to a confined doom.
The mortal moon hath her eclipse endured,
And the sad augurs mock their own presage;
Incertainties now crown themselves assured,
And peace proclaims olives of endless age.
Now with the drops of this most balmy time
My love looks fresh, and Death to me subscribes,
Since spite of him I'll live in this poor rhyme, ...

But from many of the Sonnets, it seems that Neville had been dreaming of the dark lady of death as his end, not sudden release. For all he knew, he might one day have been finally proven as being truly involved with the Essex faction, and so eventually put to death by Elizabeth - that Queenly tyrant, the 'mortal moon'. Or he might have become 'the coward conquest of a wretch's knife' - assassinated while in gaol, like his ancestor, Richard II. The Sonnets speak of his disgrace 'with fortune and men's eyes'. They speak of his name receiving a brand - and, indeed, Neville's name was branded on some of his cannons. They speak of his other roles in life besides that of a writer, so that his very nature almost became 'subdued to that it works in'. As will be described in some detail in Chapter 5, Neville sometimes embeds his own name plainly in individual Sonnets - which is only to be expected from a man who was used to working with Codes. And Neville, the diplomat, the friend of spies, certainly was used to that.

But now Neville was free and all the worst was behind him. In 1605 he was honoured with an M.A. from Oxford University, during which celebrations he and King James I witnessed a boring University play (see chapter 10) which was, nevertheless, a version of the Macbeth story. And the new King was generally pretty receptive to some of Neville's and Southampton's ideas at this time, because both of them were

87

involved in founding the Virginia Company. 'Adventurers' invested their money in the Company, and in 1609 - the year of the publication of the Sonnets - the Virginia Company received its Royal Charter, and Neville became a leading officer in the Company, being the first name mentioned after the listing of titled aristocrats. The Earl of Southampton was referred to openly as Neville's champion, so it comes as no coincidence that it was to this Earl that 'Shakespeare' had dedicated his works. This is precisely why the 'Mr. W.H.' mentioned in the Dedication is most commonly thought to have been Henry Wriothesley, Earl of Southampton, who had been reduced to plain 'Mr.' for a time after being imprisoned for treason. Thus, the mysterious Dedication to the Sonnets becomes explicable, as has been demonstrated.

But, despite promising beginnings, Neville never really got along with King James I, though he was prepared to help him with his writing, and also to try and help him rule with Parliament. But James refused to take Neville's advice, because Neville's advice involved compromise, and James was an absolutist monarch who thought he ruled by divine right. The King also suspected Neville in some measure of subversion, because Neville became a prominent member of the Mitre Club - a philosophical sister to the Mermaid Club, to which actors such as William Shakespeare belonged. Indeed, Neville's erstwhile steward in France, Sir Thomas Edmondes, was himself a member of the Mermaid Club, so there were always links between the various rather radical societies. Neville had long been known to Ben Jonson, who was also a member of the Mitre Club, and Jonson was a mutual friend of Neville's friend William Camden, the historian. Neville often spoke alongside John Donne and Inigo Jones at the Club, and Ben Jonson of course became the editor of the First Folio of Shakespeare's works. Again, then, it was surely not by mere coincidence that Jonson was the chosen compiler of the Works, nor only coincidence that he was given a post at Gresham College after he had completed his compilation - because Gresham College was founded by Sir Thomas Gresham, the great uncle who had named Sir Henry as his heir. Jonson also wrote a play in which I found that he symbolically declares Neville's authorship of the plays. In fact, in that same play, Jonson mentions a Cornish Gentlewoman, and the fact that the true writer was like a Furnace. (Neville was of course married to a Cornish Gentlewoman and once owned ironworks, in which he oversaw the work of a furnace.) The text of this play, together with my analysis, will appear as a separate publication, while a description of the play and its links with Henry Neville forms the last chapter of this book.

Neville finally succumbed to disappointment and malnutrition, dying of a mixture of dropsy, scurvy and gout in July, 1615. Nine months later, Ben Jonson went to visit William Shakespeare in Stratford, and the ex-actor died the following morning. It was Ben Jonson who organised his funeral.

There is a blank space on Sir Henry Neville's tomb where an inscription about him should be. It is said that Neville left an inscription but that his son never had it copied onto the tomb. There is just a chance that the inscription on Shakespeare's tomb was the one originally intended for Sir Henry - it is indeed more appropriate to Neville than to Shakespeare, and reads:

Iudicio Pylium, Socratem, arte Mazonem:
Terra tegit, popula maeret, Olympus habet.

(In judgement a Nestor, in genius a Socrates, in art a Virgil: The earth covers him, the people mourn him, Olympus has him.)

****

The case for Neville's authorship contains much more than all the details given here. Documentary evidence includes my discovery of some of Neville's previously unattributed papers in the Lincolnshire Archives. Neville's 'Tower Notebook', for instance, which he declares on the cover is meant for use in 'Pastimes', but which nevertheless details the history of Parliament and the coronations of Kings and Queens. These are details which were indeed used in Shakespeare's plays, this being the only sense in which such information could be called a collection used mainly for pastimes!

At one point in the notebook Neville reveals he has discovered the 1559 Law in which Justices of the Peace can decide if a play can be performed in a certain area. The act stated that the justices were to 'permyt none to be played wherein either matters of religion or of the governance of the estate of the common weale shalbe handled.' Although this had been somewhat superseded - on paper - Neville knew that the justices still wielded this sort of power and therefore seems to come to the decision that he has no option other than to continue his masquerade. After all, he was first and foremost a politician, so any justices looking into a play known to be by Neville would automatically know that a politician had written it, and therefore automatically come to the decision that it was political and thus could not be performed. So Neville then writes the words in his notebook that he must continue to 'Lie in **all**, then.'

This Tower Notebook also contains a draft of the procession of Anne Boleyn after she is crowned in London. The details in this passage are found in the play of Henry VIII, which was performed 11 years after the Tower Notebook was written. There are also suggestions for the music in this play, and for its opening scene, which I shall detail in a future Paper in *The Journal of Neville Studies*.

Many other very telling passages can be seen in that notebook too, including comments on the misgovernance of Richard II. So the question must be asked as to why Neville decided to put all this in a book he proclaimed mainly to have been kept for the purpose of 'pastimes'. And why was Neville, the politician, so interested in preparing 'Pastimes' per se? With all the foregoing evidence, the answer can surely only be that he was still writing - and revising - the Shakespeare History plays.

Neville's name also appears at the top of the well-known Northumberland Manuscript, together with a poem woven around Neville's family motto. At the foot of that manuscript, the signature of William Shakespeare is being practiced assiduously. This manuscript was found in the London home of the Earl of Northumberland (a friend and employer of Charles Paget, the spy), and it appears to have been part of a cover for other manuscripts contained within this piece of paper. Named on this cover was the banned book *Leycester's Commonwealth* , which was missing from the collection of books found together with this Northumberland manuscript. But I found two copies of *Leycester's Commonwealth* among Neville's papers in the Lincolnshire Archives. In those very copies, an annotator has written notes concerning the Red and White Roses used by Lancaster and York. This is often thought to have been an image invented by Shakespeare. Further annotations in the book similarly parallel episodes in Shakespeare's History Plays. The same annotator (who but Neville himself?) also makes notes on stereotypical human 'qualities' behind certain characters, and even writes the words 'such cruelty' against a passage describing Queen Margaret's behaviour in taunting Edward of York with the death of his son - a famous passage from the *Henry VI* trilogy.

The story of how his papers came to be in Lincoln is a long and fascinating one. Neville's second daughter married Sir Richard Worsley and went to live at Appledurcombe House on the Isle of Wight. The male Worsleys eventually died out, and a nineteenth century female inheritress married the Earl of Yarborough and took her family papers up to the Lincolnshire/Yorkshire border when she went to live with him at Brocklesby Park. A descendant of theirs placed the papers in the Lincolnshire Archives. Some of those papers even tie up with references made among the Neville Papers in the Berkshire Record Office so that, eventually, I was able to identify them positively as having been the property of Sir Henry Neville. Another book, bought by an antiquarian in York, is an annotated copy of *Hall's Chronicles* - another source of Shakespeare's History plays. This may well have been originally from the same Neville collection, as I detail in *The Truth Will Out.*[63].

Fortuitously enough, the Earl of Southampton became governor of the Isle of Wight, so it was no difficult task for Sir Henry to deposit his more risky papers on that Island, far away from the Court's prying eyes.

Much later, I was also to discover evidence for connections between Neville and the Fletcher family. John Fletcher (1579 - 1625), the playwright, collaborated with 'Shakespeare' on his later plays, *Henry VIII* and *The Two Noble Kinsmen*. Richard Fletcher, Bishop of London, had been married to Elizabeth Holland, (who, incidentally, seems to have been a relative of the Nevilles.) When Elizabeth Holland died in 1596, Richard Fletcher married the beautiful young, wealthy widow, Maria Baker. Now, the Bakers were neighbours of Henry Neville while he was, at that precise time, running his ironworks business in Mayfield, East Sussex. Indeed, Neville sold off most of that estate only in 1598, and he sold it to Thomas May, the father of a poet. Just after Neville died, the Mays sold it to the Bakers. John Fletcher had been born in Rye, where his father was a clergyman for many years. This is one of the Cinque ports which Neville was supplying with cannons to fight off the Armada. It is also a port from which ships exporting some of Neville's ordnance set sail. John Fletcher's father was a man who shared Neville's religion and outlook on life, while Giles Fletcher, John's uncle, was a famous diplomat who served in Russia. It is therefore impossible that Neville did not already know this family, even by the time they came to marry in with the Bakers. John Fletcher would then have been 17 or 18 years old, and he and his main collaborator, Beaumont, subsequently sent their manuscripts for Neville's perusal.[64]

This, then, has been just a snapshot of the total evidence in favour of Sir Henry's authorship of the Shakespeare plays. No doubt the debate will continue to rage, but it has to be admitted that finding a name in a Code and then finding that subsequent research substantiates that Code's claims are occurrences absolutely unique in the history of Shakespearean research. The name 'Vere' is also to be seen in the Code, and so the descendants of Edward de Vere, Earl of Oxford have built up a case for that man's authorship - based more on a family's fervent hope than logical argument. As further explained in the final chapter of this book, it is little wonder that 'Vere' is mentioned in the Code, since 'Elizabeth Vere' was the name of the lady whom Southampton (the Dedicatee of the Sonnets) was being urged to marry. Indeed, 'Beth' can also be seen in the Code, (plus the name 'Holland', interestingly enough, considering its links with both the Neville and the Fletcher families):

	1	2	3	4	5	6	7	8	9	10	11	12
1	T	O	T	H	E	O	N	L	I	E	B	E
2	G	E	T	T	E	R	O	F	T	H	E	S
3	E	I	N	S	U	I	N	G	S	O	N	N
4	E	T	S	Mr	W	H	x	A	L	L	H	A
5	P	P	I	N	E	S	S	E	N	N	D	T
6	H	A	T	E	T	E	R	N	I	T	I	E
7	P	R	O	M	I	S	E	D	B	Y	O	U
8	R	E	V	E	R	L	I	V	I	N	G	P
9	O	E	T	W	I	S	H	E	T	H	T	H
10	E	W	E	L	L	W	I	S	H	I	N	G
11	A	D	V	E	N	T	U	R	E	R	I	N
12	S	E	T	T	I	N	G	F	O	R	T	H

But nowhere does 'EDWARD, POET, appear, whereas HENRY clearly makes itself known, together with all the other pointers leading to NEVELL, NEVIL, etc. [as will be further outlined in a following chapter.] Besides, an attribution to the Earl of Oxford has insuperable problems of time, place, interests, experience and authorial personality to overcome. As all students of linguistics know, it is totally illogical to seek for authorial evidence where time and experience do not coincide. These are basic necessities; yet Edward de Vere died eleven years before the plays of Shakespeare ceased to be written! And he had no known metallurgical knowledge. With Sir Henry Neville, no historical problems exist. It is very unlikely that all these links could be made in such multifaceted ways, unless the Code's claims were true. Henry Neville was surely the true author of Shakespeare's works.

Chapter 4

CODES AND FUNCTIONS - THE BACKGROUND TO THE DEDICATION CODE

Knowing a little about Shakespeare, the pretender, and Neville, the secret writer, helps to put the Sonnets in their true context. Even from a quick overview of Sir Henry's life, it's easy to see why he wished to keep his authorship secret. It's also self-explanatory that he would not wish to reveal the extent of his friendship with his co-plotters - the Earls of Essex and Southampton. Yet, having written such glorious sonnets, he would have wished to see them obtain the approbation and wonderment of the reading public. Sir Henry therefore had to find a way of getting them published, yet disguising the background to, and the dedicatee of, those poems. But there must still have been a part of him that hoped his complete authorship might one day be re-discovered - one remote day, when it could no longer harm his family. What better way of doing all this than cloaking the Sonnets by re-ordering them, not explaining their background, yet creating a Code which contained his name? To be sure, the Code had to be complex enough not to be unravelled straight away, but to a man with Sir Henry's ingenuity and experience, this would not have presented an insoluble problem.

Sir Henry was used to employing the coding systems of his own day - they went with the nature of his public employment. But times change. Coding is now a computerised, more mathematical and less linguistic exercise, so it's important to look at what Sir Henry himself knew about standard coding practice in his own day. One famous exercise in code making and breaking in Neville's time involved 'framing' a Queen – a dramatic enough exercise to bring the secret world of the encoder into the public arena. This event would definitely have interested Sir Henry and other serious-minded politicians and courtiers of the day.

The Scottish Queen and the Substitution Code

In 1585 Sir Henry Neville was around 21 years old, and Mary Queen of Scots was alive, kicking and unintentionally dangerous. Neville already knew Sir Francis Walsingham - head of Queen Elizabeth I's Secret Service – and Sir Francis was determined to devise a way of ostensibly implicating Mary in a treasonable plot, in order to give the Queen of England an excuse to rid the country of her beautiful rival. Neville is not known to have been directly associated with Walsingham's plans in this respect, though he must have known something of the man's methods, since he had already accompanied him on at least one mission - and that was a mission to Scotland.[65]

The way Walsingham chose to implicate Mary in treason was by cunningly luring her into a complicated set of actions. First of all, he employed the Giffords - a Catholic family of spies and double-dealers, headed by Gilbert Gifford.[66] The Giffords put Mary in touch with militant English Catholics. Secondly, Walsingham asked Gifford to devise a simple code for the imprisoned, closely-watched Mary, so she might feel secure in secretly expressing her true, insurgent ideas.

It may seem surprising that the Protestant Walsingham found it possible to attract Catholics into his service. However, some Catholics believed that if Mary became Queen of England it would not be long before the King of Spain – to whom Mary had willed the English throne - would take advantage of the situation. **Moderate** English Catholics could not have wanted the King of Spain or the dreaded Inquisition to take over England, any more than their Protestant counterparts wished for such an event. It was thus not too difficult for Walsingham to find a moderate Catholic who would agree to be an agent provocateur and double agent in his plan to oversee the downfall of the Scottish Queen.

Some say it was Gifford who implanted in a more extremist Catholic's mind the idea of hatching a plot to kill Queen Elizabeth. This same double agent then had to lay a trail that would implicate and incriminate the Queen of Scots herself. Gifford carried out all this successfully, first by bending the ear of a romantically brave Catholic, Sir Anthony Babington, and then by bearing encoded messages between Queen Mary and Sir Anthony. But Gifford had himself devised that code, so whether incriminating material was later added to those messages by

Gifford or, perhaps, by Walsingham, is not known. Yet one thing is certain: the code itself was a simple 'substitution' cipher, and so was easier to break than a non-expert like Mary could have guessed. Walsingham had to make sure the cipher was simple – only then could he demonstrate to Elizabeth the method by which it had been 'broken' by his men. The outcome was that the Code in which Mary and Babington wrote was – predictably – cracked. Thus was the Babington plot revealed and Mary executed on a charge of treason.

The substitution cipher employed by Walsingham was quick to devise and quick to break, as are all of that ilk. This kind of code simply replaces one letter of the alphabet by another, or by a separate icon of some sort. All the letters of the alphabet are written out, together with their coded form, and kept hidden away for reference by those privy to the code. For example, the letter e might always be represented by a tree, c by a square, and so forth. But whatever the icons used, such a simple code is always easy to crack. Some letters in English are used more frequently than others, so if there are more trees than squares in a sample piece of coded writing, for example, then the tree is more likely to represent e than c, the latter being a letter which is not so frequently used.

Secondly, there are accepted phonemes in a language. For instance, the letters ztm never appear sequentially in any English word, but the phoneme (or single sound) '- ing' appears frequently, especially at the end of many words. Thus, if **i** is represented by **x** in a substitution cipher, **n** by ✢ and **g** by π, then if 'x✢π' are seen together at the end of several words, it begins to be obvious that those individual letters represent 'ing'. Next, the decoder can go back once more over the text inserting e, i, n, and g into all the words on the page, so it is not long before the whole text can be first *inferred*, and finally confirmed from the fact that the text eventually makes sense when the whole of it is read through, and from the constant representation of any one particular letter by the same icon.

Mary Queen of Scots proved fatally ignorant of codes and code-breaking. The very code which had been presented to her as a means of protection became the means of her destruction. Walsingham's plan was truly Machiavellian, as it took advantage of the specialist knowledge restricted to a very small circle. Even the Queen of England must have possessed scant knowledge of coding methodology as, presumably, she too was ultimately persuaded that Mary had indeed expressed her true, activist feelings for the first time, as any non-specialist would obviously reason that Mary only dared to do this once she thought she was protected by coded writing.

The Genre of Sir Henry Neville's Dedication Code

Codes could therefore play major and varying roles in Tudor and Stuart society. Their projected aim was usually ensured by the restricted, secretive circles in which they were created. If the function of a particular code was to deceive users into a false sense of security, then an appropriately simple code was devised. On the other hand, if its function was truly to disguise meanings and to delay knowledge of a manuscript's contents, should it fall into enemy hands, then a more complicated coding system was disseminated on a strictly 'need to know' basis only. But there was one thing all these codes had to have in common if they were successfully to fulfil their functions: they had to be devised, constructed and used by personnel who had in some way been initiated into state-of-the-art coding methodology. Sir Henry Neville had been thus initiated, but he needed to use a much more complex code to protect his identity than the one fed to Mary Queen of Scots.

The particular encoding method employed in the Sonnets' Dedication, which contains Neville's own name – and other messages too – emerges as a distinctive, yet linear development of some of the more complex systems then in use. Added to this, it is even possible that the system used in the Dedication was not yet known in England, though it had been employed in Italy around thirty years earlier. If this is the case, then knowledge of this particular coding system might have been further restricted to men who had visited that country. Sir Henry Neville fits inside both these privileged groups, in that he had lived in Italy and had also worked with Walsingham. Moreover, he actually used some of the then extant coding systems when writing the most secret parts of his diplomatic correspondence, while he was Ambassador in France.

Sir Henry Neville – the real Shakespeare – was a complex man, and the Code he created in his Dedication to the Sonnets was consequently somewhat complicated and unconventional in nature. Its lack of conventional design, however, was not occasioned merely by his own unconventional personality: the dangers and troubles Sir Henry had experienced by the time his Sonnets were published in 1609 had taught him to be very wary of revealing anything about himself and his life. Only six short years had gone by since Neville's incarceration in the Tower of London; he had lost some friends to the executioner's axe, and had been betrayed by some others. His political situation was still far from secure, and he had not found favour with the new King, James I. Neville's erstwhile good friend and relative, Sir Robert Cecil, was no longer likely to promote his interests, after Sir Henry's support for the Earl of Essex's rebellion, which had been partly aimed against Cecil himself. Henry's most staunch remaining friends and supporters were his one-time secretary, Sir Ralph Winwood, Sir Henry Savile, who had been his tutor at Oxford, and his friend and Tower companion - the Earl of Southampton. None of these men held ministerial posts in government, and none of them was particularly close to James I, so Neville was inevitably climbing the steep ladder back to Parliament and Court, slowly and cautiously.

Yet his business enterprises held more promise. He had become one of the chief officers of the Virginia Company, which received its Royal Charter in the same year as the publication of the Sonnets. Neville was also continuing to write, covertly, and must have been secretly pleased with the reception of his recent dramas. But he still dared not acknowledge them, no more than he dared to acknowledge the *Sonnets*. Doing so would have inevitably linked him to both the seditious play of *Richard II*, with its deposition of a king, and to the Earl of Southampton, to whom the early Sonnets were dedicated, and to whose later deeds some of them also referred. Any code captures a real situation existing at a specific moment in history, so its decoding necessarily involves understanding that code's historical and personal implications. As far as Henry Neville was concerned in 1609, he wanted to see his great *Sonnets* in print, but at that particular moment in time he needed to hide the background to their creation.

By publishing the Dedication Code as an Introduction to his Sonnets, however, Neville was bravely signalling that the reader should look well below the surface appearance of all those poems. To fit in with this mysterious atmosphere, he created a

Code that had some original features, even though he must have known that by composing such a cipher he ran the risk that it might be too unconventional for anyone ever to crack. He must have foreseen that its secrets would be kept for a long time, while Englishmen caught up with some of the continental ideas which had inspired Neville's invention. This strongly suggests that he was keen to protect not only himself but also the **future** interests of his family. Some of the reasons behind his great concern have been laid bare. Even more reasons for Neville's secrecy will appear during the course of this book.

Documentary evidence for Neville's interest in coding is still extant: it is in the form of a manuscript currently among Neville's papers in the National Archives at Kew. This document was given to Sir Henry by his mother in law, Catherine Killigrew. She had researched both English and Italian Codes. Sir Francis Walsingham, who ran Queen Elizabeth's rather efficient secret service[67], was a close friend of Neville's father in law, Sir Henry Killigrew. Killigrew had been an Ambassador in Scotland. It was hardly surprising, then, to find Neville in 1583 on a diplomatic mission to Scotland, headed by Walsingham and the young Earl of Essex. It was probably at this early time in his life that Neville was already being schooled for continuing diplomatic service, and being taught the ciphers employed in those circles. He was demonstrably already surrounded by in-laws who were either entrenched in the Diplomatic Service or basically interested in Coding methodology.

One coding system used in those diplomatic circles consisted of a cipher where occasional words were hidden **within** those openly used to form the *surface* meaning. It is those hidden words which form the *encoded* meaning. Nowadays, this kind of concealment is sometimes used in word games. For instance, the sentence 'On the menu today we have fish and meat' contains other words which can be read across the spaces between the words themselves. Without changing the ordering of the letters, it is possible to see at least two hidden words here – 'theme' and 'hand' – (On **the me**nu today we have fis**h and** meat.)

Knowing the conventional ciphers, Neville would have been able to create his own variations on them – a factor which immediately marks out the Dedication Code as being one which must have been fashioned by an expert. It has been supposed that Thomas Thorpe, the publisher, may have written the

Dedication Code, but when its methodology is known, it seems that, even if he helped in its compilation, he must have been informed of coding methodology by someone from the upper echelons of society - by someone like Neville himself. Thorpe certainly knew who the writer really was, a fact which, the Code tells us, he too decided to hide from the world.

So which known types of coding did Neville call upon when he created his Dedication text, and which did he eschew? He would obviously have dismissed the simple substitution cipher as being unsafe. Besides, with such a system, the coded text must appear like gibberish, whereas Neville needed to invent a Code that could also look like a plaintext, and so make some kind of semantic and syntactic sense. At the other end of the scale, the most advanced type of encoding used at the time was the Vigenere system. This has been described in many recent books on ciphers, but it would have been of little use to Neville, as it usually relied on the substitution of letters by numbers. This again would have announced itself immediately as a code, if used at the head of a book of Sonnets. Neville's first requirement was for a coding system which did not look like a code, on first sight. He must therefore have been drawn to the one resembling a word game, as described above. But Neville seems to have found ideas for *extending* this idea in the cipher system known as the Cardano (or Cardan) Grille - a code which was Italian in origin.

In this system, a piece of paper with holes in was placed over a formulated text which did not look like a code. But significant letters and words could be hidden in that text, and only the **significant** letters or words were visible through the holes in the Cardano Grille. The rest of the text – along with all the **insignifican**t letters - was obscured by the paper. First, these texts had to be copied into a grid, or grille, so that the peep-hole cards could be placed over a grid of agreed dimensions. As may be imagined, however, the kind of texts or letters that had to be written in order to embed other messages were often so strange that their hybrid purpose might be perceived. (As can be seen, this is exactly the case with Neville's Dedication text. It is indeed strangely worded.)

Though I cannot nearly approach Neville's skill, I have, by way of illustration, written a rather nonsensical text consisting of one hundred letters and spaces so that these can be set out in a 10 x 10 matrix. The size of the matrix would have been pre-arranged, so that the coded message could be carefully laid out on squared paper by the receiver.

My nonsense message reads:

TAPE . THE . SPIKE . ON . THE . ALE . SHED . ON . THIS .
PRELATE . PUT . NO . FURTHER . TO . MARRY . THAT .
STINGY . PERSON . GOOD . LUCK .

	1	2	3	4	5	6	7	8	9	10
1	T	A	P	E	.	T	H	E	.	S
2	P	I	K	E	.	O	N	.	T	H
3	E	.	A	L	E	.	S	H	E	D
4	.	O	N	.	T	H	I	S	.	P
5	R	E	L	A	T	E		P	U	T
6	.	N	O	.	F	U	R	T	H	E
7	R	.	T	O	.	M	A	R	R	Y
8	.	T	H	A	T	.	S	T	I	N
9	G	Y	.	P	E	R	S	O	N	
10		G	O	O	D		L	U	C	K

Although this is a nonsense text, it does make some sort of syntactical sense and took only a very little time to devise. But the true message is hidden **inside** this weird text, as picked out by the emboldened letters below:

	1	2	3	4	5	6	7	8	9	10
1	**T**	**A**	P	E	.	**T**	H	E	.	S
2	P	**I**	**K**	**E**	.	**O**	N	.	**T**	**H**
3	**E**	.	**A**	**L**	**E**	.	S	H	E	D
4	.	O	N	.	**T**	H	I	S	.	P
5	R	E	**L**	A	**T**	**E**		P	U	T
6	.	N	O	.	F	U	**R**	T	H	E
7	R	.	**T**	**O**	.	**M**	A	**R**	R	Y
8	.	T	H	A	T	.	**S**	**T**	**I**	**N**
9	G	Y	.	P	E	R	S	**O**	N	
10		G	O	O	D		L	U	C	K

101

The hidden message reads - TAKE THE LETTER TO MARTIN. By writing out the whole text of the original letter on a pre-arranged matrix, the text is made ready for the first stage of decoding. If we imagine that the recipient of the text has already been given a square piece of card with occasional holes in it, and that this piece of card can be fitted over the tableau text, (after that text has been written in the pre-arranged matrix), then one can see how the intended message could be read through the holes, while the insignificant letters are blocked out:

	T	A								
			K	E					T	H
E			L	E						
				T						
			T	E						
					R					
			T	O		M	A	R		
							T	I	N	

This encoding system was known as the Cardano, or Cardan, Grille because it was invented by an eccentric Italian doctor and mathematician, Girolamo Cardano (1501 -1576). Cardano worked at various universities in Northern Italy, including Padua, and it is known that Neville researched at that university during his continental tour (1578 – 83). It is therefore possible that Neville learnt of the Cardano Grille while he was in Italy. (So celebrated yet strange was Cardan, and so controversial was his life, that Italy would still have been buzzing with stories about him when Neville was there; and his coding systems were still in use.)

Neville may also have heard about the Grille from his father in law, Sir Henry Killigrew. Killigrew was in Scotland and France during the years 1560 – 63. In 1552- 4, Cardano had stayed in Scotland, where he cured the asthma suffered by the Archbishop of St. Andrews. This makes it possible that Cardano passed his encoding method on to the Archbishop, or to other

Scots, that country then being wooed by various diplomats hoping to persuade the Scots to join continental Catholic alliances. Whether **English** diplomats were using the Cardan Grille before 1609 (the year of the Sonnets' publication) is not known. If they were *not* using it, then this might be an extra reason for Neville choosing this particular system on which to base his own Code. But even if they knew it, then they would still find Neville's own Code a hard one to crack, as he varied the system enough to confuse them. This he did by combining the Cardan system with one which relied on transformations of word squares using a keyword.

Finally, there may be yet another factor which persuaded Neville to base his Code on the Cardan system. Cardano, like Neville, studied mathematics and cosmology, so Neville would have been interested in looking up his work when he stayed in Italy. Cardano also once swore an oath to a fellow mathematician, and that oath itself involved the use of a Code. He had heard of the work of Tartaglia, who had won a mathematics contest after solving cubics. Longing to know his secret methods, Cardano pestered Tartaglia for years. Finally, Tartaglia agreed to divulge everything to Cardano, provided that he would never tell anyone else, and also on the condition that if he wrote down any notes about the secret method, then he (Cardano) must write them in code. This reminded me of the scene in which the ghost of Hamlet's father calls from the depths to demand Hamlet's companions swear an oath never to tell what they have seen, and never to divulge what Hamlet is about to tell them[68]. The writer of such a work – and indeed the whole Shakespeare canon – shows signs that he himself revelled in honour, friendship, and secrets. On many occasions, those referring either to Sir Henry Neville or to words spoken by him add the fact that he wishes what he has said to remain 'secret'. After reading these reports, one is left with the distinct impression that even his friends are beginning to regard his wishes in this respect as a joke, shared between true friends who nevertheless saw Sir Henry as something of a well-loved, highly-respected, brilliant eccentric. Yet, as with Hamlet himself, Sir Henry's secrecy and eccentricities turn out to have been consciously constructed; and they ultimately became part of the defence mechanism that was finally to form the armour which saved his life.

Chapter 5

ENCODING 'NEVILLE' IN THE SONNETS AND THE PLAYS

Many of the Sonnets can already be seen to refer to episodes in Neville's life. There are, for instance, sonnets in the despairing mode of no. 29 which fits Neville's imprisoned state. But do some of the Sonnets actually also encode Neville's own name, just as does the Dedication itself?

This will be found to be the case, but there is yet another level of encoding behind the Sonnets' framework. Neville was a mathematician as well as a poet, so even the *numbering* of his sonnets sometimes has a symbolic meaning. Neville toys with us on every possible level, and uses those different levels simultaneously, so we often find several puzzles entwined in the same sonnet. Just as sonnet 29 seems to speak for Neville living through his imprisoned situation, so sonnet 111 seems at first sight to speak for Shakespeare, the poor boy who could not afford a higher education:

> O! for my sake do you with Fortune chide,
> The guilty goddess of my harmful deeds,
> That did not better for myself provide,
> Than public means, which public manners breeds:
> Then comes it that **my name** receives a brand;
> And almost then my nature **is subdu'd**
> To what it works in, like the dyer's hand.
> Pity me **then** and wish I were **renew**'d,
> Whilst like a **will**ing patient, I **will** drink
> Potions of eisel 'gainst my strong infection......

Many scholars have tried to say that 'public means' refers to Shakespeare acting before the public. But 'public means' carried one particular meaning for the Elizabethans, as for us now: it meant living on an income from state coffers, and Henry Neville was a public servant, an M.P. and sometime Ambassador, serving the people in return for some allowance from public funds. He was also the owner of a large ironworks. His ownership of the

ironworks meant that Neville's name did indeed 'receive a brand'
– his name was branded on his cannons and other iron products.
Looking again at the Sonnet above, MY NAME IS
SUBDU'D; HENRE NEWILL can be perceived (which I have
represented by bold lettering.)
The numbering of the Sonnets seems to make little sense,
on the surface. The first seventeen could certainly be addressed
to the same young man, but after this the theme changes so that a
number of men or women could be being addressed. But it does
seem as if particular numbers were chosen for certain sonnets in
the sequence so as to link up with the imagery and philosophy
expressed in those sonnets. For instance, Sonnet 8 and poem
number 8 in *The Passionate Pilgrim* both refer to music, thus
linking with the eight notes of the musical scale:

> Music to hear, why hear'st thou music sadly?
> Sweets with sweets war not, joy delights in joy;
> Why lov'st thou that which thou receiv'st not gladly,
> Or else receiv'st with pleasure thine annoy?
> If the true concord of well-tuned sounds,
> By unions married, do offend thine ear,
> They do but sweetly chide thee, who confounds
> In singleness the parts that thou shouldst bear.
> Mark how one string, sweet husband to another,
> Strikes each in each by mutual ordering;
> Resembling sire, and child, and happy mother,
> Who all in one one pleasing note do sing;
> Whose speechless song, being many, seeming one,
> Sings this to thee: 'Thou single wilt prove none'.*Sonnet 8*

> If music and sweet poetry agree,
> As they must needs, the sister and the brother,
> Then must the love be great 'twixt thee and me,
> Because thou lovest the one, and I the other.
> Dowland to thee is dear, whose heavenly touch
> Upon the lute doth ravish human sense;
> Spenser to me, whose deep conceit is such
> As, passing all conceit, needs no defence.
> Thou lovest to hear the sweet melodious sound
> That Phoebus' lute, the queen of music, makes;
> And I in deep delight am chiefly drown'd
> When as himself to singing he betakes.
> One god is god of both, as poets feign;
> One knight loves both, and both in thee remain.
> *The Passionate Pilgrim, no. 8*

Music was taught together with Mathematics at Merton, in line with the old Platonic traditions, with special emphasis on its mathematical basis. The word 'knight' on the last line of the above certainly could not apply to Shakespeare. But it does apply to Neville: I was to discover that he had probably been knighted first by the Earl of Essex at the raid on Cadiz in 1596, and may later have been received as a knight bachelor before taking up his ambassadorship of France. In those days there were several orders of knighthood. When a man was knighted by an aristocrat he owed allegiance to him for ever.

In those sonnets where their numbering symbolises aspects of Neville's life and in which the text gives anagrams of his name, it can be seen that the actual *numbers* of these sonnets are also significant. Sonnet 111 could easily be seen as the first person pronoun: I, I, I. With Sonnet 29, the 2 and 9 can be added together they make 11, which is again I, I. With Sonnet 121 ('I to myself?') we have arguably the strongest clue of all, ''tis better to be vile than vile esteemed...' Henry Neville's family motto was Ne Vile Velis – think nothing vile. In Latin, V was pronounced W. Immediately too we therefore have a version of the name 'Will.'

In the esoteric side of mathematics, the number ten was thought of as particularly significant because it comes from the old German 'tai hen' (modern zwei Hände) - two hands. In Sonnet. 20 (2 x 10) - the Master-Mistress Sonnet – we should therefore be able to discover something symbolic about that number itself. The Roman numeral for 20 - XX – was often thought to represent two antagonistic poles, especially the opposition between spirit and matter. This naturally proves to be highly significant, since this Sonnet is dominated by the opposition Master/Mistress:

> A woman's face with Nature's own hand painted
> Hast thou the master mistress of my passion,
> A woman's gentle heart but not acquainted
> With shifting change as is false women's fashion,
> An eye more bright than theirs, less false in rolling,
> Gilding the object whereupon it gazeth;
> A maiden hue all Hues in his controlling,
> Which steals men's eyes and women's souls amazeth.
> And for a woman wert thou first created,
> Till Nature as she wrought thee fell a-doting
> And by addition me of thee defeated -
> By adding one thing to my purpose nothing.
> But since she pricked thee out for women's pleasure,
> Mine by thy love and thy love's use their treasure.

If we are also meant to perceive it to include the spirit/matter opposition, then we have it represented here as the difference between platonic and physical love, a subject that is dealt with in *The Phoenix and the Turtle,* as discussed in the following chapters.

Then there are the sonnets concerned with numbers and their involvement with money – one would hardly expect the son of a Gresham[69] lady (as was Sir Henry) to omit such monetary reference! Sonnets 2, 4, 6 deal with numbers applied to making money and keeping accounts. Sonnet 6 demonstrates what a thorough and up-to-date knowledge Shakespeare (i.e. Neville) had of the law pertaining to usury:

> Then let not winter's ragged hand deface
> In thee thy summer ere thou be distilled;
> Make sweet some vial; treasure thou some place
> With beauty's treasure ere it be self-killed.
> That use is not forbidden usury
> Which happies those that pay the willing loan -
> That's for thyself to breed another thee,
> Or ten times happier be it ten for one.
> Ten times thyself were happier than thou art,
> If ten of thine ten times refigured thee;
> Then what could Death do if thou shouldst depart,
> Leaving thee living in posterity?
> Be not self-willed, for thou art much too fair
> To be Death's conquest and make worms thine heir.

Ten per cent was the legal limit of interest which usurers could charge. The writer of the above poem was therefore probably aware of the history behind this ten per cent law. In 1552, the Protestants had pushed through a Bill making it illegal to take any interest at all on money lent, but after nearly twenty years of such restraint it was becoming clear that general trading and setting up of businesses were being greatly hampered by that law, together with all sorts of underhand practices being devised to sideline the legislation. Consequently, in 1571 lending money with a view to interest was legalised again, up to a maximum of ten per cent, whereas the term 'usury' was understood as meaning the taking of excessive interest. However, there is evidence later in the Sonnet sequence that 'Shakespeare' had also read a clerical pamphlet by Miles Mosse of 1595[70] in which he not only redefines usury as being the same as the taking of *any* interest but also says the practice should again be completely disallowed. He says that the only event in which interest should be taken is if actual loss has been sustained by the lender. For Mosse, therefore, the taking of any extra money in respect of an uncomplicated loan is 'interest', whereas, he says, usury should be termed 'overplus.' In Sonnet 135, Shakespeare writes:

> Whoever hath her wish, thou hast thy Will,
> And Will to boot, and Will in overplus;
> More than enough am I that vex thee still,

But it is indeed curious that such a notoriously sharp money-lender as Shakespeare of Stratford was reputed to be, should bother to read anti-usury pamphlets, and even more curious that he should then go on to implicitly denigrate usury in his Sonnets. Neville, on the other hand, was known as a gentleman with progressive political and trading ideas who nevertheless still hung onto the old, romanticised, aristocratic, chivalric values. He was therefore just the man to write in such a mode.

When it comes to the sonnets specifically addressed to women, it may be possible to identify some of the ladies involved and link them to specific poems, but it is also possible for them to be read independently of any identification at all. Indeed, these would then have been more readily acceptable to a wider public, as they fulfil the general expectation that a male poet should address amorous sonnets to a woman rather than to a man. In other words, poems addressed to women can be accepted as what the Elizabethans termed 'Commonplaces' which can best be described as trial formulae for budding artists. The same kind of idea can be seen in needlepoint of the time, where 'samplers' were worked by young ladies practising their skill in embroidery. 'Weaving' ideas around the good, fair beauty and the dark temptress were exercises commonly indulged in by would-be poets.

However, writing sonnets to admired young *men* was innovatory. The question of whether 'Shakespeare' or Neville was merely trying to shock and to get noticed by using such a theme, or whether he had some real-life experience in mind will continue to be debated. But one thing cannot be gainsaid: the mind of 'Shakespeare' is the mind of a chivalrous lawyer and/or politician; Shakespeare of Stratford was neither, whereas Neville was skilled in politics and certainly had a knowledge of law. Not only did he debate legal matters in Parliament, but he also had a 'bed' at the Star Chamber, from which he addresses one of his letters to his secretary.[71]

Certainly, though, there were so many lawyer-politicians around at the time that without the Code it would not be easy to pinpoint the true writer. The statement that 'among a number, one is reckon'd none' (Sonnet 136) has certainly applied to many a case over the last four hundred years. A famous one during the last century concerned the late singer, Frank Sinatra. He alleged that the writer of 'The Godfather', Mario Puzo, had intended to mean him when he described how a male pop singer had had to have an operation for nodules on the vocal cords. The judge in the case found that no such specific assignment of person could be proved, since so many pop singers had abused their vocal cords and consequently suffered the same fate. To a great degree, then, the legally-minded 'Neville' may have not been really averse to waiting for some considerable time to have his earlier *Sonnets* published so that they could be added to over the years, thus making the original who, where, what and when of the WH assignment much more difficult to pinpoint. Also, they were printed a couple of months before Henry's own son was married, so even if the writer's true identity had been discovered straight away, then it may have been assumed that Neville was writing to his son, not to an Earl. However, thanks to the Code we may have been given just enough clues to attempt a coherent explanation for the whole of Shakespeare's otherwise puzzling poetic output.

Then we return once again to the French Connection. Several of Shakespeare's sonnets seem to have been partly based on those of Pierre Ronsard, a French poet who died in 1585, but who had also been at the Court of James V in Scotland. For instance, his metaphor in *Amours pour Astree,* vi, is mirrored by Shakespeare's sonnets 24 and 122:

Il ne falloit, maistresse, autres tablettes,
Pour vous graver que celles de mon coeur
Ou de sa main Amour, nostre vainqueur,
Vous a gravée et vos graces parfaites,

Ronsard

Mine eye hath play'd the painter and hath stll'd
Thy beauty's form in table of my heart ...   *sonnet 24*

Thy gift, thy tables, are within my brain,
Full character'd with lasting memory... *sonnet 122*

This Code, this 'table of my heart', did indeed have 'Henry' and 'France' at its centre, its 'sein'. And surely 'Shakespeare' was to return to Ronsard when he wrote a song in *Measure for Measure* - 'Take, oh take those lips away' which echoes Ronsard's *Deadly Kisses* :

All take these lips away; no more,
No more such kisses give to me.
My spirit faints for joy; I see
Through mists of death the dreamy shore,
And meadows by the water-side, ...   *Pierre Ronsard, 1550*

Viewed coolly, however, the most exciting and certain thing so far was that the Code had at least uncovered the identity of a man not previously widely connected with the Shakespeare mystery. But even though I remained cool, I soon had to admit that there did indeed seem to be more to it than that. The more research I did, the more everything added up. In the end, I found the great total weight of evidence provided by my research formed the strongest case for Sir Henry's authorship of Shakespeare's Works. Thus the historical evidence and the decoding complemented each other: without the starting point of the Code, I would never have discovered Sir Henry Neville, but if my subsequent historical investigations had drawn a blank, then it would have been very difficult to sustain any suspicion of Sir Henry's authorship, based on the decoding alone. But the two go hand in hand, which provides a very strong basis indeed.

NEVILLE IN THE CODE
After finding out so much about Neville's life and seeing how amazingly it meshed in with the actual works of Shakespeare, I decided to look back at the Dedication Code. I wanted to see if I could discern clues to its construction, and also to see if there was anything that I might have missed. I reasoned that the compiler might have expected anyone who had come this far to re-confirm his subsequent findings. I therefore looked at the original layout of the Dedication once more. Now, bearing in mind that Us, Vs and Ws were essentially the same letter in Elizabethan printing, and that some vowel sounds were interchangeable, anagrams of Neville's name appear at the heart of the *original* setting:

TO . THE . ON**LIE** . BEGETTER . OF
THESE . INS**VING** . SONNETS.
Mr .VV. H. **ALL**.HAPPINESSE.
AND.THAT.ETERNITIE.
PROMISED.

BY.

OVR.EVER-**LIVING**.POET.

VVISHETH.

THE .**VVELL**-VVISHING.
AD**VEN**TVRER . IN.
SETTING.
FORTH.

T.T

With the benefit of hindsight, it is possible to observe how the constructor has made sure he includes enough of the appropriate letters in the cipher to form the various versions of NEVIL. The compiler of the Code had included sufficient 'en' 'nev' and 'il' or 'ell' phonemes to ensure that the Henry Neville name would be found eventually. However, the decoding algorithm based on 'forth' was clearly the method which was designed to reveal the most - it had proved the most appropriate in that it tied up so well with the 'directions' expressed in the plaintext of the Dedication, and it had revealed a whole sentence containing the WISE THORP and his knowledge.

I now decided to see if there were any anagrams on any of the rows in the 12 x 12 setting of the Code. Row 2 proved to be a perfect anagram of TEST THE FORGE, which is of course highly relevant to Neville's ownership of the Mayfield ironworks.

	1	2	3	4	5	6	7	8	9	10	11	12
1	T	O	T	H	E	O	N	L	I	E	B	E
2	G	E	T	T	E	R	O	F	T	H	E	S
3	E	I	N	S	U	I	N	G	S	O	N	N
4	E	T	S	Mr	W	H	x	A	L	L	H	A
5	P	P	I	N	E	S	S	E	N	N	D	T
6	H	A	T	E	T	E	R	N	I	T	I	E
7	P	R	O	M	I	S	E	D	B	Y	O	U
8	R	E	V	E	R	L	I	V	I	N	G	P
9	O	E	T	W	I	S	H	E	T	H	T	H
10	E	W	E	L	L	W	I	S	H	I	N	G
11	A	D	V	E	N	T	U	R	E	R	I	N
12	S	E	T	T	I	N	G	F	O	R	T	H

The phrase TEST THE FORGE is obtained by re-arranging the columns in the order 4, 11, 12, 9, 3, 10, 2, 8, 7, 6, 1, 5. Lo and behold, this new arrangement of the columns then produces NEVIL in a straight line across row 8. Moreover, the word HENRY clusters itself around NEVIL, as seen below:

	4	11	12	9	3	10	2	8	7	6	1	5
1	H	B	E	I	T	E	O	L	N	O	T	E
2	T	E	S	T	T	H	E	F	O	R	G	E
3	S	N	N	S	N	O	I	G	N	I	E	U
4	Mr	H	A	L	S	L	T	A	X	H	E	W
5	N	D	T	N	I	N	P	E	S	S	P	E
6	E	I	E	I	T	T	A	N	R	E	H	T
7	M	O	U	B	O	Y	R	D	E	S	P	I
8	E	G	P	I	V	N	E	V	I	L	R	R
9	W	T	H	T	T	H	E	E	H	S	O	I
10	L	N	G	H	E	I	W	S	I	W	E	L
11	E	I	N	E	V	R	D	R	U	T	A	N
12	T	T	H	O	T	R	E	F	G	N	S	I

And just to prove the fact that the compiler has produced enough phonemes of Neville's name for it to appear in different layouts of the grid - once the intial decoding stages has told us what we are looking for - two independent Australian researchers also found Sir Henry's name in this Dedication Code too.

After reading my Preface to *The Truth Will Out,* where I explained how I had first discovered Neville's name, Professor James Goding corresponded with me. He was determined to see if he too could work out the Code. He was of course looking for 'Neville', but I gave him no clues, reasoning that it would be extra confirmation for my methods, if he came up with a similar process - independently. He and Bruce Leyland eventually realised a matrix must be involved, but they decided to include the hyphens given in the original text of the Dedication. They did not therefore deal with a 12 x 12 setting of the Code, yet they nevertheless came up with Neville's name too.[72]

Finally, there can be little doubt that Neville names himself in Sonnet 121:

'Tis better to be vile than vile esteem'd,
When not to be receives reproach of being,
And the just pleasure lost, which is so deem'd
Not by our feeling, but by others' seeing.
For why should others' false adulterate eyes
Give salutation to my sportive blood?
Or on my frailties why are frailer spies,
Which in their wills count bad what I think good?
No, I am that I am; and they that level
At my abuses, reckon up their own:
I may be straight, though they themselves be bevel;
By their rank thoughts my deeds must not be shown;
Unless this general evil they maintain, -
All men are bad, and in their badness reign.

Here we cannot mistake the name of Neville, spelt variously as Navile, Nevil and **Nevel.**

Line: 1.   Tis better to be **vile** than **vile** esteem'd   _____
ANVILE (Navile – a Frenchified variant of his name.)
9.   No, I am that I am; and they that **level**
10. At my abuses reckon up their ow**n:**   _____   **NEVEL**
11. I may be straight, though they themselves be **bevel;**
13. Unless this general **evil** they maintain, -
14. All men are bad, a**n**d in their badness reign.   ____ NEVIL

(Chapter 10 of this book discusses the many aspects of the above Sonnet.)

MR. NEVELL AND MR. NEVILL

The spelling of 'Nevell' (given frequently in the Code) was that used commonly by Sir Henry Neville's father.[73] Our Sir Henry usually spelt his own name 'Nevill', though he never was rule-based where any spelling was concerned. Neville's step mother also spelt her name 'Nevell', as can be proved by the fact that the music manuscript entitled *My Lady Nevell's Book* was dedicated to her. Sir Henry Neville senior was a great wit who wrote very memorable letters. He also organised a lot of Court entertainment, and owned part of what became – with his blessing – the Blackfriars Theatre. It is therefore not beyond the realms of possibility that he had a hand in the earlier, apocryphal 'Shakespeare' plays. He may also have been a co-author of *Love's Labour's Lost,* with its theme of the Dark Lady, to whom Berowne writes sonnets. 'Berowne' is a version of 'Biron', and Charles Gontaut, Duc de Biron, actually visited Nevell and hunted with him and the Queen in Windsor Forest[74].

'My Lady Nevell' – Neville senior's second wife – was none other than the half sister of Sir Francis Bacon. She was probably musical, as 'My Lady Nevell's Book' – the book of music for the virginals, based mainly themes by William Byrd – demonstrates. This also makes it quite possible that the sonnets mentioning the musical lady may have been written about her by our Sir Henry's father:

> How oft, when thou, my music, music play'st
> Upon that blessed wood whose motion sounds
> With thy sweet fingers when thou gently sway'st
> The wiry concord that mine ear confounds,
> Do I envy those jacks that nimble leap
> To kiss the tender inward of thy hand,
> Whilst my poor lips, which should that harvest reap,
> At the wood's boldness by thee blushing stand.
> To be so tickled they would change their state
> And situation with those dancing chips
> O'er whom thy fingers walk with gentle gait,
> Making dead wood more blest than living lips.
> Since saucy jacks so happy are in this,
> Give them thy fingers, me thy lips, to kiss. *sonnet 128*

Occasionally, however, the spelling 'Nevell' is encountered in one or two documents relating to our Sir Henry. One example can be seen in a manuscript now housed in the Isle of Wight Record Office:

> Letters patent granting pardon for unlicensed alienation of MANOR OF APPULDURCOMBE. Issued to **Sir Henry Nevell** senior and Sir Henry Nevell junior - ref. JER/WA/35/7 - date: 1613 June 12

And our Henry Neville is entered as 'Henry Newell' on his baptismal documents. Thus, the various spellings of Neville's name used in the Code not only accord with documentary evidence but also perhaps allow for the possibility of some collaboration by father and son.

FLESH AND BONES

Altogether, the very mathematical, geometric thinking behind the Dedication Code grid adds up to Neville. It seems he was one of the few men from England and Scotland to have had access to a calculation system which overlaps with the Code's idea of grids and moving columns. The way in which various settings of the 144 lettered cipher was being manipulated was similar to the use of Napier's rods or 'bones', but Napier himself first heard of the idea from a Dr. Craig who, like Neville, knew Paul Wittich.[75]

I began to study the history of mathematical calculation and found that Napier's had been only a kind of *literate*, Western extension of the Arabian Lattice system, the Abacus, the Roman counting board and the medieval Apice. (It had been possible to use many of these previous systems even if the user could not read or write, whereas for Napier's system, written numbers had to be known.) The way Wittich's rods were used to aid multiplication was parallel to the operations performed in solving the Dedication Code: the rods (equivalent to our columns) were separate 'sticks' with numbers on them that were arranged differently depending on which chosen numbers were to be multiplied together. Wittich was a mutual friend of Andre Dudith and Tycho Brahe, and he (Wittich) was working on his 'rods' in or before 1580 in Denmark and Breslau, where he met up with Dudith whom he took to see Brahe in Prague. From

Savile's diary, it is known that Savile and Neville went to Prague at this time, so it is reasonable to assume that they too met Brahe. Brahe had been generally travelling between Prague and Denmark, as he was building his Uraniborg observatory on an island near Elsinore between 1576 and 1580 - which years therefore encompassed the very period of Neville's Northern European travels. Brahe's ancestors, Rosencrantz and Guildenstern, appear in *Hamlet*. Indeed, it is just possible that Neville **often** sowed passing clues to his acquaintance with Brahe, since his curious 'exit pursued by Bear' stage direction in *A Winter's Tale* may be a pun on the fact that Brahe had an ongoing intellectual altercation with Nicholai Reymers Baer [often known as Ursus], for Brahe claimed that Baer had plagiarised his 'system of the world'. Moreover, the action of that part of the play takes place in Bohemia - the very country in which Neville met Brahe. Thus does the Code and its methodology meet up with both Neville and the plays in a complex yet perceivable pattern of clues, which are as randomly scattered as in any modern detective story. However, these clues tie up with no other authorship contender except Neville.

A fact demonstrating Neville's and Gresham's respect for the mathematical calculation systems of Wittich and Napier is that a mathematician called Henry Briggs was appointed as first Professor of Mathematics at Gresham College, London – the college founded by Neville's great-uncle and benefactor, Sir Thomas Gresham. Briggs once worked in conjunction with Napier, extending his work on logarithms.

Gresham College has always funded innovative research and has housed free public lectures on such research since 1597, so it would not have been surprising for work associated with that of Napier to have been disseminated to London audiences at these lectures. Recent research has shown the College to have been primarily involved with disseminating the type of mathematics that would be of practical use to artisans and merchants,[76] so calculation systems would definitely come into that category. More theoretical mathematics was left to the Universities. Indeed, it seems to have taken several years for Gresham to settle down, academically speaking, but once it did so, it became the basis of the Royal Society,[77] which needed its unique mix of academic and practical scientific interest. 'Thy gift, thy tables are within my brain, Full charactered with lasting memory' (Sonnet 122) were the lines that sprang to mind in connection with these facts.

Can we any longer be surprised at the subtle hints, changes, twists and turns that have occurred so far in our decoding? Thorpe himself would have been at one with the punning so popular with Neville. This is precisely the kind of mind needed by men who wished to condense information about a concealed identity into such a small space as the Dedication to the *Sonnets*. There were many men called Henry Neville, but only **one** who could combine the epithet OF THE SEIN, and who had a connection with the FORGE. When I at last searched the record offices for further information I found all the coded clues to have their basis in truth, and so I was able to throw off the myth of Shakespeare and welcome the great writer, politician, mathematician, entrepreneur and intellect that made up the true author.

Of course, there were many references to Nevilles in the history plays, as well as in the Code. However, I discovered one instance of Neville encoding his own name in the plays which stood out above all the rest. It is in the form of a particularly 'Shakespearean' punning game, found in *Love's Labour's Lost* - the play rightly renowned for its overflowing use of wordplay. Here, then, we have a complicated bantering masking sequence pointing to a 'fair lord' named 'no veal', i.e. Ne-veal (Neville):

KATHARINE. What, was your vizard made without a tongue?
LONGAVILLE. I know the reason, lady, why you ask.
KATHARINE. O for your reason! Quickly, sir; I long.
LONGAVILLE. You have a double tongue within your mask,
  And would afford my speechless vizard half.
KATHARINE. **'Veal'** quoth the Dutchman. Is not **'veal'** a calf?
LONGAVILLE. A calf, fair lady!
KATHARINE. **No, a fair lord calf.**
LONGAVILLE. **Let's part the word.**
KATHARINE. No, I'll not be your half.
  Take all and wean it; it may prove an ox.
LONGAVILLE. Look how you butt yourself in these sharp mocks!
  Will you give horns, chaste lady? Do not so.
KATHARINE. Then die a calf, before your horns do grow.
LONGAVILLE. One word in private with you ere I die.
KATHARINE. Bleat softly, then; the butcher hears you cry.
{ACT5|SC2 }

'Let's part the word' says Longaville; Neville, when parted, gives 'Ne-ville' (no veal), and 'Longaville' when parted directly down the middle gives 'ville' in its second half. The fact that Longaville is speaking here ensures the name 'Neville' is even more strongly underlined. Not only does 'Longaville' contain a syllable of Neville's name, but the Longavilles were ancestors of the Nevilles. We have also seen in a previous chapter (p.73) just how appropriate the description of Longaville in the play is for Henry Neville in real life. Moreover, these 'no-veal' references occur in the context of a Longaville wearing a vizard 'without a tongue'. Neville could not and did not announce his authorship of the works, yet here he was, hinting at it, but in such a complicated way that it would be missed on stage:

KATHARINE. O for your reason! Quickly, sir; I **long**. Katharine has now taken LONG away from LONGAVILLE, leaving her bantering partner with only ' AVILLE', exactly as LONGAVILLE goes on to explain:

LONGAVILLE. You have a double tongue within your mask, And would afford my speechless vizard **half**.

to which Katharine replies:
'Veal' [*a supposed Dutch pronunciation of 'Well'*] quoth the Dutchman. Is not **'veal'** a calf?

Katharine leaves LONGAVILLE with VEAL (Ville),which, she says is more like a 'calf' than a 'half'. Then she adds the word 'No' in front of her Lord 'VEAL', which of course means 'No Veal', i.e. 'Neville'. LONGAVILLE now agrees that the word (i.e. his own name) has indeed been parted, but Katherine will not agree to be his 'other half'. As if to emphasise that she means the huge man, Henry Neville himself, she hints that any child of his would more likely resemble an ox than a calf:

KATHARINE. No, I'll not be your half.
Take all and wean it; it may prove an ox.

The image of the 'ox' even holds yet another significance for a Neville: the Neville coat of arms had borne the head of a bull (or an ox) above it since the thirteenth century, when a member of the Bulmer family married into that of Neville of Raby, who were the ancestors of Sir Henry Neville.

It may also now be noted that Katharine was left with 'Long' as a name of her own. 'Long' was a name associated with working colleagues of Neville's father, and at least one woman of the family lived in Berkshire. We may therefore now be at the beginning of yet another trail of evidence.

To the modern mind, such subtle hints and encodings seem strange indeed, but the Elizabethans listened out for them. Neville had no other safe means of preserving his identification with the works. Renaissance readers and audiences were constantly on the look out for double meanings; they *expected* them. Given time enough, they may have found them. But times change, and after Neville died they changed suddenly and dramatically. That our cultural expectations changed so much with the Civil War which began to broil upon the heels of Neville's death has been a major factor in his remaining so long beneath Shakespeare's shadow.

Chapter 6

THE EARL OF SOUTHAMPTON, SIR HENRY NEVILLE AND A PLANTAGENET REVIVAL

The Dedication to Shakespeare's Sonnets was prefixed to their first complete publication in 1609, as seen in Chapter 1. It is strangely laid out and strangely expressed. The **content** of the poems themselves is mysterious too, as is the order in which they appear in the sequence, so it follows that hidden meanings are intended throughout. The writer tempts the reader into trying to perceive a story or pattern behind the whole sequence, then completely subverts this seeming intention by introducing elements that appear to be irreconcilable with any attempt to view a logical, holistic progression. The fact that the writer was unable or unwilling to name his Dedicatee also means that the author must have been working under some huge constraints.

Even before I decoded the Dedication, I suspected Mr. W.H., the Dedicatee, was most likely to have been the poet's patron and that the constraint of secrecy was therefore probably placed upon the writer by the Dedicatee himself. But a possible scenario which never occurred to me before I actually deciphered everything was the one that eventually turned out to be true: by 1609 (when the sonnets were published) both the author and his Dedicatee had featured in the same conspiracy, and subsequently been imprisoned together for two years. Here was the overwhelming reason for hiding *both* their identities.

It is quite obvious from the texts of some of the poems, however, that the author had never *originally* intended to hide the identity of his **dedicatee**. Some of the individual sonnets proclaim the writer's intention that his *dedicatee's name* should live forever. Clearly, this could not happen if the dedicatee were not named. But these same sonnets also declare that the *author's* name must remain unknown:

> Your name from hence immortal life shall have,
> Though I, once gone, to all the world must die;
> The earth can yield me but a common grave... *Sonnet 81*

The name 'Shake-speare' which appeared on some published editions of the plays, and also at the head of the Sonnets, must therefore have been nothing more than a pseudonym. It seems the writer is speaking from his heart and means what he says, yet the whole romance surrounding William Shakespeare has prevented many people from looking at the author's words dispassionately: the real writer had always hidden under another name. Only then could he declare that he would not be remembered. All these logical conclusions substantiate what I found in the Code, and the research I conducted into Sir Henry's life went on to substantiate everything further.

It is now easier to understand what was happening in Sonnet 81(quoted above). Despite its advanced number, it must have been written for Henry Wriothesley, Earl of Southampton, at a date *before* Wriothesley and Sir Henry had been charged with conspiracy in the Essex uprising. Presumably, therefore, if the earlier Sonnets had been published soon after they were originally composed, their Dedicatee could have been named, which then explains why sonnet 81 suggests that the Dedicatee's name will live forever. The writer was intending to name Southampton openly, just as he had named him as the dedicatee of *Venus and Adonis* and *The Rape of Lucrece*. But a changed situation occurred before 1609 and thwarted the author's intentions. This explains why even the eventual *numbering* of the Sonnets in the 1609 edition was meant to be deceptive, not arranged in order of their dating.

In his Hearing following that failed Uprising, Sir Henry stated that he had not seen the Earl of Southampton 'since he was a boy at my old Lord Treasurer's house.'[78] So if Neville had at any time been discovered as the man behind the Shakespeare pseudonym, and if any of the Sonnets had come under suspicion of being addressed to Wriothesley when Wriothesley was an adolescent young man, then Neville could have been accused of perjury. If Neville wrote the sonnets to a maturing Wriothesley, then Neville must have known Wriothesley for longer than he said, and that would have been key information which could have gone towards proving Neville guilty of conspiracy and treason when it came to the Essex affair. Neville had been imprisoned, but not executed, because the extent of his involvement with Essex and Southampton had not been ascertained. Under examination, he had admitted that the conspirators had mentioned their idea to him[79], but he claimed not to have known any of them very well, nor to have taken them seriously. Besides, these were great men – Earls no less – so, as he said, he was loath to bring disrepute onto their names. Sonnet 90 even suggests that he at first resisted Southampton's attempts to draw him into the Essex plot, and thus gained the Earl's disapproval for a while:

> Then hate me when thou wilt, if ever, now,
> Now while the world is bent my deeds to cross,
> Join with the spite of fortune, make me bow,
> And do not drop in for an after-loss:
> Ah do not, when my heart hath 'scaped this sorrow,
> Come in the rearward of a conquered woe,
> Give not a windy night a rainy morrow,
> To linger out a purposed overthrow.
> If thou wilt leave me, do not leave me last,
> When other petty griefs have done their spite,
> But in the onset come, so shall I taste
> At first the very worst of fortune's might.
> And other strains of woe, which now seem woe,
> Compared with loss of thee, will not seem so.

This sonnet explains exactly Neville's position at the time he returned from France. The world did indeed seem 'bent my deeds to cross'. He was under a cloud for not having gained the repayment of Elizabeth's money she had loaned to the French, and for failing to persuade the Spanish to negotiate sensibly at the Treaty of Boulogne. He was now (in late 1600) being forced by the Queen to return and finish his task. This hopelessness was finally what resulted in Neville's decision to join with the conspirators. Nevertheless, some reasonable doubt about the extent of Neville's complicity with Essex and Southampton always remained. He certainly needed a lot of persuading before he agreed to join in, and so even the suspicion which hung over him was almost dispelled when one of the accused stated from the scaffold, with his dying breath, that he was sorry if he had ever been the cause of bringing any unjustified accusations to the name of 'That noble knight', Sir Henry Neville. [80] This statement must have helped save Sir Henry's life. It also proves just how greatly he was esteemed by the conspirators – many of whom were academics and patrons of the arts. Neville's secret involvement with Essex had been kept by his dying friends, and by doing him this favour, they had helped preserve his life.

Neville therefore owed it to them too not to let out the secret they had died protecting.

Yet by the time the Sonnets were published in 1609, Neville was still mistrusted by some at Court, having been in the Tower for so long. He certainly did not wish all and sundry to know about his writing. In a 1606 letter to his friend, Ralph Winwood, Neville expresses most eloquently the legacy of mistrust that still surrounded him three years after his release from the Tower, and he also shows his humanity:

> For my own business, I am at a stand, if I go not backward. This Parliament hath done me no good, where not only speeches and actions, but countenances and conversation with men disliked, hath been observed. But in these points I cannot betray my own mind, speed as it will.
>
> Our laws against recusants have been very sharp, insomuch as we are devising already how we may qualify them in the execution....[81] *4th June, 1606*

Recusants were people who stuck to the old, Catholic religion. It must be remembered that the Earl of Southampton's background had been Catholic. By 1606, one year after the Gunpowder Plot, suspicion had fallen on just about everyone who was known to have had any connection with Catholicism, however remote. Sir Henry's *known* friendship with an erstwhile Catholic family would already have presented him with a few extra problems.

For all these combined reasons, therefore, there has always been an air of necessary mystery surrounding Shakespeare and his Sonnets, and the Dedication Code must be viewed in that context. If there had been no mystery and no intent to conceal the facts behind their creation, there would not have been a need for a Code in the first place. But a Dedication written to the Earl of Southampton by someone who had been associated with him in a rebellion would certainly be a matter needing coded concealment. Part of the mystery is thus explained. The clouds begin to roll away.

The Plantagenet Connection

But why had the Sonnets not been published earlier and named their Dedicatee? Were there perhaps even deeper and older secrets to be kept - secrets which stretched back to a time before the Essex rebellion? This may well have been the case, since the young 'Shakespeare' (or Henry Neville) must have had more than one reason for choosing the Earl of Southampton as a centre for all his poetry, and never dedicating any of it to any other lord. Of course, Neville could afford to do this, as he was not dependent on patronage for the source of his income, whereas it made no sense for William Shakespeare to write continuously for one Lord only, even though that Lord never publicly acknowledged him. But with Neville, there were different considerations at work.

Neville and Southampton were related, because both of them sprang from a common Neville ancestor - Ralph Neville, Earl of Westmoreland - and the line had also been reinforced with additional Nevilles since that time. John Neville (brother of the 'Kingmaker') had become the father of one Lucy Neville, who had produced families both with her first husband - a Fitzwilliam, and therefore an ancestor of our Sir Henry's wife - and with Sir Anthony Browne, who was the great, great grandfather of Henry Wriothesley, Third Earl of Southampton, and dedicatee of the Shakespeare Sonnets.

All this means that Neville would have jumped at the chance of writing Sonnets for the young Earl in around 1590 to 1594. And it was at precisely this time that William Cecil - then Chancellor of England - was looking for a writer to aid him in a project he had in mind. Cecil wanted to persuade the Earl of Southampton to marry his granddaughter, Elizabeth de Vere.[82] With so many family connections of his own also inclining towards Southampton and the Cecils too, Neville would be just the person to ask - he could be trusted not to give any of their plans away. Young Southampton was known to like poetry and literature. So it comes about that the first 17 sonnets are ones attempting to persuade the young man to marry - most generally considered to be the result of William Cecil's concern with persuading Southampton to marry into his family.

William Cecil's, (Lord Burghley) mother was a Neville. Henry Neville would therefore have been intent on furthering Burghley's plans, both from a family and a political point of view. He agreed that the new ministerial kind of government the Cecils had introduced was progressive, as far as the interests of the State were concerned. Without the Cecils' input, England might return to the despotism of an individual monarch. As a careful and caring M.P., Neville was out to prevent this happening, but he also knew that the people needed a visible figurehead, not a committee of invisible ministers, around whom to unite. Neville might well have had republican tendencies, but he was intelligent, humane and pragmatic enough to realise that this kind of government could not be foisted on a public which was by no means ready for such ideas. He was therefore just as worried as everyone else about the monarchical Succession. It was looking as if Queen Elizabeth I was going to be the last of the Tudors. For some reason (perhaps because she knew that she, like her sister, Mary, had difficulty in conceiving and/or bearing healthy children) Elizabeth had resisted all attempts to see her married off. This made it absolutely necessary for all men of good will to pull together and come to an early consensus concerning their monarchical candidate. Yet they could not do so openly, because Elizabeth had forbidden discussion on the subject, eventually going so far as to make it a treasonable offence for anyone to speak of who should succeed her.

The young Henry Neville had been to see King James VI of Scotland in 1583. James' possible accession to the Throne of England must have been discussed on this very occasion. But in later years, Neville and King James never really liked each other, and always stood on opposite sides of the political fence. It is therefore highly likely that there were occasional 'bad vibes' between the two men, even at their first meetings all those years before James finally came to England. This would obviously have motivated Neville to set his sites, privately, on an alternative heir to the British Throne. And who more promising or better connected - from Neville's point of view - than Henry Wriothesley, Earl of Southampton, a young man who already knew and respected him?

This opinion must have been shared by other writers, politicians and intellectuals of the time, as witnessed by a spate of 'promoters' gathering around Wriothesley from the early age of nineteen. Writers noted that Wriothesley was descended from a noble dynasty. This, together with the fact that he had been raised under the influence of successful politicians like Burghley and the Nevilles, was enough to provoke intellectuals to rally round the young Earl. They, like Neville and the Cecils, hated the possibility of a return to civil war, which they all foresaw could happen, with Elizabeth refusing to name her successor. By 1590, the Queen was already 57 years old, well past the usual life expectancy at that time, and well past her childbearing age, so the situation was becoming urgent.

Then, by the time the Queen was fifty eight, Southampton's star began to shine. He came naturally to prominence because, young as he was, he proved his bravery by going to Normandy in 1591 and declaring himself ready to fight in the cause of Henri of Navarre. (Henri was then the great Protestant hope for France, so the Earls of Southampton and Essex - who also fought for Navarre - were seen by Neville and other prominent politicians as the noblest and best dynastic descendants England possessed.)

Thus had centre stage been given over quite naturally to these two earls, even at this early date (1591). Thus it was quite natural that Neville should have devoted his early Sonnets to Southampton, based on his own personal connections, and on his political outlook. There is absolutely no need to indulge (as promoters of the Oxfordian authorship claim tend to do) in the fancy that Southampton might have been the illegitimate son of Queen Elizabeth I! He was eligible to become the centre of attention without any regard to a possible close kinship with her. It was the Earl's kinship with the *Plantagenets* which was important. After all, Queen Elizabeth was herself related to the Plantagenets, but the fear in the 1590s was that this line could be exchanged for the dreaded *Stuart* dynasty, who had many Catholic connections and who were unknown and untried as monarchs of England.

Neville, Walsingham and the rest of their entourage must have come back from Scotland full of doubts about the strange, sexually-wayward King James VI. (He was not popular amongst his own people and he tortured defenceless women under a superstitious conception of witchcraft.) On his paternal side, James VI was descended from a long line of purely Scottish noblemen. His nearest connection with the English Plantagenet Kings came somewhat late in the history of the line. Henry VII and his wife had a daughter, Margaret, who married James IV of Scotland (James Stewart) They had a son, James V, who married a French wife. Mary Queen of Scots was their daughter, so the English connection was already becoming more remote. James VI of Scotland (and, ultimately, I of England) was therefore the son of a Scottish King and the grandson of a French lady. The Catholic strain had become quite strong, and by the time James VI was born there were already closer ties between Scotland and France than between Scotland and England. This meant that the English generally felt there was very little in the dynastic inheritance of King James with which they could identify. It would have been much easier for them to see the Earl of Southampton as a possible monarch.

The reports which the Earl of Essex, Walsingham and Henry Neville, amongst others, brought back from Scotland must have been enough to prompt the English to look closer to home for a successor to the English Throne - or, at least, to keep their options open. The contemporary historian William Camden, however, expressed a fear becoming quite common at the time. This was, (as he wrote later, in 1615) that the Earl of Leicester might falsely suggest that one of his own bastards was in fact his son by Queen Elizabeth. It was therefore important that a candidate with a known *legitimate parentage and dynasty* - and, by extension, someone under the influence of the Camden circle - should be chosen and nurtured. Neville and Sir Henry Savile were well and truly in the Camden circle, as was Ben Jonson, so it is not surprising that writers quickly caught on to this circle's plans. One example of their subsequent writing in praise of Southampton follows below.

1593 saw the publication of *The Honour of the Garter* - a poem by George Peele. Peele had been at Oxford University throughout the 1570s, so there was no doubt he had known Sir Henry Savile, and through Savile he would have met or heard about Neville and Camden. Peele's poem anachronistically places the Earls of Southampton inside the early history of the Order of the Garter. This fictional device allows the writer to extol young Wriothesley, third Earl to that title, calling him 'Gentle Wriothesley, South-Hampton's Starre... 'Bright may he rise and shine immortally, with all the stars in the Queen's fair firmament,' adds Peele.

Peele is obviously trying to induce a perception of continuity between Wriothesley, ancient English honours, and the last of the Tudors. No stretch of the imagination, however, could have included the weird Scottish King in with these bright stars of Elizabeth's Court. There was inevitably going to be a problem, should the propagandists ever wish to portray James as a 'natural' successor to Elizabeth. Of course, time and events were to overtake all these masters of planned perceptions, so in a post-Essex-rebellion world the erstwhile writers in favour of Southampton had to adapt their skills to suit a different situation. But Peele was dead by then, whereas Neville was not, so Neville -

ever the pragmatist - was forced simply to make the best of a less than ideal situation.

As a footnote, it is interesting that Peele dedicated his poem to the Earl of Northumberland - the man in whose London house the famous 'Northumberland Manuscript' was discovered. The Earl of Northumberland was the patron of Charles Paget, the spy who was a friend of Neville, and who is widely supposed to have written *Leycester's Commonwealth*[83]. This latter work exposed how the Earl of Leicester was said to have been conspiring to ferment trouble between the great families at Court once more, then to put himself on the throne, amidst the ensuing confusion, which he knew could possibly amount to civil war. This is why, in *Leycester's Commonwealth,* our Neville's own father is reported as warning others about Leicester's plans. It also explains why Camden distrusted Leicester's intentions regarding his own illegitimate progeny.[84] (see also pp.84 and 85.)

Thus were the early Sonnets addressed to Wriothesley, the young Plantagenet hope, naming him as 'beauty's rose' [sonnet 1]. Not only was Wriothesley's name often pronounced 'Rosely' but he was descended from the Plantagenets, and especially from the Yorkists, whose emblem had been the white rose. Added to this, there is a group of three roses on the Coat of Arms of the town of Southampton. By Neville's time, the Tudor rose was the accepted symbol of England, so changing to another rose, rather than to the Scottish thistle, would unite English dynastic imagery too. Such devices, as any writer knows, induce important subconscious perceptions in the reader. Yet, had the true author of the Sonnets declared his name, then the true origins of the Plantagenet Rose 'conspiracy' would have been exposed. This would have been a dangerous move, especially in 1609 while a Stuart was on the Throne of England.

If the first 17 Sonnets had been published when they were first polished enough for publication - probably by around 1594 - then the Dedicatee might possibly have been named. But even so, this would have hazarded the chance of offending old Lord Burghley, because he would not have wished his failed plans for marrying his granddaughter to the Earl of Southampton to be made public. By 1609, however, it was absolutely impossible to name the Earl of Southampton in the Dedication, for this very man had represented the centre of all earlier hopes envisaging a new, liberal monarchy. Now another man was on the throne, and that man believed he ruled by divine right and so had no need of guidance from intellectuals or from Parliament.

Neville, the Earl of Southampton, and their friends seem to have been successful in ultimately persuading King James that the Essex rebellion had been concerned with seeing James' smooth passage to the English throne, whereas the actual evidence points to a very different state of affairs. The Earl of Southampton was known to have been Essex's constant companion[85], and to have been at his side during their conspiratorial meetings, and during the uprising itself. Neville, like his Kingmaker ancestor[86], was their trusted political advisor and supporter. The Essex uprising may therefore be seen as the last, failed attempt to ensure a Plantagenet succession to the throne of England.

Documentary evidence points to the suspicion that even Sir Robert Cecil may have been one of those in favour of Southampton's eventual succession to the throne, though Cecil was certainly not associated with Essex's uprising itself. After Essex and Southampton were put on trial, Cecil kept writing to everyone saying it was possible danger to the Earl of Southampton which troubled him most. Cecil did his best to protect that Earl, and it is probable that he and Neville both owed him their lives. Of the many letters Cecil wrote defending Southampton, the one to Sir George Carew - Neville's friend - is perhaps the most representative:

> It remayneth now that I lett you know what is lyke to become of the poore young Earle of Southampton who, meerely in respect that most of the conspiracies were at Drury House, where he was always cheefe, and where Sir Charles Danvers laye, those that would deale for him **(of which number I protest to God I am one, as far as I dare)** are much disadvantaged of arguments to save him, and yet, when I consider how penitent he is, and how merciful the Queen is, and never in thought or deed, but in this conspiracy he offended, as I cannot write in despaire, so I dare not flatter myself with hope."[87]

Cecil says outright that he would 'deale for him'[Southampton] which certainly seems to have some great depth of utterance. It surely suggests that he has always been one of Southampton's promoters - 'as far as I dare.' This latter remark may covertly refer to the fact that Queen Elizabeth had been very displeased at Southampton's eventual secret marriage to one of her ladies in waiting, so it was obviously not easy for Cecil to declare his support for Southampton too openly. But nowhere in his words are there any hints of condemnation that Southampton did not marry his father's choice of bride - Robert's own niece - so Cecil's support of Southampton must have had another backbone to it. Cecil, like Neville and Southampton himself, was one of those who eventually threw their weight behind the succession of James VI of Scotland, but after Southampton's disgrace and imprisonment there was nothing else left for the erstwhile Plantagenet supporters to do.

Chapter 7

THE STRANGE SONNETS AND THEIR CONCEALED AUTHOR

A woman's face with nature's own hand painted,
Hast thou the master mistress of my passion...
A man in hue, all Hews in his controlling...

The Sonnets, as presented to the world, were indeed covering up a profoundly sensitive situation, though not all of them were directly concerned with Wriothesley. Yet the presence of the writer's name in the Code also means that the true writer hoped he would eventually be discovered. It is therefore clear that Sir Henry was most anxious that readers should be intrigued enough to become involved in attempting to decode the Dedication. Yet the process of decoding was just complicated enough to make it difficult to explain and substantiate in a Court of Law. At the same time, however, the plaintext of the Dedication guides the reader to search for a specific *identity* – albeit ostensibly that of the *dedicatee* only - so this increases the chance of any would-be decoder taking notice of any name he finds there. Shakespeare-Neville thereby demonstrates his skill at using psycho-linguistic 'pointers'. The fact that he could do this while simultaneously covering his tracks is one more piece of evidence for the brilliant, 'tricky' Neville being just the person to compile the Code.

The lack of numerous Sonnets from the *young* Shakespeare's pen was always strange in itself, and definitely needed investigation. Even the evidence of literary history alone suggests that writing sonnets was an *early* exercise expected from the pen of young authors. The lack of them from Shakespeare's hand must therefore have had a reason hidden from the general reading public. According to many biographers, almost every great sixteenth century English poet had written Sonnets by the time he was twenty eight years old. The Sonnet was usually chosen as a poetic form for expressing love. Michael Drayton's sixty four sonnets longing for the daughter of his patron had 'long slept in sable night'[88] before actually being published when he was thirty.

Samuel Daniel's Sonnet Sequence addressed to *Delia* was similarly public property by the time he reached that age. Even the studious Edmund Spenser had translated Sonnets from the French and Italian before he was twenty six.

Why, then, had the illustrious thirty five year old Shakespeare, supposed author of the most famous poetic love dramas, seemingly not followed suit by sonneteering? Even when he reached the age of forty there were no published sonnets which could be definitely assigned to him. Only when he was forty five did his great sequence of 154 sonnets appear in print. Why had the great writer not tried to have them published sooner? The circumstances of Sir Henry's life could easily account for such an anomaly. Unless a suitably disguised frame could be found in which to fit his Sonnets, he would have been unlikely to publish any of them - ever. Without the explanation of Southampton's marriage, it certainly was going to be difficult to publish sonnets written to a man, in any case. Not since the homoerotic sonnets by Michelangelo had such a thing been attempted. If Queen Elizabeth had read Neville's early sonnets – including sonnet 20 (quoted at the head of this chapter) – she might well have got the wrong idea and would certainly have disapproved. And Neville could not openly explain their true background and origins. I do not think it is any mere coincidence that these sonnets from one man to another could only be published *without* a background explanation once a bi-sexual king was on the throne. As far as James I was concerned, any homosexual connotations - however mistaken - would have been far from taboo. Further sonnets, written under *different* circumstances and to different people, could also be added by this time, so to confuse the issue and thus advance the writer's intentional masquerade.

The quotation from sonnet 20 at the head of this chapter is one example of how the author purposely set out to create an ambiguity and confusion within the poems themselves, as well as in the code that heads them. This textual confusion and complexity has been the subject of debate for centuries. How could a simple country boy from Stratford, with only a primary education behind him, express himself with such erudition? And if indeed he truly overcame all disadvantages, why did he leave so little evidence of himself and his authorship to posterity? Such a 'rags to riches' actor would surely have had more to celebrate than to hide? Of course, none of this makes sense. Both the Code and the mysterious contents and ordering of the Sonnets themselves are purposefully inviting us to ask all these questions. If we, the readers, were meant to take the *Sonnets* and their declared attribution to 'Shake-speare' at surface value, then they would not have been presented in so mysterious a fashion. But not one feasible, all-encompassing explanation for all this ever made sense until Sir Henry Neville was placed in the centre of the jigsaw.

The Nature and Course of the Sonnets

Unlike the plays, the *Sonnets* are written in the first person, therefore giving the impression that the writer himself is addressing his real-life subject. Yet they are in some ways also intertextual with previous works by previous authors. However, it is well-nigh impossible to see how those specific previous works could have been accessed by Shakespeare of Stratford. Some of the works echoed in the Sonnets were written by University men of the day, whilst others were in modern foreign languages, which were not taught at the Stratford Grammar school. Even so, by the time these poems were published, *Shakespeare* was a renowned name, and no known 'disgrace' was associated with it. But when Henry Neville, the *true author,* wrote some of the sonnets he was truly 'in disgrace with fortune and men's eyes' (sonnet 29.) He had been involved with an uprising. He knew his works would be attributed elsewhere. Also, the common grave of Sonnet 81 would have always been Neville's lot: his father had built a family tomb the plaque of which, however, only names his father's generation. Even though several generations of Nevilles are said to be buried there, they are not listed. Neville knew he would die forgotten, so far as the 'common' Neville grave was concerned:

> Or I shall live your epitaph to make,
> Or you survive when I in earth am rotten;
> From hence your memory death cannot take,
> Although in me each part will be forgotten.
> Your name from hence immortal life shall have,
> Though I, once gone, to all the world must die;
> The earth can yield me but a common grave,
> When you entombed in men's eye shall lie.
> Your monument shall be my gentle verse,
> Which eyes not yet created shall o'erread,
> And tongues to be your being shall rehearse
> When all the breathers of this world are dead.
> You still shall live (such virtue hath my pen)
> Where breath most breathes, even in the mouths of men.
> *Sonnet 81*

This point is a most important one. Shakespeare, the actor and (by 1609) famous man, could never have claimed that he would not be remembered, or that he would be placed in a 'common grave'. Neither Shakespeare himself nor any of the other authorship contenders could have said that their names would be forgotten. The only person who could have declared such a thing was someone who never published **anything** under his own name, and was not a 'nobleman'. This was the case with Sir Henry Neville, and with no other authorship contender.

We may therefore also conclude from the text of the Sonnets themselves that the author was not an Earl or a Duke; indeed, not a highly titled aristocrat at all. Men born with such silver spoons in their mouths tend to see to it that monuments are erected after their death or, failing this, that trust funds promoting the arts or research are set up in their memory. If the name of the true author would die with him, then he had not obtained a sufficiently elevated position in any public walk of life for him to be remembered, and he had certainly published nothing under his own name. The true author therefore looks very much like a man who was at pains to delay the discovery of his identity by purposely concealing himself behind a mist of symbolism and distractions. We are therefore absolutely forced to conclude that he intended to use some of the Sonnets as one means of temporary disguise, while at the same time scattering clues among them - and in their Dedication - which could ultimately lead to the discovery of his name. In this case, does Shakespeare's Sonnet sequence purport to tell a *real* or *imaginary* story?

As discussed in the previous chapter, at least the first 17 of the Sonnets are addressed to the Dedicatee himself, who is, incongruously, called the 'onlie begetter' of them all. In Elizabethan times, however, 'onlie' often meant 'chief, main'.[89] This is definitely the one sense in which the word can be understood here, since there are other people in the sequence too – a dark lady, who is enticing yet disgusting, plus a 'gentle' lady, who is cultured enough to be a musician, and might also be the person compared to 'a summer's day' in Sonnet 18. There is probably more than one man addressed as well. 'Mr. W.H. is the *begetter* , but Sir Henry Neville often used the word 'beget' in its true meaning of 'started off'. On p.38 of Volume Two of *Winwood's Memorials of State* there is a letter from Sir Henry Neville in which he reports a debate he is having with other lawyers concerning moves towards an Act of Unification with Scotland. In this letter he states that 'The last Article begat more Debate and Contestation than the rest.' In the same way, the Dedication clearly indicates that 'Mr. W.H.' started off all the Sonnet sequence – perhaps the very idea of writing a sonnet sequence would never have occurred to Neville but for the start which Wriothesley's situation afforded him. I think there is evidence that at least one sonnet was addressed to the Earl of Essex and several others to Sir Henry's own son and namesake. But to explain all this would need a whole book dedicated to the Sonnets alone, such is their depth of meaning.

Having exposed the ambiguity of the 'onlie begetter, we can perhaps begin to make more sense of the individual sonnets. If the first 17 were indeed addressed to the Earl of Southampton, then it is highly likely they were written when he was a mere teenager, for the author is urging him to start thinking about getting married. Then there are other sonnets scattered among those leading up to Sonnet 126 whose content also suggests that the poet's addressee is young. Finally, at the end of the first section of the sequence, this addressee is warned that his youth cannot last, even though he is, for the present, a 'lovely boy' :

O thou, my lovely boy, who in thy power
Dost hold Time's fickle glass, his sickle hour,
Who hast by waning grown, and therein show'st
Thy lovers withering, as thy sweet self grow'st;
If Nature (sovereign mistress over wrack)
As thou goest onwards still will pluck thee back,
She keeps thee to this purpose: that her skill
May Time disgrace, and wretched minutes kill.
Yet fear her, O thou minion of her pleasure,
She may detain, but not still keep, her treasure.
Her audit, though delayed, answered must be,
And her quietus is to render thee.   *Sonnet 126*

Because, then, this sonnet seems to round off a section written to a boy not a man, it must be assumed that it belongs together with the first 17 sonnets. These first 17, followed by the sonnet now known as number 81, were therefore written long before Wriothesley's marriage in 1598, by which time he was well past boyhood. From the age of nine, however, young Henry Wriothesley, Earl of Southampton, was the ward of William Cecil, Lord Burghley, father of Robert Cecil. As noted in the previous chapter, therefore, Lord Burghley was in a powerful position from which to persuade Southampton to marry a member of his family. (He was also able to select a writer in some way under his control to compose persuasive poetry in this direction.)

So why did Burghley's plans for Southampton fail? The strongest reason was that young Wriothesley was not ready for marriage[90] Indeed - like his father before him - he even seemed unsure of his own sexuality at the time. So at first Burghley had commissioned one of his personal secretaries - John Clapham[91] - to write poems attempting to persuade the young Earl to marry soon. When these poems did not do the trick, he would have turned to the man young Wriothesley already knew and liked – Henry Neville. Young Henry Neville was a frequent visitor at the Cecils' house in the Strand, where the Earl of Southampton was usually resident with Burghley.[92] (Even the Earl of Essex also became Burghley's ward eventually, so Neville very probably first met him there too.) Wriothesley's then confused sexual perception of himself would certainly explain Sonnet 20:

> A woman's face with Nature's own hand painted
> Hast thou the master mistress of my passion,
> A woman's gentle heart but not acquainted
> With shifting change as is false women's fashion,
> An eye more bright than theirs, less false in rolling,
> Gilding the object whereupon it gazeth;
> A man in hue, all Hews in his controlling,
> Which steals men's eyes and women's souls amazeth.
> And for a woman wert thou first created,
> Till Nature as she wrought thee fell a-doting
> And by addition me of thee defeated -
> By adding one thing to my purpose nothing.
> But since she pricked thee out for women's pleasure,
> Mine by thy love and thy love's use their treasure.

The sonnet is written by a kind, understanding, jesting author who knows his subject very well. 'I can understand how your appearance could lead you to believe that you might be more of a woman than a man, but there are some important physical differences between you and the female of the species', is its message. He is clearly telling the boy to start recognising his manhood. There is numerical significance in this sonnet too, and knowing Neville's interest in mathematics and numbers, such symbolism makes sense. The Roman number 20 is represented as XX. As mentioned previously, this can also be seen as two personalities – the same as each other, yet differently placed – representing the male and the female, which refers to the very core of the poem. (This is indeed only one example of the extensive use of numerological symbolism contained in the sequence, inevitably leading to the conclusion that Neville, the mathematician, was sowing yet another clue to his identity in the otherwise rather incoherent ordering of the individual poems.)

Even the writer's punning reference to 'hues' and 'Hews' can now be explained: the Earl of Southampton ran abroad to fight with the Earl of Essex. Robert Devereux, the then Earl, was in fact Earl of Essex and 'Ewe'. (HEWS are also letters contained in the name Henry Wriothesley, so once again the complex, endlessly-punning mind of the writer is at work!) From that point, Essex and Southampton were almost inseparable, as mentioned in the previous chapter. With such an early military connection, even the '*Master*-Mistress' could be intended partly as a pun on 'Muster-Mistress'. The Muster-Master was a military post, but a 'Muster-Mistress' was a term used for a woman who ran a brothel. (As we shall see, hints of such 'ladies' occur later in the Sonnets.)

But even Neville's excellent sonnets did not persuade Wriothesley to marry. The young man soon told Burghley that he would rather fight for a cause than woo a woman. Neville then promptly wrote *Venus and Adonis,* which tells the doleful end of a man who spurned a woman in favour of pursuing the dangerous sport of boar-hunting. Venus is a beautiful woman who tries to rouse Adonis to recognise his manhood and love her. But Adonis (Wriothesley) declares that he is young and does not yet know himself; he feels he cannot therefore yet be known by a woman:

> 'Fair queen,' quoth he, 'if any love you owe me,
> Measure my strangeness with my unripe years:
> Before I know myself, seek not to know me;
> No fisher but the ungrown fry forbears:
> The mellow plum doth fall, the green sticks fast,
> Or being early pluck'd is sour to taste.

So Neville thereby symbolically implies that if the young man is too 'unripe' to love a woman, then he is too 'unripe' for dangerous blood-sports too. In trying to convince Wriothesley that Venus' bed could be just as exciting as any battlefield he is attempting to steer the young Earl onto a path of creation rather than destruction. Venus tells Adonis:

> 'I have been woo'd, as I entreat thee now,
> Even by the stern and direful god of war,
> Whose sinewy neck in battle ne'er did bow,
> Who conquers where he comes in every jar;
> Yet hath he been my captive and my slave,
> And begg'd for that which thou unask'd shalt have.

But still nothing worked. Wriothesley eventually ran away to fight with Essex for the succession of Henri of Navarre in France – i.e. for the very man who later was King at the time Neville was Ambassador.

Venus and Adonis was published in 1593. Its title page did not name any author, but its dedicatory letter was addressed to the Earl of Southampton, and the letter was signed 'William Shakespeare'. Significantly, the title page did in fact contain a Latin quotation, beginning 'Vilea miretu...' (Put together the reverse of **Ven**us with **Vil**ea, and we have '**Nevvil**') Perhaps old Lord Burghley even gave his approval to this publication, since its subject was a mythological one, therefore not easily perceived as a direct and personal suggestion that Wriothesley should begin to be interested in girls. However, if the Sonnets - openly exhorting a young man to marry - had been published around the same time, and had they also been openly dedicated to the same young Earl, then readers might begin to put two and two together. Burghley would not have liked anyone to guess at his personal schemes for marrying off the young man. It is therefore hardly surprising that the Sonnets were not published until a later date.

At the time, young Neville himself probably agreed with their publication being delayed. After all, he wanted to rise in politics and had become a Member of Parliament at the youngest possible age, and it was also Burghley who patronised him in this respect and who had introduced him to the Royal Court, so Neville was obviously anxious not to put a foot wrong with so powerful a supporter.

Over the years, Neville must have continued to write sonnets from time to time. Their individual dedicatees and individual purposes therefore diverged. Sonnet 18, 'Shall I compare thee to a summer's day', for instance, was probably written to Anne Killigrew, Neville's wife - perhaps on the occasion of her eighteenth birthday - while sonnet 26 was

138

perhaps written to Essex on the occasion of Neville agreeing to become the French Ambassador, and at the same time to serve as the Earl of Essex's personal representative over there too. However, its content might also refer to Robert Cecil's position of authority over Neville:

> Lord of my love, to whom in vassalage
> Thy merit hath my duty strongly knit,
> To thee I send this written embassage,
> To witness duty, not to show my wit;
> Duty so great, which wit so poor as mine
> May make seem bare in wanting words to show it,
> But that I hope some good conceit of thine
> In thy soul's thought, all naked, will bestow it;
> Till whatsoever star that guides my moving
> Points on me graciously with fair aspect,
> And puts apparel on my tattered loving
> To show me worthy of thy sweet respect.
> Then may I dare to boast how I do love thee;
> Till then, not show my head where thou mayst prove me.

(If this sonnet was written for the Earl of Essex, then Neville was already committed to that Earl's service, which suggests that he was indeed the Henry Neville who is listed as accompanying Essex on his 1596 Cadiz expedition, and had been knighted by him there.[93])

Old William Burghley died in 1598, and the Earl of Southampton announced his forthcoming marriage in the same year. But he married Elizabeth Vernon, one of Queen Elizabeth's ladies in waiting, not Burghley's granddaughter. There is evidence that Neville now hoped that he would at last be able to publish some of the Sonnets, and openly dedicate them to the Earl of Southampton as a wedding present. Old Burghley was dead, Wriothesley was going to be married, so a careful selection of the poems could no longer cause anyone any embarrassment. My guess is that it was at this point that Neville actually wrote what we now know as sonnet 81, declaring that Southampton would be celebrated, while he, Neville, the writer, would still not be known under his own name. 81 is of course 18 reversed, so I think this was the Sonnet intended to round off the original sequence. When Sonnet 81 is placed directly after sonnet 17, the effect is indeed one of completion:

Who will believe my verse in time to come
If it were filled with your most high deserts?
Though yet, heaven knows, it is but as a tomb
Which hides your life and shows not half your parts.
If I could write the beauty of your eyes,
And in fresh numbers number all your graces,
The age to come would say `This poet lies;
Such heavenly touches ne'er touched earthly faces'.
So should my papers, yellowed with their age,
Be scorned, like old men of less truth than tongue,
And your true rights be termed a poet's rage
And stretched metre of an antique song.
But were some child of yours alive that time,
You should live twice -in it, and in my rhyme. *17*

Or I shall live your epitaph to make,
Or you survive when I in earth am rotten;
From hence your memory death cannot take,
Although in me each part will be forgotten.
Your name from hence immortal life shall have,
Though I, once gone, to all the world must die;
The earth can yield me but a common grave,
When you entombed in men's eye shall lie.
Your monument shall be my gentle verse,
Which eyes not yet created shall o'erread,
And tongues to be your being shall rehearse
When all the breathers of this world are dead.
You still shall live (such virtue hath my pen)
Where breath most breathes, even in the mouths of men. *81*

(The androgynous Sonnet 20 would hardly have been added to a
Sonnet Sequence openly dedicated to a named man who was on
the point of marrying. I think this would always have had to wait
until the 1609 publication, where it could appear with an
unnamed dedicatee and with its origins surrounded by mystery
rather than certainty.)

That Neville had originally intended to publish a selection of
these early sonnets in 1599 is therefore witnessed partly by the
circumstantial and textual evidence given above. But there is
documentary evidence too, which should be seen in conjunction
with the circumstances outlined. In *Palladis Tamia* (published
in 1598), Francis Meres reviewed some of Shakespeare's
works, and also mentioned that there existed some 'sugar'd

140

sonnets' by that author, which were currently 'among his private friends'. Meres (1565–1647) had no known connection with William Shakespeare. He had, however, studied at both Cambridge and Oxford Universities, so he is likely to have encountered the famous name of Savile there, and to know Savile was to hear of Neville, his tutee and life-long friend. Then Meres lived in London for a while in the 1590s and made it his business to review up and coming writers. As a writer and reviewer, Meres must also have known the London publishers, so they or their employees would tell him that some of Shakespeare's Sonnets were about to appear in print. *The Passionate Pilgrim* – a collection of poems by 'Shakespeare' – appeared in 1599, but these are not all sonnets and not all by Shakespeare, and certainly not all 'sugar'd' ones, so it is impossible to believe that these were the specific sonnets to which Meres had obtained a privileged preview. Whatever the truth of the matter might be, however, the fact is that Meres had seen 'sugar'd sonnets' by Shakespeare, which would hardly have been the case unless their imminent publication was intended. His description of the ones he had seen 'among his private friends' would match the tone of the first 17 or 18 [81] *pleasant* sonnets. No unsavoury deeds inhabit those particular poems, but it would have been hard for Meres to describe the Sonnets generally in such honeyed terms, had he seen the whole sequence which we now know. As for the 'private friends', the conclusion is that in 1598 these poems were being evaluated by the writers' friends prior to publication. How Meres begged a viewing of them is impossible to say after so many years, but as any writer knows, once a work has been shown to a number of 'friends' it is virtually impossible for it not to leak out.

So what could have happened to have stopped their printing? My guess is that Robert Cecil put his foot down. He did not want his old father's ward (the Earl of Southampton) having a set of poems dedicated to him which had been commissioned by Burghley himself, in an ambitious attempt to ally the Cecils with the aristocracy. If Southampton were named in the Sonnets' Dedication, then there was at least an outside chance that some well-informed readers might guess the embarrassing truth. And if anyone at Court guessed it, then Robert Cecil might lose power through his name losing some of its dignity.

When one recognises Neville as the true poet, it does not seem mere coincidence that he was actually invited to become the French Ambassador during 1598 - the very year in which Meres had a pre-publication viewing of the Sonnets. It was also the year in which Robert Cecil became Secretary of State, which gave him extra cause for not wanting family secrets to emerge at such a sensitive time. The times were troubled by famine too, yet Elizabeth wanted to raise taxes to fund foreign wars.[94] Cecil knew Henry Neville well enough to guess that he would oppose this extra taxation in Parliament. He knew too that he was a friend of the Earl of Essex, who was already leading a faction against Cecil in Court. Essex himself therefore reasoned that his personal orders to serve in Ireland proceeded primarily from a tactic of Cecil's to get him out of the way.[95] It is no coincidence that Neville was sent to France at the very same moment. Cecil was clearly scattering his potential problems to the four winds.

We can only guess at the pressure this unwelcome offer of diplomatic service put on Neville. He could not now risk being discovered as the writer of those sonnets, because then he would also be inferred as the public playwright too. It would have been unthinkable for an Ambassador residing among foreign royalty to be known as a playwright for the public stage. Then there were the facts that he had written *Richard II* – including its deposition of a King - that he was descended from a rival dynasty, that his father and mother's union did not appear to have been 'official', (the unusual circumstances surrounding the union of Henry's father and mother will be described in a subsequent chapter) and that he was a politician – all of which had to be taken into serious consideration.

Nevertheless, Sir Henry must really have been looking forward to seeing his poems in print, even if published under his Shakespeare pseudonym. On the other hand, Cecil knew Neville hoped for high office in England, so he could always use this argument to persuade Neville to delay publication - or else!

So, for now, the sonnets dealing with Southampton's marriage had to be shelved.

But what were the other sonnets about? The most famous ones concern a dark lady, by whom the poet is simultaneously attracted and repelled. Then there are the poems to another, more cultured lady, who plays the virginals:

How oft, when thou, my music, music play'st
Upon that blessed wood whose motion sounds
With thy sweet fingers when thou gently sway'st
The wiry concord that mine ear confounds,
Do I envy those jacks that nimble leap
To kiss the tender inward of thy hand,
Whilst my poor lips, which should that harvest reap,
At the wood's boldness by thee blushing stand.
To be so tickled they would change their state
And situation with those dancing chips
O'er whom thy fingers walk with gentle gait,
Making dead wood more blest than living lips.
Since saucy jacks so happy are in this,
Give them thy fingers, me thy lips, to kiss.   *Sonnet 128*

The very fact that these ladies were included at all makes it even more difficult for any general reader to identify an author, coming as they did hard on the heels of adoring poems purportedly written to a man. Thus the writer adds one more means of authorial disguise.

The poet also expands on his male friend's virtues, giving a hint that this friend is a knight, for one of his poems repeats the Knightly attributes of being 'fair, kind and true'. (Wriothesley was entered as a Knight of the Garter at the unusually early age of nineteen.) Gifts pass between the poet and his friend – 'Thy gifts, thy tables are within my brain' - and there are also many sonnets dealing with numbers, accounting and usury.

Then there are the famous 'Will' sonnets, in which the poet is giving some indecorous hints by punning on his supposed name:

Whoever hath her wish, thou hast thy Will,
And Will to boot, and Will in overplus;
More than enough am I that vex thee still,
To thy sweet will making addition thus.
Wilt thou, whose will is large and spacious,
Not once vouchsafe to hide my will in thine?
Shall will in others seem right gracious,
And in my will no fair acceptance shine?
The sea, all water, yet receives rain still,
And in abundance addeth to his store;
So thou, being rich in Will, add to thy Will
One will of mine to make thy large Will more.
Let no unkind no fair beseechers kill;
Think all but one, and me in that one Will.

(Thus is the authorial disguise further enhanced.) And then come a large number of poems concerning age and the passing of time:

> Like as the waves make towards the pebbled shore,
> So do our minutes hasten to their end,
> Each changing place with that which goes before,
> In sequent toil all forwards do contend.
> Nativity, once in the main of light,
> Crawls to maturity, wherewith being crowned,
> Crooked eclipses 'gainst his glory fight,
> And Time that gave doth now his gift confound.
> Time doth transfix the flourish set on youth,
> And delves the parallels in beauty's brow,
> Feeds on the rarities of nature's truth,
> And nothing stands but for his scythe to mow.
> And yet to times in hope my verse shall stand,
> Praising thy worth despite his cruel hand.
>
> *Sonnet 60*

There are ones which seem to refer to specific experiences, such as bearing the Canopy and a political life, in which the poet records that he has also 'laid great bases for eternity'

> Were't aught to me I bore the canopy,
> With my extern the outward honouring,
> Or laid great bases for eternity,
> Which proves more short than waste or ruining?
> Have I not seen dwellers on form and favour
> Lose all, and more, by paying too much rent,
> For compound sweet forgoing simple savour,
> Pitiful thrivers in their gazing spent?
> No, let me be obsequious in thy heart,
> And take thou my oblation, poor but free,
> Which is not mixed with seconds, knows no art
> But mutual render, only me for thee.
> Hence, thou suborned informer! A true soul
> When most impeached stands least in thy control.
>
> *Sonnet 125*

This is indeed a most telling sonnet. As I explained in *The Truth Will Out,* Neville was a Baron of the Cinque Ports and so was qualified to 'bear the canopy' at a Coronation. He had also tried to lay 'great bases for eternity' with his national and international political work. The 'pitiful gazer' may be the Earl of Essex, who had gazed at Queen Elizabeth in her undressed state, on his return from Ireland. The 'suborn'd informer' (blackmailer) may perhaps be the wicked John Daniel, a servant of the Countess of Essex who copied out some of the letters written by her and her late husband and then tried to blackmail the Countess over their contents. Or perhaps Neville had another blackmailer in mind too, as explained in the last chapter of this book.

This latter group of sonnets, probably written after the Essex rebellion, also includes the 'disgrace' sonnets, the sonnets in which the poet is angry at 'spies' watching his movements, and the one in which he seems to be celebrating the 'eclipse' of Elizabeth, followed by his unexpected survival and freedom, the joy of which he expresses in sonnet 107.

Then comes the rival poet, or poets:

> Was it the proud full sail of his great verse,
> Bound for the prize of all-too-precious you,
> That did my ripe thoughts in my brain inhearse,
> Making their tomb the womb wherein they grew?
> Was it his spirit, by spirits taught to write
> Above a mortal pitch, that struck me dead?
> No, neither he nor his compeers by night
> Giving him aid my verse astonished.
> He nor that affable familiar ghost
> Which nightly gulls him with intelligence,
> As victors, of my silence cannot boast;
> I was not sick of any fear from thence.
> But when your countenance filled up his line,
> Then lacked I matter -that enfeebled mine. *Sonnet 86*

Many poets were then vying for the young Earl to be their patron. What is a little unusual, however, is to find a poet talking of his rivals in his own poetry. In identifying one of the rival poets alluded to in Shakespeare's Sonnets, I think I have also identified the fact that, in this case, the man who called himself Shakespeare was indeed a close friend of Southampton, his dedicatee. This is because it looks very much as if writer and dedicatee had been sharing a secret smile when reading the work of one particular rival poet, whose poetry did, on occasion, sink to the level of doggerel:

Like to the clear in highest sphere
Where all imperial glory shines,
Of selfsame colour is her hair
Whether unfolded or in twines:
Heigh ho, fair Rosaline!
Her eyes are sapphires set in snow,
Resembling heaven by every wink;
The gods do fear whenas they glow,
And I do tremble when I think
Heigh ho, would she were mine!

Her cheeks are like the blushing cloud
That beautifies Aurora's face,
Or like the silver crimson shroud
That Phoebus' smiling looks doth grace:
Heigh ho, fair Rosaline!
Her lips are like two budded roses
Whom ranks of lilies neighbour nigh,
Within whose bounds she balm encloses
Apt to entice a deity:
Heigh ho, would she were mine!

Her neck is like a stately tower
Where Love himself imprisoned lies,
To watch for glances every hour
From her divine and sacred eyes:
Heigh ho, fair Rosaline!
Her paps are centres of delight,
Her breasts are orbs of heavenly frame,
Where Nature moulds the dew of light
To feed perfection with the same:
Heigh ho, would she were mine!

With orient pearl, with ruby red,
With marble white, with sapphire blue,
Her body every way is fed,
Yet soft in touch and sweet in view:
Heigh ho, fair Rosaline!
Nature herself her shape admires;
The gods are wounded in her sight;
And Love forsakes his heavenly fires
And at her eyes his brand doth light
Heigh ho, would she were mine!

Then muse not, Nymphs, though I bemoan
The absence of fair Rosaline,
Since for a fair there's fairer none
Not for her virtues so divine:
Heigh ho, fair Rosaline!
Heigh ho, my heart! would God that she were mine!

The poem is *To Rosaline* by Thomas Lodge, and this must surely be the one parodied by 'Shakespeare' in his sonnet 21:

So is it not with me as with that Muse
Stirr'd by a painted beauty to his verse,
Who heaven itself for ornament doth use
And every fair with his fair doth rehearse,
Making a couplement of proud compare,
With sun and moon, with earth and sea's rich gems,
With April's first-born flowers, and all things rare
That heaven's air in the huge rondure hems.
O, let me, true in love, but truly write,
And then believe me, my love is as fair
As any mother's child, though not so bright
As those gold candles fix'd in heaven's air:
Let them say more that like of hearsay well;
I will not praise that purpose not to sell.

Lodge's poem fits Shakespeare's description perfectly. Firstly, the overwhelming impression Shakespeare gives is of a painted beauty, and certainly astounding colour comparisons run all the way through Lodge's poem. The 'clear in highest sphere' is the midday sun, so if Rosaline's hair is of that colour it is not just fair but dazzlingly fair. Her eyes are not merely as blue as sapphires but 'sapphires set in snow' so their colour is enhanced by the stark contrast with what must be unnaturally whitened skin. Her cheeks must really stand out against this over-white skin, being as red as a crimson cloud over Phoebus (the sun.) And her lips are probably painted in shape and colour if they resemble 'two budded roses.' Next, Shakespeare states that 'heaven itself' is used for ornament, and indeed in Lodge we have the 'highest sphere', and Love forsaking his 'heavenly fires' in order to light his brand at her eyes. Then comes the 'couplement of proud compare' with just about everything, but the fact that Shakespeare mentions specifically 'earth and sea's rich gems' makes this Lodge poem particularly appropriate.

The earthly gems include sapphire, marble and ruby, while the sea's rich gem is obviously the pearl, reference to all of which can be found at the beginning of verse 4. The 'moon' mentioned by Shakespeare is probably the orb(s) 'of heavenly frame, /Where nature moulds the dew of light' - the plural coming through Lodge's comparison with Rosaline's breasts. Finally come the April flowers: roses and lilies are both mentioned by Lodge. Altogether, the Lodge poem conforms to the modern expression 'over the top,' and we can easily sympathise with Shakespeare's suggestion that it is more like an advertisement than a work of art!

By contrast, Shakespeare does not intend to sell his addressee, and the whole tone of his critical Sonnet 21 makes us smile once we are able to read Lodge's over-exaggerated effort. Thomas Lodge was a clever satirist and prose writer, but his love poetry obviously seemed as amusing to Elizabethan readers as it does to us in this second millennium.

At this point I can imagine that some scholars are beginning to reach for their word processors in order to write and tell me that there are other love songs of the era that might fit Shakespeare's allusions just as well as the one here quoted. But I challenge anyone to find another that so fits **all** the allusions, point by point. For instance, Greene wrote some in similar vein, as did the Earl of Oxford, but there is always an ingredient or two missing; if we look at Edward de Vere's (the said Earl's) 'What cunning can express' we have the colours and the flowers but no gems of earth or sea; in Greene's 'Doron's description of his Samela' we have many of the ingredients but still lack earth's 'rich gems.' And for further corroboration of Lodge's place as the rival poet referred to here we have the startling fact that *Rosalynde: Euphue's Golden Legacie* (from which this poem is taken) was the basis of Shakespeare's cross-dressing play, *As You Like It*. Surely, then, Sonnet 21 is not placed after the 'Master Mistress' Sonnet by accident. Now we can say that the ordering of the Sonnets, their theme, their references to other works, the coding of the Dedication cipher all point to the confusion of gender brought about by disguise both on the stage and in real life: on Shakespeare's stage, men dressed as women; in real life, the young Earl of Southampton had once been doubtful about his own sexuality. Lodge's Rosaline is clearly a painted beauty, thus we are not sure what is real and what is false – just as with

Southampton's sexuality, and with the whole 'painting' of 'Shakespeare's' sonnets.

Another interesting fact is that Lodge's *Euphues Golden Legacie* was moulded around John Lyly's prose romance, *Euphues,* and this work itself contained the basic theme of the Sonnets. This basic theme (or 'frame' in which Neville deceptively chose to place his work) was that of the two male friends falling out over their love for the same girl. Place all this together with the fact that Lyly's anti-heroine was named Lucilla, and we have a basis on which to speculate about that most exciting theme, the identity of the Dark Lady, as will be discussed in the next chapter.

Chapter 8

THE QUEST FOR THE DARK LADY

Among all the different themes within the Sonnets, the identity of the dark lady has occasioned the most questing and speculation. Several identifications have been suggested, including Emilia Lanier (poetess and daughter of an Italian Court entertainer), Mary Fitton (the Queen's maid of honour who had an illicit affair with William Herbert, Earl of Pembroke), and, most intriguing of all, Lucy Negro (whose identity is variously recounted as being either a talented negro servant of the Queen, or else a prostitute. (Or is it possible that they were one and the same person?)

At such a distance in time, and with no witnesses left to question, the dark lady's trail has gone rather cold. The kind of evidence for one woman being more probable than another could never be as strong as when a five-hour-old 'scene of crime' is investigated. Thus, all that can be done is firstly to analyse the evidence of the texts of the Sonnets themselves, then look at any surviving contemporary references which seem to provide information running parallel to those texts. The final and most speculative stage is to construct alternative scenarios in which all the evidence could fit logically together, in the hope that one scenario will be watertight, or at least will produce the best possible explanation, based on all the evidence now available. In the end, it was this three-stage operation that actually led me not only to some of the real and symbolic meanings behind the figure of the dark lady but also to the discovery of an underlying, unifying concept that runs through all Shakespeare's poetic output. But this outcome would not have been possible, had I not simultaneously taken Sir Henry Neville's life and circumstances into account, meaning that when the process of investigation goes hand in hand with knowledge of Sir Henry as the true author, new insights into the Works evolve quite naturally.

Beginning with the evidence contained in the Sonnets themselves, we are told that the dark lady's hair is like 'black wires'. ('If hairs be wires, black wires grow on her head...' *sonnet 130.*) Several investigators have attempted to say that this description might suit Italian and Jewish ladies as easily as those of African origin. But, just as with the poet's insistence on his own lameness[96], I cannot see any reason to do other than take the writer's word literally as well as metaphorically. 'Shakespeare' (under any name whatsoever) was a great writer: when he was describing something, he had every linguistic means in his control to describe it accurately, or else to signal strongly that he was speaking only metaphorically, but '...black wires grow on her head'; '...her breasts are dun' surely amounts to linguistic evidence pointing more directly towards an African woman than to any other racial type. In addition to this, no Jewish people were allowed to live in England at the time.

Interestingly too, the lady's breath 'reeks'. Now, hygiene was not a strong point among the English in the 16th and 17th centuries, so many people's breath must have smelt bad, by modern standards. But the dark lady's breath obviously stands out above the unclean norm. This could suggest that she was eating non-European food. Neville would have been used to the smell of European food. Moreover, Italian women were especially famed for their cleanliness[97], so I think this latter fact alone puts an end to Emilia Lanier's claim to be this particular dark lady. Also, Mary Fitton was from an English aristocratic home, so even she would have made some effort to keep her teeth clean, and she probably would not have chewed pungent tropical fruits and nuts. All this leads to the conclusion that Lucy Negro was the most likely candidate for the poet's 'mistress' - though probably only in a metaphorical, perhaps joking, sense, as we shall see.

There is also textual and intertextual evidence that points to the first name of the woman in question being 'Lucy'. Within the Sonnets themselves, there are hints at the grisly myth of Lucy, the girl whose fiancé seemed to love her eyes more than her personality. So distressed was she with his attitude that she plucked out her own eyes and handed them to her lover on a plate, literally. Is this the Lucy hinted at in Sonnet 132? –

Thine eyes I love, and they, as pitying me,
Knowing thy heart torment me with disdain,
Have put on black, and loving mourners be,
Looking with pretty ruth upon my pain;
And truly not the morning sun of heaven
Better becomes the grey cheeks of the east,
Nor that full star that ushers in the even
Doth half that glory to the sober west,
As those two mourning eyes become thy face.
O, let it then as well beseem thy heart
To mourn for me, since mourning doth thee grace,
And suit thy pity like in every part.
Then will I swear beauty herself is black,
And all they foul that thy complexion lack.

Back in sonnet 130, the writer had declared that 'My mistress' eyes are nothing like the sun', so, unlike the dark morning or evening that is lit up by the sun or a star, the writer is communicating the fact that the dark lady's eyes match her face rather than making their impression through being of a marked contrasting nature. Unlike the sun or the evening star, they do not stand out against a contrasting background; they 'become' her. They are dark and they are not of the 'morning' but 'mourning'.

Throughout the Sonnets, the Dark Lady's eyes are mentioned repeatedly. The first time she is ever mentioned, light (from the same Latin origin as the name, Lucy) in the form of the 'sun' is said to be 'nothing like' her eyes. When one thinks about it, it is rather strange to compare anyone's eyes with the sun, even antipathetically. So what put the comparison into the poet's mind? The most logical explanation is that he wishes to emphasise what an inappropriate name she possesses. Her name means 'light', yet everything about her is dark, perhaps because - with typical punning - the name also suggests 'loose' in the moral sense. Shakespeare uses the word in this sense in *Love's Labour's Lost:*

Full of strange shapes, of habits, and of forms,
Varying in subjects as the eye doth roll
To every varied object in his glance;
Which parti-coated presence of loose love...
Have misbecomed our oaths and gravities,

And the name Lucy gets associated with immorality in that strange passage from *Richard III* in which the writer shows the extent of his extraordinarily privileged knowledge, namely that some of Edward IV's children were not legitimate - a fact only revealed in a single document housed in Rouen Cathedral:[98]

Richard Touched you the bastardy of Edward's children?
Buckingham I did, with his contract with Lady Lucy,
  And his contract by deputy in France;
  Th' unsatiate greediness of his desire,
  And his enforcement of the city wives;
  His tyranny for trifles; his own bastardy,
  As being got, your father then in France,
  And his resemblance, being not like the duke.
  Withal, I did infer your lineaments -
  Being the right idea of your father,
  Both in your form and nobleness of mind;

The lady who became pregnant when her husband was in France was Cecily Neville. Thus is Sir Henry surrounding us with complex conundrums which always lead back to his identity - of which more later! Yet though Lucy's dark, she is also 'fair':

  And yet, by heaven, I think my love as fair
  As any she belied with false compare.

So now at last he's admitted it – the comparison between the dark lady's eyes and the sun is a false one, and something about her 'belies' this. If her name is Lucy, then it certainly explains the writer's use of oppositional comparisons, and also explains one aspect of her that belies what she is, viz. her **name**. It is her *name* as well as her appearance which lead to these 'false' comparisons - just like Neville's own name and outward appearance.

But what are we to gather from all this? Is Lucy really his mistress, or is the poet also joking about a certain Lucy everyone in London knows about from her reputation? Is he trying, as usual, to add layer upon layer of confusion and complexity? Perhaps Lucy is not just one person or one single idea. Perhaps, as with all of Shakespeare's characters and scenarios, her persona includes many individuals and many metaphors.

It is probable that the rather elastic framework chosen by Neville in which to place his divers sonnets was based on John Lyly's prose work, *Euphues,* in which the fallen woman is called Lucilla. Lyly was once an Oxford tutor, so Neville must have come across *Euphues* while he was studying there. In this work, Lyly charts the history of two men's friendship, just as does Shakespeare in his *Sonnets.* The cause of a break in their friendship is also the same, viz. their mutual infatuation with a woman named 'Lucy' or 'Lucilla'. In Lyly's work, both men ultimately reject 'Lucy' because she becomes a prostitute.

So was there a London prostitute known as Lucy in Neville's time? Apparently there was. As if to prove the point that Shakespeare was also referring to a prostitute named 'Lucy', there is a satire by Thomas Lodge that mentions dark Lucy in this context. (This was the same Thomas Lodge who wove a dramatic-poetic fantasy around Lyly's *Euphues,* calling his own work, *Euphues Golden Legacy*, part of which is the story of Rosalynde – the work on which *As You like it* was based. As Frank Kermode says, one modus operandi of Shakespeare's was his extended use of connectionism based on a few words and concepts which seemed to keep buzzing around his head.[99])

Lodge's own work mentioning 'Black Luce' is entitled 'A Fig for Momus' - Momus being the god of carping criticism, while a 'fig' was the shape in which children used to hold their fingers when they meant 'I defy you'. It was rather like 'thumbing one's nose', and it is interesting that eastern european children still make a fig when they want to insult someone who has admonished them. About half way through his defiant tirade, Lodge complains that even when people know they have faults (or 'deformities', as he calls them) they still seek to hide them, and one of those regular 'deformities' appears to have been clandestine and dangerous meetings with 'Lucy':

> ...Thus, though men's great deformities be known,
> They grieve to hear and take them for their own.
> Find me a niggard that doth want the shift
> To call his cursed avarice good thrift;
> A rake-hell, sworn to prodigality,
> That dares not term it liberality;
> A lecher that hath lost both flesh and fame,
> That holds not lechery a pleasant game.
> And why? because they cloak their shame by this,
> And will not see the horror what it is;
> And cunning sin, being clad in virtue's shape,
> Flies much reproof, and many scorns doth 'scape.
> Last day I chanced, in crossing of the street,
> With Diffilus, the innkeeper, to meet;
> He wore a silken night cap on his head,
> And looked as if he had been lately dead.
> I asked him how he fared:' Not well,' quoth he,
> 'An ague this two months hath troubled me.'
> I let him pass, and laughed to hear his 'scuse;
> For I knew well he had the pox by **Luce** ...

So it was no mere 'ague' but a venereal disease that the innkeeper had contracted.

If Lucy Negro, like Lucilla in *Euphues,* became a prostitute, then she was indeed 'loose' and did not keep her infections to herself.

This can be read from sonnet 144, in which the friend may be 'fire[d] out', which meant coming out in a rash following catching a venereal infection:

> Two loves I have, of comfort and despair,
> Which like two spirits do suggest me still;
> The better angel is a man right fair,
> The worser spirit a woman coloured ill.
> To win me soon to hell my female evil
> Tempteth my better angel from my side,
> And would corrupt my saint to be a devil,
> Wooing his purity with her foul pride.
> And whether that my angel be turned fiend,
> Suspect I may, yet not directly tell;
> But being both from me, both to each friend,
> I guess one angel in another's hell.
> Yet this shall I ne'er know, but live in doubt,
> Till my bad angel fire my good one out.

Black Luce, whose real name was possibly Lucy Morgan[100] (and perhaps the wife of Thomas Morgan, the spy who allied himself with Charles Paget), may therefore well have been a model for the archetypal dark and dangerous lady portrayed as one of the women in the Sonnets. Such stereotypes persisted into the 1950s, with their personifications in the American film noir being especially memorable. So Shakespeare may have based the Sonnet character largely on popular perceptions concerning the dark lady figure, though he may also have had some sort of acquaintance with a specific dark lady in mind when bringing her to life in the poems. By using these means, at least some of his readership would have been able to imagine a flesh and blood woman when reading his Sonnets[101].

Lucy really existed and held sway in an establishment in Clerkenwell. But in January 1600 she was sentenced by a Court of Aldermen:

> Item yt is ordered that Luce Morgan alias Parker
> for that she is a notorious and lewde woman of her
> bodye and otherwise of evill conversacion shalbe
> presentlie committed to Brydewell ther to be sett
> to worke till she shall become bounde with good
> & sufficient sureties for her good behaviour
> during her naturall lief. [102]

Over one year later, we find her returned to Clerkenwell and running her business again. It seems she may have been dead even before the Sonnets were printed in 1609, and this could have been yet one more reason for their printing to have been delayed until this date. Apparently, though, she ultimately became a Roman Catholic and then died of venereal disease. I hasten to add that there was no link, other than that of timing, between the two events! However, it is just possible that in Neville's mind some sort of link was made between the Italian prostitute, Lucilla, (in Lyly's *Euphues*), Black Luce Morgan, the London prostitute, and Catholicism. To the young Neville in Padua and Venice, dark ladies and the sumptuous Catholic churches, with their alluring music and rituals, must have been a most tempting combination, especially to a young man already interested in theatre and drama. As he got older, he became gradually stronger in his Protestantism, but he had made many a Catholic friend along the way, whom he never deserted. Yet like the dark lady, the Catholic church had its dark side too. As far as Neville was concerned, its misleading beliefs, dogma, secret forces and, above all, the Inquisition, represented the unattractive, dangerous half of Catholicism. The Queen of the Night in Mozart's *Die Zauberflöte* is a beautiful, deceptive lady, who symbolises the Catholic church and represents similar feelings about it in another work of art. But in the Sonnets, the image is dark **throughout**. Not only is Luce (like the Queen of the Night) dark **inwardly** − even her **outward** appearance is distasteful. If, therefore, Neville wishes Luce to be in part a representation of the Catholic church, then his chosen metaphor is that of a woman who is so ugly and bad that only the jaundiced, warped viewpoint of the observer can make anything better of her. After saying how wiry her hair is, how smelly her breath, etc., he (in the persona of the writer) says: 'And yet, by heaven, I think my love as fair/ As any she belied with false compare'

This begins to look very much as if the writer wishes himself to be perceived as blameworthy: he is not making any excuse for being misled: from an **objective** point of view, the lady is rotten in every way. Of course, it could be just a writer wearing a mask and pretending to be someone who is easily misled, but knowing that Neville wrote the Sonnets, and that Neville (like all human beings) was sometimes guilty of wrong judgments, these self-blaming poems might be a form of confession:

In faith, I do not love thee with mine eyes,
For they in thee a thousand errors note;
But 'tis my heart that loves what they despise,
Who in despite of view is pleased to dote.
Nor are mine ears with thy tongue's tune delighted,
Nor tender feeling to base touches prone,
Nor taste nor smell desire to be invited
To any sensual feast with thee alone;
But my five wits nor my five senses can
Dissuade one foolish heart from serving thee,
Who leaves unswayed the likeness of a man,
Thy proud heart's slave and vassal wretch to be.
Only my plague thus far I count my gain:
That she that makes me sin awards me pain. *Sonnet 141*

And in sonnet 137 he admits that he has erred in not even trusting the witness of his own senses:

Why of eyes' falsehood hast thou forged hooks
Whereto the judgment of my heart is tied?
Why should my heart think that a several plot,
Which my heart knows the wide world's common place?
Or mine eyes seeing this say 'this is not',
To put fair truth upon so foul a face?
In things right true my heart and eyes have erred,
And to this false plague are they now transferred.

Neville was keen on self-analysis and wanted to be a highly moral man; and there is no doubt that he loved his wife. But might there once have been extreme circumstances which ultimately led to his going astray?

When he was staying at the Lord Admiral's home under house arrest following the Essex rebellion, Neville called the place 'an honourable prison' but listed his griefs, saying that he was '...unable to requite my pains, faith and love...'[103] The Lord Admiral was a Catholic, so Neville certainly could not hold the prayer meetings which he was wont to do with other Protestant exiles, when he was Ambassador in France. Catholicism and the lack of his wife may then have become linked in his mind, just as Catholicism and dark ladies went together in Italy. Through those lonely, pain-filled days in a Catholic household, in the absence of any other religious services, did he perhaps even become a little interested in the Lord Admiral's daily prayers and mass? Did its smelly incense simultaneously attract and repel him, just like the Dark Lady's breath? And what became of his love for his wife, once he knew he was going to be separated from her for a long time?

It is of course only possible to guess the answers to these questions. But there is textual and circumstantial evidence to suggest that Neville believed he might never see his wife again - and this thought occurred to him even *before* the Essex rebellion. In November 1600 – over three months before the Essex uprising – Neville was on what he knew would be a short break back in England. At this precise time, Sir Henry wrote to his secretary, Sir Ralph Winwood, telling him that the Queen was insisting that he should return to his duties in France. (He had been hoping against hope that he would not be sent back to France to complete his two year contract as Ambassador.) However, in this unhappy letter to Winwood, Neville states that the Queen has promised that he will be allowed home again once his contractual time is up. But Sir Henry clearly does not trust the Queen, so he has made the sad decision to leave his wife in England so that she may 'solicit' Elizabeth to remember her promise, when the time comes:

> I am now at length inforced to return into my Charge, after long contestation ... All I have won is a confirmation of the Queen's promise that I shall but serve out my two years, which how it will be kept I know not, but I have now some more ground than I had to press it, and I leave my wife hehind to solicit it. I think to set forward on my journey a fortnight hence. I put it off all I can, because I would avoid any further journey than to Paris, hoping that the King will now be thinking of his return thither to inthronize his new Queen, whereof I would have been very glad to have understood some certainty from you; and I do desire to know as soon as may be, what is the King's purpose in it, that at my coming to Paris I may be able to resolve what to do.[104]

Sir Henry is worried that he might be left in France and permanently estranged from his wife, as was a previous Ambassador, Sir Henry Unton. Unton was Neville's friend and neighbour. He – like Neville and everyone else who went to Paris at the time – suffered from an ailment affecting the liver.

This seems to have been somewhat similar to hepatitis or jaundiolaria, which is a water-borne infection. The French may have gained some resistance to this, but the English had not, so that poor young Unton died of it while in France, with never a chance to say his farewells to his young wife, having been refused the Queen's permission to return home. Neville says in an earlier letter to Cecil that he too has succumbed to that disease, but has survived it - in the short term, at least. If indeed he had hepatitis, this disease would inevitably have returned if he had not subsequently followed a strict low-fat, alcohol-free diet for a year after contracting it. It is entirely probable, therefore, that Sir Henry never felt as strong again, and that he foresaw the shortening of his life after that illness. His anxiety about travelling any further than Paris also suggests he did not feel as well as he used to. At this point, Neville must have felt he could probably die, far away from his beloved wife.

When he fled towards France after the Essex Rebellion, Neville must also have known that his involvement in the Essex affair would be discovered, eventually. Sonnet 72 therefore looks very much like the one he would have written before his flight to the land in which, whatever happened, he must perforce spend the rest of his days and then die:

> O, lest the world should task you to recite
> What merit lived in me that you should love
> After my death, dear love, forget me quite;
> For you in me can nothing worthy prove,
> Unless you would devise some virtuous lie
> To do more for me than mine own desert,
> And hang more praise upon deceased I
> Than niggard truth would willingly impart.
> O, lest your true love may seem false in this,
> That you for love speak well of me untrue,
> My name be buried where my body is,
> And live no more to shame nor me nor you;
> For I am shamed by that which I bring forth,
> And so should you, to love things nothing worth.

Neville's 'body' might well have been 'buried' in France – a circumstance which would quite naturally have led to the above lines being written.

In the end, Neville was chosen by Essex to be the next Secretary of State, had his rebellion succeeded. Thus, Essex had held out the only hope that Neville would not have to leave his wife and family and return to his duties in France. But things went dreadfully wrong: the very scheme that was intended to keep him near his wife failed. And its failure brought ignominy on Neville. Sir Henry had been witnessed secretly visiting the Earls of Essex and Southampton, and having private conversations with them and other eminent conspirators. During these meetings, he must have agreed to the performances of *Richard II* on the eve of the Essex Rebellion. Those performances had been paid for by Essex himself, because the play included the deposition of a monarch, and so Essex was hoping that those who saw the play might be spurred on to follow his stand against the Queen. Neville knew that everything - including his authorial identity - might now be revealed, after the failure of the rebellion, and he felt keenly the shame this would bring on his wife and family. So is there any evidence that Anne took the sonnet's advice and forgot him?

Anne began by writing letters to Queen Elizabeth, pleading for her husband's return from his ultimate imprisonment in the Tower. But she gave birth to another baby, over one year after he had entered the Tower of London. There are some sources which say that full visiting rights were sometimes allowed between husband and wife during sojourns in the Tower, though there are too few extant records to show whether this was a general rule or not. Neville was under suspicion of treason, so it is perhaps unlikely that he would have been allowed many visitors from the outside. David Hume actually asserts that Southampton and Neville were harshly treated, with no visiting rights. Yet there is no way of telling what the truth of the matter was, nor therefore whether the child born to his wife while he was in the Tower was Neville's or not. (There are perhaps hints in *The Winter's Tale* to there having been trouble over this.) While in the Tower, Neville might even have accepted the fact that his wife was at liberty to find a new protector for herself and their children.

From other textual evidence, it does indeed seem that the friendship between Sir Henry and the Earl of Southampton began to take the place of their own families, once they entered the Tower, as if each thought their old, married loves might be lost forever. Dr. John Casson, a distinguished researcher and drama-therapist, pointed out to me a scene from *The Two Noble Kinsmen,* in which two prisoners swear their undying love to each other. This could indeed parallel the developing situation between Neville and Southampton. So do these lines too suggest that Neville and Southampton both assumed that their spouses might find comfort elsewhere, thus leaving them free to turn their own eyes in other directions?

> ...And here being thus together,
> We are an endless mine to one another;
> We are one another's wife, ever begetting
> New births of love; we are father, friends, acquaintance,
> We are, in one another, families;
> I am your heir and you are mine. This place
> Is our Inheritance; no hard oppressor
> Dare take this from us; here, with a little patience,
> We shall live long and loving.
>
> *The Two Noble Kinsmen,* Act 2, Sc.2.

The very next scene in the play shows how all this is turned on its head and becomes comic when the two men see an attractive lady passing outside their cell window. The men who swore they would always love each other soon begin to bicker about who should woo the woman, if either of them ever gets the chance. (The theme of the Sonnets is therefore taken up once again.) Does this perhaps suggest a comic element too in what might otherwise seem the sombre side of the Sonnets? Shakespeare's later plays are all puzzling in this way – even in *King Lear* there are passages at which the audience smiles because Lear's words about himself are quite the opposite to the reality of the situation. All in all, black humour was certainly a part of Shakespeare's repertoire by the time the Sonnets were published.

Just as with Lear, therefore, the black humour surrounding the dark lady might be either a jest, or else the worst figure Neville could possibly conjure up.

One strong symbolic aspect of the dark lady could well be that she is the personification of Death. In *Venus and Adonis* death is always represented by blackness, and this is the poem, openly dedicated to Wriothesley, which emphasises the necessity of marrying and having children instead of doing battle and possibly dying young. Venus says that Adonis should have allowed *Cupid* to strike him, not *Death*: 'Love's golden arrow at him should have fled, /And not Death's ebon dart, to strike dead.' Death has an 'ebony' dart. In the same way, it is a *black* boar that kills Adonis. In 1593, with this epic poem, Neville had symbolically berated Wriothesley for preferring death in battle to life with a woman. When Sir Henry was finally imprisoned, still feeling ill, and grief-stricken by the execution of his friends, did he too begin to welcome death? -

> When to the sessions of sweet silent thought,
> I summon up remembrance of things past,
> I sigh the lack of many a thing I sought,
> And with old woes new wail my dear time's waste:
> Then can I drown an eye (unused to flow)
> For precious friends hid in death's dateless night,
> And weep afresh love's long since cancelled woe,
> And moan th' expense of many a vanished sight.
> Then can I grieve at grievances foregone,
> And heavily from woe to woe tell o'er
> The sad account of fore-bemoaned moan,
> Which I new pay as if not paid before.
> But if the while I think on thee (dear friend)
> All losses are restored, and sorrows end. *Sonnet 30*

Neville, in prison, with only his 'dear friend' Wriothesley to remind him of the turmoil in which he had lost so many other 'precious friends' had indeed reason to sigh 'the lack of many a thing I sought.'

In *Venus and Adonis,* Adonis' otherwise bright eyes become dark in death – just like the dark lady's in the Sonnets. Venus tries to awaken the dead Adonis:

> She looks upon his lips, and they are pale;
> She takes him by the hand, and that is cold;
> She whispers in his ears a heavy tale,
> As if they heard the woeful words she told;
> She lifts the coffer-lids that close his eyes,
> Where, lo, two lamps, burnt out, in darkness lies;

Perhaps the poet is also hinting at Wriothesley's early homosexual tendencies, when he declares that Adonis' beauty has brought certain temptations across his path - an evil force [spoken of as a woman in the shape of Cynthia, goddess of the moon] has 'bribed the Destinies':

And therefore hath she bribed the Destinies
To cross the curious workmanship of nature,
To mingle beauty with infirmities,
And pure perfection with impure defeature,
Making it subject to the tyranny
Of mad mischances and much misery;

Is this the same 'marrow-eating sickness' referred to in the next stanza?

As burning fevers, agues pale and faint,
Life-poisoning pestilence and frenzies wood,
The marrow-eating sickness, whose attaint
Disorder breeds by heating of the blood:
Surfeits, imposthumes, grief, and damn'd despair,
Swear nature's death for framing thee so fair.

And not the least of all these maladies
But in one minute's fight brings beauty under:
Both favour, savour, hue and qualities,
Whereat the impartial gazer late did wonder,
Are on the sudden wasted, thaw'd and done,
As mountain-snow melts with the midday sun.

The crime that dared not name itself in those days has the same effect as the one that (in the Catholic Church) gives some of its young people over to the convent, thus ensuring a 'fruitless' future. They save their oil, but at what cost? The writer says that it is wasteful to be chaste, and good to be 'prodigal' if that prodigality actually lights up the world:

Therefore, despite of fruitless chastity,
Love-lacking vestals and self-loving nuns,
That on the earth would breed a scarcity
And barren dearth of daughters and of sons,
Be prodigal: the lamp that burns by night
Dries up his oil to lend the world his light.

To have become such an expert on the subject, perhaps the writer himself also met with such temptations as a younger man. Tim Cornish – a researcher into Neville's iron working days – told me of some findings he had made. He said that Prince Maurice, son of William of Orange, lived next door to, and was a close friend of, Robert Sidney, while the latter was staying in the Netherlands. Neville apparently sold Maurice a great many guns. Neville had travelled with Robert Sidney on his grand tour from 1578 – 1583, so it could be assumed that the tour itself also had something to do with military training and selling ordnance from the business Neville had inherited on his great-uncle Gresham's incapacity in 1578, and death in 1579. A.L. Rowse says that Prince Maurice was bisexual, whereas Neville, with his twelve children, was quite obviously heterosexual. Yet the fact that he had had to deal with men who were of 'another persuasion' would have made Sir Henry the ideal person for guiding a sexually confused young man, such as was the young Earl of Southampton. Because Adonis is quite obviously unmoved by women, he dies childless. *Anything* which could lead to that particular tragedy is, in Neville's eyes, a destructive force, inevitably fatal for the human race. Lucy, the prostitute with the so very inappropriate name, with her dark nature and venereal disease, was just such another force of destruction endangering mankind.

And there was yet another source of the same threatening, fruitless mentality. At university, Neville had been the tutee of the great Sir Henry Savile, and they remained friends all their lives. Together they studied and translated Greek texts, and learned a lot about Platonism, which becomes an important mystical ingredient in Shakespeare's later plays. One aspect of Platonism, however, is just as destructive to the furthering of the human race as homosexuality and the Catholic practice of creating monks and nuns. This is, of course, 'Platonic Love'. So, a heterosexual like Neville would certainly not have failed to attack this too. Perhaps he wanted to cover this subject, just in case the impressionable Earl of Southampton came under any such influence. Anyway, I believe the result of Neville's attack on this particular kind of 'chaste' relationship between a man and a woman, or between two men, can be seen in that strange poem, *The Phoenix and the Turtle*. Perhaps the same poem also came later to represent the situation between Neville and the Earl of Southampton while they were in prison together. The lines from Act 2 Sc. 2 of *The Two Noble Kinsmen,*(quoted above) appear as an echo of the 'chaste love' presented in *The Phoenix and the Turtle*. In the play, both men accept the fact that they are now the only 'family' each of them will have, so their relationship will be as fruitless as that between the Phoenix and the Turtle – the man and the woman who agreed to live in 'married chastity':

Let the bird of loudest lay,
On the sole Arabian tree,
Herald sad and trumpet be,
To whose sound chaste wings obey.

But thou shrieking harbinger,
Foul precurrer of the fiend,
Augur of the fever's end,
To this troop come thou not near!

From this session interdict
Every fowl of tyrant wing,
Save the eagle, feathered king:
Keep the obsequy so strict.

Let the priest in surplice white,
That defunctive music can,
Be the death-divining swan,
Lest the requiem lack his right.

And thou treble-dated crow,
That thy sable gender mak'st
With the breath thou giv'st and tak'st,
'Mongst our mourners shalt thou go.

Here the anthem doth commence:
Love and constancy is dead,
Phoenix and the turtle fled
In a mutual flame from hence.

So they loved as love in twain
Had the essence but in one;
Two distincts, division none;
Number there in love was slain.

Hearts remote, yet not asunder;
Distance, and no space was seen
'Twixt this turtle and his queen;
But in them it were a wonder.

So between them love did shine
That the turtle saw his right
Flaming in the phoenix' sight;
Either was the other's mine.

Property was thus appalled,
That the self was not the same;
Single nature's double name
Neither two nor one was called.

Reason, in itself confounded,
Saw division grow together,
To themselves yet either neither;
Simple were so well compounded;

That it cried, "How true a twain
Seemeth this concordant one!
Love hath reason, reason none,
If what parts can so remain."

Whereupon it made this threne
To the phoenix and the dove,
Co-supremes and stars of love,
As chorus to their tragic scene.

Threnos

Beauty, truth, and rarity
Grace in all simplicity,
Here enclosed in cinders lie.

Death is now the phoenix' nest;
And the turtle's loyal breast
To eternity doth rest,

Leaving no posterity
'Twas not their infirmity,
It was married chastity.

Truth may seem, but cannot be;
Beauty brag, but 'tis not she:
Truth and Beauty buried be.

To this urn let those repair
That are either true or fair;
For these dead birds sigh a prayer.

(The lines 'Either was the other's mine' (v. 9, above) are surely parallel to 'We are an endless mine to one another' from *The Two Noble Kinsmen.*) So with the combined weight of *Venus and Adonis,* the *Sonnets* and *The Phoenix and the Turtle,* Neville had dealt with many threats to the continuance of the human race. These threats, according to Neville and his poems, were promulgated by homosexuality, enforced chastity (which happened to be popular with the Catholic Church), immorality (with prostitutes like Luce), and Platonic Love. In view of all this, it is therefore unlikely that Neville had practical experience of Lucy. She was probably just a shifting symbol, moving from the realm of 'wicked lady' into a representation of Death, quite effortlessly. Once Neville was ill and imprisoned in the Tower, it was death which preoccupied him most. While there, he wrote *Hamlet,* whose first entrance is marked by his soliloquy on suicide:

> O that this too too solid flesh would melt,
> Thaw, and resolve itself into a dew,
> Or that the Everlasting had not fixed
> His canon 'gainst self-slaughter! O God, O God!
> How weary, stale, flat, and unprofitable
> Seem to me all the uses of this world! *Act 1, Sc. 2*

Just before he was imprisoned, *The Phoenix and the Turtle* was published. But I think it highly likely that it was actually written around the same time as *Venus and Adonis,* and for the same purpose, i.e. to persuade Wriothesley to enter into a fruitful marriage. But, as with the Sonnets, its publication may have been finally held up by William Cecil, Lord Burghley, who would not have wished so many poems concerning Wriothesley's sexuality and proposed marriage to be published at the same time. If this had happened, then the true background to their composition would have stood a greater chance of being guessed.

In the end, then, *The Phoenix and the Turtle* was randomly placed as a work 'never before extant'[105] among other signed and pseudonymous poems said to be a tribute to the love between Sir John Salusbury and his wife, supposedly to celebrate their love and their offspring. Yet Shakespeare's poem talks of a non-sexual love which results in no offspring, making it quite different from the rest in the collection. It was, however, printed by someone who would have known both Shakespeare and Neville, so the secret of its true origin and purpose could be maintained. This printer was Richard Field, who was born in Stratford but worked in Blackfriars, where Sir Henry was born and partly raised.

Of course, there are other layers of meaning here as well, for *The Phoenix and the Turtle* is based on a poem by Chaucer, which itself contains *political, republican* symbolism; but this extra layer of meaning simply goes to prove that the political hand of Neville, the Parliamentarian and potential Essex conspirator, was the one that wrote it. But primarily, now that we know who wrote the *Sonnets*, *The Phoenix*, and *Venus and Adonis*, it is possible to link all three of them together with the overwhelming philosophy of Sir Henry Neville – breed and populate the world with good people; do not succumb to any of the temptations that would stop you in this purpose.

Death is the thing that prevents this aim, par excellence, so it is not surprising that Sir Henry feels guilty when he is wooed by the temptations of Death in the guise of the Dark Lady. Several of his friends have fallen under her power (especially since the Essex affair) as he hints in Sonnet 30. Yet none of them actively sought her out, in the manner which he now feels sometimes drawn to do:

> Thou art as tyrannous, so as thou art,
> As those whose beauties proudly make them cruel;
> For well thou know'st to my dear doting heart
> Thou art the fairest and most precious jewel.
> Yet in good faith some say that thee behold
> Thy face hath not the power to make love groan.
> To say they err I dare not be so bold,
> Although I swear it to myself alone;
> And, to be sure that is not false I swear,
> A thousand groans, but thinking on thy face,
> One on another's neck do witness bear
> Thy black is fairest in my judgment's place.
> In nothing art thou black save in thy deeds,
> And thence this slander, as I think, proceeds. *131*

(The 'one on another's neck' may well refer to the friends who lost their heads after the Rebellion. 'In nothing art thou black save in thy deeds' – the state of Death is not blackness, but the 'deeds' which lead to it certainly are.)

> Poor soul, the centre of my sinful earth,
> ...These rebel powers that thee array,
> Why dost thou pine within and suffer dearth,
> Painting thy outward walls so costly gay?
> Why so large cost, having so short a lease,
> Dost thou upon thy fading mansion spend?
> Shall worms, inheritors of this excess,
> Eat up thy charge? Is this thy body's end?
> Then, soul, live thou upon thy servant's loss,
> And let that pine to aggravate thy store;
> Buy terms divine in selling hours of dross;
> Within be fed, without be rich no more.
> So shalt thou feed on death, that feeds on men,
> And death once dead, there's no more dying then.
>
> *Sonnet 146*

Sonnet 146 certainly demonstrates Neville's personification of death. He is in the Tower, he is not outwardly rich any more, and so he will buy 'divine' terms, not by selling iron products (as once he did) but by selling dross - the scum that comes to the surface in molten metals. The worms then can only have his body – alias death – so they can feed on that, which will inevitably thereby kill death itself. By extension, if death is dead, then that particular dark lady will be no more. She has transformed herself from a prostitute to death personified. Now, like both of them, she dies.

It is highly unlikely that Neville had a *practical* acquaintance with the prostitute or that he actually attempted suicide, even though, like Hamlet, he may have contemplated it during those dark, desolate days of imprisonment, following the execution of his friends. But perhaps it is more likely that he did indeed have some sort of extra-marital love affair after leaving the Tower. The evidence for this is circumstantial, but there are so many facets to it that it must be regarded as quite strong.

To begin with, Neville's father was fond of ladies. In his 'letter to a noble Lord', Neville complains to the Earl of Southampton that he has not got as much from his father's estate as he should have done, because his father, in his will, left land to be shared between 'heirs male of his body'. Sir Henry remarked that there were 'about twelve of us'[106] at the moment (which were certainly not accounted for among his father's *legitimate* offspring.) Of course, young Sir Henry liked to give the impression that he was very different from his father in this respect, and he may well have been so, before his incarceration in the Tower. But on his release, the alteration in Neville's practical circumstances and his psyche must have been so radical that they were bound to have some sort of adverse effect. If Neville discovered – or even merely suspected – that the extra child in his household was not his, it is perfectly possible that he might have embarked on a short-lived, concealed illicit love affair of his own. If he did not, then it is difficult to explain one element in his own will and testament. As already mentioned, Neville had written to the Earl of Southampton that his own father had simply willed parts of his estate to all his 'heirs male'. However, our Sir Henry Neville was very careful when writing his *own* will to specify that the sons who should inherit were 'my heirs male *begotten on the body of my wife, Anne Killigrew.*'[107] The logical conclusion is, therefore, that there would have been no need for Henry to specify the identity of the *mother*, unless he had produced a son by another woman too.

After being so suicidal in tendency during his incarceration, Neville's sudden unexpected freedom must surely have made him want to partake in the life force once again – the same very sexual force he had been recommending to the Earl of Southampton. Indeed, one feels the surge of this life force in sonnet 107, which surely must have been written when he received news of his impending release, which came so very quickly after Queen Elizabeth's – the 'mortal moon's' - death:

> Not mine own fears nor the prophetic soul
> Of the wide world dreaming on things to come
> Can yet the lease of my true love control,
> Supposed as forfeit to a confined doom.
> The mortal moon hath her eclipse endured,
> And the sad augurs mock their own presage;
> Incertainties now crown themselves assured,
> And peace proclaims olives of endless age.
> Now with the drops of this most balmy time
> My love looks fresh, and Death to me subscribes,
> Since spite of him I'll live in this poor rhyme,
> While he insults o'er dull and speechless tribes;
> And thou in this shalt find thy monument,
> When tyrants' crests and tombs of brass are spent.

The love that looked so 'fresh' might well have been his wife, Anne, while 'thou' in line 13 is probably addressing the

Earl of Southampton – Neville's dedicatee. The 'monument' Neville finds for his patron is built on words. Sir Henry's own words at his 'Hearing' saved his life; now his words become a 'rhyme' in which he and his dedicatee will 'live' longer than the mere trappings inside which 'tyrants' enclose themselves in death. The artistry of words is a monument to life, while 'tombs of brass' commemorate death. Yet sexual life too is strong throughout the plays and the poems. If Neville had come home to a situation where his wife had sought comfort from another, then he may eventually have looked elsewhere too. But Neville never wanted to cause people pain, unless they were either threatening or hurting others, so his affair would have been necessarily clandestine.

Opportunity for something just so clandestine now soon presented itself. Neville's brother in law had died, so Sir Henry very generously undertook to protect and educate his two fatherless nephews – the children of Anne Killigrew's sister. Neville paid for them to go to Oxford University, and there are still extant letters in the Berkshire Record Office attesting to his degree of involvement with the boys' welfare. Sir Henry also presented the University with trees from his own land, as a token of thanks for the care they had taken of his young charges. He doubtless, therefore, visited Oxford, and indeed we know that he did so when he received his M.A. there in 1605 – two years after leaving prison. This also suggests he may have attended academic consultations at Oxford and so spent quite some time there preparing for his higher degree. It is during this time, in 1606, that the so-called illegitimate son of 'Shakespeare' was born in Oxford. That son was none other than William Davenant, who himself became a playwright and theatre manager.

It is often said that Davenant's mother was the wife of an Oxford innkeeper. But in fact the supposed 'inn-keeper' was more a businessman. Amongst other attributes, Davenant senior was interested in the Muscovy and East India Companies, with which Neville was also connected. So Mistress Davenant was not a common barmaid but quite a lady, of genteel origin. Young William Davenant was then put into the household of the Earl of Warwick and later sent to Oxford University. It was, however, Neville, not Shakespeare, who had influence with both those bodies, and it was with the Killigrews and Nevilles that Davenant and, later, his son were associated, not with the Shakespeare family.

The full story of the Davenants and their connections with the extended Neville family will be told in the next chapter. It is improbable that Neville himself would ever reveal the full literal story of any real extra-marital affair he might have experienced. But in sonnet 144, I think one of the covert messages he is imparting is that there are two sides to his personality: line 2 could mean that the 'two loves' seem like two spirits to the writer, and it could also mean that the two spirits of 'comfort and despair' 'suggest' (resemble) 'me' – i.e. the writer's own personality:

> Two loves I have, of comfort and despair,
> Which like two spirits do suggest me still;
> The better angel is a man right fair,
> The worser spirit a woman coloured ill.
> To win me soon to hell my female evil
> Tempteth my better angel from my side,
> And would corrupt my saint to be a devil,
> Wooing his purity with her foul pride.
> And whether that my angel be turned fiend,
> Suspect I may, yet not directly tell;
> But being both from me, both to each friend,
> I guess one angel in another's hell.
> Yet this shall I ne'er know, but live in doubt,
> Till my bad angel fire my good one out.

For once, sexual symbolism and iron imagery meet: the 'angel in another's hell' may one day give away the fact that he has been present in that hell by being 'fired out' in a rash as a sign that he has caught the bad spirit's disease. Or the good angel could be fired out by the bad one, just as a cannon ball is fired out from inside the cannon itself. In this reading, then, the cannon itself is hell and the cannon ball is the good angel. But both the cannon and the cannon ball were part of Neville's own manufacturing process; and both the 'spirits' are part of him - 'being both from me' - too. Rather than any real woman, therefore, the dark lady appears to reside within Neville's own personality. But did that dark side take over when he returned to Oxford, after such terrible incarceration? Was he tempted by Mistress Davenant?

We can only hope to come anywhere near an answer to this question by weighing the available evidence, which is what the next chapter attempts.

Chapter 9

SON OF THE DARK LADY?

John Aubrey (1626 - 1697) was the first person to record in writing a strange tradition that Sir William Davenant, the dramatist, may have been Shakespeare's illegitimate son:

> Sir William Davenant Knight Poet Laureate was borne in -- street in the City of Oxford, at the Crowne Taverne. His father was John Davenant a Vintner there, a very grave and discreet Citizen: his mother was a very beautifull woman & of a very good witt and of conversation extremely agreeable... Mr. William Shakespeare was wont to goe into Warwickshire once a yeare, and did commonly in his journey lye at this house in Oxon: where he was exceedingly respected. I have heard parson Robert D[avenant – William's older brother] say that Mr. W. Shakespeare gave him a hundred kisses. Now, Sr. Wm would sometimes when he was pleasant over a glasse of wine with his most intimate friends, e.g. Sam: Butler (author of Hudibras & c), say that it seemed to him that he writt with the very spirit [of] Shakespeare, and was seemed contented enough to be thought his Son: he would tell them the story as above, in which way his mother had a very light report, whereby she was called a whore.

This report of Aubrey's was never printed during his lifetime, but was found in manuscript form in 1680.[108] One must therefore speculate on why it was never published, and also look at the credentials of John Aubrey himself. Was this writer usually truthful, or was he merely a sensationalist? The next question must surely be whether, if the report is true, Aubrey was talking about Shakespeare of Stratford, the actor, or the writer, Sir Henry Neville.

Sir William Davenant was born in 1606, and Aubrey was twenty years younger. Aubrey was therefore born well after Sir Henry Neville died, so Davenant was the closest link he had to his and Shakespeare's times. Aubrey was probably the first English biographer, in the true sense of the word, in that he researched his subject from many angles. The latest entry for him in the Oxford Dictionary of National Biography represents, in turn, the most thoroughly researched assessment of Aubrey and his work to date. It comes to the conclusion that he was a much better and more important researcher and writer than some of his jealous contemporaries wanted to admit. Because of those contemporary rivals - such as Anthony ā Wood – Aubrey gained a reputation during his lifetime for being too gullible. Yet much of his work has ultimately turned out to have been firmly grounded. Moreover, he was for many years of his life virtually impoverished, and yet still insisted on not publishing anything which might harm someone still living. A poor man like Aubrey could no doubt have made quite a tidy sum of money by publishing 'sensations' concerning Shakespeare, as the cult was then getting underway, yet he did not publish the above report about him. Indeed, he adds at the end of the text that Davenant's own mother gained an adverse reputation through her son's loose talk when he had had a little too much to drink. It is therefore hardly likely that Aubrey would even have written the rumour down at all, unless he had believed it might contain more than a grain of truth that could be picked up by a later researcher.

It may also be significant that the person Aubrey names as knowing William Davenant's secret was Samuel Butler. Butler (the poet) was brought up on the estate of Sir John Russell of Worcestershire, and John Russell was the half-brother of Thomas Russell, the overseer of Shakespeare's will. On first view, it may therefore seem that Davenant chose Butler as a confidant because he was someone already connected with those who had been directly connected with Shakespeare. However, the Russell-Shakespeare connection has its nexus in Neville. [diagram 2]. So why does Aubrey never mention Neville's name?

Anyone who had any inkling of Neville's politics during Aubrey's lifetime would still have kept quiet about it, because of Neville's involvement with Republican ideas. Even though Neville had veered more towards a constitutional monarchy – a partnership between monarchy and parliament - than to an outright republic, the times through which both Davenant and Aubrey lived had included the Civil War, Commonwealth, and a swing back to Monarchy. No one was therefore quite sure where any declared political leanings might lead. Henry Neville's own grandson was a politician and writer who was all the while trying to persuade first Cromwell and then King Charles II not to act without a mandate from wise men. But even this young Neville's moderate stance had brought him to gaol and into disrepute with both sides. Thus, the times were still too sensitive for the true political background to our Sir Henry and his works to be brought into the public view. (It is therefore highly probable that it was during the turmoil surrounding and following the Civil War that the secret of Neville's authorship was conveniently 'lost'.)

Samuel Butler - the friend who knew Davenant's secret - had a connection with the Russells which certainly brought him into the Neville circle. Neville's daughter married Thomas Russell's nephew, and this was indeed the same Thomas Russell who had overseen Shakespeare's will. Thomas Russell's family connections included the Killigrews too. His half-brother was the radical parliamentarian Sir Maurice Berkeley, who was knighted at Cadiz alongside Henry Neville. This same Sir Maurice married Elizabeth, daughter of Sir Henry Killigrew; then Neville's daughter, Elizabeth, married Henry, the son of Sir Maurice Berkeley. Thus was it possible for the Davenant-Butler-Russell secret to be kept well within the Killigrew-Neville circle.

Thomas Russell's father died when Thomas Junior was four years old, and the boy was brought up by his mother and her second husband, Sir Henry Berkeley. His mother was Margaret Lygon, a relative of the Grevilles, one of whom had become the Earl of Warwick . (This same Earl of Warwick - Fulke Greville - was also a friend and kinsman of Sir Henry Neville.) Thomas was educated at Queen's College, Oxford – again, Oxford becomes the centre on which so many of Neville's friends and relatives converge. Thomas' wife died around 1595, after which Russell moved to Alderminster, which lies about four miles south of Stratford. In 1599 he was known to be courting Anne Digges, the widowed mother of Leonard Digges, (writer of one of the commendatory verses in the First Folio) and of Dudley Digges (future knight, Member of Parliament and member of the council for the Virginia Company.) Anne Digges had lived in Philips Lane, London, near John Heminges and Henry Condell, and she also had an estate in Rushock, Worcestershire, a few miles from Heminges's birthplace in Droitwich. Thus the wider Russell-Digges circle could well have included that of the two Globe actors who became the very men to write the Dedication to the First Folio – Heminges and Condell. (Neville was already a kinsman of Thomas Digges [1545-95], the mathematician and astronomer who had taught at Merton, where Neville was in attendance until 1578.) Neville, together with his wider family, his business and his educational connections are therefore once more right at the centre of the Shakespeare secret, and form the pivot around which the production of the First Folio revolved.[109]

Taken all in all, it is hardly surprising, therefore, that Davenant should have chosen Butler – the man who was brought up on the Russell estate – to chat with concerning his 'Shakespeare' connections. Butler was well placed enough to have known that two people – Neville and Shakespeare - had been subsumed into that pseudonymous identity. If the story of Davenant's secret parent was not true, then why did Aubrey dare to say that he had heard it all from a parson, who was also William Davenant's own brother? He might easily have attributed the tale to someone less likely to castigate him for lies than a parson.

The Oxford Connection

William Davenant's parents ran a tavern associated with Oxford University. Neville had cause to stay at Oxford around the time of William Davenant's birth – i.e. 1606 - when he, Neville, was preparing to receive his M.A. Moreover, one of the old roads from Oxford to London goes through Waltham St. Lawrence – where Sir Henry Neville's home was situated. Besides, Neville would already have known the Davenant family from their days in London. Yet Shakespeare would have been unlikely to have known them there, because the acquaintance between Neville and the Davenants would have been through Merchant Adventurer companies, with which Neville was associated but Shakespeare was not. Also, as will be demonstrated, the Davenants had other connections with the Nevilles and Killigrews, though none with Shakespeare, and these connections continued for several generations into the future. Yet there were, as already mentioned, no ongoing relations between the Shakespeares and the Davenants.

Sir Henry Neville had ongoing business in Oxford between 1604 and 1610. To begin with, he was preparing for his M.A. there, which he received in 1605. Another connection with Oxford University also ran concurrently with this: Sir Henry's brother in law had died, so Henry kindly took over the man's sons and paid for them to be educated at Oxford. Neville corresponded frequently with the Oxford lecturer who was mainly in charge of them[110]. The boys were only young and therefore cost Sir Henry more than he had at first envisaged by using up their term's food allowance in one week – on 'sweet things'. (Obviously, comfort eating was just as much a problem then as now.) All this came at a time when Sir Henry had not long been out of gaol, so must still have been adjusting to life back home with his wife. Perhaps his wife had found comfort elsewhere during his absence, or perhaps Neville felt sorrow in her presence, especially after her father had been so upset by the Essex business that he had at one time excluded Anne Neville and her children from his home in Lothbury[111]. By an especially cruel twist of fate, Sir Henry Killigrew had died only three weeks before Neville was set free, so there was not a chance for the two men – once so friendly – to renew the old trust between them.

And what was William Shakespeare doing in 1605? He seems to have been so settled in Stratford that he rented yet another cottage there.[112]   In fact, his last London stage appearance seems to have been in 1604. Not until 1608 did he become a shareholder in the Blackfriars Theatre, but even then he may not have been in London, since in 1609 he appeared in a court case in Stratford. This was to recover a debt from John Addenbrook, a Stratford man, which seems to suggest Shakespeare must have been resident there for some time, if he was having such dealings with local men. Then, in 1610, Shakespeare has more land dealings in Stratford, finally settling down in New Place, Stratford. Only in 1612, with the Bellot-Mountjoy case, does Shakespeare appear to have resumed dealings in London. So why would he have stayed at Oxford in 1605/6 'on his way to London' when he does not appear to have had anything to do with London at this time – i.e. precisely the time William Davenant was conceived and born? Indeed, it is usually assumed that all the London playhouses were often closed between 1604 and 1608, due to the plague. A middle-aged gentleman with a lucrative grain business in Stratford, who was also lending money there, would therefore hardly have been likely to have returned to the over-worked, plague-ridden theatre world of London during such a time. And if he did not travel to London, then he did not need to stay in Oxford.

Then there is the added problem that William signed no London documents during this 'Davenant' period either. Indeed, the first document we have bearing Shakespeare's signature dates from 1612. Moreover, there are added difficulties in that this and each of the other subsequent five signatures of his still in existence differ greatly from each other. This is rather surprising: many men varied their handwriting, but they did not usually employ so many different styles when it came to writing their signature at such a mature age. All this may even throw doubt on whether the three Shakespeare London signatures are signed by the same man as the three Stratford signatures at the foot of each page on Shakespeare's will.

In all these circumstances, and with Neville having to be in Oxford so often, while Shakespeare was not, it is more likely that Neville was Davenant's father. Neville may not have truly settled down again in his old home after his imprisonment. It is indeed possible that he sought comfort elsewhere, and from a statistical point of view alone it is much more likely that Davenant could have been Neville's son rather than Shakespeare's. Even if we are to believe John Aubrey, William Shakespeare only travelled once a year through Oxford, whereas Sir Henry, with his affairs at the University, would have stayed there much more frequently.

The Davenants

When the circumstances of William Davenant's life are investigated, it can be seen that other factors also add weight to the Neville theory, in addition to that of statistical probability. William Davenant was born in 1606 and was the second of four sons born to John Davenant and Jane Sheppard. The Sheppards came down to London from Durham, which was also the seat of one senior branch of the Neville family. John Davenant was born in Essex but moved into London itself as the wealth of the city began to expand. His relations included several merchant adventurers, who would therefore have known Sir Henry Neville. They were also members of the Merchant Taylors' Company, to which Neville's father was affiliated, while his mother's family – the Greshams – were prominent in the Mercers' Company. John Davenant's direct ancestors had been merchant vintners who imported wines and thus mixed with all the other Merchant Companies. John senior was a freeman of the Muscovy Company, which was eventually headed by Thomas Smythe, Neville's friend and relative. Indeed, William Davenant's grandmother was the daughter of the founder-member of that

Company, so it is inconceivable that the Davenants' paths did not coincide with the Nevilles.

Added to all this, the Davenant mother and father lived opposite to the playhouses on the South Bank, and therefore within walking distance of Neville's home with his father in law in Lothbury, with whom Neville had a very close relationship right up till the time he was accused of involvement with the Earl of Essex. It also has to be remembered that Neville conducted his ironworks business from an inn next to the Globe Theatre, and had his business letters delivered to the saddlery next door to that, so he may well have come into contact with the merchant Davenants back in the early 1590s. Indeed, the Davenants moved to their London home in the same year as Neville senior died, so our Sir Henry would have been especially active as an independent businessman after this event.

Jane, William's mother, was renowned for her beauty and wit. Her family were often courtiers, one of them being a lady in waiting to the Queen, so it is doubtful if she would have set her sights at a lowly actor. William Shakespeare was no more likely to have had an affair with an upper-class girl than was Ben Jonson! Ben knew his place when it came to class, and William Shakespeare would have done so too, though (strangely) we know nothing of William's private thoughts or aspirations, even though we know so much about Jonson's. Both the Davenant parents liked plays, though it is remarked by Aubrey that it was 'playmakers' that John Davenant really respected.

After suffering disease in the capital and losing children, John and his wife moved out to Oxford, which proved to be a much healthier place for them. There they kept a tavern, which was owned by New College, Oxford University. Even though records show that the tavern had about twenty rooms, it would only have been allowed to accommodate friends and Oxford University visitors, not paying customers, as it was not an inn. The idea that the well-connected Davenants ran a kind of public house for all and sundry is erroneous. So Neville must have stayed there because he already knew the Davenants. But Neville would definitely have been the senior guest. If the actor - rather than the writer, under his pseudonym - ever stayed with the Davenants at all, then he would have to have come through a recommendation, as the Davenant's tavern did not take in mere paying guests. If the actor was ever there, it is unlikely he would have been treated as an equal by a family with such a risen merchant and 'gentle' background as the Davenants. Besides, Shakespeare the actor had no connection with Oxford University, by whom the inn was owned, yet Neville most definitely had.

John and Jane Davenant both died in 1622, leaving a substantial sum of money to their children, hoping that their son, William, would become a merchant. However, the sixteen year old boy made his way to London, bought smart clothes and went into service at one of the Howards' houses. (Some of the large Howard family were Neville's deadly enemies, but others had been good friends of Neville's father, whereas there was no connection between the Howards and William Shakespeare.) Then Davenant, young as he was, got married, though his wife died shortly afterwards.

Now a single parent, young Davenant next became a page to Fulke Greville, Earl of Warwick. Much influence was needed for a young man to work in such an elevated home in the position of 'page', and it is certain neither William Shakespeare nor his illiterate descendants could not have wielded that kind of power. Sir Henry Neville's family, however, could easily have done so. Fulke Greville's wife was Lady Anne Neville, daughter of the Earl of Westmorland – the major branch of the Neville family, from which Sir Henry himself was descended. And Fulke knew Henry Neville, as witnessed by at least one of his letters:

> 1609 Aug 13th Eaton Letter from Sir Henry Neville to Winwood
> "Being come to Eaton upon a summons from Mr. Chancellor of the Exchequer [Sir Fulke Greville] and finding so good an opportunity as the return of young Sir Henry Savill to London ..."[113]

Greville's willingness to accept young Davenant into his household has other implications too. Firstly, it is often said that William Shakespeare may have been a friend of Fulke Greville. Yet this statement cannot be substantiated, even though at least one biographer of Shakespeare has stated it as a fact. There are absolutely no records of Shakespeare of Stratford ever having anything to do with Greville whatsoever. Yet Greville's employment of *William Davenant* is indeed recorded, even though Davenant was such a lesser playwright than Shakespeare. If, therefore, Greville had ever been a patron of Shakespeare, the Stratford actor and supposed great writer – or associated with him in any way whatsoever – then this would have been recorded. The absence of any such record strongly suggests there was never any connection between Shakespeare and Fulke Greville.

But the fact that Greville knew Sir Henry Neville can be fully substantiated. Not only were they related through the Nevilles, Beauchamps and Talbots, but Greville was also a member of the Mitre Club[114]. Sir Fulke was also a friend of the historian, Camden, who was the best friend of Henry Savile, Neville's tutor and constant companion. Moreover, Greville was a famed friend of Sir Philip Sidney - son of the best friend of Sir Henry Neville's father. And the famous story of Sir Philip giving his water bottle to a poor soldier at the battle of Zutphen comes from Greville's pen. (Once again, this proves that helping the poor was important to Greville, which again means that if he had helped Shakespeare, then the fact would indeed have been recorded. Yet from the quite substantial list of those writers whom Greville knew and helped, Shakespeare is conspicuous by his absence[115]. This fact on its own is enough to lead to the conclusion that Greville knew the Stratford boy was not the true writer, otherwise he would surely have contacted and assisted him too. After all, who was more in need of assistance than poor young William, with a wife and two young children to support in a town so distant from London, which meant that besides paying for their lodging and food he also had to pay his own rent in the Capital?)

It so happens that Davenant's first play was staged at Blackfriars – the theatre on which the Nevilles had possessed a lease. Around this time, Davenant is said to have lost part of his nose through venereal disease, though whether this is the true reason for the shape of his nose is unknown. But Dark Lucy once again rears her head again – this time in one of Davenant's plays, *The Wits*. In it, a character called Lucy speaks of 'lewd gallants' losing a nose. Davenant's condition may have been genuine, since he sought out the mercury treatment as a cure – something so threatening to health that he surely would not have done this except in a real medical emergency. Indeed, William Davenant married his doctor's widow. But again, would not the doctor's widow have been a little afraid of catching Davenant's disease, if he had truly suffered from it? Altogether, we are left with a situation where it is impossible to draw any certain conclusion.

Inexplicably, (if we see Davenant as an illegitimate orphan with few courtly connections) Davenant soon became a servant to the Queen. Henrietta Maria was particularly fond of Platonism, so the Court dramas he wrote included elements of this theme. But where he learned his Platonism is not known. However, the plays do not display such a deep knowledge of the subject as Shakespeare's late plays. It is therefore entirely possible that he learned all he needed to know from the Killigrews, some of whose family members were conversant with Platonism and Alchemy. What we do know is that once there was a respite in this turbulent period of English History, Davenant and Killigrew worked together, which argues for them having known each other for some time during the Civil War. During the time before the Restoration, Davenant also worked with Inigo Jones – Neville's old friend from the Mitre Club. By 1637 Davenant was recognised as Poet Laureate, thus following in Ben Jonson's footsteps – a phenomenal rise for the child who lost his parents at such a tender age.

During the early days of the Civil War, Davenant occasionally travelled with the Queen abroad, helping to raise money and eventually becoming one of the main communicators between King and Queen during the time when they were thus parted – a surprising office with which to have entrusted him, unless, that is, Davenant was himself descended from an old dynasty, perhaps back through the Nevilles to the Plantagenets. Davenant also had another role which was directly following in Neville's footsteps: he became lieutenant-general of the ordnance, though without some inside knowledge of his true, secret forebear – Sir Henry Neville, the ordnance manufacturer, - it is difficult to see why he would ever have been proposed for such a position.

After the execution of Charles I, arrangements were made for Davenant to run away to Virginia, but his ship was intercepted by a Parliamentary vessel, so he was brought back and imprisoned on the Isle of Wight, then subsequently taken to the Tower. (Virginia might have been the obvious destination for the son of a Neville – the man who was the first named officer in the Virginia Company, after the list of Earls, and whose son still invested in the Company. But if Shakespeare or John Davenant were his father, then there would have been no known connection between Sir William and the 'planters' with whom he would have worked when he arrived in the New World.)

On his release from the Tower in 1652, Davenant started to promote musical drama, and was the first English writer to use the word 'opera'. It may be remembered that Sir Ralph Winwood, Henry Neville's secretary, had sent Sir Henry the texts of various continental entertainments, which probably included the early opera performed at Maria de Medici's proxy wedding in Italy.[116] Neville must have been quite taken by it, because it has often been suspected that his later plays, *The Winter's Tale* and *The Tempest,* were originally performed with a great deal of music. Indeed, when Prospero declares 'And deeper than did ever plummet sound, I'll drown my book' he could mean that he is going to drown his own words in music. If this was the intention, then young Davenant knew it, because he and Dryden later turned *The Tempest* into an opera. In this case, it is noteworthy that the man to whom Davenant first showed his own opera, *The Siege of Rhodes,* was the son of a friend of Neville's. Indeed, this friend wrote an appreciation of Neville after his death. He was Judge James Whitlocke, who had long had an interest in drama:

> I was brought up at school under Mr. Mulcaster, in the famous school of the Merchantaylors in London... Yeerly he presented sum playes to the court, in which his scholers wear only actors, and I one among them, and by that meanes taughte them good behaviour and audacitye.[117]

When Neville died, Whitlocke wrote:

> he [Neville] was the most sufficient man for understanding of state business that was in this Kingdom,... and a very good scholar and a stout man, but was as ignobly and unworthily handled as ever gentleman was...[118]

Judge James Whitlocke's son was Bulstrode Whitlocke, and apparently Davenant had known him since his youth.[119] How he came to know such a family is inexplicable, unless Sir Henry Neville is fitted into the equation. Anyway, it was to Bulstrode Whitlocke that Davenant first showed his new work – the very first English opera.

Very soon after his Restoration, Charles II did two things that involved Neville's wider family. First of all, he held his Restoration Party at Billingbear House – the Nevilles' home – and then he granted Thomas Killigrew permission to form the King's Company of Players. Davenant had already gained permission from Charles I to build a playhouse in Fleet Street, so there quickly followed a re-affirmation of this promise by Charles II. Finally, the attorney general granted Davenant and Killigrew sole permission to perform Shakespeare's plays within London. Sir Henry Neville's wife was Anne Killigrew, and the playwright Thomas Killigrew was her great nephew. In fact, so many of the subsequent Killigrews became writers that it is not beyond the bounds of possibility that Anne Killigrew-Neville could have assisted her husband in his writing. The passages from *Measure for Measure* concerning Isabella's pleading for her brother's release from prison are certainly reminiscent of Anne's eloquent letters to the Queen, begging her to release 'Mr. Neville' from the Tower. Anne's great niece became a good enough poetess to receive Dryden's personal praise, even though the poor lady died in her twenties from smallpox. The Killigrew girls had obviously inherited spirit and intelligence from their Cooke ancestors, the daughters of which family were known as the best educated ladies in England.

William Davenant went on to direct new versions of *Romeo and Juliet, King Lear, Henry VIII, Macbeth, Twelfth Night* and *Hamlet.* But he was not at first so organised as Killigrew, with Samuel Pepys, the diarist, remarking that his performances began late and that the actors seemed unprepared at the openings of the plays. However, like Neville, Davenant was good at spotting 'talent' in others and eventually gained Pepys' respect for having discovered Thomas Betterton, who became known as the best actor of the age. But Betterton was humble enough to put much of his success down to Davenant's management, and what he says smacks a little of Hamlet's advice to actors:

> When I was a young Player under Sir William Davenant, we were obliged to make our Study our Business, which our young Men do not think it their duty now to do, for they now scarce ever mind a word of their Parts but only at Rehearsals.

Thomas Killigrew is noted as the first playwright and theatre manager to employ actresses, which again displays the respect for women one would expect from someone in the Killigrew-Neville family, and from someone closely associated with the true writer of the strong roles for women in Shakespeare's plays. Davenant soon followed suit, employing women in the first plays ever to include painted scenery – an innovation by Davenant himself. The Cookes of Gidea Hall – Anne Killigrew's ancestors – certainly left a strong female legacy. They included the redoubtable Elizabeth Hoby, translator and classicist, whose sternness was one reason for her sometimes being seen as the woman on whom 'Shakespeare' based his characterisation of Lady Macbeth.

Sir William Davenant's son, Charles Davenant, became a politician, and is often seen as the philosophical successor to Sir Henry Neville's grandson. Charles Davenant wrote a play before entering politics. Grandson Henry Neville was also a politician and a 'concealed poet', as one contemporary said. His works include not only poetic lampoons but also political dialogues – republican in nature – that sometimes tell the story of his grandfather's political thought. In one such dialogue, a gentleman declares that had our Sir Henry Neville's advice concerning a partnership between King and Parliament been followed, then the Civil War could have been avoided. Of course, it is the state of Civil War that our Neville, as Shakespeare, wished to prevent, firstly by demonstrating the evils of such strife in his history plays, and then by hitting his audience's emotions concerning the tragic results of continuous feuding, in *Romeo and Juliet*.

Finally, the Davenants and Nevilles pursued business interests together right into the 18th century, as a certain document demonstrates:

> Assignment of licence to erect lighthouses to
> Francis Eyles by way of mortgage; 10 Apr. 1703 First
> Party: Ralph, Lord Grey, Baron of Warke; Richard
> Neville of Billingbeare, Berkshire, Esq.; and George
> Davenant of Kensington, Middlesex, Esq. Second Party:
> Francis Eyles of London, Esq. Assignment by Neville and
> Davenant at the appointment of Grey to (2) of the licence
> to erect lighthouses, by way of mortgage to secure the
> repayment of £ 15000 and interest to (2). Recites letters
> patent of 30 Jan. 1695/96 giving (1) the right to maintain

5 lighthouses at Wintertonness and Orfordness levying 1d
per ton per voyage (inward and outward) on shipping
(split between masters/ owners, and merchants/owners) as
specified, for a term of 60 years (or 30 years from 13
Apr. 1720 if certain pre-existing letters patent remain in
force) at a rent of £ 20 p.a.
Consideration: £ 15000 by (2) to Grey (as mentioned in
an indenture of even date).[120]

Try as I might, however, I have been unable to trace any ongoing
connections between the Davenants and William Shakespeare's
descendants.

Recently, a number of supposed portraits of Shakespeare
have come under scrutiny by researchers, in association with the
National Portrait Gallery. Davenant actually owned one of these
portraits – the so-called 'Chandos', named after the Lord who
once owned it too. In fact, the Chandos portrait is the only one so
far to have been scientifically confirmed as correlating with
Shakespeare's lifetime and age at the time of painting, though the
Gallery will not go as far as to say that it is a portrait of no one
else but Shakespeare.   All the other portraits examined have
turned out to be painted at a later date – in one case the picture of
Shakespeare was painted over a religious scene.   The only other
supposed contemporary portrait is one recently discovered in
Canada, said to date from 1603.   Attempts to confirm this latter
date have so far been positive, but this does not prove that the
sitter was Shakespeare.   For one thing, the man in the painting
looks far too young to be Shakespeare at that date, and for
another, the worn label naming the sitter as 'Shakespeare' was
written on contemporary paper but bears signs of having been
actually written at a much later time.   However, the painting
shows a young man who is exactly the colouring of Sir Henry
Neville – dark, slightly auburn hair, ruddy complexion and reddish
beard - so although this is not a picture of him, it could perhaps
be a member of his family.   Moreover, I notice that the collar
worn by the sitter in the Canadian portrait bears the same design
as that on the Shakespeare engraving at the front of the First Folio.

The First Folio portrait was executed by Martin
Droeshout several years after Shakespeare's death and, as Ben
Jonson's poem below it suggests, it is not a very good likeness.
One of its strange features is that the head seems to be placed
directly on top of the closed collar, rather than attached to a
neck. The doublet below the collar looks either back to front, or

empty. It is as if the artist had been presented with a suit of clothes worn by his dead subject and then asked to superimpose a head onto these. As often remarked, there is a line around the face, as if the sitter is wearing a mask. To me, the whole impression is that an egg-shaped form, the size and approximate shape of a human head, with a wig attached, has been placed on top of that suit of clothes, then a flat portrait or mask pulled around the form – hence the line around the side of the face and the appearance of the hair being pushed back by this mask. The white, pulled-together collar below the head has a design on it which resembles the rays of the sun. The recently-discovered Canadian portrait shows a sitter wearing what appears to be exactly the same collar. It is said to be by John Sanders, and was passed down the family for four hundred years. Even though the sitter is too young to be either Neville or Shakespeare, it is strange that not only is the collar the same as that worn by Shakespeare in the Droeshout engraving, but the doublet in the Canadian picture is very like one worn by Neville in his portraits now in Audley End House. There could of course be several explanations for all this, one of them being that the Canadian portrait was not painted in 1603 at all but that the painter has instead copied elements from the Droeshout portrait of Shakespeare. Even scientific methods of dating are not proven accurate to within fifty years or so. However, this would not explain why the doublet is so like one of Neville's. So another explanation could be that, if genuine, the painting is not of Shakespeare but of one of Sir Henry Neville's sons, who has borrowed his clothes for the occasion. Neville put on a terrific amount of weight as he grew older, so presumably his earlier clothes would have to be re-cycled amongst the large number of children for whom Henry was ultimately responsible. Such an explanation would suggest that Neville knew the painter – and indeed he was on friendly terms with one well-known painter called Gheerardts, or Garret (in its anglicized form.) This may well have brought him into contact with other painters too, but unfortunately the one who is thought to have painted the Canadian portrait is not known for other works.

The painter in question is said to have been one John Sanders, who stemmed from Worcestershire (near the Russell's home.) Though no one seems to have found anything substantial about this man, I have actually traced a painter called John Saunders in the Dictionary of National Biography. This artist did indeed work in Worcestershire; the problem is, however, that he lived at a much later date than Shakespeare. Saunders was born in 1750 and died in 1825; yet this particular Saunder's son actually emigrated to Canada in 1832. Perhaps he was a descendant of the man who painted the 1603 portrait. Something is obviously afoot, but I fear more research is needed to discover what is actually going on. To end on a positive note, however, there may just be something significant in the design of the collar worn in both the Sanders and the Droeshout painting: the pattern is like the rays of the sun, and the symbols of the rays of the sun were carried on the banners the Nevilles bore into battle, ever since the appearance of the three suns at the Battle of Mortimer's Cross during the Wars of the Roses. Indeed, the closed collar in the Droeshout engraving resembles the form of a shield.

So was Davenant really Sir Henry Neville's son? In the absence of documentary evidence, no one can ever say for certain. But in such delicate matters documentary evidence has always been missing. However, Neville did specify in his will that only his sons *by his wife* should inherit parts of his estate. This is indeed difficult to explain if he had had no sons by any other woman. Moreover, the dates and circumstances of Davenant's birth correlate with Neville's known movements at the time. Then there is the ongoing relationship between the Davenants, Killigrews and Nevilles, plus the shared political philosophy of Charles Davenant and Sir Henry Neville's grandson. Davenant also followed Neville's wider relatives and connections with the Russells, and with Sir Fulke Greville , Earl of Warwick. If there were absolutely nothing in the theory, then all this would be very difficult to explain away.

Our initial shock at these possible circumstances is surely somewhat ameliorated by the fact that very few of us, fortunately, are in a position to know what scars might have been left with Neville after he was shut away in the Tower for almost three years, constantly dreading that he might at any moment be 'the coward conquest of a wretch's knife'. And we must also be realistic: anyone who could plot and write the plays had to have a certain hidden ingredient his nature. Neville and his family were self-confessed disguisers, and he could duck and dive with the best of them when it came to working out political strategies too. Everyone was astounded to find that he had been involved with the Essex affair – he was clearly able to hide his revolutionary and republican tendencies very efficiently. His fellow MPs were equally astounded when they discovered that he had been the chief Parliamentary undertaker, that is, the person who reported to the King everything that happened in Parliament, 'undertaking' to manage the politicians for him, in return for certain assurances of the Commons' rights and privileges. For aught his fellow politicians knew, Neville was the most vociferous of them all in openly opposing King James I, but there he was, leading a double life.

Another surprisingly deceitful, amusing, yet somewhat vengeful side of Neville's character showed itself in an incident reported by the Court gossip, John Chamberlain. After his daughter Frances' marriage to Sir Richard Worsley, Neville often went to visit the couple on the Isle of Wight. When on his way there one day, a horse and rider, recognising Sir Henry's Coach, galloped towards them. The rider was the Spanish Ambassador – a man from a family whom Henry disliked, and whose brother he had spent his time avoiding while in France. The Spaniard doffed his cap, while someone - perhaps in Neville's carriage or perhaps another rider - snatched the hat from him. The Spanish Ambassador was clearly expecting a greeting but had his hat stolen instead, along with a precious jewel which embellished it. Sir Henry's voice was heard ordering his coachman to speed on his way. According to Winwood, a member of this Spaniard's family had spread the most terrible rumours about Sir Henry. The Ambassador himself had also been trying to discredit the Virginia Company with King James I, so Neville clearly had no interest in protecting the man. But this particular action or omission on Neville's part does perhaps display a surprisingly opportunistic side of Neville, which had been further underlined by his actions during the planning of the Essex uprising.

It has to be remembered too that Neville was also a Gresham. His great uncle – Thomas Gresham, from whom he inherited the ironworks – had an illegitimate child. It is also rumoured that Neville's own mother had had a daughter by Lord Grey. No one is sure about the identity of the mother of Thomas Gresham's daughter; but it is known that he left a substantial sum of money for the care of the 'fallen women' of London. Someone had to oversee the administration of that part of the will. Was Neville the inheritor who did so? The ghosts of all the Lucy Morgans and Doll Tearsheets in town must have haunted Gresham's descendants.

Chapter 10

NEVILE , BEVILE AND THE KING'S SECRET WRITER.

Neville actually revealed his name and his background once or twice in the Sonnets, as well as the plays, as detailed in Chapter 5. The symbolic numbering given to some of his poems often points out a sonnet or two in which he strongly displays his name and personal feelings, sonnet 121 ('I to myself') being a prime example:

> 'Tis better to be vile than vile esteemed,
> When not to be, receives reproach of being,
> And the just pleasure lost, which is so deemed,
> Not by our feeling, but by others' seeing.
> For why should others' false adulterate eyes
> Give salutation to my sportive blood?
> Or on my frailties why are frailer spies,
> Which in their wills count bad what I think good?
> No, I am that I am, and they that level
> At my abuses, reckon up their own,
> I may be straight though they themselves be bevel;
> By their rank thoughts, my deeds must not be shown
> Unless this general evil they maintain,
> All men are bad and in their badness reign.

It is easy to see 'Nevel', Nevil and 'Nevile' incorporated in the text of this sonnet. But the *semantics* of the sonnet also demand attention to detail, and these details reveal Neville behind their practical reality. The writer is first of all complaining that he has been reproached for something which he is *not*, viz. 'vile' (*line1*.) He obviously perceives himself as proceeding from good motives, though with the knowledge that he has some human 'frailties'(*line 7*) too. He also tells us that he receives his 'pleasure' (*line 3*) not from the inward 'feeling'(*line 4*) that he knows he is **not** 'vile' but from others' recognition of his basic goodness. Occasionally he is 'sportive' (*line 5*). At the time, this word often referred to sexual activity, but it could also encompass the fact that he writes entertainments. Yet he does not wish people to 'give salutation' (*line 6*) to him for that, but rather to value him for being generally good rather than 'vile'. Yet 'frailer' (*line 7*) people than he are spying on his 'frailties', and these people have different values from his, to boot - '... in their wills count bad what I think good'. So, by extension, these Neville-detractors are ultimately incapable of discerning absolute right from wrong. They are set to spy upon him merely because they view the world from a different angle. They have different values from those held by the writer of the sonnet. And in the last two lines we are told about the misanthropic outlook of these spies: 'All men are bad and in their badness reign.'

If we take those last words literally, the writer, unlike the spies surrounding him, is definitely concerned about *who* reigns. As Neville was a politician, this concern makes sense. We could therefore here be witnessing the early expression of the writer's worries about the Succession - a topic of discussion forbidden by law under Queen Elizabeth. But this looks like a later poem - a bitterness from his post-imprisonment days has crept in. So was there another point in time when the question of adequate kingship also arose? Only by examining the available clues can there be any attempt at a likely explanation. The people who are spying on the poet don't think it makes any difference who reigns, because 'all men are bad' anyway. The writer obviously disagrees with them. This basic differing of value-systems between Neville and the spies watching over him makes him resentful: 'I am that I am', he confidently declares in line 9, and what he *is* is 'not vile' (*Ne*-vile). How could he be counted as such just for believing that certain people are capable of reigning in a better way than other rulers?

Thus has Neville (Ne-vile) revealed his own name and some of his basic beliefs; but within the text of Sonnet 121 (perhaps its numbers also signify 'eye to eye') he appears possibly to have gone one step further and encoded the name of one of the spies watching over him too. 'Tis better to **be vile**...' the writer begins. Just as 'Ne-vile' is a name, so is 'Be-vile', or 'Beville'. Only one letter is changed, yet a complete opposite is formed. Surprisingly (or perhaps unsurprisingly, since so many links between Neville and the Works of Shakespeare have now become clear) there was a Sir William Beville who would definitely have been known by Neville.

Sir William Beville and his wife, Frances Knyvett-Beville, were courtiers who owned a manor house in Wiltshire. The Jacobean Court - like its predecessor - was full of 'factions', and the bad news was that Lady Frances Beville's sister was married to a member the 'Howard faction', which was then directly opposed to the Nevilles. Indeed, Lady Beville's sister was the mother of Frances Howard, the girl who had been forced by her ambitious uncle to marry the young son of the Earl of Essex, when she was only thirteen years old. This uncle, Henry Howard, had always displayed great power over his young niece, and he was Neville's worst enemy, setting spies on him and using his influence against him in every way possible. The Knyvett connection could therefore not have escaped the Howard uncle's attention: he would use it whenever and however the opportunity arose.

Running parallel to all this, Neville was secretly inside a circle of writers who lived on the margins of Court life. Perhaps his closest contact in this circle was Sir Thomas Overbury, who was, at first, a great friend of Ben Jonson. Jonson wrote Court Masques and was privy to Court gossip - probably mainly through Overbury's good offices. Beaumont and Fletcher, who sent their works to Neville for assessment, were part of this circle too. From letters received by Neville and ones written by others at the time[122], we know that Neville kept a close eye on Overbury's progress. As well as being useful from a literary point of view, Overbury was secretary and confidant to the King's favourite, Sir Robert Carr. This being the case, Overbury was the most likely member of the literary/court circle to be allowed to see some of Neville's draft manuscripts.

But certain complications arose. Sir Thomas Overbury fell in love with Elizabeth Sidney, who was then Countess of Rutland. Ben Jonson discovered that he himself was unwittingly being used as a go-between by Overbury[123], because Elizabeth Sidney was Jonson's patron. Jonson became openly angry about this, but the affair must have quietly affected Neville too, because the Duke of Rutland's brother was now married to none other than the widowed Lady Beville, i.e. Frances Howard's aunt. At the same time, Frances Howard (still married to the young Earl of Essex) was having an affair with Robert Carr, the King's favourite.

Carr and Sir Thomas Overbury had been friends for many years, Overbury having ultimately become Carr's secretary. However, Overbury hated and mistrusted the beautiful yet deadly Frances Howard and was doing his best to put an end to her affair with Carr. Wicked uncle Henry Howard, however, encouraged the affair, hoping that he himself - not Overbury or Neville - would thereby have access to the King's favourite. Yet it was this same wicked uncle who had arranged the marriage between the young Earl of Essex and his own twelve year old niece - a marriage which was still in force. The extent to which women were used as political pawns by men in those days was disgraceful, so Sir Henry Neville definitely stood out as being very different from the mysogenistic norm.

Judging by the anger expressed in Sonnet 121, and by what was then happening at Court, Neville must have been discovered as a writer by this Howard faction, and in some way compromised. The remaining evidence for what actually happened begins with the fact that Neville was at Court for the Christmas Entertainments of 1604:

> *Letter from Dudley Carleton to Ralph Winwood, January, 1604 [1605 in the new calendar]*
> Your Friends are well, Mr. Chamberlain at Knebworth, Mr. Gent in London. Sir Henry Nevill went yesterday from thence.[124]

In the same letter, however, Carleton tells how Neville has been unpredictably passed over when it comes to gaining plum appointments in the new year 'round':

> Sir Henry Maynard prepares for France. Sir Thomas Bodley hath been much laid to by my Lord of Cranborne to accept the place of Secretary, and I doubt not but you hear how he refused it. This Offer is made an Act so meritorious, that it is bruted *a son de trompette* in all Places, but some malicious Fellows talk as fast of Sir Walter Cope, as if he were designed to that place, and that the other was only ad faciendum populum. Sir Henry Neville sits by all this while unthought of, but 'tis hoped by many honest Men, the Necessity of the Time will lay the Place upon him.

So something had clearly happened to dash Neville's prospects. Why had he not been offered a promoted office? Carleton seems to hold the clue to what precisely had been going on. Earlier in that same letter, he had mentioned that Lady Beville had been acting in a Court Masque by Ben Jonson[125] - the *Masque of Blackness* - alongside King James I's Queen. Lady Beville would, therefore, have had the Queen's ear during rehearsals. Had she learnt that Neville was a secret playwright? It would certainly have been a relevant piece of news to tell the Queen at such a moment. And it is not difficult to see how Lady Beville would have heard about this: the Duke of Rutland's wife - Elizabeth Sidney, Jonson's patroness - could have discovered Neville's secret through her admirer/lover, Sir Thomas Overbury. If she then told her husband, he could easily have told his brother, who would then have told his own wife, Lady Frances Beville, full knowing that she was interested in plays and masques. It is of course also probable that Lady Rutland (Overbury's lover) knew her sister in law well and told her Neville's secret directly.

However, the fact that Sir Henry Neville was a playwright may not, **on its own**, have been enough to cause him to be completely overlooked when it came to receiving Christmas appointments and honours. But the dating of these events - 1604/1605 - was a time when something momentous was happening on the Shakespeare front, and this could have been the cause of a misunderstanding. At this precise time Shakespeare-Neville was writing *Macbeth*. If, therefore, the Countess of Rutland had been told that Neville was not only a playwright but that he was currently writing a play about a wicked Scottish king, then a rumour like that would certainly have been enough to compromise Neville's position in both Court and politics! Such specific misleading information would at last explain the enigmatic ending to Sonnet 121:

> By their rank thoughts my deeds must not be shown,
> Unless this general evil they maintain,
> All men are bad, and in their badness reign.

Is the writer trying to say that Lady Beville has put an incredibly pejorative slant on his work? By writing *Macbeth,* Shakespeare-Neville did not wish to suggest that James was a typically bad 'Scottish king'. Quite the opposite, in fact: he wished to show him as 'good' by contrast with Macbeth, and as springing from a different, better ancestry than Macbeth's . At the same time, the play describes how Duncan's sons came to England for assistance, thereby demonstrating just what great things can be achieved when England and Scotland act together. And, on a personal level, King Duncan was an ancestor of Neville himself.

Neville therefore was not 'vile' and had just cause to complain about a certain Lady 'Bevile' who had come by her information through 'others' false, adulterate eyes' - i.e. through Thomas Overbury's affair with Lady Beville's sister in law. Indeed, here we have, for the first time, a literal explanation for the use of the adjective 'adulterate' since Neville's secret would have been gained through the Countess of Rutland's suspected adultery with Sir Thomas Overbury. (Everything was destined to end in tears a few years later when Frances Howard conspired to trap Overbury in a compromising situation too, which led to his being placed in the Tower, where Frances apparently engineered his murder through poisoning, all the joint efforts of Neville, the Killigrews and the Earl of Pembroke - patron of the First Folio - having failed to save Overbury's life.)[126]

Neville would finally have confessed to the King that he actually was a writer, but he would have told him about the true purpose of his Scottish play too. The King's reaction seems to have been favourable, for this then explains why James I eventually visited Billingbear specifically to ask for advice concerning his own writing.[127] The King's favourable reaction would also explain why Neville appears to have been offered the chance, soon after the new year, to take the King to the place where he had studied - namely, Oxford University.

This visit to Oxford happened in 1605. Neville received his M.A., and arranged entertainments there for the King. Thanks to John Chamberlain, we know something about those entertainments. Neville's scribe, John Packer, also notes the occasion, so we have a short account of what took place, and it is indeed interesting that the entertainments included plays and poetry:

> The Disputations for the most part were well performed and pleased the King exceedingly, for he had a great part in them, and spake often and to the purpose; but he was so continually interrupted with applauding, that he could not express himself so well as he wish'd; yet he found Taste in that Distaste, and was never a whit offended.

> But the plays had not the like success,
> especially Magdalen's tragedy of Ajax which
> was very tedious, and wearyed all the
> Company. But the Day of Departure, an
> English Pastorall of Samuel Daniel's presented
> before the Queen made amends for all; being
> indeed very excelent, and some Parts exactly
> acted.[128]

However, it is highly significant that Packer stopped short of detailing another play which was performed at the same occasion. This was one which paralleled *Macbeth*, written by Matthew Gwinne (1558 - 1627), a fellow of St. John's College, containing an explanation of King James' ancestry from a different line![129] It is certainly very difficult to explain the concurrence of all these known events, unless we put Sir Henry Neville and Lady Beville's treachery firmly into this equation, the consequent theory being that Neville would have suggested the Macbeth theme to Gwinne, in order to demonstrate to the King how his own play would carry a 'good' message - just as Gwinne's had now done.

But the evil will and bad feeling between the Beville/Knyvett/Howards and the Nevilles seems to have continued, as witness a strange incident several years later. In 1609 Sir Henry Neville's eldest son (also Sir Henry) was arrested and beaten - to within an inch of his life - by officers in Cornwall who (allegedly) mistook him for Henry Knyvett[130]. It is difficult to explain this misunderstanding unless the officers were really illiterate and read Knyvett as Neville, which is not very likely. More likely is that there was some **wilful** misunderstanding involved. One suspects that these officers had been well paid for their 'mistake', because such a serious error would otherwise have led to financially crippling fines and the added possibility of their never being able to find such work again. Besides, there are no records of any subsequent arrest of any Henry Knyvett, so it is very strange indeed that the Knyvett name was ever mentioned in association with the deed.

What actually happened was that young Henry Neville, who was staying in Cornwall with his Killigrew relatives at the time, had been accused of piracy by a Frenchman. The whole case seems rather scurrilous, as this Frenchmen never produced any proof of young Neville's supposed 'crime', and, in the end, Sir Francis Bacon was able to defend young Neville and get the case dismissed[131]. So how did the Knyvett name come to be mentioned? The officer surely gave the game away: it was probably the Knyvetts who had hired him and his colleagues to carry out the attack on young Henry Neville, purposely striking a blow against the whole Neville family.

After all, by the time this disturbing attack occurred, even more water had flowed under the bridge. The Gunpowder Plot had put Catholics like the Howards quite out of the running as far as the King's favour was concerned. Catholics generally had supposed that Robert Cecil might even have engineered the plot in order to bring about this end, and Neville was perceived as well and truly back in favour with Cecil by that time. Neville was of course also related to the Cecils, so there must have been a general concern among the Howard faction that this was becoming too strong an alliance for them to resist. Sir Henry Neville had gained a lot of strength and fortitude from his Tower experience, and the Knyvetts and Howards had found out by past experience that Neville was strong enough and intelligent enough to gainsay them. Thus it looks very much as if they made the dastardly and cowardly decision to harm one of his family - thus striking at Neville's emotions rather than his impenetrable intellect.

Frances Knyvett-Beville actually died four years before the publication of the Sonnets (in 1609), and so Neville must have thought he was able to hit back at her in his Sonnet - non-violently and without any threat of further action:

> Sir Lewis Lewkener hath buried his new young Lady that was Argalle's widow, and Sir Francis Manners his Lady Bevill, both of the Small Pox, which have raigned and raged here this summer exceedingly. *John Chamberlain to Ralph Winwood, 12th October, 1605*[132]

The attack on Sir Henry's son, however, followed hard on the heels of the appearance of Sonnet 121, i.e. in April, 1609, so it seems that this attack itself may have been a direct reprisal from the rest of the Knyvett family in response to the publication.

But the question as to why the Knyvetts and Howards did not, at the same time, publicly reveal the secret of Sir Henry's writing must also be asked and answered. To begin with, such a revelation would have done Neville much good in the eyes of the public - amongst whom the Shakespeare plays were popular -

whereas it would have done the Howard faction no good at all to demonstrate to the wider world that they were in conflict with such a great writer, popular politician, and intellectual. Secondly, I suspect the King himself did not wish the secret to be revealed, and probably therefore sent a private edict to this effect around those who already knew. The King would not wish Neville to rise in popular esteem to such an extent that he might outshine the present monarchy itself - especially as Neville had already been involved in the Essex anti-monarchical attempted coup. Moreover, any intelligent Neville was especially dangerous when associated with popular opposition to the King, because in an age obsessed by ancestry, the Nevilles were perceived as having strong dynastic rights. Thirdly, James must have reckoned that he might be able to use Neville's newly-revealed skills, if he played his cards correctly. James himself liked writing and wanted to perfect his books. Knowing that Neville wished his playwrighting to be kept away from prying eyes, King James could gain Neville's expert assistance without ever publicly revealing that he had had access to it. That way, James himself could take all the credit for his writing.

The whole secrecy surrounding Neville may well have other implications too. Ever since Richard Neville, Earl of Warwick, had become known as the King Maker, the Nevilles had been cast in senior advisory roles. When one thinks about it, just such a recognised and continuing role is essential for the smooth running of the State - or it certainly was in the past, when there were many fewer educated people around to help in such matters. Over the years, the Nevilles had built up a body of very valuable knowledge concerning State procedures and statecraft. The essential problem with the English monarchical system is the danger that a monarch is chosen purely on the basis of inheritance. Indeed, the Shakespeare 'Wars of the Roses' plays illustrated just what tragedies are unfortunately inherent in such a system. As happened with Henry VI himself, a monarch can succeed to the throne when he is only a child, and therefore demonstrably incapable of ruling. But unless there is an agreed, longstanding and (privately) acceptable fall-back to tide the State over in such dangerous circumstances, then things can - and did - go very wrong. The Nevilles were powerful and clever enough to take on the temporary task of settling the State during such emergencies, and also the task of tutoring and advising any maturing monarch. These very circumstances came to pass during the reign of the boy king Edward VI, when Sir Henry Neville senior undertook this role and also called on the aid of the eminently bright and able Sir Henry Killigrew, so the country was well and humanely governed. Since that time, there may even have therefore been a private agreement that the Nevilles would always be there if any tiding-over of the State was needed. The system broke down temporarily when the Catholic Queen Mary - daughter of Catherine of Aragon - succeeded to the throne, as she was not prepared to listen to these Protestant Nevilles. Neville Senior had indeed tried to put Lady Jane Grey on the throne, and had decided to exile himself abroad when this attempt failed. Once again, the Nevilles were still the potential King and Queen makers. But Sir Henry Senior survived, and was back in England again when Elizabeth came to the throne, with the Cecils (Neville's friends and relatives) having taken on the now traditional Neville role in his absence. It was only natural, therefore, that our Sir Henry himself - with the coming of King James - should hope for a return to the status quo.

To a certain extent, then, Neville must have succeeded in explaining all this to the Scottish King, and James was able to accept it, once he saw what an able man and writer Sir Henry truly was. But it was nevertheless - and probably always will be - the fate of the Nevilles to be occasionally perceived as potential rivals by successive monarchs, not simply as 'supports'. There was, and remains, little which can be done to prevent this, and one suspects the Nevilles were well aware of the problem. Yet, ever since Warwick the King Maker, the Nevilles have gone out of their way to demonstrate that they have no personal wish to take over the throne for themselves.

Our Sir Henry clearly saw one way of helping James to perceive him as an assistant rather than a rival. He told him of his plan to 'manage' a partnership between King and Parliament, so that if the Nevilles were ever unable to fulfil their unsung yet palpable role, then Parliament could tide the State over in any instance of monarchical crisis. He said he was also able to advise the King on how to approach Parliament so that they too became allies, not rivals. It was none of Sir Henry's fault that King James I was not ready for such a progressive philosophy. King Charles II, however, was a different kind of person. The very fact that he held his Restoration Party at Billingbear House with Richard Neville as the Master of Ceremonies surely indicates his acceptance of the situation first outlined by our Sir Henry himself: the Nevilles could 'undertake' to manage the State for the King, just as Henry VI had requested Richard Neville to do in *Henry VI, part 3:*

> KING HENRY VI ...Warwick, although my head still wear the crown,
> I here resign my government to thee,
> For thou art fortunate in all thy deeds.
> ... Warwick, thou art worthy of the sway,
> To whom the heav'ns in thy nativity
> Adjudg'd an olive branch and laurel crown,
> As likely to be blest in peace and war;
> And therefore I yield thee my free consent.
> *ACT4|SC6*

Again, one is forced to ask who but a Neville would have written such words from a King to a Neville?

But what came of Sir Henry Neville's secret writing? Did the secret get passed down the generations? There is some evidence contained in the next chapter to suggest that it did, but to a very limited extent[133]. What would seem to have been passed down to us all, however, is King James I's private edict not to talk about the Shakespeare authorship. Although James' embargo could be viewed as only a theory on my part, the evidence presented here and in the following chapters all point that way. Furthermore, it must be remembered that King James was then seriously considering promoting Neville to the post of Secretary of State, should anything happen to the disabled and ailing Robert Cecil. The King therefore certainly could not allow details about Neville's secret career as a playwright to get out. Indeed, this - rather than any other factor - may have been James' real reason for not finally giving Neville that powerful position.

By ultimately choosing Ralph Winwood for the post of Secretary, James knew he would be getting Neville's policies anyway, as Neville and Winwood worked so closely together. Indeed, Dudley Carleton wrote to John Chamberlain saying that both he and Chamberlain knew this would be the case. If James had really wanted *completely* different policies from those outlined by Neville, then he would have chosen someone other than Neville's best friend as Secretary. Ideally, King James wished to be an absolute monarch, but finding great opposition to this in the English Court and Parliament, he may finally have been afraid that by letting go of Neville's statecraft and influence over Parliament, he could have stumbled into unguided danger. He would also have been bereft of the Nevilles' expert and traditional role.

Chapter II

THE DARK GHOSTS OF NEVILLES PAST

The Nevilles were no common family, in any sense of the word. They were born into riches and influence which made them the subject of aristocratic and intellectual attention. They, unlike less privileged families, knew of their ancestors' deeds, going right back to the Norman invasion. Skeletons were therefore bound to be hidden in some of their cupboards. So the fascinating image of Dark Ladies and all their shadowy connotations so popular with Shakespeare-Neville had its origin in the specific' dark' circumstances and shadowy ladies inhabiting the realm of Nevilles past. But I have discovered that Neville must also have been aware of certain shadowy circumstances surrounding his own beginnings. These circumstances, plus the requirements of Neville's diplomatic career, re-inforced his initial fascination with mystery and secrecy, and he wrote with obvious delight to Cecil about his own and others' simulations and disguises.[134] At the same time, 'Shakespeare' wrote of the dark, mysterious Rosaline in his early play, *Love's Labour's Lost,* and of Jews, businessmen and the dark, lovely Jessica in *The Merchant of Venice.*

For Neville, however, Blackness and Darkness stem back to a time even before these plays were written - right back to a time before he was born – back to his parents and a dark secret which threatened his mother's honour and his own lands.

Sir Henry Neville's father (also called Sir Henry Neville) was a Protestant and so decided to spend many years of the Catholic Queen Mary's reign abroad.[135] However, before leaving England, he married Winifred Losse in 1551[136]. Then, quite unexpectedly, and ten years after this marriage, Sir Henry's first child - a daughter, Elizabeth - was born in 1561, soon followed by our Henry Neville himself.

But both these children are registered as being born to **Elizabeth Gresham**, not Winifred Losse. Yet the marriage between Elizabeth Gresham and Sir Henry Neville senior did not take place until 1568[137]. Moreover, this 'marriage' is recorded only as 'in settlement', which usually means an agreement for a marriage to take place at a future date. Search as I might, however, I can discover no formal record of an actual wedding ceremony between Elizabeth Gresham and Sir Henry Neville. Additionally, some documents also record Elizabeth Gresham as being already 'matched' with Thomas Mason, son of Sir John Mason, the diplomat and Treasurer of the Queen's Chamber.[138] This was recorded only two years before Elizabeth Gresham became pregnant with a child by Neville, thus suggesting that she had preferred Neville all along, but there had been some impediment to their marriage. Again, no formal 'match' or wedding between Elizabeth Gresham and Sir Henry Neville was ever announced. All this leads one to suspect that our Henry was born out of wedlock. Had the spotlight therefore been turned in his direction, Henry could have lost his own and his children's inheritance - a good enough initial reason to hide from the limelight, right from the beginning of his writing career! The first questions to ask, however, must concern Winifred Losse, Sir Henry senior's first wife. As there are no clues to her fate, then perhaps we might discover something by looking at her parentage.

Winifred Losse was the daughter of Sir Hugh Losse, surveyor to Henry VIII. Among other tasks, this Sir Hugh carried out the surveying of Blackfriars Priory, which was acquired by Henry VIII after the dissolution of the monasteries.[139] Hugh Losse, being the father in law of Sir Henry Neville, senior, was therefore in a position to gain his son in law part of the Blackfriars property in 1560. Yet Sir Henry Neville senior was not offered a chance to buy a Blackfriars apartment through his father in law, even though he wanted to acquire it. Instead, he had to purchase a 60 year lease from his friend, Sir William More.[140] It is therefore entirely possible that there had been a breakdown in the Neville-Losse marriage. A certain Paul Gresham also obtained a lease on part of the same building. (One wonders if Sir Henry senior met Elizabeth Gresham through him, though it is also true that Sir Henry possessed lands in Wiltshire and that both he and Elizabeth Gresham were already in mutual contact with the owners of Longleat House, where documents bearing their names are still stored.)

But whatever the manner of their meeting, it is a fact that our Sir Henry and his older sister were born to Elizabeth Gresham and Sir Henry Neville at Blackfriars and not at their father's main home of Billingbear in Berkshire. Indeed, our young Henry Neville's own birth date is so uncertain that it is even possible he and his sister Elizabeth were twins. But a boy would inherit property and land, so here were reasons why this early date for his birth might initially have been kept secret, as it was not until seven years later that even a marriage *settlement* between the parents was announced, though Oxford University later listed out Henry's birth year as 1562.

What is the most likely explanation for all this confusion of dates? The University's dating probably reflects the true birth date of our Henry Neville, as Elizabethans sometimes kept the numbering of the *previous year* right up until March 25th of the new year, but sometimes did not do so. It is therefore quite possible that Church authorities noted the birth of Neville's sister Elizabeth as 1561 (if she was born between January and March 25th 1562), whereas the Oxford authorities could have used a different notation and listed Henry's birth as 1562. This would indeed mean that Elizabeth and Henry were probably twins. At very least, it would mean that there was under a year's difference between them.

On 30th May, 1564[141] our Sir Henry was baptised at St. Anne, Blackfriars, which was at least two years after the actual birth date recorded at Oxford University. It is therefore probable that Henry was ill at this time, which would have made his parents rush to baptise him, in case he died. There must therefore always have been some confusion between what Henry was told to say, and what was perhaps part of some kind of cover-up. Even the Oxford Dictionary of National Biography now lists his birth date as between 1561 and 64. If Henry was in fact born as a twin of his sister Elizabeth, and if his parents were not yet married, they might well delay his baptism, perhaps hoping that they could be married in time to 'legitimise' their child in some way. To have delayed the child's baptism for at least two years, they must have been worried about the possibility that, as an illegitimate son, he would not be allowed to inherit. (It is of course also notable that if our Henry was in fact a twin, then the inclusion of twins in so many of the plays is finally explained.)

So what was happening at Blackfriars, Henry's birthplace? And why did Elizabeth Gresham give birth to, and baptise, her first two babies there? Blackfriars monastery had been dissolved by King Henry VIII. It was a huge building which was split up into separated units (defined by Hugh Losse) that were sold separately and then split further by their new owners so that smaller units could be sold on to various interested parties. Sir Henry senior was obviously not invited to tender for one of the lots, and so had to be content with the 60 year lease there for his London base. But, significantly surely, the part of the Blackfriars property he chose was situated on the site of the Office of the King's Revels. This section of the property was then his own to enjoy and dispose of during those 60 years, subject only to the payment of ground rent to Sir William More.

Sir Henry senior must have purposely sought out the Revels area of the property, for he was himself instrumental in devising Court entertainments[142]. It therefore comes as no surprise that he himself had many connections in the world of Elizabethan entertainment, and so eventually re-let part of his own, leased property in the area to his friend, the musician and theatre-manager, Richard Farrant. In order to do this, Neville senior had to get Sir William More's approval, so Neville and Farrant both wrote to him on the same day, 27th August, 1576:

SIR WILLIAM
After my hearty commendations unto you and to Mrs. More. I am to request your good friendship unto my very friend Mr. Farrant, who understanding that your house which I had of you is to be let, either presently or very shortly, that he may be your tenant thereof, giving unto you such rent as any others will. It may do him at this present great pleasure, and no man shall be readier to requite your friendship than he, I dare answer for him. If you may pleasure him without prejudice to yourself, I pray you certify your man that keeps your house of your pleasure, and accordingly he shall deal with you. ... from Phyllyngber this 27th August.

Yours to his power,
Henry Neville[143]

RIGHT WORSHIPFUL
... where your Worship doth mind to let your house in the Blackfriars, late in the Lord Cobham's hand, I am earnestly to request your Worship if I may be your tenant there if the Italian may be removed[144], as it appeareth somewhat to me, it were easily done. If it be your pleasure to accept me, though unacquainted unto you, I hope in God you will not mislike with me in any dealings concerning the rent or any other things to be performed. If it be my chance to have that favour at your hands, thus yet farther am I to request: that I may pull down one partition and so make of two rooms – one; and will make it up again at my departure, or when my lease shall end. ...With my humble and hearty commendations. I commit you to the Almighty. From London this 27th of August.

Your Worship's to command,
Richard Farrant[145]

I think we may now infer many background facts from all the above. Firstly, by 1576 something had happened to cause a complete change in Neville senior's personal circumstances: when he took on the Blackfriars property in 1560 he obviously intended to live there, since it is reported that he changed the layout of the rooms shortly after moving in, even moving and replacing a whole staircase in order to create more convenient living quarters for himself.[146] When put together with the fact that his daughter (and probably our Henry too) was born there the very next year, this suggests that Henry senior needed to live there with the woman who was pregnant by him, viz. Elizabeth Gresham. Had he remained at Billingbear, it is possible that servants or other workers on his estate could have begun to gossip – they must perforce have known about Winifred Losse. By moving into a London house next to his 'revelling friends', however, Sir Henry senior was free to employ different servants who knew nothing of another wife.

Winifred Losse, his first wife, never appeared to live at the Blackfriars property and was still nowhere to be seen in 1576. Yet in 1560 Henry Neville senior could not have been in a position to marry Elizabeth Gresham, otherwise he would surely have done so before he 'settled down' with her to such an extent that he had three children by her before making a marriage settlement with her in 1568. By 1568, therefore, something must have happened which gave him the freedom to promise himself in marriage. But whatever had happened to Winifred – whether she was divorced or whether she died - it was not recorded. (However, there is also no record of Sir Hugh Losse ever complaining about Neville's earlier relationship with a woman other than his daughter.) By 1576, – the year Neville senior made over part of his leasehold property to Richard Farrant – Elizabeth Gresham-Neville had been dead for three years, having borne him six children.

The upshot of all this is significant for Henry Neville's early introduction to the world of drama and secrecy. If Henry senior did not return to live permanently at Billingbear until after his quasi-marriage to Elizabeth in 1568, then our Sir Henry – their first son - had been born, baptised and raised in the midst of the Office of the King's Revels – indeed, right next to where the King's costume wardrobe was kept for celebratory and ritualistic occasions. (This is the origin of the strangely named 'St. Andrew by the Wardrobe' Church in Blackfriars – the very Church which took over the role and records of St. Anne, where young Neville was baptised.) The fact that Neville senior did not sell a part of his lease at Blackfriars until 1576 suggests that he used the Blackfriars property up till that time. Thus our Sir Henry would have spent the first fourteen years of his life partly in the area where Royal entertainments were rehearsed and performed, interspersed with visits to Billingbear, in whose surrounding countryside and woods he picked up his early knowledge of horticulture and country pursuits.

The cover-up concerning Elizabeth Gresham and her children born out of wedlock may have been performed with the help of Sir Thomas Cawarden - Master of the Revels - as that man began to take over St. Anne's Church in 1555 – the very Church in which the (illegitimate) children of Elizabeth Gresham and Sir Henry Neville were later baptised. Only when some parishioners complained was Cawarden forced to stop annexing the Church as part of his Revels offices, though even by 1585 there was still a dispute as to whether St. Anne's was really church land at all.[147] There seems to have been no regular vicar in charge, otherwise he would have been named as having been involved with the parishioners in their disputation over the ownership of the Church. There is no record of any ordained clergyman **ever** joining in the complaints, which means that the 'occasional' clergymen who led services at St. Anne would not have known the parish or its inhabitants particularly well. It would therefore have been much easier for Sir Henry senior to have his children baptised there at St. Anne's – with few questions asked – than anywhere else, and a proven church baptism was probably enough to make the outside world believe that a child must be legitimate.

It is only possible to speculate on what actually happened to Winifred Losse, however. Judging by the fact that she and Sir Henry married when the latter was around 31 years old but that they had had no children by the time he was forty, it is probable that she was sterile. Perhaps her infertility had been practically proven, since Neville junior was later to say that he had about 11 brothers[148] who, however, have never been counted as sons of either Winifred Losse or Elizabeth Gresham. Perhaps, Ophelia-like, Winfred retired to a nunnery, or similar institution, at last leaving Neville senior free to re-marry, though in 'settlement' only. Such happenings would indeed explain why the whole Office of the Revels would have been sympathetic enough to keep the secret of Sir Henry's new affair and resultant children. Sir Thomas Cawarden, Master of the Revels, was a friend of Henry Neville senior, and seven years had elapsed between the birth of Henry's first child and his 'settlement marriage' to her mother. 'Seven years' might itself be significant: after precisely such a lapse of time, a missing person is presumed dead, thus leaving a spouse free to re-marry; it was also a long enough period of time for an injured party to divorce someone for desertion. But under the laws then existing, none of these possibilities could have legitimated our young Henry Neville: it was a family secret which had to be kept in perpetuity.

Indeed, the strange inscription on the Neville Tomb in St. Lawrence's Church at Waltham St. Lawrence suggests that later generations of the Neville family may have attempted to continue this 'cover-up'. The Tomb's inscription has several strange features. Firstly, it is very difficult to work out its semantics:

> Here lyeth Buryed SR Henry Nevill knight, descended of the Nevills Barons of Abergavenny who were a branch of the House of Westmorlande. He was (besyde martial services) of the Privie Chamber to Henry The 8 and Edward 6. He died in January Ao 1593. Issue he had only by Elizabeth sole Heyer to Sr John Gresham Knight by Dame Frances sole Heyer to Sr Henry Thwaites Knight Which Dame Elizabeth died 6 November 1573. Dame Frances are both here allso buryed with Elizabeth Nevill the oldest daughter.

The above is in fact understandable, except for the last sentence. Dame Frances refers to Frances Thwaites, Elizabeth Gresham's mother, and so it must be assumed that she came to live with her daughter and son in law after she was widowed. However, this fact neither explains the strange semantics, nor the effigies which appear above the inscription. Here, there is a representation of Sir Henry senior, with two ladies grouped side by side behind him. Of course, the inscription wishes us to assume that one of these ladies is Elizabeth Gresham, while the writing also guides the reader into believing the other figure represents either his mother in law or his daughter. But, again, this is strange, since it is usually the case that the effigy of a daughter would be placed either well behind or below her parents, and it is altogether out of the ordinary that an effigy of a mother in law should appear on the tomb at all. It looks very much as if the person who ordered this inscription was trying desperately to account for the effigies of the two/three women seen directly behind the effigy of Sir Henry, Senior. The inscription also makes the point that he had 'issue' only by Elizabeth Gresham. But absences speak as loudly as presences: nowhere does it state that Elizabeth Gresham was Sir Henry's wife, and nowhere does it mention Winifred Losse who, however, is officially listed as his wife (in the annals of Parliament)[149]. Yet the fact that the two female effigies are placed side by side suggests two wives of Sir Henry senior are buried here. If Winifred had simply died young, then surely she would have been recorded in the inscription itself. If, however, she outlived Sir Henry senior, then she could indeed have been buried eventually in the tomb alongside Sir Henry.

It is therefore beginning to look as if poor Winifred may have been 'set aside' for some unknown reason. It is, moreover, impossible that one of the ladies on the tomb could represent Elizabeth Bacon-D'Oyly – Sir Henry's third wife – since she outlived him and is buried in Henley on Thames with her third husband, Lord Periam. One wonders if the Neville Monument inscription itself was actually written long after Sir Henry and his household had died, perhaps in order to perpetuate the myth of the legitimacy of his children. There is perhaps some artificial ageing in the form of language used; for instance, it is strange that the word 'Buryed' in the first line begins with a capital letter. Capital letters were normally used for nouns only, during the 16th 17th and 18th centuries, just as is customary in present-day German. Also, the term 'oldest daughter' sounds distinctly more 19th or 20th century, since 'first-born' was the common usage before that time. Indeed, 'Shakespeare' never used the term in connection with a family relationship. Additionally, Sir Henry senior is described as having died 'in January Ao 1593'. This cannot be *Elizabethan* Calendar dating by the Church, otherwise it would have been termed as '1592', Sir Henry Senior being known to have died in 1593 according to the *new* calendar only. As Church dating was numbered in what was known as 'Old Style', where the new year started only in March, it is likely that a *later generation* would have written this kind of date. Nineteenth century genealogists were researching the Nevilles, so some of the inscription itself may have been placed there in the hope of preventing further investigations.

In an 1846 edition of *The Gentleman's Magazine,* Lord Braybrooke (the then owner of Billingbear House) wrote a stern reply to a Mr. Doyly-Bale who suggested that Sir Henry Neville senior had been married *three* times. Braybrooke insisted that Neville's only wives had been Elizabeth Gresham and Elizabeth Bacon-Doyly.[150] It can be seen from this that Lord Braybrooke quoted only Neville historians and the 'evidence' of the Neville Monument to substantiate his case that no wife existed prior to Elizabeth Gresham. It could be argued, however, that it would have been far easier to pretend that the first wife had died, as it is highly unlikely that such an eminent, eligible, handsome man as Sir Henry Neville senior would not have been initially married off at a much younger age than when he 'married' Elizabeth Gresham, already in his forties. It could be, therefore, that there may be evidence - somewhere - that Winifred Losse actually died at a date later than Sir Henry senior's alliance with Elizabeth Gresham. Finally, there is proof that the then Lord Braybrooke was either covering a secret or else very confused: he declares in his letter (see endnote, numbered above) that the effigies on the tomb are of Sir Henry's *two* wives. But Braybrooke names only two ladies - 1)Elizabeth Gresham and 2)Elizabeth Bacon-D'Oyly - and the latter simply cannot be represented on Neville senior's tomb, since we know that Elizabeth Bacon was not buried in the Neville Monument but with her third husband in Henley on Thames Parish Church. Indeed, there still exists a splendid monument there to her memory. Neville senior must therefore have had two other wives buried with him, one of whom was Elizabeth Gresham, and another whom Lord Braybrooke refuses to acknowledge, even though other researchers named her as Winifred Losse.

So what could have been going on? Before the Settled Land Act of 1925, successive owners of Billingbear House and its extensive lands could well have feared that their inheritance might be handed to another branch of the family, had the illegitimacy of Sir Henry Neville senior's children ever have been suspected. The 1925 statute, however, strengthened the rights of those actually in **possession** of land, therefore going a long way towards preventing would-be claimants raking up ancient historical reasons for a better right to property. Before that date, however, the Nevilles would have had the strongest of all possible reasons for not wishing the spotlight to be turned on that era in the family's history, with our Sir Henry himself having been especially cautious about allowing his name to appear on any publication whatsoever.

Above a second, blank plaque on the Neville Memorial there are effigies of another man and woman. These very probably represent our Sir Henry and his wife, Anne Killigrew-Neville. It could be asked why Anne would be buried here and not with her second husband, George Carleton – Neville's old friend. The answer is that she seems to have outlived them both and so would probably have chosen to be buried with the man by whom she had known issue. As for the plaque being left blank, one wonders whether there might not be two reasons behind this fact. Firstly, it is just possible (as discussed in the previous chapter) that Anne finally took Sir Henry at his word when he wrote her sonnets telling her to forget him, because he thoroughly expected not to survive his Tower experience. We know that she had at least one child during the time he was imprisoned and, if David Hume is to be believed, Neville was so persecuted during this time that he would not have been allowed visitors.[151] Neville even writes to tell Winwood that he 'cannot requite my love', and Anne writes many letters to the Queen, begging that 'Mr. Neville' might be restored to her and the children. She would surely hardly have been so fervent, had she and the children been allowed visitation rights. So, altogether, it seems rather difficult to imagine that the child born to Anne over a year after Henry entered the Tower, was his. But if this were the case, Henry would have understood the situation and accepted the child as his own. Yet such a circumstance would have made it difficult for Henry's children to be mentioned on the tombstone.

The second reason for the empty plaque may be that the inscription placed on Shakespeare's tomb might indeed have been meant for Sir Henry. Its references - which speak of Socrates and Nestor - seem much more appropriate to Sir Henry than to Shakespeare.

But whatever the circumstances of the situation, there is no doubt that our Sir Henry was brought up surrounded by the Revels and the Theatre. By 1576 the widowed Sir Henry senior saw to it that some of his Blackfriars property was re-let to his 'dramatic' friend, Richard Farrant. In 1564 Farrant had become Master of the Children of Windsor[152], so he obviously then had a home quite close to Billingbear. In 1576 Farrant also became Deputy Master of the Children of the Chapel, having in 1567 begun a series of Court plays with the Windsor Children[153]. This means that, besides spending his young years next to the Office of the Revels, our Sir Henry had probably continued to know the company of 'theatrical' men and children even after going to live in Berkshire. Farrant was close enough to Sir Henry senior to be allowed to lease rooms at Blackfriars under his recommendation, and it was these rooms which he ultimately converted into the first Blackfriars Theatre, which was where the Windsor Children then gave their first *public* performances. Young Sir Henry must already have seen these children at work in Windsor, so which 12/14 year old boy would not have begged his father to take him back on visits to his Blackfriars birthplace just to see how the new Theatre was coming along? After all, Sir Henry senior still had some rooms left there. Besides, he now had a new wife – Elizabeth Bacon Doyly – who could oversee the care of the younger children back in Billingbear. Indeed, it is not unlikely that Sir Henry senior had quite a big say in the office of the Revels. Between 1573 and 1579 there was only an 'acting' Master of the Revels, so presumably this meant he was only expected to perform a limited number of the tasks. As Cawarden's friend, and a known deviser of entertainments, Sir Henry Neville senior would have been the very man to call upon for assistance. Besides, he then still possessed the remainder of his Blackfriars property situated right by the office of the Revels.

The word 'black' had therefore signalled the beginning of Henry junior's life – he was not born at Billingbear but at **Black**friars. The secrecy he must later have been told to retain concerning his origins would always be associated with Blackfriars, the Theatre and his mother. The theatre itself would therefore easily become yet another of his alluring 'Dark Ladies' – dark enough to stand alongside, and to symbolise, his mother's dark secret. The public Theatre reeked every bit as much as the Dark Lady's breath in Sonnet 130. Besides, the theatre district of London was itself then situated next to the brothel district, so it tended to suffer by association. Black Luce and her cohorts would have been at the back of people's minds whenever the theatres were mentioned.

The impact of these new discoveries on the interpretation of the plays

It is at last explicable that (as Sir Frank Kermode says) 'Shakespeare' shows an inside knowledge of the Theatre even in his very early plays, especially in *King John*.[154] This means that we can now dare to date *King John* as having been written during the threat of invasions by the Spanish Armadas. Though the play may not have been written before the actual 1588 invasion, it has to be remembered that the Earl of Essex and a certain Henry Neville went to Spain in 1596 to burn the ships in Cadiz harbour - the Spanish navy was being built up to produce another Armada in order to attack England again. This would date the play as being meant for performance in 1595 at the latest. Indeed, King Phillip of France utters the word 'armado' in Act 3   Sc.IV :

King Philip So, by a roaring tempest on the flood
A whole armado of convicted sail
Is scattered and disjoined from fellowship.

Some scholars have therefore been tentatively suggesting this early dating of the play for years – and their suggestions are based on a logical reading of this very patriotic, rousing text. Yet by assuming that the play was written before 1596 we are saying that 'Shakespeare' must have had inside knowledge of both politics and the Theatre by that early date. This is why scholars have been so tentative about their otherwise logical conclusion – there is no evidence that the Stratford boy ever saw a theatre at such an early time in his life. But now Sir Henry is put in the place of William Shakespeare, we need be tentative no longer. Everything is explained: the dating of the play, its imagery, characterisation and politics all add up to Sir Henry Neville – M.P. since the age of about twenty one - and to no one else. But in order to understand the various reasons that prompted Sir Henry to write *King John* at such an early age, it is necessary to look at further episodes which influenced the young artist's life.

By the time he was around 18 years old, young Sir Henry Neville undoubtedly began to meet with dark ladies in new, unfamiliar settings. He was then heading for Venice. I am able to say he 'undoubtedly' met dark ladies there because the iron and cannon industry of that city had been centred on the ghetto – the very area where the Jews were forced to live at the time – and Neville was taking a European 'study tour' partly in preparation for his coming role as an iron and ordnance manufacturer. (The word 'ghetto' was itself a Germanicised version of 'getto' - from gettare, to throw, or cast. Cannons were once cast in this part of the city mainly by immigrant German Jews, and the fact that Shylock had once been in Frankfurt is actually mentioned in *The Merchant of Venice.*) By Neville's time, the Venice cannon works had been moved to the Arsenale, but access to this was very restricted. Thus, Neville's best plan would have been to visit the site of the *old* iron forges and cannon works in the ghetto, in the hope of questioning the Jews there about their memories of iron working. Altogether, Neville's Tour was to prove seminal to all his later creative activities – in every area of his life.

I have discussed some Shakeespearean threads connecting with Sir Henry's European tour in *The Truth Will Out,* but I shall here concentrate on a new aspect of my research – the discovery that Neville must have visited Denmark.

Neville was accompanied on his tour by his kinsman and tutor from Merton College, Oxford, Sir Henry Savile, the mathematician, astronomer and Platonist. He enlisted Neville's services in searching for ancient Greek manuscripts. The Platonism and knowledge of Greek legends (especially evident in Shakespeare's later plays) no doubt have their origins in this early shared interest. Their shared sojourns with leading European humanists of the day contributed to the great humanism in Shakespeare's Works.[155] But what was it that initially prompted the Oxford group to stray from England, and from Oxford academia, for so long? Who might have funded their meandering, expensive journey? The answers to these questions lead down a trail that begins with Gresham cannons destined for Elsinore[156] – the setting of *Hamlet.* Neville once more is clearly evidenced as the only Authorship Contender in which all the seemingly-disparate strands within the plays are united, and this particular strand opens with a dying relative and a shipwreck.

In 1578, Neville's great uncle, Sir Thomas Gresham, was fading fast. The years of incessant business dealings at home and abroad had certainly taken their toll. Nevertheless, he had reaped the rewards of his endless toil: he had grown extremely rich, but he had no legitimate children who could benefit from his prosperous 'empire'. Thus, the young Henry, freshly emerged from University, was in the enviable position of being one of Sir Thomas' chief heirs. To him Gresham had willed his iron and ordnance business[157]. Gresham's frailty now dictated that young

Henry should begin to take over, and there was already an urgent situation emerging. The Danish King Frederick II had been buying cannons from all over Europe in order to enforce rights over a very profitable shipping lane, and some of those cannons had been purchased from Gresham's ironworks in Sussex. King Frederick built a fortress from which to command the Oresund Straits, so that he could levy customs from all shipping that passed through that strip of sea between Denmark and Sweden. Cannons were therefore important artefacts in his grand, if aggressive, designs.

However, the Gresham cannons shipped out to him in 1578 never arrived. Through archaeological explorations carried out in 2003[158], it is now known that the ship carrying these cannons sank in the Thames estuary. The shipwreck may well have been known at the time too, but the lack of mechanical recovery aids would have prevented its heavy cargo from being retrieved.

The size of the cannons already recovered from the Thames' wreck demonstrates that King Frederick's custom was too important to be lost. The very rich Sir Thomas Gresham would certainly have been willing to fund an expensive tour in order for his heir to maintain the Danish business, and for him to view ordnance design and manufacture throughout Europe. Gresham had received two licences to export ordnance to Denmark – in 1574 and 1578[159]. It was this latter shipment which went down, and too much to be mere coincidence that Henry Neville began his continental tour that very same year. Indeed, he must have dutifully studied the design of cannons wherever he went, for later in his career we find him exporting his own cannons to the Low Countries, and these were his own invention, based on a French design called the Falconette.

Gresham also exported bar iron, and this too was found aboard the wrecked ship. The largest iron product manufacturers, like Gresham, based their trading in London, even though their manufacturing was carried out in Kent and East Sussex. The bars were either brought to London overland to be shown to foreign customers or to begin their journey along the Thames and out to sea. Or sometimes the bars started their export journey by sea from the Port of Rye (one of the Cinque Ports, of which Henry Neville was entitled to be called a baron.) Later, Sir Henry Neville traded his iron in London too, and, significantly, the base he chose for this purpose was the

Talbot Inn, next to the Globe Theatre.[160] Gresham actually died in 1579 while Neville was still on his tour, so from the time of his return to England in 1583, Neville became involved in manufacturing an increasing number of cannons for the Cinque Ports, as part of the preparations to defend against the 1588 Spanish Armada.[161] No doubt he viewed this role and his later assistance in Cadiz as having 'laid great bases for eternity' (see Sonnet 125.)[162] Little wonder, then, that Neville always tried to export his cannons to the Protestant North in Europe rather than the Catholic South, and little wonder that Gresham – an ardent Protestant with an export business based partly in Antwerp – would have felt it quite urgent that Neville should go to Denmark to re-establish confidence with the Protestant King there.

All this being the case, 'Elsinore' was probably one of Neville's first stops on the continent. In fact, King Frederick's castle was called 'Kronborg', and the port itself 'Helsingor', so it is not difficult to see that only someone who had actually travelled there (or heard of it through a direct connection, such as Gresham) could have invented the name 'Elsinore' in *Hamlet.* Frederick's great, forbidding fortress would naturally have come to Neville's mind whenever he saw the Tower of London. Then, after the Essex rebellion, the Tower began to look like his ultimate destination, meaning the connections between it and the Helsingor fortress would have become gloomily twinned in Neville's mind and heart. It was during Neville's time in the Tower that *Hamlet* was written.

Illegitimacy and Cannons

Cannons themselves were a physical presence linking Helsingor and the Tower in which Neville was now imprisoned, and it is the word 'cannon' which affords an insight into the workings of the true writer's mind at these two separated points in his life. 'Cannon' is a word used in many of the plays – and even in *Lucrece* – but its most frequent and repeated use occurs in two plays: *Hamlet* and *King John.* For the first time, then, we can see the writer's mental connectionism across time, and begin to examine the writer's various reasons for perceiving these links between those two plays. Following on from this, comparisons between further contents of the plays themselves will perhaps enable us to perceive new points concerning their dating, and their ideology.

The nature of the final speech in *King John* (c.1595) leads to the conclusion that it was written partly as a rallying call for all Englishmen to unite and face the great force of shipping being built up once more in the Spanish main:

Bastard. ...This England never did, nor never shall,
　　　　Lie at the proud foot of a conqueror
　　　　But when it first did help to wound itself.
　　　　Now these her princes are come home again,
　　　　Come the three corners of the world in arms
　　　　And we shall shock them. Naught shall make us rue
　　　　If England to itself do rest but true.

The words therefore echo the spirit of the day. It is very interesting too that the writer gives this last speech to 'Bastard.' This was Phillip, illegitimate son of Lady Falconbridge (or Fauconberg, or Faulconbridge) and Richard I. The Fauconbergs were ancestors of the Nevilles, (just as were the Longuevilles, a variant on which name appears in another early play – *Love's Labour's Lost.*) Moreover, another, later kinsman of Sir Henry Neville's was also known as The Bastard of Fauconberg. This was Thomas, the illegitimate son of William Neville of Fauconberg, Earl of Kent. This latter 'bastard' was in fact a cousin of Richard Neville, Earl of Warwick (known as the Kingmaker) whom 'Shakespeare' was to place prominently in his Henry VI plays. Like Richard Neville, Thomas was apt to change sides in the War of the Roses, ultimately becoming a Yorkist along with the Kingmaker himself.

Why, then, did Sir Henry place words advocating English **unity** in the mouth of one whose name must have echoed 'Civil War' in the minds of those few people in the audience who knew something of the Wars of the Roses? Firstly, the young Henry Neville was now attempting to produce a new public image for his own family. The Nevilles had played prominent parts in Civil strife, but Sir Henry – the writer - wished his and their name to become associated with an anti-civil war stance. At the same time, he wished to influence the theatre-going public to oppose all forms of civil war too. Moreover, he was always personally ambitious for the political role of Secretary of State – advisor to the monarch. Here, in *King John,* we are shown the first image on stage of a Neville-Plantagenet (viz. Phillip, the Bastard) falling into his 'natural' role as chief commentator on, and advisor to, the State. Richard Neville, Earl of Warwick, takes up this same mantel in *Henry VI,* parts 2 and 3, while in *Henry IV,* part 2, it is yet another

Neville who interprets Prince Hal's behaviour for the King[163]. But it was probably also Neville's knowledge of his own, technically illegitimate, origins that decided him to cast the 'Bastard' as the hero of *King John*. By giving the Bastard worldly-wise soliloquies and wise, patriotic speeches, young Henry was implicitly bolstering his own ego. Moreover, this particular 'bastard' had been openly accepted into the Falconbridge family earlier in the play, when the grandmother admits him as her true grandson. In just the same way, the Nevilles and Greshams must have covered up the circumstances of their first-born son's birth and agreed to accept him as one of their own.

In those days, the subsequent marriage of parents did not legitimize any previous children, so no wonder Henry Neville was rather reluctant to have spotlights turned upon him. If he had become a famous writer under his own name, it was to be expected that later researchers would look at his life closely, but if they did so, then Sir Henry's descendants would have stood a chance of losing their inheritance.

Now, discovering Sir Henry as the true writer (in an age where his family can no longer be harmed) has at last opened up the correct pathway to understanding the Shakespeare plays. Only now does it become possible to see the edifices along that avenue in their correct order and thus give them their true significance, for the first time. Indeed, near the beginning of *King John* we are given a hint of the Bastard's ancestry when he proclaims 'I come one way of the Plantagenets' (*King John*, V.vi.12). Henry Neville was directly descended from Edward III, so he too was a Plantagenet. It is therefore not stretching a point too far to say that the Bastard in the play spoke with the voice of the writer himself. As far as the audience is concerned, the Bastard's last speech transcends the historical time-line and speaks to them of the terrible civil wounds the country received during the Wars of the Roses. The Bastard is bemoaning the fact that England once did indeed 'wound itself', and this theme of feuding, framed in such a way that the audience laments it, becomes the backbone of the early History plays, and of *Romeo and Juliet*. The writer is, after all, a politician and a businessman who believes in, and needs, a united country in which to work.

Earlier in the play the Bastard utters a cry which might well come from Henry's own lips too, given the circumstances in which he was born some 4/7 years before his parents were married:

Bastard ...
    Heaven guard my mother's honour, and my land! (*Act 1, Sc.1*)

The writer certainly knew the then existing law on legitimacy:

King John Sirrah, your brother is legitimate;
    Your father's wife did after wedlock bear him,
    And if she did play false, the fault was hers -
    Which fault lies on the hazards of all husbands
    That marry wives.

Neville would definitely have known, therefore, that the fact of his own illegitimacy was not protected by the law outlined in this speech. Henry was not born to his father's official wife, Winifred Losse. For him, there could be no cover-up if the secret ever came to light: his mother was not married to his father when he was born. If the truth were ever known, then he would have been labelled as illegitimate by everyone, and forever, and this would automatically disinherit his children and their children, for as far ahead as Henry could possibly see. Had he been legitimate, however, he would probably have been born and baptised at Billingbear, in which case the young Henry would probably never have had such an early introduction to the theatre and Revels. His illegitimacy was inexorably bound up with his place of birth – Blackfriars and its Theatreland. No wonder, therefore, he sought out a 'frontman' from within the Theatre itself – and a frontman who was, at the same time, a distant kinsman of his. If William Shakespeare were ever, accidentally, to discover Sir Henry's identity, then he would have known Sir Henry was rich enough to reward him. William would have been left in no doubt that he stood and fell by Sir Henry's fortune. But should he ever be imprudent enough to give the secret away, then William and his theatre company would be investigated and the plays banned because of their identifiable political origin.[164] It would not therefore have been in Shakespeare's interest to reveal the secret.

    The question of whether Shakespeare, the actor, knew anything about the origin of the works published under his name is a vexed one. My own guess is that he probably did not, (though Professor Rubinstein insisted on placing the opposite point of view in *The Truth Will Out*.) I think it more likely that material was passed to Shakespeare through a network of contacts, as I explain in my Paper *Sir Henry Neville and the Iron*

Men of the Theatre.[165]. But the important point is that, whether he knew anything or not, it was in Shakespeare's own interest to keep quiet about it. After all, by the 17th century he was beginning to seek out ennoblement for himself and his family in the form of securing a Coat of Arms, and this scheme would certainly have come to naught, had his status as a mere frontman become publicly known. If he did indeed find out Sir Henry's identity, then there must often have existed a state of extreme tension between the two men.

As already mentioned, the word 'cannon' is employed most frequently in *King John,* but its usage in *Hamlet* comes a very close second. Altogether, there are 7 uses of the word 'cannon' or 'cannoneer' in the earlier play, and 6 in *Hamlet*. The word is again present in many of the other plays, even the Comedies. (Even though it exists only as a single usage in the other plays, however, the fact that it is used so frequently really does suggest that the writer found 'cannon imagery' coming to him in nearly every circumstance. This is hard to explain when any other authorship contender is viewed.) Its usage is perfectly explicable when we recognise Neville as the author. Henry returned from his continental tour in 1583, went on a diplomatic mission to Scotland with the Earl of Essex, and then came down to Mayfield in Sussex, where he saw to it that Gresham's cannon works continued producing ordnance, eventually changing their brand to 'Neville'. Neville therefore now produced cannons to defend the Cinque Ports, so it was hardly surprising that this artefact should be at the top of his mind when he wrote *King John.*

With Neville's presence, there are indeed observable, palpable links between the early play of *King John* and the later one, *Hamlet.* In both plays there is a claim that the monarch on the Throne is not there by true right. In Hamlet's case, it is an uncle that has gained the throne though murder, while King John was regent because his brother, King Richard, was away fighting in the Crusades. The point of the play is also that John continued in office, despite others having a better claim to the throne. A Neville writer would have been aware that his own then monarch – Queen Elizabeth Tudor – also had less right to the throne than members of his own family. The young Sir Henry would therefore have comforted himself with just such thoughts when he learned about his own illegitimacy. (If Queen Elizabeth could take the English throne - illegitimately, as far as many were concerned - then how could it be wrong for Neville himself to succeed to his father's and great uncle's possessions?) Thus did illegitimacy and all forms of inheritance become linked in his mind - and especially that of monarchical inheritance. In the case of *King John,* the play actually opens with a reference to the fact that King John is not a 'legitimate' King of England:

> **King John** Now say, Chatillon, what would France with us?
> **Chatillon** Thus, after greeting, speaks the King of France
> In my behaviour to the majesty,
> The borrowed majesty, of England here.
> **Eleanor** A strange beginning - "borrowed majesty".
> **King John** Silence, good mother; hear the embassy.
> **Chatillon** Philip of France, in right and true behalf
> Of thy deceased brother Geoffrey's son,
> Arthur Plantagenet, lays most lawful claim
> To this fair island and the territories,
> To Ireland, Poitiers, Anjou, Touraine, Maine,
> Desiring thee to lay aside the sword
> Which sways usurpingly these several titles,
> And put the same into young Arthur's hand,
> Thy nephew and right royal sovereign.

In both plays - *Hamlet* and *King John* - there is a brother reigning instead of the true King. In both plays this false-playing brother either murders or attempts to murder a kinsman who stands in his way. The mother of the character after whom the play is named is present in both too. In his book, *Shakespeare's Language,* Sir Frank Kermode does not note these overlapping *circumstances* of the two plays, but his specific study of their *language and characterisation* causes him to draw parallels. Kermode remarks that *King John* is a strange mixture of the old and the new when it comes to writing style and theatrical awareness. We can now add that this is precisely what one would expect if Neville wrote the play. He had seen 'old' style performances at Blackfriars, but his own experiences and studies made him aware of 'new' ideas, especially those emanating from the humanists he met on the continent. Neville's special area of study at Oxford had been astronomy – a subject which was then being flooded with 'new' controversial ideas and discoveries. Kermode therefore unconsciously and perceptively picks up a reflection of Sir Henry's spirit in both *King John* and *Hamlet.*

Hamlet contains references to 'infinite space'. This was a new concept which Neville's kinsman, Thomas Digges, had taught at Oxford. To Neville, therefore, the mixture of old families and new ideas came naturally. As Kermode says, the characterisation of the Bastard is completely new, and so is his quipping language, though this is surrounded by some 'old-style' speeches, such as the lament for Prince Arthur. (One cannot help remarking on what has now – with the discovery of Sir Henry – become obvious: Prince Arthur was a 'boy', and Neville had seen the 'boy' actors of the Chapel at work under Farrant, using 'old-style' speeches.)

Sir Frank also notes that King John's quasi-Protestant stance against the Pope is brought out as a *positive* element in the Play. (Again, there is simply no evidence that the real Shakespeare ever sided with Catholicism.) But the negative side of John's personality is brought out most strongly, and that negative concerns King John's nature as a murderer of the true inheritor to the throne. In *Hamlet*, Claudius too had murdered the true monarch, even though the audience is never presented with any evidence that he was a bad king for the State. Not only was this ambiguity of perception typical of Neville but if *King John* was written in around the late 1580s and early 1590s, then it was entirely **topical** as well. The controversy over Mary Queen of Scots was gaining more heat. Walsingham's campaign to impugn Mary with treason was well underway (see Chapter 2). Moreover, by 1585 Mary had been put into the 'care' of none other than Sir Henry Neville senior and Ralph Sadler, a diplomat who had spent much of his time in Scotland.[166] Sadler and Neville were reluctant to become Mary's jailers, and Sadler certainly had enough experience of Scotland and of Mary's sad situation to see both sides of the problem. Young Henry Neville had himself been on a mission to Scotland in 1583 and had also spent much of his European Tour in the company of Arthur Throckmorton, whose family were Catholic and had great sympathy with the Scottish Queen. The duality of perception regarding *King John* and Claudius, then, was one that young Neville himself often felt about most monarchs, and how he felt about religion too. Whereas the Catholic Cardinals are painted as bad lots in *King John* and in the *Henry VI* trilogy, Neville never did - in real life - assign this kind of bad nature to every Catholic. Mary, Queen of Scots, was executed in February, 1587, which left the English public – and Queen Elizabeth herself – with many ambivalent feelings. Everyone felt sorry for Mary on a personal level, but at the same time they disliked the thought of militant Catholicism and must now have felt that her death would be the spark that would light the Spanish Armada's course towards England, as indeed it did. *King John,* then, hit exactly the mood of the people throughout the late 1580s and 1590s.

A *physical* knowledge of the Theatre is also present in the play, (which is again just what one would expect from a writer with Sir Henry Neville's specific access to the building of the Blackfriars Theatre):

> **Bastard** By heaven, these scroyles of Angiers flout you, kings,
> And stand securely on their battlements
> As in a theatre, whence they gape and point
> At your industrious scenes and acts of death.
> Your royal presences, be ruled by me.
> Do like the mutines of Jerusalem:
> Be friends awhile, and both conjointly bend
> Your sharpest deeds of malice on this town.
> By east and west let France and England mount
> Their battering cannon, charged to the mouths,
> Till their soul-fearing clamours have brawled down
> The flinty ribs of this contemptuous city. ... *Act II, Sc.1*

There can be little doubt that, in the above text, the English and the French may stand for the Elizabethan audience's consciousness of Protestants and Catholics, while Angier represents Spain. What Catholics and Protestants are now being asked to do in effect, therefore, is to forget their differences for a while and stand up against Spain – their common enemy. What's more, they are being asked to do this by a 'Bastard' who is using theatrical imagery to embellish his point. Sir Henry Neville is definitely the man speaking for himself here!

When imprisoned after the Essex uprising, Neville must have therefore have begun to analyse how all his good intentions (so far as England was concerned) had been 'clean perverted.'[167] He would necessarily have mentally returned to the two most seminal experiences in his life – the European Tour and his Ironworks. 'Denmark's a prison', says Hamlet, and indeed that portion of Denmark which Neville must have visited on behalf of Gresham – the Helsingor Fortress - certainly resembled such an institution.

Ralph Berry's article *Shakespeare's Elsinore - place in 'Hamlet'* [168] very efficiently ties up the references in the play with the actual location. Berry argues that only someone who knew Kronborg Castle in the 1500s could have written it. 'The castle/palace was burned down in 1629, then rebuilt by Christian IV with a virtually unchanged exterior.' Once again, however, when Neville is placed in the equation, even more connections are explained. *Hamlet* actually opens with a scene on the battlements – the part of the fortress that Neville, the budding ordnance manufacturer, would have noticed first and foremost.

As far as characterisation goes, Hamlet – in his merrier moods - has something of the wit and confidence of the Bastard in *King John*. John describes the Bastard as 'madcap', and Hamlet too shows signs of a lack of equilibrium. Neville had encountered just such traits in the Earl of Essex. In *King John,* then, we find echoes of Neville's early encounters with the Earl. Neville would have known him through the Cecils, and then met him again on his diplomatic mission to Scotland in 1583. Thus, with the dating of *King John* now suggested as 1587-1595, we can infer that part of the Bastard's madcap spirit may well have been inspired by Essex. That Earl died proclaiming just the same irrepressible nature, dressing dramatically and quipping to the end. So Hamlet becomes yet another combination of Neville's intelligence and Essex's spirit – just like the Bastard in the earlier play.

Hamlet **and the Bible**

One great difference, however, between the plays of *King John* and *Hamlet* is that the latter contains a constant trail of images from the New Testament within its text. Again, this is what we might expect with Neville as the author, since before and after writing *Hamlet* Neville was involved with Savile in looking at early Christian history, and indeed working towards a new translation of the Bible[169]. Savile's magnum opus was a book about St. John Chrysostom, an early Saint of the Eastern Orthodox Church. Christianity in its various forms was therefore as much a part of Neville's and Savile's consciousness as their study of the Greek and Roman philosophies. In the first half hour of *Hamlet,* the reference to the cock crowing is reminiscent of Peter's betrayal of Jesus:

Re-enter GHOST.
    But soft, behold! Lo where it comes again!
    I'll cross it though it blast me. Stay, illusion.
    [GHOST spreads its arms]
    If thou hast any sound or use of voice,
    Speak to me.
    If there be any good thing to be done
    That may to thee do ease, and grace to me,
    Speak to me.
    If thou art privy to thy country's fate -
    Which happily foreknowing may avoid -
    O, speak.
    Or if thou hast uphoarded in thy life
    Extorted treasure in the womb of earth,
    For which, they say, your spirits oft walk in death,
    Speak of it, stay and speak!
    [The cock crows]

... **Barnardo** It was about to speak when the cock crew.

Horatio And then it started like a guilty thing
    Upon a fearful summons. I have heard
    The cock, that is the trumpet to the morn,
    Doth with his lofty and shrill-sounding throat
    Awake the god of day, and at his warning,
    Whether in sea or fire, in earth or air,
    Th' extravagant and erring spirit hies

The cock's crowing in the Bible signifies betrayal, and Hamlet's father has indeed been betrayed. But Neville was a man who had lived with forest people too, both at his early home of Billingbear on the outskirts of Windsor Forest, and in East Sussex, where his iron works was based. He knew of folklore and myths, as well as being familiar with the old Greek learning, and all this had taught him there was nothing new on Earth. Even Jesus' story had been pre-figured by older myths of goodness and betrayal, so Marcellus next gives a speech which shows the strange mixture of Christianity and paganism, thus reflecting the various aspects of Neville's erudition:

> **Marcellus** It faded on the crowing of the cock.
> Some say that ever 'gainst that season comes
> Wherein our Saviour's birth is celebrated,
> The bird of dawning singeth all night long,
> And then, they say, no spirit dare stir abroad,
> The nights are wholesome, then no planets strike,
> No fairy takes, nor witch hath power to charm,
> So hallowed and so gracious is that time.

The writer thus gives us a feeling that Christianity has not even yet truly won out. Neville, after all his studies, may well have been in two minds about its veracity, yet he never doubted its ethics. He lived by them; he was a Christian 'inwardly', as his father in law once commented in a letter to him[170]. Perhaps, however, this pagan/Christian dual-consciousness was what Neville blamed for all the terrible injustices and unchristian events that were then occurring in the State. Certainly, when it comes to the play of *Hamlet,* there is a whole war going on between Claudius' pagan wassailing and Hamlet's internalisation of the Christian ethic:

> **Hamlet** The king doth wake tonight and takes his rouse,
> Keeps wassail, and the swagg'ring up-spring reels,
> And, as he drains his draughts of Rhenish down,
> The kettle-drum and trumpet thus bray out
> The triumph of his pledge.
> **Horatio** Is it a custom?
> **Hamlet** Ay, marry, is't,
> But to my mind, though I am native here
> And to the manner born, it is a custom
> More honoured in the breach than the observance.
> This heavy-headed revel east and west
> Makes us traduced, and taxed of other nations.
> They clepe us drunkards, and with swinish phrase
> Soil our addition; and indeed it takes
> From our achievements, though performed at height,
> The pith and marrow of our attribute.

Then the writer goes on to draw a parallel, which begins with a comparison that is truly relevant to Neville's own situation:

So, oft it chances in particular men
That for some vicious mole of nature in them,
As in their birth, wherein they are not guilty,
Since nature cannot choose his origin,
By their o'ergrowth of some complexion,
Oft breaking down the pales and forts of reason,
Or by some habit that too much o'erleavens
The form of plausive manners, that these men,
Carrying, I say, the stamp of one defect,
Being nature's livery or fortune's star,
His virtues else, be they as pure as grace,
As infinite as man may undergo,
Shall in the general censure take corruption
From that particular fault. The dram of evil
Doth all the noble substance of a doubt
To his own scandal.

Thus does Neville sum up not only Denmark's, Claudius' and Hamlet's case but also his own. Neville was obviously very conscious of his illegitimacy. The very first simile he chooses to underline his meaning in this speech of Hamlet's is of someone whose 'birth' has flaws in it. Claudius too had suffered a birth problem: he was the second son, not the first. From this one flaw – which, like Neville's own birth, was no fault of his own - the rest of his actions and character took their origins.

The Ghost's oration also contains several passing references to phrases used in the King James version of the Bible. Sir Henry Savile oversaw this translation, and since the 1590s he had been asking several English diplomats abroad to use their good offices to try and obtain certain manuscripts which might help him in his project.[171] Just as Sir Henry Neville had been at Eton with Savile assisting him with John Chrysostom, he must have been helping him with the Bible project too, and the references he uses in *Hamlet* appear to underline this assertion. It is often said that some of the Biblical translations in the Authorised Version resemble Shakespeare's language, though until Neville was placed in the picture it was impossible to see how this could have been the case. However, if we look at some of the Ghost's language and imagery – and even some references made by young Hamlet himself – there is little doubt that the writer had in mind passages from Revelations and from certain other books of the Bible too.

To begin with, we have the Ghost's intonation of 'Horrible, horrible, most horrible'.[172] The word 'horrible' is surprisingly little used in the Bible, but many in the audience at the time would have been well-versed in some of the translations then extant – especially the Geneva Bible - which enjoyed a great sale throughout England. 'Horrible' appears only six times, but at least one of those six references had reason to find its echoes in the minds of both Neville and the audience. It occurs in Jeremiah Chapter 18, in which there is a warning of 'Judgments threatened to Judah for her strange revolt.' This was of course relevant to the Essex revolt which had just taken place. But the passage also condemns 'the virgin of Israel'

> Therefore thus saith the Lord; Ask ye now among
> the heathen, who hath heard such things: the virgin
> of Israel hath done a very horrible thing.
> *Jeremiah, Chap. 18, verse 13*

For those who understood the political significance of this reference, therefore, there was a double message: the revolt against Elizabeth was wrong, but she herself – the Virgin Queen – was not blameless. She was surely yet another of Neville's 'Dark Ladies.' She had done **two** 'horrible' things in Neville's eyes: firstly, she had forbidden discussion of the monarchical succession, thus endangering the state, and secondly she had executed the Earl of Essex who, in fact, had led what would now be termed a civil protest rather than a bloody revolution. To have attracted the following of so many intellectuals and men who were truly concerned about the country's welfare, the Earl could not have been, ab initio, simply a 'madcap'. Even his performance at his trial – where he seemed to admit that his actions were provoked merely by personal ambition – could have been just as much an 'act' as was Essex's feigned madness. With Hamlet, the 'madness' had been assumed so that his presence at court might be ignored, in the hope that no one would suspect that he was all the while researching the guilt of his uncle and plotting his revenge. With Essex, the 'confession' of his own ambition, and his ridiculous blaming of his sister for allegedly encouraging him to believe it was possible he might become King, was probably a similar mere device. Essex wished to concentrate the minds of the prosecutors on *him* and away from his *supporters*, in the hope that they would then be freed. If the

Earl of Essex had been able to persuade the judges that he was acting alone, then his friends might be allowed to live. (In this context, it begins to look very much as if Essex's poor, blameless sister might have been cast in the role of Ophelia, who is perceived – erroneously – by some characters in the play as the source of Hamlet's madness.) If this is true, then Essex was certainly an embodiment of the Christian ethic in that he was willing to sacrifice himself for his friends. This may be the very reason for Neville now choosing to include so many (albeit oblique) Biblical references in this particular play.

The term 'prison house' is also used by the Ghost, and in the Bible. The Ghost says:

> ... But that I am forbid
> To tell the secrets of my prison-house
> I could a tale unfold whose lightest word
> Would harrow up thy soul, freeze thy young blood,
> Make thy two eyes like stars start from their spheres,
> Thy knotted and combined locks to part,
> And each particular hair to stand an end
> Like quills upon the fretful porcupine. *Act 1, Sc. 5*

Again, its use in the Bible is rather rare, there being only 4 instances. Perhaps the most telling is Isaiah, Chapter 42, verses 6 and 7, for it carries the theme of redemption, just as the Ghost now hopes to be redeemed by undergoing his purgatorial trials:

> I the Lord have called thee in righteousness,
> and will hold thine hand and will keep thee,
> and give thee for a covenant of the people, for
> a light of the Gentiles; To open the blind eyes,
> to bring out the prisoners from the prison, and
> them that sit in darkness out of the prison
> house.

Yet the Ghost's speech in tota resembles nothing so much as the spirit of a book from the New Testament – viz., Revelations. The Ghost alludes to the secrets and horrors of purgatory, and Revelations was written when the early Christian Church was undergoing severe trials, and was under pressure to express itself in secrecy too, just like Neville. Like the play of *Hamlet,* it had to carry a meaning but at the same time cloak it; and like the Ghost's speech, it was full of warnings about unspeakable horrors to come. Like Neville now writing in prison, the Church had to be simultaneously comforting, optimistic yet also cautionary. And that caution had to be expressed horrifically enough to ensure people would take due care in their actions yet still keep the faith. *Hamlet* opens with friends working together, so can be viewed as optimistic, though they hint at sinister happenings presaging what is to come. In the same way, Revelations hits a similar note of comfort and caution at its very start:

> Blessed is he that readeth, and they that hear
> the words of this prophecy, and keep those
> things which are written therein: for the time
> is at hand. ... Fear none of those things
> which thou shalt suffer: behold, the devil
> shall cast some of you into prison, that ye
> may be tried; and ye shall have tribulation ten
> days: be thou faithful unto death, and I will
> give thee a crown of life *Verses 3 and 10.*

Neville knew that eventually the Queen would die and that, with care on everyone's part, the King of Scotland would succeed her, just as the King of Norway succeeds to the Danish throne at the end of *Hamlet*. But he did not really expect to live to see this come about, so must have found comfort in those words from Revelations. To judge from the beginning of *Hamlet* and its hints at the cold weather and the coming of 'our saviour' Neville was optimistic that what the State was now undergoing was a period of Advent, therefore suggesting better times to come.

But Hamlet, like Neville, does not share this optimism for himself personally. His very first appearance is framed by melancholy and blackness. His first soliloquy concerns a wish for his own death:

Hamlet O that this too too solid flesh would melt,
 Thaw, and resolve itself into a dew,
 Or that the Everlasting had not fixed
 His canon 'gainst self-slaughter! O God, O God!
 How weary, stale, flat, and unprofitable
 Seem to me all the uses of this world!

There is surely little doubt that we are here listening to the voice of the dead Essex conjoined with Neville. Neville is the survivor, but undergoing similar imprisoned misery to that once suffered by his dead Earl, so he has no use for the world. And within this speech we also have the almost Joycean connectionism between the words: 'a dew' and the Ghost's 'Adieu, adieu, remember me'. Thus, in Neville's complex mind, the connections between words and homophones become connections in the real world. He is certainly making us alert to the fact we should be listening out for his choice of words and their internal and external textual resonances.

This being the case, we must certainly begin to ponder on Hamlet's use of the word 'Wormwood' when he is viewing the play within the play. The Player Queen is saying that if her husband died, then she would nevertheless stay true to him, and not marry again:

Player King Faith, I must leave thee, love, and shortly too.
My operant powers their functions leave to do;
And thou shalt live in this fair world behind,
Honoured, beloved; and haply one as kind
For husband shalt thou -
Player Queen O confound the rest!
Such love must needs be treason in my breast.
In second husband let me be accurst;
None wed the second but who killed the first.
Hamlet [Aside] Wormwood, wormwood.
Player Queen The instances that second marriage move
Are base respects of thrift, but none of love.
A second time I kill my husband dead,
When second husband kisses me in bed.
Player King I do believe you think what now you speak,
But what we do determine, oft we break.
Purpose is but the slave to memory,
Of violent birth, but poor validity;
Which now, the fruit unripe, sticks on the tree,
But fall unshaken when they mellow be.
Most necessary 'tis that we forget
To pay ourselves what to ourselves is debt.
What to ourselves in passion we propose,
The passion ending, doth the purpose lose.
The violence of either grief or joy
Their own enactures with themselves destroy.

There are so many levels of action pertaining here. First and foremost, Hamlet wishes Claudius and his mother to see themselves reflected in these stage characters. After all, Hamlet himself has had a hand in the text of the play. At this point, he wants his mother to repent of her action in marrying Claudius after his father's death. But it is also true that Neville's own situation is paralleled here too. He has been placed in gaol for an indefinite time; he does not expect to survive the experience and, just like the Player King, he has told his wife (in the Sonnets) to forget him. But the word 'wormwood' could seem an odd aside for Hamlet to use. Not even the Arden edition of *Hamlet* attempts to explain it. However, read in conjunction with either the Geneva or the Authorised version of the Bible, it is strangely resonant. Like some other Biblical references the writer uses in the play, it is found in Revelations:

> And the third angel sounded, and there fell a great star from heaven, burning as it were a lamp, and it fell upon the third part of the rivers, and upon the fountains of waters. And the name of the star is called Wormwood: and the third part of the waters became wormwood; and many men died of the waters, because they made bitter. *Chapter 8, vv. 10 and 11.*

By implication, here is a warning indeed. Perhaps Neville is hinting that Hamlet should remember that the Ghost told him not to bring distress to his mother. The 'wormwood' (bitterness) he feels at her actions should not be allowed to spread and poison others. But during the wife's speech in the Play within the Play the use of the word 'Wormwood' in Proverbs, 5, vv.3 and 4 is surely uppermost in Neville's and Hamlet's conjoined mind:

> for the lips of a strange woman drop as an honeycomb, and her mouth is smoother than oil: But her end is bitter as wormwood, sharp as a two edged sword.

There are similar uses of 'edged' and 'sword' in some earlier plays:

French King ...And, with spirit of honour edged
More sharper than your swords, hie to the
field. *Henry V*

La Pucelle I am prepared: here is my keen-edged sword,
Decked with five flower-de-luces on each
side, *Henry VI, 1*

Among other things, therefore, we may be nearing a conclusion that Savile and Neville had already translated large passages of the Bible together, even before James I gave his approval and took the kudos for the whole project. Or Sir Henry may simply have been reading the Geneva Bible - the forerunner of the Authorised Version – while he was imprisoned. Either way, Shakespeare's works are the product of a mind that has been accustomed to reading the Protestant rather than Catholic canon.

....

The inscription on Neville's portrait (now in Audley End house) reads: 'Everywhere without visible signs', which thus becomes a most appropriate description of his role in so many areas of life, and also encapsulates his concealment of his own identity, necessitated both by the circumstances of his birth, and by the areas of State Affairs in which he later moved. It is a quotation from Thucydides:

> *The whole earth is the tomb of heroic men, and*
> *their story is not graven in stones over their clay*
> *but abides everywhere without visible symbol,*
> *woven into the stuff of other men's lives.*

Neville, as Ben Jonson says of him, took care to make his 'lent life' good against the Fates.[173] He had therefore to hide his life within those to whom he lent it, and that included lending it to, and hiding it within, the characters he created in the plays themselves.

Chapter 12

THE LANGUAGE OF SHAKESPEARE AND NEVILLE

Language is itself a code, and without language there could be no codes. From the type of coding methods used in the Dedication to Shakespeare's Sonnets, we were able to form a partial profile of the person who could have constructed it. For instance, its basically mathematical construction gave away the fact that its compiler was interested in that particular subject. Furthermore, this code contained some ideas from a multiplication system. When the Sonnets were published, some aspects of the Dedication's particular coding methodology were known abroad but not in the British Isles, so the compiler had to be someone who had travelled on the continent. We were able to narrow this down further to someone who had visited Italy and also either Prague or Denmark, because these were countries where inventors whose methods had some bearing on the Dedication Code lived and worked.

In much the same way, a writer's construction of language leaves a trail too. Although it is possible for a skilled writer to vary his or her usage - in just the same way as it is possible for an encoder to base his work on different ideas - linguistic style and usage at least enables one to narrow down the field when searching for a profile of an unknown author, or when trying to work out whether two supposedly separate writers are in fact one and the same person.

Comparing the language of Shakespeare in his plays with that of Sir Henry Neville in his letters leads to some significant findings. However, they happen to share so many similarities of style, content, collocation and vocabulary that this single chapter can do nothing more than touch the surface of what I hope will eventually grow into an ongoing examination of various aspects of the topic.

The linguistic/computer analyses I have undertaken support the theory that Henry Neville was Shakespeare, but, in line with all such analyses and gathering of evidence, certain factors must be constantly borne in mind. When any formal linguistic analysis is attempted, it is always difficult to separate vocabulary from style, and style from content. This chapter will therefore occasionally allow one area to stray into another. But with the development of computer applications, word frequency analysis is one specific area of linguistic examination that has become easier and more accurate, so that this is the first test I shall attempt to apply to the subject.

Even before the computer was developed to its current advanced state, statisticians began to analyse texts from a word frequency point of view. They claim to have discovered that the frequency with which certain words are employed could be considered as a hallmark for a certain writer. Their claims have inevitably been debated and sometimes disputed, but their theories are now so easy to apply that this kind of analysis has become rather popular. The general consensus is that prepositional use is an especially tell-tale sign of a certain author. Experts begin by seeking out at least two passages for comparison in this respect. In the case of Shakespeare and Neville, therefore, one passage should be (reputedly) by Shakespeare and the other by Neville. However, the statisticians have been careful also to say that it is not worth even beginning to employ their methods unless *external* evidence already leads to a strong suspicion that the two passages under consideration might have been written by the same person. For example, it would be no use comparing a passage by Shakespeare with a passage by Tennyson in the hope of proving such a thesis, because Tennyson and Shakespeare were not contemporaries, even if their linguistic styles might occasionally overlap.

Where authorship is in doubt, analysts all affirm that, first and foremost, the *life* of the suspected author should contain a weight of knowledge and chronology which overlaps with that displayed in the *texts* of the pseudonymous author. Without such correlation it would of course be senseless to theorise that the two writers might be the same person. Thus, this total weight of external evidence must precede any linguistic analysis. Linguistic analysis can provide extra *support* for a historically-based, logical theory, but it can never be used as *primary* evidence. It cannot stand alone, so it cannot completely deny circumstantial, cultural and documentary evidence, although if two entirely different tones, or prepositional usage, or an entirely different vocabulary were consistently chosen by two authors, it would be very difficult to conclude that the two authors were one and the same person.

As with handwriting, linguistic style can change over time, even within the writing of the same person. But handwriting provides even less conclusive evidence of authorship than does linguistic usage. Scribes were often employed by those who could afford them, and sometimes whole passages of a writer's work could be edited by an assistant.[174] Moreover, every educated man at the time was taught several handwriting styles, and also taught how to disguise his handwriting. (We find Robert Cecil praising Neville's messenger and scribe in France [Aurelian Townsend], for instance, for his mastery of 'different hands'.[175] But, as with handwriting, linguistic style can be altered, imitated or disguised at will, whereas it is impossible to 'fake' true background knowledge gained through particular, individual experience at a particular juncture in time. In other words, it is the total, combined weight of the macroscopic evidence which counts, not that gained solely by staring down a microscope. The type of evidence to be expected in a four hundred year old case will obviously not be of exactly the same order as that to be gathered at a five hour old scene of crime! When one, minute piece of material is separated from all the rest then taken as overwhelmingly indicative in any investigation, injustices and wrong conclusions may follow, so it is always a good idea to keep the whole picture in mind when looking at any thesis, of whatever age.

Linguistic analysis therefore tends to tunnel the vision. It certainly is more multi-faceted than merely studying handwriting, but nevertheless it is still an instrument which must be used with care. Whenever a linguistic analysis is attempted, certain ground rules must always apply. First and foremost, the passages chosen should be carefully selected: they should be similar in content and intended function.

In the case of Neville and the Shakespeare texts, overlapping chronology, knowledge and opinion are there in plenty, but we have the problem that Neville's only known writing is in the form of his private and diplomatic letters. We are fortunate that he produced a tremendous weight of the latter, but the problem is that the *function* of Neville's known writing is therefore very different from that of the plays of Shakespeare. There is the added difficulty that Neville writes in prose, whereas the largest part of the plays consists of iambic pentameters.

But even when all this is taken into consideration, it is often possible to perceive a balance and rhythm beneath Neville's known writing which itself rings with an almost poetic resonance. This is a topic I shall return to later. But it was indeed a difficult task to find a passage from both authors that overlapped in their *function*. And even when I finally found two pertinent passages, they were shorter than I would have liked. Experts stress that the material should be of sufficient *quantity* if it is really going to lead to anything approaching a definite conclusion on its own. In other words, data has ideally to be functionally similar, and sufficient in quantity.

Yet the analysis I made can be labelled an interesting phenomenon – at very least. And if taken together with all the other evidence – just as the experts advise – it becomes one more piece in the jigsaw's picture.

I began by looking for a passage from Shakespeare that was not from any play. Letters of Dedication precede his *Rape of Lucrece* and *Venus and Adonis,* and it is the form of the 'letter' which represents Neville's known body of writing, so this seemed the most logical area upon which to focus. Luckily, Shakespeare also wrote an 'Argument' to introduce his *Lucrece.* He was therefore telling a story in prose – which is precisely what Neville does in many of his news-based Diplomatic dispatches. It was for these reasons that I examined Shakespeare's own preamble to *Lucrece:*

THE ARGUMENT

Lucius Tarquinius, for his excessive pride surnamed Superbus, after he had caused his own father-in-law Servius Tullius to be cruelly murdered, and, contrary to the Roman laws and customs, not requiring or staying for the people's suffrages, had possessed himself of the kingdom, went, accompanied with his sons and other noblemen of Rome, to besiege Ardea. During which siege, the principal men of the army meeting one evening at the tent of Sextus Tarquinius, the King's son, in their discourses after supper everyone commended the virtues of his own wife; among whom Collatinus extolled the incomparable chastity of his wife Lucretia. In that pleasant humour they all posted to Rome; and intending by their secret and sudden arrival to make trial of that which everyone had before avouched, only Collatinus finds his wife, though it were late in the night, spinning amongst her maids; the other ladies were all found dancing and revelling, or in several disports. Whereupon the noblemen yielded Collatinus the victory, and his wife the fame.

At that time Sextus Tarquinius, being inflamed with Lucrece' beauty, yet smothering his passions for the present, departed with the rest back to the camp; from whence he shortly after privily withdrew himself, and was, according to his estate, royally entertained and lodged by Lucrece at Collatium. The same night he treacherously stealeth into her chamber, violently ravished her, and early in the morning speedeth away. Lucrece, in this lamentable plight, hastily dispatcheth messengers, one to Rome for her father, another to the camp for Collatine.

They came, the one accompanied with Junius Brutus, the other with Publius Valerius; and finding Lucrece attired in mourning habit, demanded the cause of her sorrow. She, first taking an oath of them for her revenge, revealed the actor and whole manner of his dealing, and withal suddenly stabbed herself. Which done, with one consent they all vowed to root out the whole hated family of the Tarquins; and, bearing the dead body to Rome, Brutus acquainted the people with the doer and manner of the vile deed, with a bitter invective against the tyranny of the King; wherewith the people were so moved that with one consent and a general acclamation the Tarquins were all exiled, and the state government changed from kings to consuls.

The ending of the passage contains the very *political* statement that 'the state government changed from kings to consuls' and this was something that coincided with Neville's ideas, and with his profession as a diplomat and politician. I could therefore think of no more appropriate passage from Shakespeare to light upon in my quest to be able to compare like with like. I noticed straight away that the Shakespeare extract used the same kind of sentence length as Neville's general rule in his diplomatic letters. Regarding its *style* too, it bore the hallmarks of several of Neville's political dispatches, a most cogent one being as follows:

There happ'ned upon Corpus Christi Day last at Limoges, a matter which doth easilye discover the Passion and Malice yet remayning in the Popish syde heere, against the Protestants. Certain Priests themselves went into the Churche in the Night, and brake down som Images, and (as they say) cast the Sacrament about the Churche. In the Morning, the People assembling, a great Exclamation was made by the Priests of this Outrage, and som principall Men of the Religion in that Towne, charged by Name to be the Doers of yt. The People by and by grew in Fury, and would have proceeded to the present Execution of them, taking Armes, as I am informed, for that purpose, and the other syde arming themselves likewise for theire Defence.

Monsieur de Saligna, Governor of the Towne, arriving and examining the matter, found that one of the Relligion was charged by Name to have bin an Actor in yt, who had bin in his Company all that Night. Whereupon, suspecting the matter, he caused som of the principall Accusers to be severely examined, and **namely one** offered to depose, that he had seene this Man there, whom Monsieur de Salignac knew to be absent. And threatening him with the Torture, drew the Confession from him of the whole Practice, and that they had done yt to the intent to move the People to a Sedition, and to have cut the Throats of them of the Relligion. Hereupon, som of them were apprehended and som fled. What justice will be don is muche expected ...

Letter to Robert Cecil, dated 6th June, 1599, Paris

In this particular letter, Neville is telling a story, just as is Shakespeare in his introduction to *Lucrece*. This was probably the closest I was going to get in finding two extracts which were functionally similar.

Even a quick reading of both passages demonstrates the very similar style of the two excerpts. On further analysis, extra confirmation appears: firstly, there is an identical use of some less usual nouns – 'Passion' and 'Actor' appearing in both of them. Most interestingly too, Neville's dispatch contains the word 'torture' which is said to have been a word used first by Shakespeare - in stanza 184 of *Lucrece*. Then there is a tell-tale use of the same prepositions – all factors which linguistic experts find very convincing. In this case, it is the word 'Whereupon' that is similarly used. (It was, significantly, the word 'upon' that gave away which of two possible authors had written a certain article concerning the Constitution of the U.S.A. [176] Indeed, the computer/language analysts involved with this investigation laid down the basic rules for applying statistical analyses to language, and it is their precepts which I have followed throughout.)

It is possible to subject the first two paragraphs of the *Lucrece* introduction and the above 'Dispatch Story' to statistical analysis, since both contain about 250 words each. Ideally, we would have passages of 1,000 words each, but in this case it is difficult to find functionally similar passages containing such a large number of words.

We can begin by looking at the small, frequently-used words, then go on to the less common ones. Statisticians advise that if significant correspondences are found, then such evidence would go to *support* historical and other external data. Looking at the table below, we can safely conclude that this evidence is indeed confirmatory:

word	Lucrece (frequency)	Dispatch story (frequency)
to	10	9
upon	0	1
also	0	0
and	10	13
this	1	2
of	8	9
though	0	1
on	0	0
whereupon	1	1
they	2	2
it (or yt)	1	3
actor	1 (in final paragraph)	1
passion	1	1
one	2	2
caused	1	1
done	1	2
principal	1	2

Of course, we are not exactly comparing like with like here, in that we are looking at the *beginning* of *Lucrece,* whereas the other extract is taken from half way through a Dispatch. It must be recognised too that the *message* would have taken precedence over *style* in the Dispatch, and that it would have therefore been less subjected to revisions.

Even so, there are clear stylistic correspondences with Shakespeare in this and other of Neville's letters. It is also significant that many of the words and phrases used by Neville in his dispatch occur frequently throughout the Shakespeare works. One favourite phrase is 'by and by' which is used in the above dispatch - and elsewhere in Neville's correspondence - as well as appearing 49 times in the Shakespeare works. As one further example - again from *Lucrece* - Shakespeare's 1593 Dedication of that work to the Earl of Southampton can be compared with extracts from a letter Neville wrote to that same Earl in c. 1604, begging his help to try and find money-making projects to recoup what he had lost on his expenses in France and in fines paid to Elizabeth following the Essex affair:

Shakespeare's Dedication

To the Right Honourable Henry Wriothesley, Earl of Southampton, and Baron of Titchfield.

The love I dedicate to your Lordship is without end; whereof this pamphlet without beginning is but a superfluous moiety. The warrant I have of your honourable disposition, not the worth of my untutored lines, makes it assured of acceptance. What I have done is yours; what I have to do is yours; being part in all I have, devoted yours. Were my worth greater, my duty would show greater; meantime, as it is, it is bound to your lordship, to whom I wish long life still lengthened with all happiness.

> Your lordship's in all duty,
> William Shakespeare.

Neville's Letter

Right Honourable and my very good Lord

Finding my self, either out of the inverility of my nature or the abundance of my love and respect unto your Lordship, which is ever accompanied with reticence and reverence, that I cannot so fully and freely expresse my self by speech unto your Lordship as my occasions require, I have adventured to do it by writing, humbly praying your favourable interpretation...

My professions and demonstrations of duty and service unto your Lordship, and to you only, being so open as all men that know me well take knowledge of it, I cannot entertaine any thought or feare that your Lordship stands any otherwise affected towards me than when you dismissed me at that time from your presence, as full of Joy as ever I was in my life.

...I have thus opened my want and my sute. It is in your power to suffer me to continue in necessyties and all the inferences that accompany it, or to releave me, as I conceave, with a word. The example cannot be ill ...in respect of your self, to do good to one that is so nearly tyed unto you by so many bonds. **And the lesse precedent merit there hath bin in me, the more noble will your favour be** and bind the more hereafter.

I can say no more, but that whatsoever it shall please your Lordship to do for me shall be receaved with an honest thankfull mind. And in that I compassed all offers and assurances of love, duty and service. And so praying humbly pardon of this boldness, I rest

Most ready and dutyful at your Lordship's Commandment

The same sentiments are expressed in both pieces of writing, and Neville certainly possesses the same emotional power in his words as Shakespeare. And notice the poetic alliteration - 'reticence and reverence', 'fully and freely...' It is lovely to see too that elsewhere in his long letter to the Earl, who definitely would have known about his writing (he was Neville's 'champion' and sometime patron) Henry includes a simile, which is a luxury he does not allow himself very often when merely writing to fellow diplomats and purely business associates:

> yet may my case be little better, if you stir me up no friends, than the poore cripple who lay long by the poole without cure for want of some to stir. This help I neither wish nor hope for from any but your Lordship.

(I have printed part of Neville's letter in bold because its opinion reminds one of Hamlet's feelings, similarly expressed, in Act 2 Sc.ii of that play) :

> Use them after your own honour and dignity; the less they deserve, the more merit is in your bounty.

Returning, however, to his ambassadorial dispatches, Neville sometimes begins these by stating his premises in a way that appears complex, yet condenses all the necessary meanings, just

240

as in the Introduction to *Lucrece*. Only later in his letter does his style begin to 'flow.' (This kind of 'slow start' happens especially when Neville is tired, depressed or unwell.) We may take as an example the opening of the letter from Neville to Cecil, dated 15th June, 1599, while Neville was suffering from jaundice:

> Yt may please you to remember, that at one of the last tymes I wayted upon you, I desyred to understand as muche of her Majestie's general Intentions as she would be pleased to think me worthie to be trusted with; to the end I might serve her the better in my Negotiations here, by directing them in particular, unto those generall Ends which she had proposed to her selfe. The Conveniency or rather Necessitie of which Course, doth daylie more and more discover yt selfe unto me. And that I may both explain my Meaning, and the Reason of that Proposition, I beseeche you give me leave to exemplifie yt in this matter of the Peace with Spaine;

This is very similar to the opening of the *Lucrece* 'Argument'. There is surely a parallel to this in *Henry V* and other early plays – and indeed some later ones too, especially the beginning *Cymbeline* – where the first scenes are of such a complexly condensed linguistic style that they are a little hard to grasp until one can view them in hindsight against the later text, as one watches the play. The device used to cloak this problem in *Henry V* is that of the Chorus' opening poetic declamation, which I presume would have been added by the author after he completed some of the main text. It is a master stroke by a man in a hurry! Neville was in Paris when putting final touches to the play (as I explain in *The Truth Will Out*) so he needed to complete it quickly, as he knew he must soon travel to Boulogne to attend the Treaty negotiations there. Since writing *The Truth Will Out*, a correspondent from Hanover University has informed me that he was already examining relative speech lengths in Shakespeare's plays when my book was published. He had noticed how they became generally shorter during and after the writing of *Henry V,* which, as he said, certainly could point to an author whose life-style had changed at that very moment. This was indeed the case with Sir Henry Neville.

It is sometimes as if our playwright's first ideas are hitting his mind and the page so much in parallel that they form a ball of thread that cannot be untangled until it has been first thrown intact. Indeed, Ben Jonson accused Shakespeare of such problems with his writing for the stage, saying that his ideas were often too complex, philosophical or poetic to be immediately understood by the audience. He claimed that Shakespeare's works were therefore often more poetry than drama, which is precisely what one would expect from an author who was so highly educated and was also constrained to follow another profession, and thus able to attend stage performances only fitfully, once daily work intruded. They are surely *not* the kind of plays one would expect to be written by an *actor,* who would have constant contact with the stage and thus be gaining constant feedback from his fellows. Yet *Shakespeare* was an actor, while Neville was basically a politician and lawyer – eventually becoming a sometime judge in the Star Chamber – concerned above all with helping to draft Statutes[177], with civil rights, responsibilities and Justice, which could be worked out through the arts of Rhetoric, Dialogue and Jurisprudence. Rhetoric was taught as a matter of course at Merton, where much learning was gained through debate, which obviously stood any potential playwright in good stead. But a playwright from such a background and with Neville's kind of profession would necessarily begin his thought processes in a rather erudite way, only gradually becoming involved with the *action* of the play itself.

Neville's knowledge of Jurisprudence can be seen in one aspect of the character of Henry V, who is surely based on Neville himself. When he goes amongst his men in disguise – and Neville self-confessedly sometimes disguised himself too[178] – he lectures them on facets of the philosophy of Law:

King Henry   So, if a son that is by his father sent about merchandise do sinfully miscarry upon the sea, the imputation of his wickedness, by your rule, should be imposed upon his father that sent him. Or if a servant, under his master's command transporting a sum of money, be assailed by robbers, and die in many irreconciled iniquities, you may call the business of the master the author of the servant's damnation. But this is not so. The king is not bound to answer the particular endings of his soldiers, the father of his son, nor the master of his servant; for they purpose not their death when they purpose their services. Besides, there is no king, be his cause never so spotless, if it come to the arbitrement of swords, can try it out with all unspotted soldiers. Some, peradventure, have on them the guilt of premeditated and contrived murder; some, of beguiling virgins with the broken seals of perjury; some, making the wars their bulwark, that have before gored the gentle bosom of peace with pillage and robbery. Now, if these men have defeated the law and outrun native punishment, though they can outstrip men, they have no wings to fly from God. War is His beadle, war is His vengeance; so that here men are punished for before-breach of the king's laws,in now the king's quarrel. Where they feared the death they have borne life away, and where they would be safe they perish. Then if they die unprovided, no more is the king guilty of their damnation than he was before guilty of those impieties for the which they are now visited. Every subject's duty is the king's, but every subject's soul is his own. Therefore should every soldier in the wars do as every sick man in his bed - wash every mote out of his conscience; and dying so, death is to him advantage; or not dying, the time was blessedly lost wherein such preparation was gained. And in him that escapes, it were not sin to think that, making God so free an offer, He let him outlive that day to see His greatness and to teach others how they should prepare.

In real life too, Neville was quick to point out anomalies in reasoning concerning matters of Law. In 1606, he suggested that English 'Gentlemen' volunteers going over to help the Netherlanders in their fight against Spanish rule should have to take an oath of loyalty, if they were Catholics. (This was presumably because some 'Gentlemen' English volunteers had become double agents for the Spanish over there. Neville did not wish the rule to be extended to all poor soldiers.) Neville's friend, Ralph Winwood, was very much on the Netherlanders' side, like Sir Henry, so Neville wrote to tell him what had happened to his ideas once they reached the House of Lords:

> There was one point proposed, first by my self, and intended to the good of your side, and so it passed the Lower House, but afterwards the Lords altered it, so as I doubt rather it may do harm. It was thus at the first:
> That all the subjects of this realm which should go over to serve, or should serve any foreign Prince in his wars which professed the Romish Religion, not having before their going out of

England taken an Oath newly prescribed – and if they were Gentlemen and Officers of Bands, not having entered into Bonds at the Port where they shipped, with two sureties of £20 at the least, with condition not to be reconciled to the Pope or Church of Rome, nor to entertain or conceal any traitorous attempts or practice against the King or this State - should be felons.

This being particular at the first is made *general* by the Lords' alteration, and extended to **all** that shall serve any foreign Prince or State whatsoever. The inconveniency that I apprehend will follow thereof is that our Voluntaries which go over to serve your side will not be so forward hereafter, when they shall see they shall adventure the peril of felony, if they either do not this which is required of them, or be not able to prove it when they shall be called in question.

Thus is my good intention clean perverted, and I have told my Lord of Salisbury what I conceive of it... *4th June 1606*[179]

[From a linguistic point of view, it can be seen straight away that Neville is - as usual - employing the prepositions 'thereof' and 'hereafter' so preferred by Shakespeare. 'Thereof' is used 40 times in Shakespeare, and 'hereafter' 52 times in Shakespeare. The word 'traitorous' is also used here and appears 8 times in the plays. So here again we have extra proof, from the statisticians' point of view.]

Allowing for the gap in time between the two extracts, and for the fact that the above is a private letter to a friend, and therefore an unrevised text, the similarities between Neville and Shakespeare can still be seen. Separating style from content for a moment, it is noticeable that Neville the politician often dealt with legalities surrounding soldiers. In the 1590s, he was responsible for introducing a Bill for the reform of the 'outmoded' recruitment methods.[180] This was mirrored in the recruitment scene in *Henry IV, part 2*. The next Bill he introduced was for the reform of the 'licentious and lewd soldiery', and following that we find the same concern with the behaviour of soldiers echoed in *Henry V*. Then in 1606, we discover Neville once again concerned with the law surrounding soldiers – this time more worried (after his experience in the diplomatic service) about the possibilities of 'gentlemen' soldiers becoming double-agents. Rosencrantz and Guildenstern in *Hamlet* are surely his dramatic precursors of this particular concern – and he had direct experience of such men. Altogether, there is surely no other authorship candidate whose professional knowledge so nearly matches incidents and references within the plays. Neville's whole concern with legal matters – together with the style and vocabulary – overlaps with that of Shakespeare. And there is one especially indicative use of a word by Neville, which precedes even the Oxford English Dictionary's reference to its supposedly first use. This word is 'delinquent'. The Oxford English Dictionary finds that Caxton used a Frenchified form of the word, but avers that that word as we know it today was first used in 1603. However, I have discovered Neville using it in 1599: "I fynd yt directly contrary to all our Treaties, that any *Letters of Mart* should be grauted but against the principall Delinquents, and their Goods and Factors....' *Letter from Sir Henry Neville to Mr. Secretary Cecyll, Orleans, 14ᵗʰ July 1599, (Winwood's Memorials, Vol.1 p. 68.)* Then, 'delinquent' is subsequently used by Shakespeare in *Macbeth* (c. 1606) :

> Did he not straight,
> In pious rage, the two delinquents tear
> That were the slaves of drink and thralls of sleep?
> Was not that nobly done? Ay, and wisely too, *Act 3, sc.6*

The next use of the word noted by the OED is not until the 18ᵗʰ century.

This evidence is indeed important and highly significant. There is no explanation for the fact that Neville used the word far earlier than anyone else, and that it should then turn up in a text by Shakespeare, other than that the same writer wrote both works. The word was so new when 'Shakespeare' employed it that he uses it only once throughout the canon. Indeed, the vocabulary employed by Sir Henry in his letters is frequently inventive and unusual, and frequently overlaps with Shakespeare's, as will be seen in the 'Concordance' tables overleaf.

[The References to Neville's writing come from his letters in *Winwood's Memorials,* unless otherwise stated]

WORD OR PHRASE	NEVILLE *examples of incidence*	SHAKESPEARE *examples of incidence*
With a pretence	**Vol. 1, p. 17, 26 April 1599** ..to passe forthwith to Molins..with a pretence to go to Bathes at Pogues	Why hast thou abused so many miles with a pretence?- *Cym iii 4*
Advertise (to tell)	**ibid**.... and from thence to the court to advertise the King [used frequently in diplomatic correspondence]	Wherein he might the king his lord adveritse Whether our daughter were legitimate *Hen VIII ii 4*
Exceeding (meaning 'very')	**Vol.1, p.18, 27 April** ..whereof I am exceeding glad	Many occurrences, e.g. How doth the King? – Exceeding ill *2HenIV ii2*
Such sort	**ibid.** I will endeavour in such sort as your Honor prescribes	I defy all angels, in any such sort.. *Mer Wiv ii2*
Procure that..	**ibid,** ..to procure that the King shall send over some personage of Quality...	Procure that Lady Margaret do vouchsafe to come *1Hen VI v5*
Torture (often said to have been first used on stage by Shakespeare, and not used generally elsewhere)	(see Neville's dispatch, 6th June, 1599, quoted above)	46 uses in Shakespeare, beginning with *Lucrece:* And that deep torture may be called a hell, When more is felt than one hath power to tell.

Poor thing	**Vol. 1, p.45** I never saw a poorer thing	I never saw such noble fury in so poor a thing *Cymbeline*
Play false	**Vol. 1. 26 Jan 1599** ..but I fear he will play false in it..	**King John** Sirrah, your brother is legitimate; Your father's wife did after wedlock bear him, And if she did play false, the fault was hers [Plus 3 further instances]
Open-eyed	**15th Nov 1600** ..they be jealous enough of it and therefore open-eyed to observe what is done	Open-eyed Conspiracy his time doth take *Tempest ii 1*
Clean (absolutely, completely)	**4th June 1606** Thus is my good intention clean perverted	Roaming clean through the bounds of Asia *Com of Err. i 1* Though not clean past your youth *2 Hen IV i 2*
contumely	**ibid.** ..some particular contumely to the King personally	The oppressor's wrong, the proud man's contumely *Hamlet iii 1*
oeillades (glances)	A very French term, and only used once by Shakespeare – in the *Merry Wives*, i.e. after Neville has been French Ambassador	...examined my parts with most judicious oeillades: *Merry Wives, 1 ,3*

in what estate	**Vol.1 ibid** p. 85 .. that he now found in what estate those customs stood	**3rd Watchman** Ay, but give me worship and quietness; I like it better than a dangerous honour. If Warwick knew in what estate he stands, *Henry VI, part 3: Act 4, sc 3*
make love to	**Vol.1 ibid** p.86 *According to the OED, the use of this term was first recorded as a* **spoken** *term by John Lyly in 1580. Lyly was taking his M.A. in Oxford while Neville was there, so it is possible Neville first heard it there too.*	All instances of this in Shakes come *after* Neville's use, e.g. *Merry Wives*: **Falstaff** No quips now, Pistol! Indeed, I am in the waist two yards about, but I am now about no waste; I am about thrift. Briefly, I do mean to make love to Ford's wife.
flank	**Vol.1 ibid** p. 86 ....his thrust lighted lower than he intended and ranne him into the Flank ...	Used twice by Shakespeare – both times in *Venus and Adonis*
the first motion	**Vol.1 ibid** p.89 ...Her Majestie would, at the first Motion, and as it were upon even hand, receave him to her Grace	*Julius Caesar*: Brutus ... Since Cassius first did whet me against Caesar I have not slept. Between the acting of a dreadful thing And the first motion, all the interim is Like a phantasma or a hideous dream:

like enough	**Vol.1 ibid p.90** ... and like inoughe there may be good use made of him ...	Nine instances in the plays
Peremptorily	**Vol.1 ibid 93** ...answered very peremptorily that all the world should not perswade him to favour the King of Spaine against his good Sister of England...	**Falstaff** ...Harry, I see virtue in his looks. If then the tree may be known by the fruit, as the fruit by the tree, then, peremptorily I speak it, there is virtue in that Falstaff: *Henry IV, 1*
distemperature	**Vol.1 ibid p. 94** ... which makes me almost gladd of that little Distemperature I have now upon me, for a pretext neither to visit, nor to be visited, till I may be able to deliver som Certayntie of these Bruits, whereof all men expect to know the Trueth by mee. ...	Distemper and distempered used in 27 instances, but it is remarkable to find 'distemperature' as well: *Mids. N's Dream*: **Titania** ...That rheumatic diseases do abound. And thorough this distemperature we see The seasons alter. and in *Pericles*: **Lysimachus** Upon what ground is his distemperature? Of pale distemperatures and foes to life? Plus 2 further instances, found in *Romeo and Juliet,* and *The Comedy of Errors*

Bruit	In many of HN's diplomatic letters. This was in fact a word used mainly in diplomatic circles, as was 'advertise'. It is hardly a coincidence, therefore that Shakespeare was the first writer to use these terms on the stage.	And the King's rouse the heaven shall bruit again, Bespeaking earthly thunder. *Hamlet,* 1.ii As common bruit doth put it.*Timon* **5.i** The bruit is Hector's slain, and by Achilles. ***Troilus & Cressida* 5.ix**
let slip	**Vol 1**, p.292 …having let slip the best opportunity	**Julius Caesar:** Cry havoc and let slip the dogs of war **Measure for Measure** Which for this fourteen years we have let slip
hollow (used as an adjective)	p. 53 'Mr. Gray is …hollow and venal'	52 uses in Shakespeare, e.g. The most hollow lover - *AYLI -* act4, sc.1 But hollow men, like horses hot at hand, Make gallant show and promise of their mettle; *Julius C* act4 sc.2 His eye is hollow, and he changes much. *H.IV, pt 2*
dis + many words not usually preceded by this prefix	Disfurnish, disaccommodate,etc., throughout Neville's diplomatic correspondence	*Richard II :* Dispark'd my parks and felled my forest woods

Petit	Winwood, p.83, *given with the French spelling,* ...they would not upon such petit respects as profit urge anything that they saw by evident proof so prejudicial unto us...	*Hen V,* **French Soldier** Petit monsieur, que dit-il? Act 4, Sc.1
good pleasure	**Vol.1 ibid** p.20 I signified my arrival unto him...and prayed audience, as soon as it might stand with his good pleasure	I am Robert Shallow, sir; a poor esquire of this county, and one of the king's justices of the peace. What is your good pleasure with me? *HenIV, part 2*
Sifted	**Vol.1 ibid** p. 95 ...In which Practize, there was a dangerous Reache, and not thoroughly sifted *Sir Henry's usage coincides with that of Shakespeare, who only uses it twice:*	*Hen VI part 1* Beside, I fear me, if thy thoughts were sifted, The king, thy sovereign, is not quite exempt From envious malice of thy swelling heart. *Hamlet* **Polonius** Affection! Pooh! - you speak like a green girl Unsifted in such perilous circumstance.
cold comfort (often said to have been invented by Shakespeare.)	*Winwood, vol 1, p.161:* Notwithstanding the **cold comfort** I gave him lately...	I do not ask you much; I beg cold comfort; *KING JOHN* she being now at hand, thou shalt soon feel to thy cold comfort, for being slow in thy hot office? *T OF THE SHREW*

conveniency	Neville to Cecil, dated 15th June, 1599 The Conveniency or rather Necessitie of which Course	But with all brief and plain conveniency MER OF VEN ACT4|SC1 keepest from me all conveniency OTHEL ACT 4/ SC.2
Vehemency	**ibid** ...with such Vehemency and Celerity as conveniently you may *Winwood, vol 1 p. 248*	with what vehemency Th' occasion shall instruct you. *Henry VIII, ACT5|SC1* ...That with such vehemency he should pursue Faults proper to himself. *Measure for Meas. ACT5|SC1*
Celerity	**ibid**	she hath such a celerity in dying. *ANT & CLEO {ACT1|SC2*
question-less	*Winwood, ibid.* Questionless, if your peace succeed not, ...	She, questionless, with her sweet harmony and other chosen attractions, would allure, *PERICLES* That I should questionless be fortunate. MER OF VEN

The table of concordances between Shakespeare and Neville could be greatly expanded. The words and phrases mentioned above, however, are generally not very often used by other writers of the time, and the use of the 'Neville word' **delinquent** is especially telling.

We should probably also add the strange word 'prenzie' to the list above. 'Shakespeare' uses this in just one play - *Measure for Measure* - in Act III, scene 1 where there is talk of the 'prenzie Angelo' and his 'prenzie guards'. At least, this is how the word appears in the First Folio. Since that time, editors have seen fit to change the word to 'precise', though there seems no logical reason for doing so, other than that the word 'prenzie' is not one in English usage, either now or, it seems, during Shakespeare's time. Scholars have tended over the years to believe that the transcribers and printers of the First Folio were therefore misreading 'precise' for 'prenzie'. However, the word 'precise' is used elsewhere in the play, so the transcribers would have no reason not to recognise this word, because it would have appeared more or less the same throughout. Besides, the words 'prenzie' and 'precise' looked nothing like each other in the old Secretary Handwriting style used by 'Shakespeare' and his contemporaries. The 's' of 'precise' would have stood out a mile, while the 'c' in that word looked like our modern handwritten 'r'. The 'n' of 'prenzie' would also have been impossible to confuse with the Elizabethan 'c'. Altogether, then, one is forced to conclude that the writer did indeed use the word 'prenzie'.

A writer who was capable of inventing new words and coining some from foreign languages - as Neville did - would have been just the man to introduce the word 'prenzie'. This would have been especially true of someone who had been recently in France, for the words 'prenable' and 'preneur' would readily spring to the mind of such a person. 'Prenable' means 'corruptible' while a 'preneur' is a lessee. Both of these words would make sense, when it comes to Angelo in *Measure for Measure*. (Angelo was eminently corruptible - and so were his guards - and he was also a 'lessee' in the position of governor of the town, as the Duke had placed him in that role while he was supposedly abroad. A man who had been a diplomat in France was the likeliest person to have invented this new word. Neville, when he was Ambassador in France, encountered corruptible people, and 'deputies' - 'preneurs' who, like Angelo, conducted themselves less scrupulouusly than they ought.

Form and Content

Added to all these individual words and phrases, the *form* of the linguistic usage is just as telling. A good writer always tends to be seeking new vocabulary and novel phrases, not daring to presume that he may himself have set a trend in new expressions. But, as Frank Kermode says in his book, *Shakespeare's Language,* there are total linguistic structures which Shakespeare seems to enjoy using at certain points in his writing. It is exciting, therefore, to discover that Neville uses them too, at the same juncture in time. Indeed, many of Neville's letters and diplomatic dispatches to Robert Cecil are marked with the rhetorical devices one might expect from someone accustomed to writing for the stage.

For example, on 7th August, 1599, Neville wrote a letter to Cecil containing an account of the actual speech he delivered to Henri IV and Villeroy, his secretary. As one of my correspondents pointed out (after reading an extract from the letter on my website), "If the speech was delivered in English, the intricacy of language would have been lost on the French (certainly on Henri), and, if translated into French, a waste of time." [181] It looks very likely, therefore, that Neville first wrote the contents of the letter as a draft speech in English, intending this for his own use, but finally translated it before he spoke to Henri:

> I told him I was sorry that the great deserts of her Majesty, and the reason and justice of her demands, (which they did so fully acknowledge) together with the insistence and solicitation I had used ever since my coming, had wrought so little effect for her Majesty's contentation.
>
> I put him in mind of that speech I had before used to the Counsail, namely, that I prayed them to consider to whom it was that they were to give an answer, and upon what subject and occasion. That it was to a great Princess, who had most faithfully and sincerely assisted the King in his greatest extremity, and that, having means, and great opportunity to have dismembered and ruined the Crown of France, and perhaps to have taken a good portion of it herself, (as many other Princes would gladly have done, and some did, detaining it to this day) chose rather to employ her uttermost means and forces to preserve it, and had effected perhaps more therein than all the rest of the

friends and allies of the Crown of France, neglecting in some sort her own affairs for that purpose, and not refusing to bring herself into some want to supply them.

That *she* - now demanding nothing but some part of her own, whereof she had disfurnished herself to furnish them - and that not upon any light occasion, but being (as they all knew) in actual war, both at home within her own realm of Ireland and abroad, against one of the greatest and most potent Princes of Europe, whose continual attempts and designs against her she could not repel as she had done, but with great and continual charge – deserved at their hands a more than ordinary acknowledgment and care to content her.

My correspondent noticed quite separately from me that Neville's phrase "disfurnished herself to furnish them" is very like Polonius' to Reynaldo in Act 2, Sc.I of *Hamlet,* "by indirections find directions out." Indeed, I had placed the extracts on my website without comment, in the hope that readers would independently notice their Shakespearean structure. As Sir Frank Kermode points out, *Hamlet* "is dominated to an extent without parallel in the canon by one particular rhetorical device: it is obsessed with doubles of all kinds, and notably by its use of the figure known as hendiadys."

The language Neville employs in the above letter – written only a few months before being sent to the Tower, and only a few months before the writing of *Hamlet* - is lavishly supplied with the 'doubles of all kinds' to which Kermode refers. Neville uses: **merits and occasions, attempts and designs, reason and justice, proceedings and acknowledgement; acknowledgement and care, insistence and solicitation.** Other Neville letters of the time also bear just such doublings, for example:

Armed and strengthened – 1st Aug. 1599
Wrong and injustice – ibid

Examples paralleling this in the Shakespeare plays include:

TITUS ANDRONICUS
armed and appointed

HAMLET
reason and sanity
duty and obedience

MEASURE FOR MEASURE
reason and discourse

OTHELLO
reason and compass

MERRY WIVES OF WINDSOR
rhyme and reason

RAPE OF LUCRECE
Respect and reason
reproof and reason

TROILUS AND CRESSIDA
Reason and respect

TWELFTH NIGHT
judgment and reason

KING JOHN
stern injustice and confused wrong

HENRY V
care and valour

HENRY VIII
Zeal and obedience
etc., etc.

Neville also frequently displays the alliteration of a poet, often at the very same time as he iterates word doublings. (This is a noticeable trait in the 'Shakespeare' usage too!) When reporting to Cecil his first conversation with King Henri, Neville repeats the actual words he spoke to him. Here we find 'glad ...God ... greater good', and 'obedience and obligation' placed close to each other in the text:

> ... and that she [Queen Elizabeth] was very glad (seeing God had so ordained it for his greater good) that he had found some difficultie and opposition in the passing of it, that so his said subjects of the Religion [i.e. Protestantism] might now receive and acknowledge it wholly from himself and render him that entire love, obedience and obligation, that so great a favour deserved.

This was written at the same time as Henry V, whose opening Chorus contains alliteration in line 4:

And monarchs to behold the swelling scene,

which is soon followed by 'affright the air at Agincourt' and 'two mighty monarchies', and 'your humble patience pray'.

In a later paragraph of the same letter, Neville becomes interested in alliterations beginning with 'p' and 'c', so that within the space of two lines he writes of '...the Punishment of those that were past;...by publishing the Proclamation... of extraordinary Commission to certain chosen Persons of wisdom and integritie...'

Further down the same page we have '...restrain the carriage of corn by his subjects into Spain'. Indeed, Neville hardly seems to be able to prevent himself rhyming in this paragraph, since he begins '..your Honour's letters of the first of May, the very same day I went to Moret...

Frank Kermode also notes that *Hamlet* begins the series of what are often called the 'problem plays'. As noted in *The Truth Will Out*, the themes of the dramas change suddenly from histories and comedies to the darkest tragedies. Neville's dramatic arrest and imprisonment at just that moment elucidate this change in a way unparalleled by any other explanation. But, in addition, Neville's incarceration in the Tower explains what Kermode notes as a sudden change in Shakespeare's language too. The plays, as he says, become 'word-obsessed' and also begin to display a disgust with sexuality. Neville's incarceration away from the world of 'action' explains both these factors. It is known that Southampton's wife was not allowed to visit her husband for over a year after he had been imprisoned. It is therefore hardly likely that Neville would have been allowed such visits either. In a letter to Winwood while Sir Henry was under house arrest in Chelsea, Neville tells his friend that he is in 'an honourable prison' but that he cannot requite his love. The resulting obsession with words rather than action peaks in *Troilus and Cressida,* a play which combines political debate with somewhat disjointed sexual innuendos, plus a suggestion that women, when under trying circumstances, can't help being unfaithful!

Up until this point in his life, Neville had ostensibly been very happily married and, to judge by his condemnation of Henri IV's womanising, true to his wife:

> The King rode post yesterday to Paris, upon no occasion but to see Madamoiselle d'Entragues; which needs not, for he hath not been idle, neither at Orleans nor here, but hath had varietie brought him out of all parts; and for anything I see, he minds little else but that and hunting, and will hardly stay one day with his Counsail.[182]

However, in former days he nevertheless shared Shakespeare's enjoyment of a sexual 'merriment', as can be seen in an earlier letter to Robert Cecil:

> He told me also a merriment, that he understood the Archduke, that night he was married, was not able to consummate matrimony with the Infanta, which he had likewise related to the General of the Cordeliers, who had answered that it might well be, for he had heard the Archduke's Consellor affirm, that he knew when he was 37 years old he had never touched Woman. Thus, praying pardon of your Honour, if whiles I thought to relate you all that passed, I have troubled you with more than needed...

This kind of 'merriment' is entirely consistent with the type and nature of Shakespeare's sexual innuendos in the plays before *Hamlet*. That a jaundiced notion of women's faithfulness, sets in at the time Neville enters the Tower makes this sea change entirely explicable. Just as Kermode further remarks, "...it remains true that the work of a writer changes under pressures that can be regarded as partly private as well as responsive to more public, cultural pressures."[183]

While in the Tower, then, Neville had time to experiment, and *Troilus and Cressida* must be one of his most experimental works, in that its *action* is secondary to its discursive exploration of the politics of the State, and the politics of all kinds of relationships. These would of course have been the two concerns uppermost in Neville's mind, under the circumstances. And at the very basis of every type of politics is the question of *worth*. Is it possible to assess the intrinsic worth of people, or is worth simply a variable, always relative to other factors? These are questions which are implied throughout *Troilus and Cressida*. By extension, had Neville set the Earl of Essex's value too high? Was he guilty of ignoring Essex's shortcomings simply because he was an Earl? This was indeed one of the implied excuses Sir Henry gave for not having told the Queen about Essex's projects. At his Hearing, he suggested that the high *rank* of the person whom he would have accused should be remembered:

> ...an imbecility and weakness of my own nature, (if so it be to be termed) which could not resolve to become an accuser – which how odious a thing it is, all the world knoweth, especially in respect of the person whom I must have accused who I desire may be considered not as he hath been found since, but as he was reputed[184].

So perhaps Neville was able to turn a blind eye to Essex's shortcomings merely because of his rank. But take 'rank' away from a person or from society, and what dangers might be inherent in such a re-tuning of the strings of government:

Ulysses But when the planets
    In evil mixture to disorder wander,
    What plagues and what portents, what mutiny,
    What raging of the sea, shaking of earth,
    Commotion in the winds, frights, changes, horrors,
    Divert and crack, rend and deracinate,
    The unity and married calm of states
    Quite from their fixure! O, when degree is shaked,
    - Which is the ladder to all high designs -
    The enterprise is sick. How could communities,
    Degrees in schools, and brotherhoods[185] in cities,
    Peaceful commerce from dividable shores,
    The primogenity and due of birth,
    Prerogative of age, crowns, sceptres, laurels,
    But by degree stand in authentic place?
    Take but degree away, untune that string,
    And hark what discord follows: each thing meets
    In mere oppugnancy. The bounded waters
    Should lift their bosoms higher than the shores,
    And make a sop of all this solid globe;
    Strength should be lord of imbecility,

Even the unusual word 'imbecility' is present in *both* Ulysses' and Neville's speeches. But Neville knew he was merely playacting on both occasions. Ulysses represents the old, confined concepts. In the ancient geocentric theory of the universe, Earth was a captive entity in the middle of the planets and the sun, which moved around the Earth and kept it fixed in immobility . Degree was therefore viewed as being as natural as the fixed position of the Earth itself. Yet Ulysses' metaphor of re-tuning one string of a musical instrument opens up an unstated possibility – that the other strings are not fixed but can also be re-tuned so as to harmonise with the new positioning. And such a great writer must have been *conscious* of using an open-ended metaphor here, even though the character speaking the lines in the play did not perceive its shortcomings. In just the same way, the true, heliocentric universe, with a wandering, explorative planet Earth, never entered Ulysses' philosophy, but it was an ever-present factor in Neville's own armoury of knowledge. The writer has Ulysses call the sun a planet, knowing that this is what the Ancient Greeks believed, but also being aware that their perception was untrue. Historical accuracy in relation to astronomy was a particular hallmark in Shakespeare and Neville, for Shakespeare portrays Hamlet as being aware of Thomas Digges' concept of 'infinite space'. Hamlet was therefore a conscious portrayal of a historical but more 'modern' man, in that he was a mirror of both Essex and Neville himself. By extension, therefore, Hamlet represents the new, expansive, relativistic thinking of the new age, while Ulysses is stuck in the past. Ulysses could not retune all the strings but, given the chance, Neville believed in his heart of hearts that he and Essex could have done so. As far as Neville is concerned, Ulysses is therefore an example of a man praising a political stance which he, Neville, knows is relative not absolute. Ulysses' idea of respecting 'rank' might be a very good thing in a *wartime* situation – and the framing of his whole speech is that of the Trojans discussing reasons for their present failures in combat. But in peace, the same rules should not necessarily apply. This is a subject eventually explored in depth in *Coriolanus.* Surely only a politician and astronomer was capable of combining such thoughts and structuring such stage rhetoric.

Thus, in *Troilus and Cressida*, we are treated once more to Neville's ever-present concern with the legal and moral position of soldiery. Helen of Troy has been the cause of many a soldier's death, as we are reminded in that play:

Diomedes She's bitter to her country. Hear me, Paris;
    For every false drop in her bawdy veins
    A Grecian's life hath sunk; for every scruple
    Of her contaminated carrion weight
    A Trojan hath been slain. Since she could speak,
    She hath not given so many good words breath
    As for her Greeks and Trojans suffered death.

The whole play is populated by soldiers. Soldiers and individual fighters are, arguably, the most active partakers in it, apart from Cressida herself. Sir Henry Neville is the only authorship candidate who ever wrote about, and was concerned with the plight of, soldiers. Throughout the plays of Shakespeare, there are altogether no fewer than 539 instances of the word 'soldier' within the texts and the stage directions. Ultimately, soldiers are the practical guardians of the state, and Neville was a statesman.

The pastoral side of Neville's knowledge was witnessed by Queen Elizabeth herself, who ordered Sir Henry's area of Windsor Forest to be closed to hunting while Neville remained in France for, she affirmed, no one knew how to manage it so well as Sir Henry. Neville's friend and neighbour, Sir Henry Unton, was similarly a 'forest man'. He is the gentleman whose life (including his wedding) is celebrated in a famous picture, which is often used to illustrate *A Midsummer Night's Dream.* Strangely enough, with knowledge of Henry Neville's authorship comes the possibility – even probability – that it was indeed Sir Henry Unton's marriage which was celebrated by that play.

Similarly, we have Windsor present in *The Merry Wives,* and a forest and hunting as part of *Love's Labour's Lost.* Neville and his forefathers had been keepers of Windsor Forest, so there was no difficulty for Neville in producing local references, and naming forest plants and herbs.

But Neville had a large vocabulary which encompassed every area of life, and was also extremely adept at inventing his own words too. Below are some of his favourites, some of which (like disaccommodate and complementize) he appears to have invented. All of them sound 'Shakespearean', but none of them is actually used in the plays, whereas Neville seems to use everything found in Shakespeare's plays, while also, therefore, adding to them in his personal correspondence:

Disaccommodate, inthronize, reservedness, concurrence, intermedler, Passionateness, Signification, Tergiversations (letter to Winwood, 1605) inconveniency Complementize – letter to Cecil, Paris, 15 May 1599 (p.24)

Among the many very Shakespearean passages to be found in Neville's letters, the ones below are interesting:

14 Jan 1599

I fynd a great Concurrence towards some Alteration in those Parts, and many are wonne to the adverse Syde; which will not declare themselves till the instant, and in the meane tyme hold false Fellowship with our Syde, to doe the greater harme. (Alliteration such as this is frequently used in the Shakespeare canon.)

29 Jan 1600 (to Winwood)

All this tends little to the sweetning of my Entertainment there, or to the enabling me to effect any gratefull Service; but I must have Patience.

Shakespeare is likewise fond of gerunds, so that phrases parallel to ...'the sweetning of...' occur quite frequently. For example:

MEASURE FOR MEASURE
I'll take my leave,
    And leave you to the hearing of the cause,

HAMLET
No, not to stay the finding of the axe,

HENRY IV *PART 1*
Upon the parting of your wives and you.

MACBETH
By the pricking of my thumbs...

HENRY IV *PART 2*
I have lost it with hallooing and singing of anthems.

Begotten and *All Happiness* [reminiscent of the Dedication to the Sonnets]are also to be found in the same letter from Neville to Winwood, dated 11th March, 1605.

Metalworking imagery is also to be found in plenty in the plays, and Neville is the only authorship candidate to have had knowledge of this:

Charge you and discharge you with the motion of a pewterer's hammer – HenIV iii2

I saw a smith stand with his hammer , thus – K/ John, iv 2

With busy hammers closing rivets up - Hen V i Prol

Mechanic slaves With greasy aprons, rules and hammers – Ant and Cleo v 2

I cannot do it; yet I'll hammer it out – Rich II

And wilt thou still be hammering treachery – 2 Hen VI i2

I give thee my apron and, Will, thou shalt have my hammer – 2 Hen VI ii 3

"Unannealed" is used in *Hamlet*. [Annealing is certainly part of specialist metallurgical terminology. It is a process of removing the stresses from metals by heat and has the effect of softening the metal and so making it less prone to cracking. It is indeed difficult to explain how any other authorship candidate would have known the word.]

References to, and imagery based on, gun production are quite frequent in the Shakespeare Works. They certainly betray an inside knowledge of iron production and furnaces in general:

Venus and Adonis.

Or like the deadly bullet of a gun,
His meaning struck her ere his words begun.   *line 160*

As from a furnace, vapours does he send.
His eye which scornfully glisters like fire
Shows his hot courage and his high desire." *ll. 294 - 296*

An oven that is stopp'd, or river stay'd,
Burneth more hotly, swelleth with more rage. *ll, 331 -2*

"Cynthia for shame obscures her silver shine
Till forging Nature be condemn'd of treason,
For stealing moulds from heaven that were divine." *ll. 728 -730*

> Here overcome, as one full of despair,
> She vail'd her eyelids, who like sluices stopp'd
> The crystal tide that from her two cheeks fair
> In the sweet channel of her bosom dropp'd;
> But through the floodgates breaks the silver rain,
> And with his strong course opens them again. *ll. 955 - 960*

The Rape of Lucrece.

> O night, thou furnace of foul-reeking smoke... *l. 799*

> As smoke from Aetna, that in air consumes,
> Or that which from discharged cannon fumes. *ll. 1042 - 3*

Love's Labour's Lost

> MOTH. You are too swift, sir, to say so:
> Is that lead slow which is fir'd from a gun?
> ARMADO. Sweet smoke of rhetoric!
> He reputes me a cannon; and the bullet, that's he;
> I shoot thee at the swain.
> MOTH. Thump, then, and I flee.
> *Act 3, Sc.1*

Henry VI, part 2

> QUEEN. Enough, sweet Suffolk, thou torment'st thyself;
> And these dread curses, like the sun 'gainst glass,
> Or like an overcharged gun, recoil,
> And turns the force of them upon thyself. *ACT3|SC2*

Romeo and Juliet

> Shot from the deadly level of a gun,
> Did murther her; as that name's cursed hand
> Murder'd her kinsman.
> *ACT3|SC3*

King John

> BASTARD. An if thou hast the mettle of a king,
> Being wrong'd as we are by this peevish town,
> Turn thou the mouth of thy artillery,
> As we will ours, against these saucy walls;
> And when that we have dash'd them to the ground,
> Why then defy each other, and pell-mell
> Make work upon ourselves, for heaven or hell.
> *ACT2|SC1*

King Henry V

Chorus ...   Work, work your thoughts, and therein see a siege;
Behold the ordnance on their carriages,
With fatal mouths gaping on girded Harfleur.
Suppose th' ambassador from the French comes back;
Tells Harry that the King doth offer him
Katherine his daughter, and with her to dowry
Some petty and unprofitable dukedoms.
The offer likes not; and the nimble gunner
With linstock now the devilish cannon touches,

[Alarum, and chambers go off]

And down goes an before them. Still be kind,
And eke out our performance with your mind.   Exit
ACT3||SC1, PROLOGUE

WILLIAMS. You pay him then! That's a perilous shot out of
an elder-gun, that a poor and a private displeasure can do
against a monarch! *ACT4|SC1*

Henry VI Part I.

I'll to the Tower, with all the haste I can,
To view the artillery and munition. *Act I, Sc.i.*

The Merry Wives of Windsor

MRS. PAGE. Come, to the forge with it then; shape it. I
would not have things cool.   *ACT4|SC3*

...Plus dozens more. Some of the inclusions of 'cannons' have
of course already been dealt with in a previous chapter.

The following information was supplied by Tim Cornish of
Mayfield, Sussex, where Neville owned his ironworks:

Peter Quince in Midsummer Nights Dream calls to the rude
mechanicals to *Meet me in the palace wood a mile without the
town.* (I.i.93) One of his company is Francis Flute the bellows
mender.

Henry Neville delivered some of his guns by road to
Southwark, where they crossed the river by the only bridge and
were taken to the Tower of London. A letter from William Luck
in Mayfield to Henry Neville in 1595 is to be left at Richard
Merch the saddlers, next to the Talbot Inn in Southwark.

William Boyd writes: *Shakespeare's working life was in Southwark, south of the river, and London Bridge, a noisome, rank and dangerous district, freer of the City of London's legal edicts by virtue of its location and home to its theatres, pleasure gardens, bear-fighting pits, innumerable taverns and brothels.*

....

As I said at the very beginning of this chapter, there are inevitable problems in comparing the language of Neville with that of Shakespeare. However, what evidence there is can be said to be highly persuasive. But Neville was hiding his identity, so he did not leave manuscripts of a poetic nature behind him. Yet he lived in with the Killigrews, where his father in law's second wife - Jael de Payenne - held literary soirees, and who were about to spawn a succession of playwrights. One of those Killigrews – his nephew, Robert – possessed a manuscript copy of a slightly different version of Shakespeare's Sonnet number 2[186]. This has never been explained, though it has often been thought that Robert's manuscript version was probably written by Shakespeare himself! (Robert was a son of Neville's father in law's brother, William Killigrew, who was an especial friend of Neville and lived at Lothbury with him.[187])

The Tower Notebook is a notable exception to the rule that Neville was careful not to betray his identity, but this lay concealed in his daughter's house on the Isle of Wight.[188] Together with the two annotated versions of *Leycester's Commonwealth* found alongside it, the book contains notes overlapping with the *content* of a number of the History plays. But these are only note-books and background material for the plays, and thus hold few clues to the actual linguistic style of the author. So, as I have endeavoured here to treat mainly style and vocabulary and, as far as possible, separate this from content, this is not the place for a detailed discussion of these notebooks. They are better treated separately, where there is space for their content to be laid open to view. Like the notebooks of Leonardo da Vinci they require a specialist study of their own. Until then, a review of some of their content is given in *The Truth Will Out*. Altogether, as every specialist involved with computer-based linguistic analysis affirms, the most persuasive evidence in this kind of case is that of overlapping knowledge and step by step chronology, concerning the two writers under review. The meshing together of Shakespeare and Neville in these respects is second to none. Moreover, Neville is the only authorship contender ever to have been found in possession of notebooks which contain material that overlaps with the History plays of Shakespeare. Consequent, demonstrable overlapping of linguistic usage between Shakespeare and Neville now adds icing to the cake.

Chapter 13

BEN JONSON, THE CORNISH LADY, AND THE FIRST FOLIO

Many of the old plays written prior to
the outbreak of the Civil War seem
greatly to resemble the modern
detective story because, to understand them,
it becomes necessary to follow up the clues -
more or less obvious - they give.
Lansdown Goldsworthy, 'Ben Jonson and the First Folio'

Lansdown Goldsworthy's Paper, *Ben Jonson and the First Folio*[189], led me to a work which actually contains an oblique reference to the Sonnet Code cryptogram - and to Thomas Thorpe, the man who 'hid' Neville. As with the Code itself, however, it is necessary to examine the background to this work in order to understand its cryptic clues.

Goldsworthy observed that many Elizabethan and Jacobean writers wrote in a manner which paralleled the genre of the Detective Story. Using this analogy brings modern readers closer to what is actually going on in these allegorical works: the writers were peppering them with clues towards a particular topical mystery or subject of discussion. Goldsworthy's Paper was written seventy four years before the publication of my theory concerning Henry Neville, but he too was convinced by his own research that Ben Jonson's works regularly addressed the Shakespeare mystery. (This in turn underlines the fact that the mystery was already occupying the minds of some educated people, even during Jonson's own lifetime.) Jonson therefore knew about the concealed poet behind the Shakespeare pseudonym. Besides Ben Jonson's poem to Sir Henry Neville leaving cryptic hints in this direction, one of his *plays* also contains a similar message. Evidence now points to that play, *The Staple of News,* having been written with the express purpose of marketing the then recent First Folio edition of Shakespeare's collected plays in 1623. And, as Goldsworthy says in his Paper about the play, Jonson took the opportunity to leave in it plentiful clues to the identity of the true writer of the Shakespeare works. Thus far, then, Goldsworthy and I are in agreement. However, he did not undertake a thorough analysis of the play, leaving whole passages, incidents and characters unexplained.

Since Goldsworthy wrote his Paper in 1931, there appears to have been few attempts to solve the core conundrum at the heart of Jonson's play. In trying to come to grips with the work, other literary critics have tended to concentrate on the picture Jonson painted of early newspapers and their misinformation. But a more holistic concept is needed here. Newspapers and their misinformation were true occurrences at the time, therefore certainly a fruitful individual source for Jonson's satire. But the point is that their misinformation is used by Jonson as a clever device: it forms a background against which he can expose the fact that the Shakespeare myth is of the same order as these invented, far-fetched items of news. As with any modern detective story, therefore, the clues are there, and once certain key facts are worked out, the whole scenario becomes crystal clear. By laying linguistic and circumstantial clues, Jonson is making it possible for discerning members of his audience to clap their hands and shout 'I've got it'. But this discernment is itself only possible for those who have already gone some way towards working their 'little grey cells' on the Shakespeare mystery, the times in which he lived, and the circle of persons, locations, knowledge and situations reflected in contemporary plays.

Ideally, it would be pleasurable for any potential student of Jonson's play to read it first and, as with a detective novel, see if he or she can work things out. However, as nearly four hundred years have elapsed since the play's first performance, its clues and the nature of its satire are now quite remote from our experience; so I have ventured to tackle the problem in reverse by introducing the play, its background and unavoidable interpretation before presenting the work in its entirety. However, my own edition of the text of Jonson's play will be published separately.

It is not surprising Ben wanted to advertise the publication of the First Folio. It had been a tremendous, and tremendously expensive, undertaking. Jonson himself had given his time and resources to editing, and generally putting together, the Shakespeare plays. The 1625 opening performance of

The Staple of News, therefore also proclaimed Jonson's involvement in that process - allegorically - and came only two years after the publication of the First Folio itself. The first 'complete' collection of Shakespeare's dramas may have proved a little slower to leave the shelves than the publisher would have hoped. Jonson would have expected this might be the case, given the then general prejudice against printed versions of plays. Poetry was considered respectable literature for wealthy members of society to read, but stage plays were not. Quartos of individual plays had sold - students and poorer but literate members of society could afford them - but the whole collection of 'Shakespeare's plays' in one was an expensive volume. Jonson therefore actually admits in the spoken Epilogue to *The Staple of News* that his primary purpose in writing this propagandist play has been both 'to profit and delight'. In the written version, he even precedes the play with a Latin quotation to this effect too. As always, Jonson intends his words to encompass at least two meanings: the main purpose of the play - from Jonson's point of view - was to market the First Folio of Shakespeare's works, and so personally 'profit' thereby. But he also wished to convince his target audience - the learned and the wealthy - that they too would 'profit' intellectually by reading the plays. And Jonson certainly needed to do this, if he hoped to sell to this class of society.

Jonson, however, was faced with a dilemma. If he, or any of the other producers of the First Folio, had been free to proclaim the name of the true author, then the rich and learned members of his audience would have realised that the writer sprang from their own class of society. They would then immediately have been more interested in buying the First Folio to see what the plays actually had to say. But - even from a reading of Jonson's play itself - it becomes clear that he was not allowed to tell his secret. There were presumably many overt and covert factors pressing down on Jonson in this respect. The overt ones would have been more obvious then than now, because many references in the Shakespeare works were topical. Though we have by now lost the immediacy of their meaning, the Shakespeare plays sometimes dealt with what were politically sensitive issues at the time. The great soliloquies - nowadays so treasured for their linguistic perfection and universal connotations - include a specific extra dimension for contemporary audiences. They are the first instances of the ruling classes' thought processes being laid bare before the public. Moreover, there were the occasional Court and State 'confidences' encapsulated either within some double-entendre lines in the plays, or within the depiction of some of their characters. If, therefore, any figures in authority were able to **prove** that the true source of the works was none other than a Member of Parliament who was also descendant of an old ruling dynasty, they would certainly wish these facts to be suppressed, hoping that public audiences would then not be especially listening out for the plays' implicitly political and otherwise sensitive messages. Jonson's own play also hints that *personal* strictures bound him to secrecy too - a prior legal agreement or personal oath, together with an understandable loyalty to a man whom he respected so much, and whom he knew to have such powerful connections and personal status. Most excitingly too, *The Staple of News* also reveals some of Neville's *personal* circumstances leading to his own decision not to have his name connected with the plays - and they are revealed as the very circumstances deduced throughout this book. Jonson certainly could not have proclaimed all this **openly**, in a play. The work simply had to be clouded by allegory and symbolism.

So Jonson had to face his problems head on: he could not directly state the very thing which would, above every other factor, persuade his target audience to re-assess the First Folio and consider it a wise purchase in the first place. The plays' connection with the little-respected, unlearned boy from Stratford was a positive drawback for sales amongst this wealthy group. Few of the aristocrats, courtiers or upwardly-spiralling merchants who attended *Jonson's* plays would have stooped to consider purchasing collected works by such an 'unworthy' fellow as Shakespeare who, from aught they knew, did not even have a named patron. True, they would have known that 'Shakespeare' had once sought to gain the Earl of Southampton's favour, but there had never been any open information that he had been successful in this attempt. Besides, that Earl had been disgraced after the Essex rebellion, yet no subsequent potential patron had been linked with, or sought by, Shakespeare. Thus 'Shakespeare' remained, for this kind of audience, a very shadowy figure. After all, everyone knew for certain the identities of Jonson's patrons. They knew too about Jonson having been specially selected, and personally taught, by Camden. But what did they know for certain about Shakespeare's education and patronage? Precisely nothing. Shakespeare himself would be blazoning the names of his patrons in his poetic works - just like Jonson did - had he truly found any. Yet even his great Sonnets had been dedicated to an unknown person.

This sophisticated target audience also knew that any patrons should have been boasting all round court about their patronage of such a poet; yet no one had done so. Fulke Greville had been proud to publicise his patronage of Jonson and others. Goodere had made no secret of the fact that he supported Drayton, and Drayton had loudly proclaimed that Goodere was his employer. Yet from Shakespeare's own and his possible patrons' lips came not one word. So this target audience would necessarily have suspected that both Shakespeare and his possible patron had something to hide. If they were seen to be actually reading plays by such a suspicious person, therefore, might it not be possible that they themselves could become perceived as complicit? Was there, perhaps, even some sort of unlawful activity going on behind the mystery? They did not know, so could not take the risk of being seen with such a purchase. Books were dangerous commodities - mere ownership of some 'suspicious' works had been enough to have men tortured by such notorious super-interrogators as Topcliffe.[190] Only if Jonson could hint at the great ancestry and respectability behind the Shakespeare plays could he be assured that such an audience would feel free to go out and buy.

But this learned audience was intrinsically not stupid; they now needed to be guided towards the truth. Any mere *pretence* on Jonson's part concerning the true identity of Shakespeare would not have been credited by them. Yet in *The Staple of News*, Jonson expressly states that those who know, or have now guessed the secret, should not tell. Thus Jonson makes it absolutely clear that he too knows, but must not directly say. In fact, he exhorts those who have understood his clues to 'rest quiet'. And in choosing such words Jonson knew there were two meanings within what he said: 1) that people should keep quiet about it, and 2) that once they had guessed the name of the true author, eminent members of the audience could 'rest quiet' in the knowledge that they would not bring any disrepute upon themselves by owning a work with such a respectable provenance. Jonson therefore cleverly weaves relevant information into the very fabric and construction of his play, knowing that only those who have been 'insiders' themselves will be able to put two and two together.

Only by doing this could he overcome innate prejudices. After all, Thomas Bodley himself had specifically opposed printed plays being bought for the Bodleian Library. Indeed, it was only through a legal anomaly that a copy of the First Folio was finally purchased by Oxford University. In 1611 there had been an agreement with the Stationer's Company that one copy of every book they approved should be sent to the Bodleian. They approved the First Folio, so Oxford University was forced to accept a copy of it.

The patronage of First Folio by the Earls of Pembroke and Montgomery was obviously helpful in selling the book, but prejudice about printed plays per se could not be entirely overcome by their involvement. Additional publicity of various kinds was essential, if the book were to receive a wider circulation. Even though some noble friends of the Earls purchased the First Folio, there were initial losses to be borne, because some expensive promotional copies had been sent out free. It was obviously a case of 'all hands on deck' for everyone involved in its production to think of ways they could help to promote sales. In the end, it was only after Jonson's groundbreaking and continuous insistence that 'Shakespeare's' plays were **poetry** too, and stemmed from a respectable source, that it became truly 'respectable' to read them[191].

Some early attempts to promote the plays of 'Shakespeare' as an art form.

In their earlier attempts at making the Shakespeare works respectable and acceptable, the 'Neville circle' had attacked the problem from a different angle. They had tried to ennoble Shakespeare, the Actor, hoping that this would then automatically ennoble the works too. Jonson's former tutor, William Camden, (who was also a great friend of Henry Savile, Neville's tutor, lifelong friend and executor of his will) had tried to help in this respect. Camden did this by supporting William of Stratford's claim to a Coat of Arms. But his attempt misfired, bringing as it did the opposition of one or two respected Heralds of Arms, who guessed there might be some underhand movement behind such an unviable case. It is therefore significant that the First Folio did not - indeed could not - carry a copy of the Arms which a disgraced, corrupt Herald granted surreptitiously to Shakespeare. This fact alone is enough to prove that people were not going to be fooled. Clearly, therefore, Jonson needed to do something drastic. If the works could not be ennobled by these means, then the only thing he could do was **hint** at the **truth**. Great thanks are owed to Jonson and his unrelenting efforts to turn round general opinion in every respect, and *The Staple of News* is definitely one means by which he attempted to do so.

Synopsis of Jonson's play, *The Staple of News*

Jonson began his play by cleverly appealing to his target audience's concepts of separateness and superiority: he flattered them by writing a play especially for them, making it plain that his work contained cryptic information which only they would understand:

The P R O L O G U E for the C O U R T.
A Work not smelling of the Lamp, to night,
  But fitted for your Majesty's Disport,
  And writ to the Meridian of Your Court,
We bring; and hope it may produce Delight:
The rather, being offered as a Rite
        To Scholars, that can judge, and fair report
        The Sense they hear, above the vulgar sort
Of Nut-crackers...

Jonson openly states that his production is 'offered as a Rite to Scholars', and we have to bear in mind that the audience would only *hear* the word 'Rite' spoken, so that 'offered as a *Right* to scholars' is also an intended meaning. The words therefore suggest that Scholars have a right to know what was going on - a 'Right' which the 'vulgar' do not have. The writer implies that 'Scholars' have gained this 'Right' because it is only they who can properly report the 'Sense they hear'. In other words, Scholars will break through to, and convey, the 'sense' of what they hear, without giving everything away, if they would rather not do so. Jonson therefore produced a play constructed on the principle of the old Roman satires, which he knew Scholars would latch onto straight away. However, we - the modern audience - are not so schooled in quickly recognising classical allusions, quotations and parallels as were the Jacobeans. We are also faced with the added problem that Jonson was writing a *contemporary* satire too. There are thus several scholarly 'spots of time' involved in his play. We live in a different time and a different world - lifestyles, personalities, values, seemingly everything, has changed. Political satire has the disadvantage of dating so rapidly that its topical allusions are quickly forgotten. We could therefore be forgiven for having to read, re-read and study the play in order to understand it.

The first thing that strikes us on **reading** the play is the strange naming of the dramatis personae. As with all Jonson's plays, the names themselves often give clues to real-life identities, while at the same time representing abstract qualities and/or inanimate objects. But the audience of the time would have been expecting this; they knew that Jonson and other satirists borrowed such devices from the ancient Greek and Roman plays, so the naming of the dramatis personae was very important:

PENNYBOY JUNIOR, the Son, the Heir and Suitor.

PENNYBOY CANTER, the Father, the Canter.

PENNYBOY SENIOR, the Uncle, the Usurer.

FASHIONER, the Taylor of the Times.

PICKLOCK, Man o' Law, and Emissary West- minster.

CYMBAL, Master of the Staple, and Prime
Jeerer.

FITTON, Emissary Court, and Jeerer.

ALMANACK, Doctor in Physick, and Jeerer.

SHUN-FIELD, Sea-Captain, a Jeerer.

PYED-MANTLE, Pursuivant at Arms, and Heraldet.

SHOE-MAKER,

REGISTER, of the Staple, or Office.

SPURRIER,

PECUNIA, Infanta of the Mines.

MORTGAGE, her Nurse.

BROKER, Secretary, and Gentleman-Usher to her Grace.

STATUTE, first Woman.

BAND, second Woman.

WAX. Chambermaid.

LICK-FINGER, a Master-Cook, and parcel-Poet.

MADRIGAL, Poetaster, and Jeerer.

LINENER,

HABERDASHER,

NATHANEEL, first Clerk of the Office.

THO. BARBER, second Clerk of the Office.

CUSTOMERS, Male and Female.

PORTER,

DOGS II.

The actual story of the play doesn't seem to matter very much. As is usual with Jonson, episodic action, characterisation and allusion mean more than narrative.

The play opens with Pennyboy Junior counting the minutes to his coming of age. His clothiers then enter and kit him out in a completely new suit. Thom Barber, his barber and assistant, pleases Pennyboy so much that he tells him he will grant him a favour. Thom begs Pennyboy to recommend him as a clerk in the new press office, which Jonson calls 'the staple of news'. (The word 'staple' is cleverly chosen, because Jonson wishes it to incorporate more than one meaning. Firstly, he wants the press office to be seen as a 'staple' meaning a product 'manufacturer' and 'merchant', so that it immediately becomes clear that the office's business is not the dissemination of raw truth but rather the manufacturing of news items for sale. Secondly, 'staple' implies the fastening together of written pages, which could refer to the binding together of news sheets, and also to the binding of the First Folio.)

Pennyboy Canter now enters onto the scene, singing. He is a beggar, whom Junior calls his Founder because, he says curiously, he brought him news of his father's death one week earlier. They all go off to see the press office and its work, during which visit Jonson takes the opportunity to run down what he calls the 'weekly cheat sheets'.

Soon, we meet Pennyboy Senior, Junior's rich uncle. He has a ward called Pecunia (a Cornish gentlewoman), and decides that she should now meet Junior, with a hope that they might team up. Junior and Pecunia get on well straight away, and Pecunia is very proud of her ancestry, which, with the help of a Herald of Arms, she recites. The press workers and rest of the company, and their retinue - minus Pennyboy Senior - eventually go off for a dinner together at a tavern, during which the Cook treats them to a great speech on the art of poetry, containing allusions to one he calls, 'the master-cook', whom no one knows, nor can know until they have studied him, in his many capacities, for years.

This 'master', says the Cook, is so many things, astronomer, gourmet, soldier, politician, mathematician, geometrician, architect, raiser of 'bulwarks' designer, inventor and - even though none of them knows it - a poet too. The rest of the company then indulge in witty talk, by the end of which, no one any longer believes the obviously-learned Pennyboy Canter is a mere beggar. (Nor, by this time - if they have understood the allegory - do the audience believe that the unlearned Shakespeare is the Writer of the plays in the First Folio.) Pennyboy Junior is indeed so taken with Canter's knowledge and wit that he wants to found a college for 'Canters' [beggars] based on his ideas. Pennyboy Canter now throws off his cloak and reveals he is none other than Junior's father, who has been in disguise after giving out that he was dead.

Picklock, the lawyer, however, now begins to attempt to take advantage of the situation. It is revealed that Canter, before he disguised and pretended to be dead, left his property in trust to his son. His son became 21 years old at the beginning of the play, and so inherited. But Picklock now tells Canter that he - Picklock - has all the deeds and never actually wrote down anything about a Trust. Also, Picklock reminds Canter that he knows his secret about the 'sinister' way in which he himself inherited the Estate. By these means, he attempts to take the Pennyboy inheritance. However, unbeknown to him, various unseen protectors of Canter have heard his threats and offer to stand up for Canter, should Picklock ever be so dishonest as to press the point.

Pennyboy Senior, meanwhile, has been going quietly mad. He thinks his two dogs, Lollard and Bloc, have betrayed him, so has them locked up in privies, which he names after them. He also purposely ignores anyone who comes to speak to him. All those surrounding him are ready to insult him, but no one seems able to resolve the situation until Pennyboy Canter now approaches 'like a furnace' and sweeps all his ineffectual companions away. Canter says he can cure Senior, whose 'fit' he thinks is occasioned more by anger than true madness. Senior is delighted and amazed to see Canter is alive after all, and takes all his advice to heart - he will free his dogs and no longer be so mean with his money.

At the end of the play, the Staple of News is abolished, Pecunia and Junior agree to marry, Senior leaves his property to his nephew, and everything quietens down and returns to sanity, including Pennyboy Senior himself.

The play is interspersed throughout with commentary from on-stage spectators, bearing such significant names as 'Gossip' and 'Tattle', and with reference to the Freemasons, including more than one character's quite overt statement regarding this and similar secret societies:

Thom. The measuring o' the Temple: a Cabal
Found out but lately, and set out by Archie,

Cla. Shut up the Office, gentle Brother Thomas.
Thom Brother Nathaniel, I ha' the Wine for you.

Pen Sen. ...If they be rude, untrained in our Method,
And have not studied the Rule, dismiss 'em quickly. .

Is by the Brotherhood of the Rosie Cross,
Produc'd unto Perfection,   *etc*

Interpreting the Allegory within the Play

The first character to appear in the play proper is Pennyboy
Junior, and the unravelling of his identity enables us gradually to
recognise who the other characters are meant to be. Junior soon
leaves us a verbal clue by echoing a word which appears later in
the Prologue. That word is 'Follies', and this was a term often
used at the time to indicate such things as stage plays. Pennyboy
Junior is taken up with 'follies' in general: right at the start, his
main concern is how he is going to be newly fitted out with a suit
of clothes, now that he has reached his twenty first birthday (the
spelling is the original, throughout the extracts):

Pennyboy Ju.
*His Shoemaker has pull'd on a new Pair of Boots; and
he walks in his Gown, Wastcoat, and Trousers, expecting
his Taylor.*
Gramercy Letherleg: Get me the Spurrier,
And thou hast fitted me.
Lether-leg.
I'll do't presently.

P. Ju. Look to me, Wit, and look to my Wit, Land,
That is, look on me, and with all thine Eyes,
Male, Female, yea, Hermaphroditick[192] Eyes,
And those bring all your helps and Perspicills,
To see me at best advantage, and augment
My Form as I come forth, for I do feel
I will be one, worth looking after, shortly.

'Wit' itself must notice Pennyboy Junior, as must all the 'Land'.
He will indeed be 'one' [just as the works of Shakespeare are

278

now bound into one volume] who will be 'worth looking after, shortly'. In the same way, the complete volume of the Shakespeare plays has just come of age too. It too is concerned about its new presentation, and the way it will be fitted out and covered. Jonson has made a Folio from a Folly; Pennyboy Junior is 'Follies' personified: **he can be none other than the personification of the First Folio itself.** And once we perceive Pennyboy Junior's true identification, we begin to realise how the playwright is constantly producing overlapping meanings between the cladding of Junior and the covering of the book. For instance:

> And Liberty, come throw thy self about me,
> In a rich Sute, Cloak, Hat, and Band, for now
> I'll sue out no Mans Livery, but mine own,
> I stand on my own Feet, so much a year,
> Right, round, and sound, the Lord of mine own Ground,
> And (to Rime to it) Threescore thousand Pound!

The 'threescore thousand pound' emphasises the great expense behind the production of the First Folio. And the 'so much a year' metaphorically refers to the subscriptions which buyers could pay to purchase the book. Like Junior, the Folio was now going to *earn* 'so much a year' too, while Junior's insistence on a 'Rime' hints that we are indeed here dealing with a volume of 'poetic' works.

Pennyboy Junior [the First Folio] has a' Fashioner' [tailor]. The 'Fashioner' is therefore none other than Ben Jonson himself - the book's editor and producer ['moulder'] - who now has to assure his fashionable, fastidious audience that cheap 'musty' leather has not been used in the binding of his book:

P. Ju. Nay, Fashioner,
> I can do thee a good turn too, be not musty,
> Though thou hast moulded me, as little Thom says,
> (I think thou hast put me in mouldy Pockets.)
> [*He draws out his Pockets,*
Fas. As good,
> Right Spanish Perfume, the Lady Estifania's,
> They cost Twelve pound a Pair.
P. Jun. Thy Bill will say so.
> I pray thee tell me, Fashioner, what Authors
> Thou read'st to help thy Invention? Italian Prints?
> Or Arras Hangings? They are Taylors Libraries.
Fas. I scorn such helps.

P. Jun. O, though thou art a Silk-worm!
    And deal'st in Sattins and Velvets, and rich Plushes,
    Thou canst not spin all Forms out of thy self;
    They are quite other things: I think this suit
    Has made me wittier then I was.
Fas. Believe it, Sir,
    That Clothes do much upon the Wit, as Weather
    Do's on the Brain; and thence comes your Proverb;
    The Taylor makes the Man:

Jonson is bolstering his own reputation here! He is hinting that his editing and design has done much to improve 'Shakespeare'. This would indeed accord with Jonson's opinion - expressed in *Timber*, another of his works - that 'Shakespeare' often went on too long. In turn, this remark accords with Bacon's description of Neville's speech at his trial as being very 'long, continued and symbolical'. Note, however, that Jonson - the *literary* man - does not complain of Shakespeare's over-use of symbolism, unlike Bacon, the prosaic.

    The general point to be made already by this time in the play, however, is that the upper classes - who loved codes and conundrums - would hardly have been able to resist Jonson's challenge. In this respect, Jonson's play was similar in purpose to the coded Dedication to the Sonnets. And the first step in solving the play's conundrum is even easier than taking the first step towards solving the Dedication Code. The overlapping of 'Folly' and 'Folio' would have made the audience laugh too: plays were follies, as far as they were concerned, so committing them to a complete **Folio** must have seemed a somewhat 'foolish' enterprise. But if seeing Jonson's play then reading the First Folio would solve an actual *conundrum* - a respectable courtly pursuit - then they would be ready to lay down their prejudices in the interests of furthering their personal knowledge. They too would then feel free to 'profit' by and 'delight' in this shared activity.

    And the Jonson conundrum, like the Dedication Code, has a numerical dimension too. At the beginning of the play, Pennyboy Junior declares that he is standing at the very moment of becoming 21 years old - and reveals that there has been a bond not to allow him to be 'fashioned out' until that term expired. Once we realise that he is the First Folio, and then count back to twenty one years before its publication, we arrive at 1602. At this point, Neville was still in the Tower, and probably despairing of surviving the experience. That he was allowed to act in a legal capacity, however, is witnessed by the fact that he is recorded as having signed papers to endorse the appointment of a vicar at Wargrave, so it is highly likely that this was the very year in which he would also have agreed to sign over to Ben Jonson the rights to edit and 'fashion' his works. (Why Shakespeare, Oxford, Bacon or anyone else would have seen fit to sign away their works at such a point in time is entirely inexplicable.) For Neville to have considered it necessary for a term of twenty one years to have expired before Jonson was allowed to deal with those works, however, there must have been surrounding circumstances the author thought best hidden. The very reasons behind the author's decision in this respect are voiced later in Jonson's play, and those reasons accord perfectly with Neville's own circumstances, as will be seen.

But what of the other characters in the play? To begin with, there are three characters whose names are preceded by 'Pennyboy'. From reading the whole play I was able to see that this epithet was applied to those persons or institutions who held - or once had held - some sort of rights over the plays themselves. The Pennyboy title was therefore appropriately given to those whose actions had a bearing on the profit produced by the sale of the First Folio. Now knowing that Pennyboy Junior represented the First Folio itself, I was forced - by the framing, naming and strong pointers within the work - to come to the conclusion that Pennyboy Canter is the writer, and Pennyboy Senior represents general Authority, at whose behest the works can either be sold or withdrawn from sale. Jonson can therefore make Pennyboy Senior at one moment a general representation of Authority, or, at another, a specific person of authority, sometimes even King James I himself. In other words, the Pennyboys are the characters whose direct involvement generated the 'pennies' or royalties due to those who worked in some capacity on the plays' behalf. The inclusion of the word 'pen' in Pennyboy also extends the epithet to signify someone who was in some way associated with writing or publishing as a profession. It is therefore interesting that Jonson indicates that a kind of quasi-masonic brotherhood - in addition to a family relationship - joins these Pennyboys to each other and also to most of the other characters in the play, including Statute, Broker, Mortgage, Almanack, Shunfield (a military man), Pyed-Mantle (a Herald and Pursuivant at Arms) Register, Fitton (a courtier, whose name meant 'liar' in those days) Picklock (a lawyer) and the mysterious Thom Barber.

There are on-stage commentators, 'disguising' as on-stage spectators, but apart from one or two of these, there is only one female character in the main body of the play. This is Pecunia, who is a 'Cornish Gentlewoman' and clearly represents the original manuscripts of the plays. Even the naming and characterisation of the dramatis personae, therefore, already start to have some connections with Neville. Neville was the elected messenger and spokesman for the Commons, therefore a 'Canter'; he had been an M.P. for Cornwall and was married to a Cornish Gentlewoman who, by the time Jonson wrote *The Staple of News,* would most likely have inherited her husband's manuscripts. Perhaps this also, however, incorporates the image of Anne Killigrew-Neville's daughter, who now possessed the Tower Notebook and other of her father's documents.

But wait - more connections follow, and they come thick and fast. Pennyboy Canter (Neville) is really the father of Pennyboy Junior (the First Folio) but in the first half of the play disguises as a beggar, pretending that the Canter has died. This particular form of disguising is a typical action of Neville's - he confessed that he had gone in disguise to the memorial service of the King Phillip II of Spain, and also wrote and told Cecil that if he were not allowed to return from France, then he would come back to England disguised as a Hermit and go and live in the 'Forest'. (Soon after this, the character of Jacques appeared in *As You Like It.*) And just in case the audience missed these connections, Jonson soon reveals that Pennyboy Junior - who truly believes his father dead - has named this particular Pennyboy 'Beggar' as his 'Founder'. The word 'Founder' suggests both 'originator' and also 'Foundry' (just as surely as 'Folly' suggests 'Folio'). To add to this image, other characters compare Canter's entrance with a 'Furnace':

> **Shun**. A Furnace.   **Alm.** A Consumption,
> [They all run away.
> Kills where he goes.

(In view of Jonson's already-stated connection with a Cornish Gentlewoman, I think we may be entitled to read the last line also as "'Kill[igrew]'s where he goes". [This is analogous today with comedians' occasional use of 'Tony Blur' for Tony Blair.] Perhaps there is also an inference that Anne Killigrew helped with writing the plays, which would certainly be within the bounds of possibility considering her mother's learning and learned ancestry, and the fact that so many of the Killigrews were to become increasingly associated with writing and the theatre.) Of course, the Furnace and the Foundry are direct connections with Neville's profession as an ironworker, and his cannons might well 'kill' where he (or simply his name on his cannons) 'goes'. Making Pennyboy Canter - revealed as the 'father' figure - represent the true writer also accords with the metaphor Heminge and Condell used in their Dedication of the First Folio to the Earls of Pembroke and Montgomery. They too spoke of the writer of the works as a 'Father', in that they called the works his 'Orphanes' for whom they wished to procure 'Guardians'. This alone, then, would make it logical and fitting to see Pennyboy Junior, the 'orphaned' son, as the writer's 'works' and Pennyboy Canter, his disguised father, as the 'author himself', even without all the linguistic clues and telling metaphors with which Jonson has filled the text of his play.

By this time in the play, Jonson has been steadily building up a picture of Neville in other ways too, getting 'Lickfinger, the Cook' (spirit of poetry) to describe the concealed writer thus:

> ...Seduced Poet, I do say to thee,
> A Boyler, Range, and Dresser were the Fountains
> Of all the Knowledge in the Universe.
> And they 'are the Kitchens, where the Master-Cook —
> (Thou dost not know the Man, nor canst thou know him,
> Till thou hast serv'd some years in that deep School,
> That's both the Nurse and Mother of the Arts,
> And hear'st him read, interpret, and demonstrate!)
> A Master-Cook! Why, he's the Man o' Men,
> For a Professor! he Designs, he Draws,
> He Paints, he Carves, he Builds, he Fortifies,
> Makes Citadels of curious Fowl and Fish,
> Some he dri-dishes, some motes round with Broths.
> Mounts Marrow-bones, cuts fifty angled Custards,
> Rears Bulwark Pies, and for his outer works
> He raiseth Ramparts of immortal Crust;
> And teacheth all the Tacticks, at one Dinner:
> What Ranks, what Files, to put his Dishes in;
> The whole Art Military. Then he knows
> The influence of the Stars upon his Meats,

And all their Seasons, Tempers, Qualities,
And so to fit his Relishes, and Sauces,
He has Nature in a Pot, 'bove all the Chymists,
Or airy Brethren of the Rosie-cross.
He is an Architect, an Ingineer,
A Soldier, a Physician, a Philosopher,
A general Mathematician.
Mad. It is granted.
Lic. And that you may not doubt him for a Poet —
Alm. This fury shews, if there were nothing else!
And 'tis Divine! I shall for ever hereafter,
Admire the wisdom of a Cook!
Ban. And we, Sir!

Neville was fond of his food. He was also a member of the Mitre Club in Bread Street, where wit and philosophy mediated themselves over dishes of venison and glasses of wine - just as they did in the scene from Jonson's play in which the Cook appeared and gave this speech. Neville also did indeed assist a Professor - namely Sir Henry Savile, his kinsman and lifelong friend. He was therefore indeed 'the Man o' Men, For a Professor!' Even when he was a teenager, we find Dudith, the Hungarian philosopher, writing to Neville and asking him to try and tutor Sir Henry Savile in the 'new' mathematics of Thomas Digges. Not only was Digges - a Copernican - the inventor of the telescope, he was also a relative of Neville's and had lectured at Merton College, which Neville attended. Moreover, Digges was the first person to posit the theory of infinite space, to which Neville has Hamlet refer in passing. But for a long while, Savile stayed with the Ptolemaic system, saying he had looked at Digges' astronomical ideas but thought he was wrong! So Neville was schooled in both Astronomy (in which he majored at Oxford) and Astrology, because of Savile's Platonist beliefs. Jonson is therefore correct in saying that the 'Master-Cook' [i.e. Neville, the poet] knows about the stars and the seasons, for Neville, was ever the observer of the *practical* rather than just the *mystic* in Nature.

The 'fifty-angled custards' mentioned by Jonson in the above extract from his play almost certainly refers to Neville's mathematical abilities, and to the fact that he assisted Savile, who became Professor of Geometry at Merton.

Digges also wrote a famous treatise on military tactics, which Neville would most certainly have been obliged to read while preparing for the business of producing cannons, and this facet of the 'poet-chef' is also mentioned by the Cook in his great speech. As for the mention of the brethren of the 'Rosie-Cross', this particular secret society seemed to have much more to do with Astrological beliefs than did the Freemasons, of which latter society William Herbert, Earl of Pembroke and patron of the First Folio, was made Grand Master.[193] And here, Jonson is saying that the 'Master Cook' - therefore 'Master of the spirit of poetry' - knows more about science than do those 'airy' Rosicrucians. It follows logically, therefore, that Jonson is saying that Neville was not a Rosicrucian, so we are inevitably narrowing down the brotherhood to which he belonged to be the Freemasons which, though it may have encapsulated some Rosicrucian symbolism, had enough of a practical side to involve itself in business dealings and in the founding of the Royal Society[194].

After completing his editing of the First Folio, Jonson was given a paid position in Gresham College - often thought to be the predecessor of the Royal Society, and therefore also linked with Masonic symbolism in its inception.[195] Moreover, Thomas Gresham is also said to have been an earlier Grand Master of Freemasonry. No one has ever explained why Jonson happened to begin an association with Gresham College at precisely the time the First Folio of Shakespeare's works appeared, but knowing that Gresham was Neville's great uncle and benefactor offers the perfect explanation of both time and place. Jonson would therefore also have been hoping that the nobility - and Freemasons - would buy the First Folio, once they guessed its relevant associations. Indeed, it would probably be only the nobility, rich merchants, or public institutions who would have been able to afford it. Thus, hinting at the truth - that the real writer was from their own background and not from the 'common actor' origins which had been painted - was surely likely to assist its sales. The past was certainly a different country - the classes kept almost hermetically divided, possibly as much from the fear of disease as from snobbery. But the upper classes were also afraid that their 'superior' thought processes - born after careful nurturing and expensive education - might be prone to infection too. Jonson therefore had every reason to demonstrate to them that this would not be the case if they bought and read 'Shakespeare'. As the Cook describes, the real man behind the works is certainly a fit person to be read by them.

Throughout the play, Jonson is also making references to mining, metals and 'ores':

Pecunia [*Original MSS., and Cornish Gentlewoman*]. My Pedigree?
I tell you Friend, he must be a good Scholar
Can my Descent: I am of Princely Race,
And as good Blood as any is i' the Mines
Runs through my Veins. I am, every Limb, a Princess!
Duchess o' Mines was my great Grandmother;
And by the Fathers side, I come from Sol
My Grandfather was Duke of Or, and match'd
In the Blood-Royal of Ophyr.

Pecunia is not primarily speaking of her **own** but of the **Manuscripts**' inheritance. She **is** the Manuscripts. With our present knowledge of Neville's hand behind those manuscripts, and with the Neville 'theory' now being strongly endorsed by Jonson's play, we are able to understand every one of Pecunia's references:

- 'he must be a good Scholar Can my Descent' 'Can' is here used in the present-day Germanic sense of 'können' - i.e. can do, or (here) can discern something. The Neville Descent is particularly difficult to discern. It involves senior branches, junior branches and the inter-marrying between them. In the same way, the conundrum of who really wrote the Manuscripts is a difficult one to solve.
- 'I' [meaning, the Manuscripts] am of Princely Race' - true! The Nevilles were descended from the Plantagenets.
- 'As good Blood as any is i' the Mines Runs through my Veins'. As we have seen, Henry Neville was connected with iron; iron ore comes from mines. Moreover, Pecunia is here speaking in her dual capacity as a Cornish Gentlewoman: Neville's wife - Anne Killigrew - had a father who came from Cornwall, where much wealth was built up from the tin, and some silver, mines too.
- 'Duchess o' Mines was my Great-Grandmother.' Neville's great-grandmother was the wife of Baron Bergavenny, who owned some Welsh mines.

286

- 'And by the Father's side I come from Sol' - Sol, the Sun (or three suns) was the sign under which the Plantagenets went into battle, as I explained in *The Truth Will Out*. Also, on Neville's portrait in Audley End, there is a finger ring containing a jewel inside which is fashioned the sign of the sun surrounding the face of a lion.

- 'The Duke of Or' can be taken as a reference to the iron ore involved with Neville's inheritance from Gresham who, though no real noble, could easily take the joking title of the Duke of Ore, being the greatest iron founder in England. At the same time, 'Or' is 'gold' in heraldic terminology, and the Nevilles and Greshams were certainly rich.

- The location of 'Ophyr' or 'Ophir' (mentioned in the Bible) is not known, but it is associated with a region from which Solomon gained all his gold. The connection with Solomon, therefore, may well suggest both the wealth of the Nevilles, and also Solomon's temple and the Crusades, in which the Nevilles were active. It may suggest again Neville's Masonic connections, and wisdom too.

But it is the Welsh connection which is finally underlined, and Neville's ancestry was most definitely connected with that. Through his ownership of the Mayfield iron works he also became a neighbour of his cousins, the Barons Bergavenny (who took their name from Abergavenny in Wales):

Pyed Mantle [the Herald]. The Mines o' Hungary, this of
    Barbary.
    But this, this little Branch?
Pec. The Welsh Mine, that.
    I ha' Welsh Blood in me too; blaze,
Pye. Sir, that Coat
    She bears (an't please you) Argent, three Leeks vert,
    In Canton Or, and tassel'd of the first.
P. Ca. Is not this Canting? do you understand him?
P. Jun. Not I; but it sounds well, and the whole thing
    Is rarely painted: I will have such a Scroll,
    What ere it cost me.
Pec. Well, at better leasure
    We'll take a view of it, and so reward you.

The Neville family was also descended from a Bohemian line[197], hence 'The mines o' Hungary'. In addition to that, Neville had been greatly influenced by Dudith, the Hungarian Humanist, so that he too had become a 'mine' of inspiration for his works. Elsewhere in the play, the Manuscript is associated with the West Indies too, which doubtless reflects the Tempest, and Neville's own counsellorship in the Virginia Company. Pennyboy Canter is still in disguise as a beggar, and so pretends not to understand what the Herald of Arms is saying. This of course mirrors the situation of Neville 'disguised' as Shakespeare - the poor Stratford boy could never have understood all these ancestral connections, and yet a knowledge of them is variously stated, inherent and implied in the plays, par excellence in *Henry V,* where the long recital of European family trees becomes almost comic - as in Jonson's scene here too. But the point is that Pennyboy Canter (if we view him as Shakespeare, the unlearned, which his disguise now proclaims him to be) would not have been able to achieve the conceptualised knowledge of European ancestry apparent in this speech, whereas Pennyboy Canter - Neville, the true writer and canting politician - would have imbibed it all with his mother's milk:

> ...There is no bar
> To make against your Highness' claim to France
> But this, which they produce from Pharamond:
> 'In terram Salicam mulieres ne succedant'-
> 'No woman shall succeed in Salique land';
> Which Salique land the French unjustly gloze
> To be the realm of France, and Pharamond
> The founder of this law and female bar.
> Yet their own authors faithfully affirm
> That the land Salique is in Germany,
> Between the floods of Sala and of Elbe;
> Where Charles the Great, having subdu'd the Saxons,
> There left behind and settled certain French;
> Who, holding in disdain the German women
> For some dishonest manners of their life,
> Establish'd then this law: to wit, no female
> Should be inheritrix in Salique land;
> Which Salique, as I said, 'twixt Elbe and Sala,
> Is at this day in Germany call'd Meisen.
> Then doth it well appear the Salique law
> Nor did the French possess the Salique land
> Until four hundred one and twenty years

After defunction of King Pharamond,
Idly suppos'd the founder of this law;
Who died within the year of our redemption
Four hundred twenty-six; and Charles the Great
Subdu'd the Saxons, and did seat the French
Beyond the river Sala, in the year
Eight hundred five. Besides, their writers say,
King Pepin, which deposed Childeric,
Did, as heir general, being descended
Of Blithild, which was daughter to King Clothair,
Make claim and title to the crown of France.
Hugh Capet also, who usurp'd the crown
Of Charles the Duke of Lorraine, sole heir male
Of the true line and stock of Charles the Great,
To find his title with some shows of truth-
Though in pure truth it was corrupt and naught-
Convey'd himself as th' heir to th' Lady Lingare,
Daughter to Charlemain, who was the son
To Lewis the Emperor, and Lewis the son
Of Charles the Great. Also King Lewis the Tenth,
Who was sole heir to the usurper Capet,
Could not keep quiet in his conscience,
Wearing the crown of France, till satisfied
That fair Queen Isabel, his grandmother,
Was lineal of the Lady Ermengare,
Daughter to Charles the foresaid Duke of Lorraine;
By the which marriage the line of Charles the Great
Was re-united to the Crown of France.
So that, as clear as is the summer's sun,
King Pepin's title, and Hugh Capet's claim,
King Lewis his satisfaction, all appear
To hold in right and title of the female;
So do the kings of France unto this day,
Howbeit they would hold up this Salique law
To bar your Highness claiming from the female;
And rather choose to hide them in a net
Than amply to imbar their crooked tides
Usurp'd from you and your progenitors.

HENRY V, Act 1, Sc.2

By repeating and prolonging such privileged and involved
knowledge, the true writer is simultaneously declaring his own
'insider information' and also subverting the idea of anything

being based on ancestry rather than merit or expediency. Jonson, however, was trying to sell to a courtly audience, so he makes Canter's mocking of the Herald very gentle!

A specific family connection of Neville's is also referred to in Jonson's play. This is a member of the Bulmer family (see diagram 3). The Bulmers married into that of the Nevilles more than once, which led to the sign of the Bull becoming one of the heraldic badges of the Neville Family. Raby Castle - ancestral home of the Earls of Westmorland, the main branch of the Neville family - even has a Bulmer Tower. In this scene, Jonson jokingly refers to Sir Beavis Bulmer as Bevis Bullion:

> **P. Jun.** Do'st thou want any Money, Founder?
> **P. Ca.** Who, Sir, I?
> Did I not tell you I was bred i' the Mines,
> Under Sir **Bevis Bullion**.
> **P. Jun.** That is true,
> I quite forgot, you Mine-men want no Money,
> Your Streets are pav'd with't: there, the Molten Silver
> Runs out like Cream on Cakes of Gold.
> **P. Ca.** And Rubies
> Do grow like Strawberries.
> **P. Jun.** 'Twere brave being there!

Perhaps Jonson is here also hinting that the true writer was rich enough not to need a patron. The Scholars in the audience would certainly have picked this up as one of the meanings. But might he also be hinting at Anne Killigrew's step-mother's possible contacts in Silver Street, London? This was where the French Huguenot Mountjoy family lived - the family with whom 'Shakespeare' was said to have lodged. Jael de Payenne, Anne Killigrew's step-mother, was a French Huguenot, and the Mountjoys communicated in French, so it would have been very surprising indeed if William Shakespeare of Stratford was really the man who had lodged with them, as he did not speak French and had no known Huguenot contacts. Canter's assertion that 'Rubies Do grow like Strawberries' seems to be warning us that we must here start sorting out truth from fiction!

Besides being a mining engineer, Beavis Bulmer was also, like Neville, involved in bringing a water supply to various parts of London[198]. He, like Neville too, worked with Richard Martin, whose treatise on the Royal Mint - now among Neville's papers in the Worsley Collection at the Lincolnshire Archives - was written out by none other than Packer, Sir Henry Neville's own scribe. Over and over again, Jonson is sowing his whole text full of clues that lead back to Neville. Indeed, so many verbal and circumstantial clues are given that I finally decided the only way to demonstrate the totality and irrefutable nature of Sir Henry's identity as drawn in Jonson's play was to reproduce and annotate the whole text (which will be published soon after this book).

Alongside all this, Jonson is also keen to show the manufactured nature of news as a 'commodity'. Most telling of all, he points out that the purveyors of news feel quite easy about manufacturing stories for the masses. In the following note, he jokingly undermines characters of his own creation:

To the R E A D E R S.

IN this following Act, the Office [of the Press] is open'd, and shew'n to the Prodigal [Pennyboy Junior], and his Princess Pecunia, wherein the Allegory, and purpose of the Author hath hitherto been wholly mistaken, and so sinister an Interpretation been made, as if the Souls of most of the Spectators had liv'd in the Eyes and Ears of these ridiculous Gossips that tattle between the Acts. But he prays you thus to mend it. To consider the News here vented to be none of his News, or any reasonable Mans; but News made like the *Times* News, (a weekly Cheat to draw Money) and could not be fitter reprehended, than in raising this ridiculous Office of the Staple, wherein the Age may see her own Folly, or hunger and thirst after publish'd Pamphlets of News, set out every Saturday, but made all at home, and no Syllable of truth in them; than which there cannot be a greater Disease in Nature, or a fouler scorn put upon the Times, And so apprehending it, you shall do the Author and your own Judgment a Courtesie, and perceive the Trick of alluring Money to the Office, and there coz'ning the people. If you have the Truth, rest quiet, and consider that
Ficta, voluptatis causa, sint proxima veris.

The last line is from Horace's *Art of Poetry*: 'Fictions, in order to please, should approximate to the truth.' Horace was one of Neville's favourite writers.[199]

The Staple of News which Jonson invented for the play was like a press office into which all kinds of people brought all gradations of 'news'. But the kind of news Jonson chose jokingly to foreground in the play was of the variety which could be labelled as nothing but false, so incredible was it. For instance the news of an ale-house keeper who was said to have discovered perpetual motion:

> **Tho.** The perpetual Motion
> Is here found out by an Ale-wife in Saint Katherines,
> At the Sign o' the dancing Bears.
> **P. Jun.** What, from her Tap?
> I'll go see that, or else I'll send old Canter.
> He can make that discovery.

It is interesting that, even here, Jonson adds that Pennyboy Canter, the true author, is the best person to send to check out this discovery. Neville, as Jonson knew, was keen on science and mathematics. But the list of impossible 'news' grows ever longer:

> **Tho.** They write here one Cornelius-Son,
> Hath made the Hollanders an invisible Eel,
> To swim the Haven at Dunkirk, and sink all
> The shipping there.
> **P. Jun.** But how is't done?
> **Cym.** I'll shew you, Sir.
> It is an Automa, runs under Water,
> With a snug Nose, and has a nimble Tail
> Made like an Auger, with which Tail she wrigles
> Betwixt the Coasts of a Ship, and sinks it streight.
> **P. Jun.** Whence ha' you this News.
> **Fit.** From a right Hand I assure you,
> The Eel Boats here, that lye before Queen-Hythe,
> Came out of Holland.
> **P. Jun.** A most brave Device,
> To murder their flat bottoms.
> **Fit.** I do grant you:
> But what if Spinola have a new Project:
> [*Spinola's new Project; an Army in Cork-shooes.*]

> To bring an Army over in Cork-shooes,
> And land them here at Harwich? all his Horse
> Are shod with Cork, and fourscore Pieces of Ordinance,
> Mounted upon Cork-carriages, with Bladders
> In stead of Wheels to run the Passage over
> At a Spring-tide.
> **P. Jun.** Is't true?
> **Fit.** As true as the rest.
> **P. Jun.** He'll never leave his Engines: I would hear now
> Some curious News.
> **Cym.** As what?
> **P. Jun.** Magick or Alchimy,
> Or flying i' the Air, I care not what.
> **Cla.** They write from Libtzig (Reverence to your Ears)
> The Art of drawing Farts out of dead Bodies,
> *[Extraction of Farts.]*
> Is by the Brotherhood of the Rosie Cross,
> Produc'd unto Perfection, in so sweet
> And rich a Tincture —
> **Fit.** As there is no Princess,
> But may perfume her Chamber with th' Extraction.

I imagine the phrases in Italics might be posted up on banners around the on-stage 'news office' to represent headlines, which the actor points out as he talks of them, thus adding to the comic effect. But Jonson's message is clearly that the idea of an uneducated boy with no courtly or political connections being capable of writing the works now printed in the First Folio is just as nonsensical as all the other manufactured 'news'! This piece of 'ficta' comes no nearer to approximating to the truth than do all the others repeated by this spurious Press Office, or Staple of News. I venture to suggest that this is why Jonson abolishes the Staple of News at the end of his play, leaving us with only the symbolism in his play to rely upon for information. He is in effect saying that those in the audience who understand his true meaning should now abolish the 'vulgar' untrue news regarding Shakespeare's authorship. Yet this news was allowed to masquerade as truth whereas, ironically, Jonson's 'fictional' conundrum is the thing that really tells you truth - but 'If you have the truth,' you should 'rest quiet,' he says.

So why does Jonson exhort those who have solved the conundrum not to tell it? Well, first and foremost, he lets us know that the author did not wish his name to be associated with his plays, for the time being, mainly because of the misconceptions it might bring upon him. Moreover, he hints that, as a politician, he may not 'prostitute' himself. His name in the play, 'Canter', has many meanings, and the character in the play realises that what he has written could be misconstrued. Indeed, one definition of the word 'cant' can itself embody the meaning of something to be 'looked down upon'. It can, in fact, mean any or all of the following, and each one of them suggests a misconstruction of the true worth of the author:

1. boring talk filled with clichés and platitudes
2. hypocritical talk: insincere talk, especially where morals and religion are concerned
3. jargon: the special language or vocabulary of a particular group, especially a group whom some people look down on

[All these meanings were current in the mid-16th century. The word probably stems from Latin cantare "to sing"; perhaps from an ironic comparison between a church choir's singing and the speech of beggars and criminals.]

Jonson must have intended the character's name to carry even this latter sense, since Pennyboy Canter is dressed as a beggar. Neville was also perceived as a criminal by some for becoming involved with the Essex rebellion. Yet many courtiers had sympathised with Essex and some still revered his memory, so the author's association with him may not have diminished sales of the Folio. As Jonson had already implied in his epigram to Sir Henry, however, Neville himself feared 'what posterity shall think' of him - a concern which the following extract from the play also reveals:

> **Pen. Ca.** ...Will it manage well?
> My Name must not be us'd else. Here 'twill dash.
> Your Business has receiv'd a taint, give off,
> I may not prostitute my self. Tut, tut,

The 'it' to which Canter obliquely refers is the First Folio. Public stage plays, as a business, had certainly received a taint. Neville, as a diplomat and politician, plus a member of a Royal family, certainly could not prostitute himself. As for the 'tut, tut', Jonson had edited the works and knew this was an exclamation used predominantly in the History plays, and predominantly by courtiers. Indeed, Canter, in the passage quoted above, purports to be imitating the language of courtiers.

Canter goes on to say, metaphorically, why he did not oppose the printing of individual plays, and yet is now not sure he wants them all published together in one volume:

> That **little** Dust I can blow off at pleasure -
> Here's no such Mountain. Yet, i' the **whole Work!**
> <u>But a light Purse may level.</u>   [*The work is cheap, from the rich writer's point of view - he thinks anyone could afford it.*]

The writer thinks that putting all the plays together gives them meanings which he did not intend. Collectively, they might seem to imply something which is not to be applied universally but only within the context of one particular play.

It is at this point in Jonson's play that Canter's companions suddenly see the light - this beggarly Canter is not what he himself seems to be, (any more than Shakespeare was what he seemed either):

> **Fitton** [a courtier]. This is some other than he seems!
> **P. Jun.** How like you him?
> **Fit.** This cannot be a Canter!
> **P. Jun.** But he is, Sir,
>   And shall be still, and so shall you be too:
>   We'll all be Canters. Now I think of it,
>   A noble Whimsie's come into my Brain!
>   I'll build a Colledge, I and my Pecunia,
>   And call it Canters Colledge: sounds it well?

So Pennyboy Junior - the personification of the First Folio - sees things quite differently from his disguised father, who is Canter, the author. Junior says that when the works are all put together they produce enough of a scholarly basis on which to found a college. He will award Professorships to virtually the whole cast of the play:

> **Alm**. Excellent!
> **P. Jun.** And here stands my Father Rector,
>   And you Professors. You shall all profess
>   Something, and live there, with her *Grace and me*,
>   Your Founders: I'll endow't with Lands and Means,
>   And Lickfinger shall be my Master-Cook.
>   What, is he gone?
> **P. Ca.** And a Professor.
> **P. Jun.** Yes.

P. Ca. And read Apicius de re Culinaria
　　To your brave Doxy and you!
P. Jun. You, Cousin Fitton,
　　Shall (as a Courtier) read the Politicks;
　　Doctor Almanack he shall read Astrology;
　　Shunfield shall read the Military Arts.
... **P. Jun.** And Horace here the Art of Poetry.
　　His Lyricks, and his Madrigals, fine Songs,
　　Which we will have at Dinner, steept in Clarret,
　　And against Supper, sous'd in Sack.
Madrigal. In troth,
　　A divine Whimsie!
Shun. And a worthy Work,
　　Fit for a Chronicle!
P. Jun. Is't not?
Shun. To all Ages.
P. Jun. And Pied-mantle shall give us all our Arms:
　　But Picklock, what wouldst thou be? Thou canst cant too.
Pic. In all the Languages in Westminster-hall,
　　Pleas, Bench, or Chancery. Fee-farm, Fee-Tail,
　　Tenant in Dower, at Will, for Term of Life,
　　By Copy of Court-Roll, Knights Service, Homage,
　　Fealty, Escuage, Soccage, or Frank almoigne,
　　Grand Sergeanty, or Burgage.

Neville's stress on the importance of education, and his founding of Grammar Schools on his Yorkshire lands, is thus celebrated, in an extract which also implicitly advertises Gresham College - the foundation bearing Neville's mother's name, where Jonson himself was then employed! [I have italicised the words 'Grace and me' in the quotation above, because it may well be a pun on 'Gresham'] So it is at this point that we realise many of the other characters in the play were sometimes the embodiments of the different facets of the true author's own multiple personality. It must have seemed to Jonson that Neville possessed all the skills of the various professors at Gresham. Neville knew, for instance, about cookery, mathematics, astronomy, astrology, medicine, politics, rhetoric, law, - he was once even a judge in the Star Chamber - heraldry and the military arts, etc., etc.,. He was therefore (in addition to being Pennyboy Canter) Fitton, the courtier and politician, Picklock, the lawyer, etc. all rolled into one.

Yet Jonson wants to make sure that every thing and every person in the play is somehow connected with the First Folio, so that there can be no mistaken interpretation regarding that fact. After all, the plays are just as multi-faceted as their author - a point he is also stressing in the above extract. Jonson therefore names his characters appropriately and/or points out what they are meant to symbolise. Hence the name of the Courtier in the play - Fitton. Mary Fitton was the erstwhile mistress of William Herbert, Earl of Pembroke, patron of the First Folio, and Jonson knew that this fact would not be missed by his courtly audience. But 'fitten' also meant a liar. One may wonder at the extent of Jonson's daring in so naming a character in his play, but everyone by now accepted Ben as a larger-than-life, extreme individual, whose outrageous characteristics had to be tolerated along with his humour and genius. As we will discover, Picklock's name was also instantly recognisable among the courtiers and men about town of the time, yet Jonson appears to have suffered no adverse effects from his risk-taking in this respect either.

In fact, it is Picklock, the lawyer, who later in the play finally hints that perhaps one hidden reason why Neville does not want to be named is because there is a dark secret concerning the inheritance of his estate:

> **Pic.** I will tell you, Sir,
> Since I am urg'd of those, as I remember,
> You told me you had got a grown Estate,
> By griping Means, sinisterly.

The word 'sinisterly' echoes the heraldic term of the 'bar sinister' - a sign of illegitimacy, which is exactly the conclusion I reached quite independently when viewing the strange circumstances surrounding Henry Neville's birth.

Canter's breath is taken away for the moment by Picklock's remark; he is speechless, for once. Then, little by little, Picklock begins to metamorphose from the family advisor and protector into someone ready to blackmail in order to gain what he suspects may become a precious commodity - the original manuscripts of the Shakespeare plays:

Pic. ...

> You told me you had got a grown Estate,
> By griping Means, sinisterly.

(P. Ca. How!)

Pic. And were

> Ev'n weary of it; if the Parties lived,
> From whom you had wrested it —

(P. Ca. Ha!)

Pic. You could be glad

> To part with all, for satisfaction:
> But since they had yielded to Humanity,
> And that just Heaven had sent you for a Punishment
> (You did acknowledge it) this riotous Heir,
> That would bring all to Beggery in the end,
> And daily sow'd Consumption where he went —

P. Ca. You'ld cozen both then? your Confederate too?

Pic. After a long, mature deliberation,

> You could not think where better how to place it —

P. Ca. Than on you, Rascal?

But who might this Picklock be meant to represent from real life? At this distance in time, it would be quite difficult to identify him, without the 'Neville key'. But Jonson gives us a few clues to the identities of one or two other characters he mentions in the play. For instance, Pecunia - owner of the manuscripts - is a 'Cornish Gentlewoman'. Pennyboy Canter is Neville, and Neville was a spokesman (Canter) for the House of Commons; Sir Bevis Bullion (a named individual in the play) is really Sir Beavis Bulmer, a relative of Neville's. And so it seems that with 'Picklock' Jonson is making a similar play upon names, because the real life lawyer represented here can surely be none other than James Whitelock. Whitelock became a Judge, as well as a Parliamentary supporter of Neville's, and his is seemingly the only posthumous eulogy on Sir Henry to have survived. Whitelock's relatives became associated with Gresham College, and his son himself was a friend and literary associate of William Davenant (see Chapter 8.)

In many ways, Whitelock seems to have been a good man in many respects, and is portrayed as such by Jonson right until the end of the play. Moreover, he was viewed by the Herberts - the patrons of the First Folio - as any ally.[200] He may also have been associated with Neville in an Arminian church movement - the forerunner of Methodism. He was, however, fond of his food, like Neville, and his friends noted that he became increasingly witty over a meal, which is just as he is portrayed in the play. But the times were harsh: Whitelock had an increasingly large family to feed; he had also been imprisoned already by James I, following the publication of an essay on the necessity of the King ruling with Parliament. The last thing he would have needed, therefore, would for it ever to become known that he was associated with the dissident Neville's dissident plays. It seems, then, that Picklock might be talking on two levels here: he knows about Neville's illegitimacy and so is able to try and blackmail him. But the 'estate' he's seeking may well not be his Billingbear home but Neville's manuscripts.

Of course, there was the straight financial incentive too, in that by keeping the original manuscripts he would have been able to charge any interested publisher or theatre company for a viewing of them, plus simultaneously keeping an eye on the possibility of their being a future family asset.

Whitelock's identity accords completely with what Pennyboy Junior and others say about Picklock in the play, before that character makes his entrance:

Cym. One Master Pick-lock,
    A Lawyer, that hath purchas'd here a Place
    This morning, of an Emissary under me.
Fit. Emissary Westminster.
Cym. Gave it into th' Office
Fit. For his Essay, his Piece.
P. Jun. My Man o' Law
    He's my Attorney, and Sollicitor too!
    A fine Pragmatick! what's his Place worth?

The fact that Picklock [Whitelock] knew of Canter's [Neville's] 'sinister' extraction, and his consequent wrongful inheritance, also accords with Whitelock's known purchasing of lands in the Berkshire area, during which exercise he - a skilled lawyer - would have investigated all ownership titles. Bulstrode Whitelock (James' Whitelock's son) lived at Chilton Lodge, which was part of the Hungerford estate once owned by John of Gaunt, and therefore definitely once in the Neville family. James Whitelock (Picklock) was, moreover, patronised by Sir Francis Bacon, who was the half brother of Neville's step-mother, so who better to know his family secrets? Moreover, Neville himself had had altercations with his still-living step mother concerning the inheritance of part of the Berkshire estates[201], which Elizabeth Bacon reckoned should have been hers. Bacon

- a man known to betray his friends - would not have shrunk from revealing all this to Whitelock, especially if Whitelock had tried to buy some of her estate. Bacon was just the man to join with Whitelock on a complete investigation into titles, which could have revealed some of the circumstances surrounding Neville's birth. However, Francis and Elizabeth Bacon would have been the last people to want all this to become public knowledge, as no one knew where such family investigations might lead. In any case, there would certainly be little hope of the childless Elizabeth Bacon inheriting Billingbear, as such estates were usually in 'tail mail'.

Then Whitelock eventually had reason to *fear* Bacon too, because it was Bacon who gave a report on Whitelock's quasi-antimonarchical writings to the Privy Council.[202] It is therefore perfectly possible that Whitelock might for a while have been himself under pressure to do Bacon's bidding, and courtiers in Jonson's privileged target audience would have known all this. Jonson's aspersions would therefore be more likely put down to Bacon's schemes than Whitelock's machinations. But perhaps Jonson was hinting that if anyone in the audience wanted confirmation about who wrote the original manuscripts on which the First Folio was based, then they should seek out the Whitelocks. Bulstrode Whitelock (son of James) was also the man to whom Davenant showed his early manuscripts, so it is highly likely that this family had seen Neville's plays too.

By the time Jonson wrote the play, he would have had no fear of disguisedly placing either Bacon or Whitelock into its framework in this daringly pejorative manner, since King James I was by then displeased with them both. He had indeed already imprisoned each of them - Whitelock because of his essay against absolute monarchy, and Bacon because of his bribery and corruption. As Whitelock was known for his daring political Essay, and Bacon was even better known for his many Essays, it is probable that when the word 'Essay' was mentioned by Fitton, the audience would put these dastardly actions down to Bacon rather than Whitelock. Jonson often used the device of allowing one character in a play to subsume another too, so once again his target audience would listen out for every possibility. Moreover, Picklock's attempt at blackmail was a perfect vehicle in which to allow Jonson to convey the knowledge that there were personal as well as public reasons behind Neville's wish to remain pseudonymous.

The Shakespeare's Plays implied in the Text of Jonson's Drama

Just in case any 'scholar' in his audience - in 1625, or now - ever doubted the fact that the whole of *The Staple of News* was intended as an allegory about the First Folio and its author, Jonson - in addition to all the other clues - also peppered his drama with passing echoes from the Shakespeare plays. The following is just a sample of his technique in this respect:

Picklock
How do's the Heir, bright Master Penny-boy?
Is he awake yet in his One and twenty?
Why, this is better far, than to wear
Dull smutting Gloves, or melancholy Blacks,
And have a pair of Twelvepenny-broad Ribbands
Laid out like Labels.

Pennyboy Junior has been wearing black since he heard of the death of his father. The passing reference to the 'melancholy Blacks' therefore immediately suggests *Hamlet* :

Queen. Good Hamlet, cast thy nighted colour off,
And let thine eye look like a friend on Denmark.
Do not for ever with thy vailed lids
Seek for thy noble father in the dust. *Hamlet*

And the reference to the 'Dull smutting Gloves' is probably meant as a jibe at Shakespeare, the son of a glover. Now that the true, elevated ancestry of the Works is being revealed, the image of the glover's son can be cast away, making the appreciation of the plays 'better far' - as Jonson hopes. And Jonson continues to underline his own play's satirical association with *Hamlet,* :

Alm. ... a brave piece of Cookery! at a Funeral!
But opennyng the Pot-lid, he made us laugh,
Who' had wept all Day! and sent us such a tickling
Into our Nostrils, as the Funeral Feast
Had bin a Wedding-dinner.

This can be no other than a direct reference to the Shakespeare play:

301

Hamlet ...The funeral bak'd meats
Did coldly furnish forth the marriage tables.

Similarly, Pecunia's love at first sight when she meets Pennyboy Junior echoes Miranda's exclamation on first seeing Ferdinand, in the Tempest:

Pec. And I have my desire, Sir, to behold
That Youth and Shape, which in my Dreams and Wakes
I have so oft contemplated, and felt
Warm in my Veins, and native as my Blood.
When I was told of your arrival here,
I felt my Heart beat, as it would leap out
In Speech; and all my Face it was a Flame:
But how it came to pass, I do not know. *The Staple of News*

Pecunia too, like Miranda, has been locked away from the society of men.

Then we have one of Pennyboy Senior's dogs committing the same outrageous act as that of Launce's in *Two Gentlemen of Verona:*

Pen Sen. Where did you lift your Leg up last? 'gainst what?
Are you struck Dummerer now, and whine for Mercy?
Whose Kirtle was't you gnaw'd too? Mistris Band's?
The Staple of News

Launce "Did not I bid thee still mark me and do as I do?
When didst thou see me heave up my leg and make water
against a gentlewoman's farthingale? Didst thou ever see
me do such a trick?" The Two *Gentlemen of Verona*

And thus the references continue!

But what of the 'prodigal son', the 'riotous heir' of Jonson's play? Is it possible that he was partly trying to portray Sir Henry Neville's real-life son within his characterisation of Pennyboy Junior? Well, if the prodigal son is merely seen as the First Folio itself, then this publication was never allowed to be associated with Sir Henry, so it may not mean any more than a book produced 'waywardly' - i.e. without Sir Henry's knowledge. But if the prodigal is also identified as Sir Henry's real-life eldest son, then the known facts point towards something of a beggarly end.

The story is a sad one. In the early part of the 17th century, Sir Henry's son chose to return to France and study

302

there[203]. Neville was given a passport to travel with him when he wished, but he first sent an educated manservant - Simons - to watch him. Simons constantly wrote back to Neville telling him of his son's extravagant tastes and spending sprees[204]. After his student days ended, the boy returned to England, but appears to have gone to lodge with his mother's relatives down in Cornwall - the free-booting side of the Killigrew family - for it is there we discover him being arrested by officers for piracy. Dudley Carleton says that he was beaten during this arrest, so it is possible that he received a brain injury which sent his behaviour from mildly exuberant to positively perverse. We shall probably never know. The times were harsh. Neville and Sir Francis Bacon did their best to get the boy's arrest legally registered as a case of mistaken accusation and mistaken identity, but one is left thinking that the harm was done.

Despite all this, the young man, however, made a favourable marriage. But then, in 1621, young Henry is said to have mortgaged out at least one of his estates. (Perhaps this is why Pecunia - the personification of the original manuscripts - has a nurse called Mortgage in the play.) Jonson would probably have heard about the estate's misfortune by the time he wrote his play, since John Chamberlain hints that young Henry, like his father, was a member of the Mitre Club, which Jonson also frequented[205]. Other hints at the author's son's prodigality are also contained in Theobald's revision of *Cardenio*[206], so all in all, it does look as if his reputation could be a true one, which sad fact now serves further to confirm Sir Henry Neville's true authorship, in accordance with Jonson's clues.

Our Neville himself had written to the Earl of Southampton, saying that he had eleven brothers, so one is forced to conclude that some of these were either born to his father's first wife, Winifred Losse, or else to other unnamed women. What happened to her and them, however, still remains a mystery. Only Jonson's 'factional' play serves as any small light. If Jonson speaks the truth, then all these half brothers - who possibly should have had the Billingbear inheritance - must have been dead by the time the First Folio was published.

With such dark family secrets and such political considerations, no wonder Neville hid his identity. But in hiding it behind the mask of an uneducated man, perhaps he did his readers no favours. 'Nothing can come of nothing' says King Lear, and if the fable of William Shakespeare has given even a hint of an impression to Englishmen that brilliance is more a matter of inspiration than perspiration, then it is a great pity. As Neville and Jonson both knew, 'a true poet's made as well as born'[207].

Like King Richard II, however, Henry Neville junior seemed enough of a prodigal to be over-fond of his clothes, according to Simons, at least, and this aspect of his personality may have been what sparked Jonson's portrayal of him as a bright character in the play. Jonson had the brilliant idea of turning him into the character of Pennyboy Junior, the man who is coming of age at the beginning of the play and waiting for his 'Fashioner' to fit him with a new suit of clothes. As will be seen from the my annotations to the complete version of the play, this device has made it easy for Jonson to overlap Pennyboy Junior's outfitting with the binding and covering of the First Folio, in so many different 'conceits'. Jonson has also cleverly portrayed himself as the 'Fashioner'; there could hardly be a better metaphor for the editor of the Folio and the writer of the play, who are of course one and the same person.

Thom Barber and Thomas Thorpe

The character of Thom Barber, I think, also corresponds to a real person, rather than an abstract quality or inanimate object. I believe he may well represent Thomas Thorpe, publisher of the Sonnets. From what is said to him, Thorpe may have actually helped with the coding of the Dedication too:

> **Fashioner** [*addressing Pen Jun*]. ... I am bound unto your Worship.
> **P. Ju.** Thou shalt be, when I have seal'd thee a Lease of my Custom.
> **Fas.** Your Worships Barber is without.
> **P. Ju**. Who? Thom?
> Come in Thom: set thy things upon the Board,
> And spread thy Clothes, lay all forth in procinctu,

Besides Fashioner's [Jonson's] pun in being 'bound unto' Pennyboy [the First Folio] we have Thom indulging in metaphorical activities too. He is setting things 'upon the Board' - and that was exactly what TT's Code was all about. And laying 'all forth in procinctu' describes the decryption process.

Finally, after Pennyboy Canter reveals himself as the father of Pennyboy Junior - the First Folio- Jonson allows him to reveal himself in the Nevilles' favourite role - that of advisor

304

to the King. Pennyboy Senior [the personification of authority] now becomes specifically King James I. Canter comes back from the (supposed) dead and sweeps away all the King's 'misleaders':

Pennyboy Ca. You see by this amazement and distraction,
    What your Companions were, a poor, afrighted,
    And guilty Race of Men, that dare to stand
    No Breath of Truth; but conscious to themselves
    Of their no-wit, or Honesty, ran routed
    At ever Pannick Terror themselves bred.
    Where else, as confident as sounding Brass,
    Their tinkling Captain, Cymbal, and the rest,
    Dare put on any Visor, to deride
    The wretched, or with Buffoon Licence jest
    At whatsoe're is serious, if not sacred.
P. sen. Who's this? my Brother! and restor'd to Life!
    [*Pennyboy sen. acknowledgeth his elder Brother.*
P. Ca. Yes, and sent hither to restore your Wits,
    If your short Madness be not more than Anger,
    Conceived for your Loss! which I return you.
    See here, your Mortgage, Statute, Band, and Wax,
    Without your Broker, come to abide with you,
    And vindicate the Prodigal from stealing
    Away the Lady. Nay, Pecunia her self
    Is come to free him fairly, and discharge
    All Ties, but those of Love, unto her Person,
    To use her like a Friend, not like a Slave,
    Or like an Idol. Superstition
    Doth violate the Deity it worships,
    No less than Scorn doth. And believe it, Brother,
    The Use of things is all, and not the Store:
    Surfeit and Fulness have kill'd more than Famine.
    The Sparrow, with his little Plumage, flies,
    While the proud Peacock, overcharg'd with Pens,
    Is fain to sweep the Ground with his grown Train,
    And load of Feathers.
P. sen. Wise and honour'd Brother!
    None but a Brother, and sent from the Dead,
    As you are to me, could have altered me:
    I thank my Destiny, that is so gracious.
    Are there no Pains, no Penalties decreed
    From whence you come, to us that smother Money
    In Chests, and strangle her in Bags?

Pennyboy senior is able to call Pennyboy Canter 'brother' for more than one reason. Not only are they brothers in the play, but King James I was accepted into a Masonic order in Scotland.[208] Once inside the lodge, therefore, he - like all the other brethren - had to refer to every other member as a 'brother'. While a parliamentarian, Neville had indeed warned James of the dangers of over-taxing his subjects - warned him, in Jonson's words, of 'Intolerable Fines, and Mulcts impos'd!'[209] The 'Money' kept 'In Chests' probably represents James' restrictive attitude to trade. Right from Richard Neville, Earl of Warwick, onwards, the Nevilles had encouraged moves towards capitalist expansion, and thus defended the needs of the merchants. Sir Henry was a Gresham too, therefore doubly convinced that this was the way to advance the 'Common wealth'. But King James no doubt viewed such policies as a route towards empowering another class in society, other than the 'nobles'; so he had often opposed Neville's ideas. Gradually, however, merchant wealth did predominate; but the merchants still did not have their taxes reduced nor their grievances addressed, nor laws altered in their favour, which all ultimately led to a repeat of Civil War, just as Neville had feared.[210] There was to be none of the Constitutional Monarchy urged by Neville, until after monarchy had learnt its lesson through the tragic suffering of itself and the nation.

But what did Lansdown Goldsworthy finally make of the play? Goldsworthy came to no really firm, specific and all-inclusive conclusions in his Paper, except that he was sure Jonson's play was wholly concerned with marketing the First Folio, and that the writer was seeking to persuade the rich and privileged to buy it. We must all be grateful to Goldsworthy for pointing this out, but it must be admitted that he skirted over whole passages, characters and allusions in the play as being 'mainly intended to form a framework to carry the allusions to "Shakespeare"..'and 'it is not proposed here to attempt any lengthy inquiry into this.'[211] But in not doing so, Goldsworthy stopped short of tackling, researching and analysing the play in holistic depth. As becomes clear when viewing (or reading) the whole of the original play, every character and every allusion carries specific meanings. Of course, as with all art, these meanings are often more complex than a simple one-to-one equivalence, but their multiplicity and complexity within this play always lead back to Neville. Goldsworthy, however, had not hit upon this key factor. But because he appears to have been the only person previously attempting any real interpretation of the play in modern times, one of his theories must be examined and discussed: Goldsworthy thought the play purposely sought to exclude Edward de Vere, Earl of Oxford, from being erroneously identified as the author[212].

It may well be asked why Jonson would have bothered to do this as, at such an early date, de Vere had rarely been mentioned in that context. Did Goldsworthy perhaps think Jonson knew the Dedication to Shakespeare's Sonnets was a Code[213] containing the real author's name? And had Goldsworthy also discovered that the Code contained the word 'Vere'? Did he therefore also believe Jonson considered the possibility of a confusion in the mind of a reader who could see VERE as an anagram of EVER (as in EVER-LIVING POET)? Perhaps. However, it is really highly unlikely for this to have crossed the very logical Jonson's mind, as de Vere died eleven years before the time during which the later Shakespeare plays were written.

Now I have laid bare the process by which that Code is decrypted, and found Sir Henry Neville at its core - identified most specifically, and symmetrically in the Code by so many different means[214] - it also becomes clear why the name 'Vere' is present too. The first 17 of those Sonnets were written with the intention of persuading the Earl of Southampton to marry Burghley's granddaughter, Elizabeth **Vere,** and Jonson would have known all this. Indeed, BETH, VERE and BEN HID IT can be seen in the Code's very first setting, as of course, can NEVELL too. Yet the words BETH and VERE are never placed symmetrically or in a block, whereas NEVELL certainly is:

	1	2	3	4	5	6	7	8	9	10	11	12
1	T	O	T	H	E	O	N	L	I	E	B	E
2	G	E	T	T	E	R	O	F	T	H	E	S
3	E	I	N	S	U	I	N	G	S	O	N	N
4	E	T	S	Mr	W	H	x	A	L	L	H	A
5	P	P	I	N	E	S	S	E	N	N	D	T
6	H	A	T	E	T	E	R	N	I	T	I	E
7	P	R	O	M	I	S	E	D	B	Y	O	U
8	R	E	V	E	R	L	I	V	I	N	G	P
9	O	E	T	W	I	S	H	E	T	H	T	H
10	E	W	E	L	L	W	I	S	H	I	N	G
11	A	D	V	E	N	T	U	R	E	R	I	N
12	S	E	T	T	I	N	G	F	O	R	T	H

BEN HID IT; BETH; VERE;

As has been demonstrated too, the 'fourth settings' of the Dedication arrive directly and symmetrically at the phrases THE WISE THORP HID THY POET and HE ONLIE BE OF THE SEIN[E] - HENRY, POET NEWELL, etc., whereas no algorithmic decryption leads to Vere and his attributes which would in any way suggest Edward de Vere as a possible author.

Goldsworthy, through his lack of the 'key' and lack of an overall concept and thorough analysis of Jonson's play, somewhat tentatively began to think Sir Francis Bacon might have been hinted at as the real Shakespeare. He took the character of Lickfinger, the Cook, to be a reference to the Cooke family. However, Jonson would have known that Sir Henry had connections with the Cooke family too. Bacon's mother was Anne Cooke, but her sister, Catherine Cooke, was Neville's mother in law. The Cooke girls were reputedly the most educated ladies in England, and Catherine was interested in Codes, presenting a Latin treatise on some coding methodology to Sir Henry - a document which is still among his files in the National Archives at Kew. It details a code known to have been used by Sir Francis, which is quite different from the strides Sir Henry made in developing his Dedication Code as an extension of the Cardano Grille and Keyword systems (as described earlier in this book.) The fact that Sir Henry's stepmother was Elizabeth Bacon - half sister of Sir Francis - must also have been taken into account by Jonson. Indeed, Sir Francis and Sir Henry sat in Parliament at the same time too, so it is logical to assume that they had much contact with each other, especially before the catastrophic Essex rebellion. After this their paths definitely diverged, with Henry becoming more progressive and Bacon going in precisely the opposite direction. Bacon opposed Neville on his liberal politics (as Owen Lowe Duncan points out on pp.266 -267 of his Thesis on Sir Henry), favouring absolute rule by the King and advising James I to proceed with that policy - most definitely not the elements which made up the work of the true poet and dramatist! If Bacon had ever had a poetical or dramatic turn of mind, he would not have expressed such an absolutist opinion.

Besides, Bacon himself always protested that he had no poetical skills; he was a brilliant lawyer and laid down rules for empirical research, and for the discernment of science from magic. Such men, such rules and such ideas are needed in the practical world. But he possessed neither the flights of fancy nor the true emotions necessary for the creative artist - as he himself would surely have been the first to admit. As already noted, at the Earl of Essex's trial, Bacon remarked disdainfully that Neville had indulged in a 'long, continued and symbolical speech' in his own defence, whereas a poet and dramatist would have admired, not castigated, such an utterance. On the other hand, it is precisely the kind of speech the real Shakespeare would have made.

Moreover, just to underline Neville's association with Cookery, there is still, among the Duke of Rutland's papers, an invitation to come and hear Sir Henry Neville, Inigo Jones and John Donne speak at a dinner in the Mitre Club. (Oh, that time travel had already been invented!) Francis Bacon, however, was not a Mitre member. Perhaps there is a possibility that Bacon had a hand in discussing the early plays, and Neville must have known Bacon's philosophical essays concerning 'qualities' - such as ambition, or greed - being encapsulated within certain personalities, because Neville points out just such ideas in his annotations of *Leycester's Commonwealth.* But this was old hat even by Bacon's day - it was the stuff of Medieval Mystery plays. I venture to suggest this is one reason why Neville is scribbling down a list of some of Bacon's essays on the Northumberland Manuscript - if Neville's mind was running along the drama track, then he would have seen that Bacon's essays borrowed extensively from the old Medieval plays. Further down the page there are more 'modern' works mentioned, such as *The Isle of Dogs*.

There are indeed impossible discrepancies present in trying to identify Bacon as the man referred to in Jonson's play, one of them being that such an identification would have done nothing, in 1625, to recommend the Shakespeare plays to a 'respectable' audience. On the contrary, associating the plays with Bacon would certainly have discredited them with the King and his Court, since Bacon was by then thoroughly disgraced for bribery and corruption. Indeed, he had just been imprisoned for these crimes. No taint of corruption ever touched Neville, and his association with the Earl of Essex would have done no harm to his reputation, as far as the Stuarts and many courtiers and academics were concerned.

By recognising a few key facts, therefore, it has been possible to name at last the true identities of the dramatis personae in Jonson's play, and thus make better sense of its action. I would like to add one more identity to the list, however, as I believe it will put the seal on Jonson's connecting thread running through the whole of this play. The identification of Dr. Almanack might seem unimportant, as there were so many extant doctor-astrologers at the time. However, it *is* important that Pennyboy Senior is seen as mistrusting his skills, precisely because of Almanack's connection with astrological beliefs. The work of moving towards a more scientific basis for knowledge was definitely promoted by King James [Pennyboy Senior], and by Gresham College, and this became the basis of the Royal Society, which had a Stuart monarch for its patron. So the identity of Dr. Almanack is probably going to lie amongst those people respected by Gresham College for *some* of their abilities, but whose *astrological* beliefs cut no ice with the more practical, progressive scientists. It therefore seems most likely that Dr. Almanack was Thomas Bretnor (1570/71–1618) astrologer and medical practitioner. He settled in London about 1604, and became known through his fluency in Latin, French, and Spanish.

Bretnor, significantly, also published a series of almanacs for the years 1607 to 1619, but in them he defended astrology.

Bretnor's almanacs, however, became popular, probably due just as much to their little aphorisms and forecasts as their astrological basis. Ben Jonson actually mentions him by name in *The Divell is an Asse* (I. ii), while at the same time talking of a certain 'Gresham', so it is not in any way fanciful to suggest that Jonson's mind is running along the Gresham track throughout more than one of his plays.

But Jonson and the Greshamites would have taken Bretnor seriously for the other side of his work, for he included land and quantity surveying, map-making, and navigation amongst his list of skills. In fact, despite his astrological convictions, Bretnor was a friend of Edmund Gunter, professor of astronomy at Gresham College. Jonson, therefore, really was making use of his own time at Gresham College to fuse a thread of connection between himself, the true writer of the Shakespeare plays - Neville - and the production of the First Folio. The increasing popularity of Gresham College as a place for both rich and poor to study, along with its associations with the Gresham-Nevilles, would have definitely increased the sale of the First Folio. And it was Jonson who laid bare this College's connections with the true Shakespeare, in his allegorical *Staple of News*. In his almanacs, Bretnor also drew attention to Napier's work on logarithms, and Napier's associate, Briggs, became professor of mathematics at Gresham. Thus the background to part of the inspiration for the Sonnet Code was also made clear to anyone who might have already cracked it. Once the key to his play is perceived, therefore, Jonson is making sure that all his characterisations and allusions become homogenous. Bretnor also wrote a treatise on the medicinal use of opium, so one is left with a little guess that hallucinations from opium - one of the few painkillers, surely, available to Neville for relief from his bodily afflictions - may have been responsible for parts of *Cymbeline* and *The Tempest*.

We are therefore now able to list some of the real-life identities behind Jonson's characters. The real-life equivalents appear in italics:

PENNYBOY JUNIOR, the Son, the Heir and Suitor = *First Folio, and Henry Neville, the son.*

PENNYBOY CANTER, the Father, the Canter = *Sir Henry Neville, the true Shakespeare.*

PENNYBOY SENIOR, the Uncle, the Usurer = *Authority, sometimes King James I.*

FASHIONER, the Taylor of the Times = *Ben Jonson, author of the play, editor and devisor of the First Folio.*

PICKLOCK, Man o' Law, and Emissary West- minster = *Sir James Whitelock, Judge.*

PECUNIA, Infanta of the Mines = *The original mss of the Plays (with whom Pen. Jun - the First Folio - must be united, and also hinting at Anne Killigrew-Neville.*

MORTGAGE, her Nurse.

BROKER, Secretary, and Gentleman-Usher to her Grace.

STATUTE, first Woman.

BAND, second Woman.

ALMANACK, *Thomas Bretnor*

WAX. Chambermaid.

LICK-FINGER, a Master-Cook, and parcel-Poet = *Spirit of Poetry;*

MADRIGAL, Poetaster, and Jeerer = *possibly Thomas Lodge*

THO. BARBER, second Clerk of the Office = *Thomas Thorpe, publisher of the Sonnets and the Sonnet Code.*

DOGS II. *named 'Lollard and Block' in the play - the Nevilles had been ancestrally associated with the Lollards and Henry Neville with blocking Kings in Parliament. King James - and other authority figures - could therefore well have perceived Neville as having both the Church and Parliament under their own control.*

Thus, all through this case, it has surely been most convincing how carefully-chosen metaphors within the Shakespeare plays themselves, and in the works of his contemporaries, collide with real life, in the most unexpected, totally unpredictable, ways. One way of appreciating how rare such a conglomeration of collisions actually is, is to think of them in topological terms. Poincarré, the 'father' of topology, pointed out that if two bodies are orbiting around each other, then the imaginary paint trails which they leave can be seen to meet at certain definable, predictable points. However, once *three* bodies begin such intertwined orbits, then a very complex situation arises. The coordination points of their paint trails are difficult - almost impossible - to predict. The complexity and unpredictability increases if more orbiting bodies are added to the equation. I venture to suggest, therefore, that the inverse of this situation is also true. Where coordination points arise again and again within these complex paint trails and yet leave a discernible pattern, capable of an explanatory, all-encompassing theory, then this theory is likely to be true.

For instance, one 'orbit' in which Sir Henry moved was that of iron and cannon manufacture. This fact focused our attention on the references to iron and ordnance within the plays. Many references were found, including specialist terminology usually restricted to workers in that field. Yet surely few scholars had previously glanced in this direction. Why not? Precisely because this 'orbit' was never suspected in Shakespeare's identity. Yet when it began to leave its visible paint trail, there it was, meeting up with all the other orbits. The discovery of Jonson's play, with its re-iteration of connections between the writer, iron and military science, showed how all these orbits again coincide. The coordination points between Shakespeare's and the iron's 'orbits' were therefore looked at again, and found to be intertwining, from every perspective. The Jonson 'orbit' had now been added to the others, and, surprise, surprise, its coordination points matched those of the other orbits. The Cornish orbit was also noticed - again not a location previously considered very often in connection with the plays supposedly stemming from the hand of a Midland author who is never known to have seen the sea - but there it was in the true author's life, as is surely hinted at in the pirates' characterisation in *Hamlet, Pericles, Twelfth Night, Measure for Measure* and *Henry VI part 2*. Then again, the never-suspected Cornish connection appears in Jonson's play too. Next, par excellence, there is the political orbit. This is certainly obvious within the plays, yet inexplicable if we think of Shakespeare as the author, for he never travelled in any such orbit, so left no paint trails which could possibly coordinate with the plays, nor with all the other orbits now perceived. Sir Francis Bacon travelled in the political orbit, but not in the orbit of iron working, so once again the multiple paint trails left by these other multiple orbits do not all have coordination points with Sir Francis'.

One point Poincarré also made very clear was that shapes were not topologically similar unless they could be easily pressed to re-form themselves into other shapes, without having to slice them up. This indeed defines the basic difference between topology and geometry. Altogether, Sir Henry Neville's case (or 'shape') can be extended in all directions to conform to that within the plays and within all the other evidence leading to the correct identification of him inside the authorship question. Unlike the case of the Earl of Oxford, there is no 'slicing' off at a crucial point in the appearance of the plays which, even without the fact that the Earl's orbits also leave divergent paint trails from those left by the plays, would discount him completely, topologically speaking. Sir Henry Neville's case, on the other hand, is topologically sound. Moreover, his case now stands up to scrutiny based on every other type of perception and analysis too. There can now truly be little doubt that Sir Henry Neville is Shakespeare.

Addendum

THE CODE AND ITS DOUBLE

Having spent so much time analysing the Dedication Code, I eventually became brave enough to attempt to construct one of my own, on the same model and with parallel, but substantially different, inclusions. By doing this, I reasoned that I should be able to settle once and for all two major questions that arise from its solution: 1) Is it possible that the words in the Dedication grid appear just by chance, even in their transformations? and 2) Is it really possible to predict how the transformations will turn out and, therefore, possible to construct a similar code using some sort of plan?

In order to answer the first question, I wrote several tracts consisting of random and unencrypted texts, then subjected these texts to various transformations to see if any consistent sense could be made from them. A selection of the results - printed at the end of this chapter - seems pretty conclusive. Common words are sometimes formed by re-arranging the letters in the texts, but they do not form and re-form either proper names or significant phrases. By 'significant phrases' I mean phrases that can be deduced to stem from the wording and hints contained within the original plaintext. For instance, in the Dedication Code, we have the words SETTING FORTH, and it is subsequently in the **fourth** setting that a linear message appears. Added to this, we have the embedded phrase HE ONLIE BE OF THE SEIN(E) with the word HENRY in a straight, vertical line beneath it. Then we have various spellings of the name NEVILLE throughout the settings of the text, plus factors associated with his life.

Predictably, no such consistencies appeared in settings of the random texts. Another feature these random texts had in common was that they looked less 'contrived', more natural than the text of the Dedication Code.

Next, I tried a simple encoding of the names SIMON, GLANVILLE and NEVILLE within a text of my own. All I did

315

was consciously to use and re-use phonemes that were included in these names. At this stage, I did not attempt to construct overlapping messages that could appear in different settings, as I felt I needed to begin to practice with a simple task. Only after doing this would I feel confident enough to construct a more advanced code - more advanced, that is, in the sense of being specifically planned to give more than a one word message in the fourth setting.

Even though this initial text was only to encode three simple names, the restrictions produced by this requirement made the difference from the *random* texts I had constructed immediately noticeable: in order to include these phonemes the text had to become quite strangely-worded. It was impossible to let it flow. However, if I had been prepared to spend more time on it, I had no doubt that I could then have constructed a better text. The time factor was indeed a huge consideration, and so by attempting my own code construction I was made even more aware of the fact that whoever constructed the Dedication Code must have had hours of uninterrupted time to spend. This is obviously consistent with Neville's sojourn in the Tower, but is difficult to explain if it was indeed written by any busy professional engaged in the hurly burly of the world, such as an actor like William Shakespeare or a publisher like Thomas Thorpe.

I constructed my 12 x 12 grid and soon became aware of the difficulties. I wanted the names of my encoded subjects to link together in some way, if possible. This was the best I could come up with after ten minutes' experimentation: the need to encode the names SIMON, GLANVILLE and NEVILLE certainly led me to construct a silly text.

TO . THE . BEST . HELPING . HAND .
MY. OWN . GLAD . ONE . WILL .
EVER . HAVE,
I . GLADLY . GIVE .
AN . AMUSING . FEW . LINES .
AMONG . THE . MANY . SONGS .
I . HAVE . SPENT . MY . TIME . SAVING .
LAND . LIFE . NO . EVIL .
LONGING .
WILL . BE .
HIS . LOT .

Yet, however silly, it is at least a plain text. The only features that tell us it may be encrypted are indeed those very features that tell us that the Dedication to the Sonnets is also a code:

1) It is laid out in a peculiar fashion
2) It contains some unusual words, and sometimes these words are even used more than once [GLAD, GLADLY, which rather parallels WISHETH THE WELL-WISHING., as appears in the Dedication Code.] (I did this in the hope of getting the GLA to become part of GLANVILLE, just as Thorpe hoped all that WISHING would become part of WISE. Thorpe had cleverly used EVER-LIVING to form the VIL of NEVIL, so I tried to vary this by using the word EVIL in my own text.)
3) Its phrases are strange and hard to interpret. (Like Thorpe, I was constrained by the need for certain phonemes to cluster together, so had to use an unusual sequence of words.)

I used 144 letters, just as in the Dedication Code, and I constructed my last line so that it consisted of whole words when transformed into a 12 by 12 matrix:

1	2	3	4	5	6	7	8	9	10	11	12
T	O	T	H	E	B	E	S	T	H	E	L
P	I	N	G	H	A	N	D	M	Y	O	W
N	G	L	A	D	O	N	E	W	I	L	L
E	V	E	R	H	A	V	E	I	G	L	A
D	L	Y	G	I	V	E	A	N	A	M	U
S	I	N	G	F	E	W	L	I	N	E	S
A	M	O	N	G	T	H	E	M	A	N	Y
S	O	N	G	S	I	H	A	V	E	S	P
E	N	T	M	Y	T	I	M	E	S	A	V
I	N	G	L	A	N	D	L	I	F	E	N
O	E	V	I	L	L	O	N	G	I	N	G
W	I	L	L	B	E	H	I	S	L	O	T

I found that if I used the last line WILL BE HIS LOT as my keyword, I did indeed get repeated instances of SIMON, GLANVILLE and NEVILLE (variously spelt.) I also managed to design the grid so that the name SIMON GLANVILLE appeared in a hidden cluster in the first setting, just as with HAREE NEVELL in the true Code.

Here is my code and its first few transformations:

1	2	3	4	5	6	7	8	9	10	11	12
T	O	T	H	E	B	E	S	T	H	E	L
P	I	N	G	H	A	N	D	M	Y	O	W
N	G	L	A	D	O	N	E	W	I	L	L
E	V	E	R	H	A	V	E	I	G	L	A
D	L	Y	G	I	V	E	A	N	A	M	U
S	I	N	G	F	E	W	L	I	N	E	S
A	M	O	N	G	T	H	E	M	A	N	Y
S	O	N	G	S	I	H	A	V	E	S	P
E	N	T	M	Y	T	I	M	E	S	A	V
I	N	G	L	A	N	D	L	I	F	E	N
O	E	V	I	L	L	O	N	G	I	N	G
W	I	L	L	B	E	H	I	S	L	O	T

L	H	B	E	T	O	T	E	H	S	T	E
W	G	A	N	P	I	N	H	Y	D	M	O
L	A	O	N	N	G	L	D	I	E	W	L
A	R	A	V	E	V	E	H	G	E	I	L
U	G	V	E	D	L	Y	I	A	A	N	M
S	G	E	W	S	I	N	F	N	L	I	E
Y	N	T	H	A	M	O	G	A	E	M	N
P	G	I	H	S	O	N	S	E	A	V	S
V	M	T	I	E	N	T	Y	S	M	E	A
N	L	N	D	I	N	G	A	F	L	I	E
G	I	L	O	O	E	V	L	I	N	G	N
T	L	E	H	W	I	L	B	L	I	S	O

E	E	O	T	L	H	B	T	S	E	H	T
O	N	I	N	W	G	A	P	D	H	Y	M
L	N	G	L	L	A	O	N	E	D	I	W
L	V	V	E	A	R	A	E	E	H	G	I
M	E	L	Y	U	G	V	D	A	I	A	N
E	W	I	N	S	G	E	S	L	F	N	I
N	H	M	O	Y	N	T	A	E	G	A	M
S	H	O	N	P	G	I	S	A	S	E	V
A	I	N	T	V	M	T	E	M	Y	S	E
E	D	N	G	N	L	N	I	L	A	F	I
N	O	E	V	G	I	L	O	N	L	I	G
O	H	I	L	T	L	E	W	I	B	L	S

T	T	H	B	E	E	O	L	E	T	S	H
M	N	G	A	O	N	I	W	H	P	D	Y
W	L	A	O	L	N	G	L	D	N	E	I
I	E	R	A	L	V	V	A	H	E	E	G
N	Y	G	V	M	E	L	U	I	D	A	A
I	N	G	E	E	W	I	S	F	S	L	N
M	O	N	T	N	H	M	Y	G	A	E	A
V	N	G	I	S	H	O	P	S	S	A	E
E	T	M	T	A	I	N	V	Y	E	M	S
I	G	L	N	E	D	N	N	A	I	L	F
G	V	I	L	N	O	E	G	L	O	N	I
S	L	L	E	O	H	I	T	B	W	I	L

H	B	E	O	T	T	H	E	T	L	E	S
Y	A	N	I	M	N	G	O	P	W	H	D
I	O	N	G	W	L	A	L	N	L	D	E
G	A	V	V	I	E	R	L	E	A	H	E
A	V	E	L	N	Y	G	M	D	U	I	A
N	E	W	I	I	N	G	E	S	S	F	L
A	T	H	M	M	O	N	N	A	Y	G	E
E	I	H	O	V	N	G	S	S	P	S	A
S	T	I	N	E	T	M	A	E	V	Y	M
F	N	D	N	I	G	L	E	I	N	A	L
I	L	O	E	G	V	I	N	O	G	L	N
L	E	H	I	S	L	L	O	W	T	B	I

As can be seen, I got versions of SIMON, GLANVILLE, NEVILLE everywhere, sometimes overlapping. Admittedly, I also got words which I had not planned, like GAVEL, but these were not often repeated and did not detract from the words I had consciously pre-planned. I also did not get many words of more than four letters. Indeed, it is statistically unusual to find unplanned words of more than four letters forming randomly. Likewise, one can now see how unusual it is to find any whole phrases linked within any settings of such a Code, again confirming that THE WISE THORP HID THY POET could not have appeared by chance. Neither did I find any misleading words or phrases. In any case, I reasoned that given time and the will to do so, I could change words and phrases here and there, if any formed that were misleading.

Of course, this was a mere beginning to my task. I realised that my next task must be to work out how Thorpe (or Neville) managed to overlap his settings, so that in the 15 across grid he got HENRY appearing in a straight vertical line, while it appeared in a diagonal one in the 16 across setting, and at the same time reproduced a message in the fourth transformation of the 12 x 12 grid.

But before I embarked on this daunting task, I had to bear in mind that Thorpe was telling us about a real live person and his attributes, which included both his writing and other activities, so that the phonemes Thorpe used would have been designed to form words concerned with all the aspects of the poet's life. So now I invented a name and a life. My fictional poet would be called Henry Darcy (I used Henry because it would then be reminiscent of the true Code, and Darcy because it contained some less-used letters of the alphabet.) I reasoned that if I could make the word Darcy appear, then it would certainly be only by design, not accident. Then I thought of embedding meanings in my first two lines, just as in the true Code. In order to do this, I now needed to write Darcy's biography.

My Henry Darcy was a sixteenth century shepherd who worked on the land of a certain Duke – was he his illegitimate son? Yes, perhaps so, because this shepherd had managed to gain a good education. He began to write poetry, and was soon in demand among the aristocracy of the north of England. He had a wife called Angela.

As I worked out my grid, I tried to think of words associated with shepherding. Strangely, the constraint produced by the need for certain letters to be placed in specific cells in the grid made it possible for me to use the words 'crook' and 'bleat.' (I remembered how appropriate the words BEGETTER, ETERNITIE, EVER-LIVING and ADVENTURER were to the prodigious Henry Neville. He was a **begetter** of at least eleven children, so his family seemed sure to be an **ever-living eternity**. He was also an **adventurer** in the Virginia Company.)

This is how I worked out the Henry Darcy code. I decided to give my linear message in the fourth setting, just as in the true Code, so first of all I set out this linear message as I wished it to appear in that setting:

1								
2								
3								
4								
5								
6								
7					y			
8				r				
9			n					
10		e						
11	t	h	e	b	e	s	t	
12								

My main message would be HENRY, THE BEST. As it was to appear in the fourth setting, I could not form the rest of the grid or the column numbering at this stage. I had to work back to the first setting and then form the other words and the column numbers around this first setting. In other words, I had to reverse the process described in Chapter 4. It is here I must warn the reader that the process becomes very involved - it is one of those tasks that has to be performed to be understood properly! The only way to get to grips with it is to begin by setting out the whole task on squared paper and working stepwise through the processing. In fact, I eventually constructed a wooden model for demonstration purposes. I purchased 12 strips of wooden doweling, printed out each column of the Dedication Code, then pasted the letters from each column onto the doweling. Next, I produced a horizontal row of numbers from 1 to 12, below which row I placed the strips. I then produced another horizontal strip containing the keyword ordering of the columns. By moving each column to its appropriate new place, I could actually observe the process in physical operation. This kind of construction could easily have been made in Neville's day too.

Indeed, the Napier's bones type of calculators were formed in this way, with the columns or 'bones' being placed in a box so as to keep them from slipping out of their new order when they were moved.

So now that I had the order of columns for the fourth setting I could label my linear message table with the '4th setting' numbers and then transfer those columns to their first setting positions, so that column 7 of my fourth setting became column 1 of my first setting, etc. The resultant First Setting of my grid therefore looks like this:

	1	2	3	4	5	6	7	8	9	10	11	12
1												
2												
3												
4												
5												
6												
7								y				
8									r			
9			n									
10						e						
11			h	b		e		t	s	e		t
12	S	A	T	I	S	F	A	C	T	I	O	N

I now had to form a text that incorporated the letters of my message above in their First Setting positions, while the keyword SATISFACTION could now also be placed in its correct order. This meant that I could now weave a First Setting Plaintext around those letters, secure in the knowledge that it would be transposed into the message I originally designed by the time I reached the Fourth Setting.

But I also wanted to make sure that I could include the word DARCY in a vertical column straight down a 15 across grid, in just the same way as HENRY had been placed in the true Code. To do this, I had to set out a 15 across grid and place the set letters of DARCY and HENRY so that they would appear in this new setting. So as to be clear about this, I first labelled each cell in the 12 x 12 setting with its own reference number, so that

I could then carry these same individual reference numbers over to the 15 across setting.

	1	2	3	4	5	6	7	8	9	10	11	12
1	1a	2a	3a	4a	5a	6a	7a	8a	9a	10a	11a	12a
2	1b	2b	3b	4b	5b	6b	7b	8b	9b	10b	11b	12b
3	1c	2c	3c	4c	5c	6c	7c	8c	9c	10c	11c	12c
4	1d	2d	3d	4d	5d	6d	7d	8d	9d	10d	11d	12d
5	1e	2e	3e	4e	5e	6e	7e	8e	9e	10e	11e	12e
6	1f	2f	3f	4f	5f	6f	7f	8f	9f	10f	11f	12f
7	1g	2g	3g	4g	5g	6g	7g	8g	9g	10g	11g	12g
8	1h	2h	3h	4h	5h	6h	7h	8h	9h	10h	11h	12h
9	1j	2j	3j	4j	5j	6j	7j	8j	9j	10j	11j	12j
10	1k	2k	3k	4k	5k	6k	7k	8k	9k	10k	11k	12k
11	1m	2m	3m	4m	5m	6m	7m	8m	9m	10m	11m	12m
12	1n	2n	3n	4n	5n	6n	7n	8n	9n	10n	11n	12n

Now I knew that, for example, cell 3m – i.e. row 11, column 3 – in whichever grid it appeared, - must contain the letter H.

With this in mind, and keeping the individual cell reference numbers, I now set out my 15 across grid, labelling each square or 'tile' with the reference numbers I had given them in the 12 x 12 matrix:

	1	2	3	4	5	6	7	8	9	10	11	12	13	14	15
1	1a	2a	3a	4a	5a	6a	7a	8a	9a	10a	11a	12a	1b	2b	3b
2	4b	5b	6b	7b	8b	9b	10b	11b	12b	1c	2c	3c	4c	5c	6c
3	7c	8c	9c	10c	11c	12c	1d	2d	3d	4d	5d	6d	7d	8d	9d
4	10d	11d	12d	1e	2e	3e	4e	5e	6e	7e	8e	9e	10e	11e	12e
5	1f	2f	3f	4f	5f	6f	7f	8f	9f	10f	11f	12f	1g	2g	3g
6	4g	5g	6g	7g	8g	9g	10g	11g	12g	1h	2h	3h	4h	5h	6h
7	7h	8h	9h	10h	11h	12h	1j	2j	3j	4j	5j	6j	7j	8j	9j
8	10j	11j	12j	1k	2k	3k	4k	5k	6k	7k	8k	9k	10k	11k	12k
9	1m	2m	3m	4m	5m	6m	7m	8m	9m	10m	11m	12m	1n	2n	3n
10	4n	5n	6n	7n	8n	9n	10n	11n	12n						

Onto this 15 across grid, I superimposed the word DARCY and also embedded a message within the first two rows, just as HE ONLIE BE OF THE SEIN(E) is embedded in the true Code, while still keeping the necessary letters from my 12 x 12 grid in their required cells. (The lower case letters represent the requirements of that other grid):

	1	2	3	4	5	6	7	8	9	10	11	12	13	14	15
1	1a	2a	3a	T	H	E	G	R	E	10a	11a	12a	1b	2b	3b
2	4b	5b	6b	A	T	M	A	N	S	1c	2c	3c	4c	5c	6c
3	7c	8c	9c	10c	11c	12c	1d	D	3d	4d	5d	6d	7d	8d	9d
4	10d	11d	12d	1e	2e	3e	4e	A	6e	7e	8e	9e	10e	11e	12e
5	1f	2f	3f	4f	5f	6f	7f	R	9f	10f	11f	12f	1g	2g	3g
6	4g	5g	6g	7g	8g	y	10g	C	12g	1h	2h	3h	4h	5h	6h
7	7h	8h	9h	**r**	11h	12h	1j	**Y**	3j	**n**	5j	6j	7j	8j	9j
8	10j	11j	12j	1k	2k	3k	4k	5k	**e**	7k	8k	9k	10k	11k	12k
9	1m	2m	**h**	**b**	5m	**e**	7m	**t**	**s**	**e**	11m	**t**	S	A	T
10	I	S	F	A	C	T	I	O	N						

As can be seen above, I wrote THE GREAT MAN'S above DARCY and decided to weave the rest of my inscription in with all this.

In all, the whole exercise took about three hours. In the seventeenth century, the grids would probably have been drawn out on a large piece of paper and individual cards or tiles with letters on one side and cell references on the other, which would have made the job almost as easy as with a computer. My resultant plain text, though once again a rather silly one, made some sort of sense and was arguably only a little less intelligible than the Dedication Code itself:

	1	2	3	4	5	6	7	8	9	10	11	12	13	14	15
1	T	H	A	T	H	E	G	R	E	W	H	E	N	B	E
2	I	N	G	A	T	M	A	N	S	I	O	N	S	O	F
3	T	H	E	D	R	E	A	D	L	O	R	D	S	O	F
4	T	H	I	S	S	T	R	A	N	G	E	L	A	N	D
5	I	S	N	O	S	E	C	R	E	T	N	O	W	W	I
6	T	H	M	A	N	Y	A	C	R	O	O	K	E	D	L
7	I	N	E	R	E	A	D	Y	O	N	C	E	A	G	A
8	I	N	H	I	S	D	U	K	E	A	S	K	S	W	H
9	I	C	H	B	L	E	A	T	S	E	N	T	S	A	T
10	I	S	F	A	C	T	I	O	N						

Set down as an inscription, the text reads:

THAT . HE . GREW . WHEN . BEING . AT .
MANSIONS . OF . THE . DREAD .
LORDS . OF . THIS .
STRANGE . LAND .
IS .
NO . SECRET .
NOW, WITH . MANY .
A . CROOKED . LINE . READY.
ONCE . AGAIN . HIS . DUKE .
ASKS .
WHICH . BLEAT .
SENT .
SATISFACTION .

With more time and inclination on my part, the whole exercise
could have been more expertly executed, no doubt. But it surely
has served to make the point that, if one wishes to obtain
anything like regular patterns and word clusters, then the whole
operation must be painstakingly planned. The regular and
discernible word clusters in the Dedication Code to the Sonnets
could not have happened by chance. This is especially true
when one also considers the number of hints towards the Code's
solution which are placed in the original text of the Dedication.

Set out below are the first few 12 X 12 transformations of my own code, with HENRY, THE BEST appearing, *as planned*, in the fourth setting:

FIRST SETTING:

	S	A	T	I	S	F	A	C	T	I	O	N
	9	1	11	5	10	4	2	3	12	6	8	7
	1	*2*	*3*	*4*	*5*	*6*	*7*	*8*	*9*	*10*	*11*	*12*
1	T	H	A	T	H	E	G	R	E	W	H	E
2	N	B	E	I	N	G	A	T	M	A	N	S
3	I	O	N	S	O	F	T	H	E	D	R	E
4	A	D	L	O	R	D	S	O	F	T	H	I
5	S	S	T	R	A	N	G	E	L	A	N	D
6	I	S	N	O	S	E	C	R	E	T	N	O
7	W	W	I	T	H	M	A	N	Y	A	C	R
8	O	O	K	E	D	L	I	N	E	R	E	A
9	D	Y	O	N	C	E	A	G	A	I	N	H
10	I	S	D	U	K	E	A	S	K	S	W	H
11	I	C	H	B	L	E	A	T	S	E	N	T
12	S	A	T	I	S	F	A	C	T	I	O	N

SECOND SETTING:

E	T	H	H	W	T	H	A	E	E	R	G
M	N	N	N	A	I	B	E	S	G	T	A
E	I	R	O	D	S	O	N	E	F	H	T
F	A	H	R	T	O	D	L	I	D	O	S
L	S	N	A	A	R	S	T	D	N	E	G
E	I	N	S	T	O	S	N	O	E	R	C
Y	W	C	H	A	T	W	I	R	M	N	A
E	O	E	D	R	E	O	K	A	L	N	I
A	D	N	C	I	N	Y	O	H	E	G	A
K	I	W	K	S	U	S	D	H	E	S	A
S	I	N	L	E	B	C	H	T	E	T	A
T	S	O	S	I	I	A	T	N	F	C	A

THIRD SETTING:

E	E	R	W	E	H	T	H	G	T	A	H
S	M	T	A	G	N	N	N	A	I	E	B
E	E	H	D	F	O	I	R	T	S	N	O
I	F	O	T	D	R	A	H	S	O	L	D
D	L	E	A	N	A	S	N	G	R	T	S
O	E	R	T	E	S	I	N	C	O	N	S
R	Y	N	A	M	H	W	C	A	T	I	W
A	E	N	R	L	D	O	E	I	E	K	O
H	A	G	I	E	C	D	N	A	N	O	Y
H	K	S	S	E	K	I	W	A	U	D	S
T	S	T	E	E	L	I	N	A	B	H	C
N	T	C	I	F	S	S	O	A	I	T	A

Though not quite the name I want, HENRY DARY has appeared in this, the third setting, because I used the phonenemes of this name within the text. Significantly, the Australian enthusiasts found 'Nivil' in the first setting of the text, which is as far as they went, as they had not discovered the keyword system.

FOURTH SETTING:

G	E	A	E	T	W	E	R	H	H	H	T
A	S	E	G	I	A	M	T	B	N	N	N
T	E	N	F	S	D	E	H	O	O	R	I
S	I	L	D	O	T	F	O	D	R	H	A
G	D	T	N	R	A	L	E	S	A	N	S
C	O	N	E	O	T	E	R	S	S	N	I
A	R	I	M	T	A	Y	N	W	H	C	W
I	A	K	L	E	R	E	N	O	D	E	O
A	H	O	E	N	I	A	G	Y	C	N	D
A	H	D	E	U	S	K	S	S	K	W	I
A	T	H	E	B	E	S	T	C	L	N	I
A	N	T	F	I	I	T	C	A	S	O	S

One fact here is absolutely plain: never once does the name NEVILLE or any of its variants appear where the phonemes have not been specifically designed for it to do so.

In the 16 x 9 setting, we again get DARCY in a diagonal line, with the name of his wife ANGELA attached to it:

1	2	3	4	5	6	7	8	9	10	11	12	13	14	15	16
T	H	A	T	H	E	G	R	E	W	H	E	N	B	E	I
N	G	A	T	M	A	N	S	I	O	N	S	O	F	T	H
E	D	R	E	A	D	L	O	R	D	S	O	F	T	H	I
S	S	T	R	*A*	*N*	*G*	*E*	*L*	*A*	N	D	I	S	N	O
S	E	C	R	E	T	N	O	W	W	I	T	H	M	A	N
Y	A	C	R	O	O	K	E	D	L	I	N	E	R	E	A
D	Y	O	N	C	E	A	G	A	I	N	H	I	S	D	U
K	E	A	S	K	S	W	H	I	C	H	B	L	E	A	T
S	E	N	T	S	A	T	I	S	F	A	C	T	I	O	N

Again, this was designed, not the work of chance.

After the experience of planning out this Code, I began to think of analogous activities. The nearest I could come to it from my own experience was a game of cards. It was something like the most complicated solitaire game I know, where one deals out piles of three cards from a randomly shuffled pack and then must abide by certain strict rules of ordering and moving from one pile to another so as to form sequences from which the suits can ultimately be sorted in ascending order. At each turn, one required move is restricted by another, so that the player must carefully pre-plan every move so as not to block the rest. The spatial element of the Code's requirements and its complex need to combine one grid with the requirements of another, and to choose a text that hints at its subject while at the same time fitting in with the restricted placement of the letters, produce the same confusion as that complex game of cards, or perhaps a similarly complex game of chess, where once again the grid comes into play.

Or another analogy might be tiling a complex, Roman-type floor. The placement of the tiles must be pre-arranged, even though some individual tiles must look confusing when seen in isolation from the whole picture, just like a jigsaw puzzle. Each tile must be labelled on its back and placed according to a diagrammatic grid. Nothing can be left to chance in any of these operations. So was it pure chance, I wonder, that the man who tiled the floors of Billingbeare House – the home of Sir Henry Neville – was called Thorpe? Was he perhaps related to the code-maker? I wonder if we shall ever be able to find the answer; at least the quest should be interesting and may provide answers to questions we have not even thought of asking.

EXPERIMENTAL POSTSCRIPT

Here, as promised, are the results of a **random** inscription experiment I carried out after constructing the Code above. This was the random, uncoded text I invented:

> I DEDICATE THESE POEMS
> TO THE RIGHT
> HONOURABLE
> AUGUSTUS MUNSTER
> TO WHOM I WISH
> LONG LIFE
> HEALTH AND
> HAPPINESS
> STRENGTHENED BY
> A CONSTANT DESIRE
> TO SEND MANY
> MORE SOON

Points I noticed about the random, **uncoded** text I produced are as follows:

1) To begin with, as I was *not encrypting* the text, I did not feel constrained to produce 144 letters. With the randomly-produced 138 letters of my text above, there is no squared number to be found. I said what I wanted to say, and did not produce the number of letters that could fit perfectly into any squared grid, whereas the **true Code** fits into 12 x 12, 16 x 9, 9 x 16,

8 x 18, 18 x8, 6 x 24, and 24 x 6. This fact alone is the very first sign that we are dealing with a **code** in the Dedication to the Sonnets. How many other dedications or inscriptions are formed with exactly this number of letters, thus proclaiming their intent and at the same time affording us the very best chances of forming subtexts?

2) If I attempt to place my uncoded dedication onto a perfect 12 x 12 grid, no obvious keyword appears.

3) If I give the text the 'benefit of the doubt', however, I suppose BLE AUGUSTUS M (line 4 of the attempted grid below) comes closest to a usable keyword, so I tried what happened when I used this.

4) New words do indeed appear in the transformations of the 12 x 12 settings, but there is no connection between them and they are in no way connected with the text itself. Neither does there appear to be any pun in the text to give a clue towards any method of decipherment.

5) No linear message appears.

6) There is no name that can link us to the creator of the code or the author, whereas Thorpe was the name of the printer and, perhaps, co-compiler of the Dedication Code, and it is Thorpe's name that forms itself in the linear message of the true Code.

7) The words BRINY and GOATS appear diagonally in the 16 across setting, but since these do not refer to anything else in the inscription, and are certainly not named persons, they cannot be counted as significant. In the true Code, words within the plaintext, plus words within the transformations confirm each other's existence, as they do in my own 'parallel code.'

8) This Dedication has a more normal appearance of plain text than does that of the true Code. There are no repeated words, and not one V in sight, so the name Neville could not form itself unless we use a W as a double V. But in the true Code, the inventor made absolutely certain the name would form and re-form itself by contriving to use both Vs and Ws.

For interest's sake, then, the results of the random test now follow, though I would argue that without the indication of a perfect square number of letters being used, then no one would suspect them of being encrypted in this manner. This argument alone therefore should almost be enough to prove in the first instance that we are dealing with intentional encryption in the true Dedication Code to the *Sonnets*, and that it was indeed intended to be laid out first in a perfect square.

(N.B. The letters 'zo' appear in the squares which remain unused.)

keyword	B	L	E	A	U	G	U	S	T	U	S	M
	2	5	3	1	10	4	11	7	9	12	8	6
	1	*2*	*3*	*4*	*5*	*6*	*7*	*8*	*9*	*10*	*11*	*12*
1	I	D	E	D	I	C	A	T	E	T	H	E
2	S	E	P	O	E	M	S	T	O	T	H	E
3	R	I	G	H	T	H	O	N	O	U	R	A
4	B	L	E	A	U	G	U	S	T	U	S	M
5	U	N	S	T	E	R	T	O	W	H	O	M
6	I	W	I	S	H	L	O	N	G	L	I	F
7	E	H	E	A	L	T	H	A	N	D	H	A
8	P	P	I	N	E	S	S	S	T	R	E	N
9	G	T	H	E	N	E	D	B	Y	A	C	O
10	N	S	T	A	N	T	D	E	S	I	R	E
11	T	O	S	E	N	D	M	A	N	Y	M	O
12	R	E	S	O	O	N	zo	zo	zo	zo	zo	zo

SECOND SETTING:

D	I	E	I	T	D	H	A	E	E	T	C
E	E	P	S	T	O	H	S	O	E	T	M
I	T	G	R	U	H	R	O	O	A	N	H
L	U	E	B	U	A	S	U	T	M	S	G
N	E	S	U	H	T	O	T	W	M	O	R
W	H	I	I	L	S	I	O	G	F	N	L
H	L	E	E	D	A	H	H	N	A	A	T
P	E	I	P	R	N	E	S	T	N	S	S
T	N	H	G	A	E	C	D	Y	O	B	E
S	N	T	N	I	A	R	D	S	E	E	T
O	N	S	T	Y	E	M	M	N	O	A	D
E	O	S	R	zo	O	zo	zo	zo	zo	zo	N

THIRD SETTING:

I	T	E	D	E	I	T	H	E	C	A	D
E	T	P	E	E	S	T	H	O	M	S	O
T	U	G	I	A	R	N	R	O	H	O	H
U	U	E	L	M	B	S	S	T	G	U	A
E	H	S	N	M	U	O	O	W	R	T	T
H	L	I	W	F	I	N	I	G	L	O	S
L	D	E	H	A	E	A	H	N	T	H	A
E	R	I	P	N	P	S	E	T	S	S	N
N	A	H	T	O	G	B	C	Y	E	D	E
N	I	T	S	E	N	E	R	S	T	D	A
N	Y	S	O	O	T	A	M	N	D	M	E
O	zo	S	E	zo	R	zo	zo	zo	N	zo	O

FOURTH SETTING:

T	E	E	I	C	D	A	T	E	D	H	I
T	E	P	E	M	E	S	T	O	O	H	S
U	A	G	T	H	I	O	N	O	H	R	R
U	M	E	U	G	L	U	S	T	A	S	B
H	M	S	E	R	N	T	O	W	T	O	U
L	F	I	H	L	W	O	N	G	S	I	I
D	A	E	L	T	H	H	A	N	A	H	E
R	N	I	E	S	P	S	S	T	N	E	P
A	O	H	N	E	T	D	B	Y	E	C	G
I	E	T	N	T	S	D	E	S	A	R	N
Y	O	S	N	D	O	M	A	N	E	M	T
zo	zo	S	O	N	E	zo	zo	zo	O	zo	R

FIFTH SETTING:

E	C	E	T	D	I	H	A	E	I	T	D
E	M	P	T	O	E	H	S	O	S	T	E
A	H	G	U	H	T	R	O	O	R	N	I
M	G	E	U	A	U	S	U	T	B	S	L
M	R	S	H	T	E	O	T	W	U	O	N
F	L	I	L	S	H	I	O	G	I	N	W
A	T	E	D	A	L	H	H	N	E	A	H
N	S	I	R	N	E	E	S	T	P	S	P
O	E	H	A	E	N	C	D	Y	G	B	T
E	T	T	I	A	N	R	D	S	N	E	S
O	D	S	Y	E	N	M	M	N	T	A	O
zo	N	S	zo	O	O	zo	zo	zo	R	zo	E

1	2	3	4	5	6	7	8	9	10	11	12	13	14	15	16
I	D	E	D	I	C	A	T	E	T	H	E	S	E	P	O
E	M	S	T	O	T	H	E	R	I	G	H	T	H	O	N
O	U	R	A	*B*	L	E	A	U	*G*	U	S	T	U	S	M
U	N	S	T	E	*R*	T	O	W	H	*O*	M	I	W	I	S
H	L	O	N	G	L	*I*	F	E	H	E	*A*	L	T	H	A
N	D	H	A	P	P	I	*N*	E	S	S	S	*T*	R	E	N
G	T	H	E	N	E	D	B	*Y*	A	C	O	N	*S*	T	A
N	T	D	E	S	I	R	E	T	O	S	E	N	D	M	A
N	Y	M	O	R	E	S	O	O	N	zo	zo	zo	zo	zo	zo

1	2	3	4	5	6	7	8	9	10	11	12	13	14	15
I	D	E	D	I	C	A	T	E	T	H	E	S	E	P
O	E	M	S	T	O	T	H	E	R	I	G	H	T	H
O	N	O	U	R	A	B	L	E	A	U	G	U	S	T
U	S	M	U	N	S	T	E	R	T	O	W	H	O	M
I	W	I	S	H	L	O	N	G	L	I	F	E	H	E
A	L	T	H	A	N	D	H	A	P	P	I	N	E	S
S	S	T	R	E	N	G	T	H	E	N	E	D	B	Y
A	C	O	N	S	T	A	N	T	D	E	S	I	R	E
T	O	S	E	N	D	M	A	N	Y	M	O	R	E	S
O	O	N	zo	zo	zo	zo	zo	zo						

In conclusion, it is demonstrably certain that the main messages and names given in the Dedication Code were pre-planned. Thorpe and Neville refined their planning to a much greater degree than I did, even in my 'parallel code'. This means that many of the other words associated with Henry Neville – e.g. WINSER FOREST, PARIS TRAETEE - were probably also pre-planned. Where planning ends and chance begins in the *transformations* is a little difficult to say, but as we are pointed to the fourth setting by the very text of the Dedication itself, it is safe to say that most significant finds within the first four settings of their tableaux are probably intended. In the *first settings* of all the true Code's grids, we find words and phrases that are relevant, and contiguous within regular shapes; the chances of this occurring by mere accident are negligible, especially given the spatial and linguistic restrictions, as I have demonstrated, and it is almost impossible to contemplate how any relevant linear message could appear unintentionally.

Henry Neville - The Real Shakespeare

**Summary of his life including further notes [in Italics]
concerning links with the plays
of 'William Shakespeare of Stratford'**

Henry Neville was born circa 1562, at Blackfriars, London, to Sir Henry Neville of Billingbear, near Windsor, Berkshire, and Elizabeth Gresham, daughter of a rich Norfolk merchant, niece of Sir Thomas Gresham, founder of Gresham College and The Royal Exchange. Henry Neville was baptised in May 1564 at St. Anne's, Blackfriars.

Henry Neville's father owned the property which eventually became the Blackfriar's Theatre, at which many of the later plays of Shakespeare were performed.

Henry had a sister, Elizabeth, who was very near in age - possibly a twin. Instances of twins occur in 'Twelfth Night' and 'The Comedy of Errors'. Sonnet XX - the Mater-Mistress sonnet, could also suggest a consciousness of boy/girl twinship.

67 – birth of brother, Edward Neville, followed in circa 1570 by the birth of a sister, Katherine Neville.

73 – death of Elizabeth Gresham.

78 – Henry Neville graduates from Merton College, Oxford but remains Henry Savile's tutee and research assistant. Neville embarks on Grand Tour with Henry Savile and Robert Sidney (brother of Sir Phillip Sidney), travelling first through France and the Low Countries to Breslau (then in Russia). The group later proceeds through Germany and Austria and into Italy. Neville's great uncle, Thomas Gresham, has just sent a shipment of cannons to the King of Denmark at Elsinore, but the ship has been wrecked en route. Gresham is too old and feeble to travel to Denmark, so Neville (his heir) was probably sent there in his place.

At Breslau, the party stays with the Hungarian humanist philosopher, Dudith, who recommends a visit to Wittich, one-time professor of Mathematics at Wittenberg. Dudith also had links with Tycho Brahe of Denmark. *Wittenberg was Hamlet's University, while Tycho Brahe was the man with Rosencrantz and Guildenstern in his ancestry. Brahe sends an engraving of himself to Savile's brother, requesting him to send it to 'the friends' in England. The engraving contains Rosencrantz and Guildenstern's names and coats of arms on its border. Elsinore was the setting for 'Hamlet'.*

1579 – Great Uncle Gresham dies, leaving his Mayfield Ironworks in trust to Henry Neville via his father until Henry Neville 'comes of age' at 21years old.

There is certainly a stress on cannons in 'Henry V' and ironworking imagery generally in the plays. For example, the very specific and technically correct understanding of the term 'un- anneal'd' displayed in 'Hamlet' would not be knowledge available to anyone outside the metal working industry.

November 1580 – Henry Neville meets Arthur Throckmorton and William Ashby in Nuremberg. They then all travel together, visiting Prague, Vienna, Padua, Venice and Vicenza (a town neighbouring Verona.) Dudith had also lived in Verona.

'The Merchant of Venice' shows specialist knowledge of the Jewish trading merchants and of Venice itself. No such knowledge was then available to the 'untravelled' masses of the English public. The play also contains a knowledge of some of the Jews of Venice having once been in Frankfurt, Germany. Henry Neville had stayed in Germany and so would know this; but it was knowledge very few Englishmen shared at the time. Henry Neville attended a University College where gentrified sons of merchant traders were allowed entrance, but this was the lowest class even he would converse with, and he was not a titled nobleman, so sustained contact between a titled nobleman and a poor actor is extremely unlikely. Henry Neville, however, was considered both 'noble' and middle class, due to his 'dual ancestry'. He was eventually chosen by the House of Commons as their 'messenger' or go-between to the House of Lords. Shakespeare's plays contain mainly the language register of the middle and noble classes, rarely giving a voice to the common man, and even then allowing him to speak with a more elevated register than most would have possessed in reality.

Vienna was the setting for 'Measure for Measure' and it is known Henry Neville came into contact with the Puritan faction there, who were trying to make fornication a punishable offence. This contact was made through Savile. William Shakespeare of Stratford did not possess a passport and, besides, had neither the money nor the sponsorship for travel on the continent.

Verona is the setting for 'Romeo and Juliet' and it is surely unthinkable that Henry Neville would not have spent at least one day there, as it is so near Vicenza.

82 – Henry Neville returns to England.
Between now and 1586 Henry Neville first meets the boy Earl of Southampton at his Cecil friends' home. (The Earl had become a ward of William Cecil, Lord Burghley, in 1582, when he was nine years old.)

The first 17 'Sonnets' are most commonly associated with the Earl of Southampton. Yet if they were written when that Earl was young – as is suggested by their content, which refers to him as a 'lovely boy' – there is absolutely no chance that they could have been written by a man from the lower classes, because Lord Burghley, as a very careful guardian, would never have allowed the young Earl near a member of the lower classes. However, Henry Neville was a close friend of the Cecils, while old William Cecil, Lord Burghley, was perhaps closer to Henry Neville's father than to any other man alive. Burghley's own mother had been a Neville. It would therefore have been quite natural for him to commission those early Sonnets (persuading Southampton to marry) from among his close friends, and from someone he knew was already friendly with the young Earl. (It was Burghley's own granddaughter that the old man wanted the Earl of Southampton to marry.)

83 – Henry Neville travels in the Earl of Essex's diplomatic mission to James VI of Scotland, led by Francis Walsingham, Elizabeth's spymaster and personal friend of Sir Henry Killigrew, Henry Neville's future father-in-law. The place where all English diplomatic missions stayed was Glamis Castle, as its owner was known as 'the leader of the English faction' in Scotland.

The play 'Macbeth' which is set in Glamis Castle displays a detailed knowledge of Scotland and its history. Glamis Castle was not in reality Macbeth's castle but was probably the only one Henry Neville knew well, so he would have felt more secure about setting his play there. At that time, Scotland was a foreign country, so it was necessary to possess a passport to go there. The Scots were especially meticulous when it came to paperwork and keeping records. William Shakespeare of Stratford never possessed a passport and his presence in Scotland was never recorded or spoken of.

1583 – Henry Neville returns to England, stopping at Sunninghill in Berkshire, where Sir Henry, his father, was then entertaining Queen Elizabeth, plus Henri of Navarre and the Duc de Biron. Both Nevilles (senior and junior) then instruct the queen in hunting and assist her in killing a young deer (see Victoria County History of Berkshire.)

Ferdinand of Navarre and Biron (or, sometimes, Berowne) are characters in 'Love's Labour's Lost', as is Longueville, a name which appears in the Neville family tree, and which also shares the second syllable of Neville's own name. The incident of helping the Queen kill the deer actually happened to Neville and his father in Windsor forest, and the Duc de Biron records the marvellous sight of Queen Elizabeth and her maids in waiting on horseback in the forest, trying to hunt.

1583 – Henry Neville quarrels with Ambrose Dudley, Earl of Warwick, over the right to cast and sell ordnance. (Perhaps this was the start of Henry Neville's quarrel with the Dudley family, which led to his belief in Paget's charges against Robert Dudley, Earl of Leicester, famously set out in the booklet known as *Leycester's Commonwealth.* This booklet catalogues the many alleged murders committed by the Earl of Leicester throughout his career in pursuit of his ambition for the throne of England.) Many earlier historical accounts suppose that it was Henry Neville senior who was involved with this quarrel, but further research (by researchers for the new Oxford Dictionary of National Biography, and by Tim Cornish, an independent researcher) has shown that our Sir Henry was personally in charge of the Sussex Ironworks at this time.

Two manuscript versions of 'Leycester's Commonwealth' were actually in the possession of Henry Neville, who also defended Paget and continued to argue for his 'pardon' even when it was clear this course of action was making the Queen and Robert Cecil very angry. *The incidents of 'accidental' poisoning in 'Leycester's Commonwealth' are very similar to those later described in 'Hamlet.' Meanwhile, Henry Neville's future father-in-law, Sir Henry Killigrew, had also had trouble with the Earl of Leicester. Killigrew had been appointed leader of the English 'contingent' in the Netherlands and was having to spend much time and energy overcoming Leicester's bad reputation there, thus affording Henry Neville a double reason to portray Leicester – the Earl of Essex's step-father in real life - as Claudius, the wicked uncle cum step-father, in 'Hamlet.'*

84 – Henry Neville is sworn a burgess of Windsor and 'brother assistant of the Company of the Guildhall.' From now on is recognised by the Queen as one of the best keepers of his area of Windsor Forest.

'The Merry Wives of Windsor' shows a knowledge of that town and of the Berkshire country legend of Herne the hunter, while both Henry Neville and his father before him became overweight and grew increasingly like Falstaff. Falstaff was originally named Oldcastle, which could be read as the exact opposite to Neville, in the sense of 'New Villa.' There is also a constant display of botanical knowledge in the plays, which is an unusual feature to find alongside knowledge of the Court and politics too. It is difficult to think of any other Elizabethan who possessed all this specialist knowledge besides Henry Neville.

89 – Henry Neville is elected a Knight for Sussex (which qualified him to be 'Baron of the Cinque Ports'.) He was probably given this title in respect of already being a major trader there from his great uncle's Mayfield Ironworks in that county. In fact, Henry Neville was known as the head of the Ironworkers in Sussex, and also supplied cannons to the Cinque Port defences – yet another reason for him to have been allowed into the ranks of the 'barons of the Cinque Ports'). His cannonry was also exported through the Cinque Ports of Rye and Winchelsea, where cannons are still occasionally found buried in the gardens.

Those allowed to carry the canopy at a coronation had to be drawn from barons of the Cinque Ports. Henry Neville knew this, as shown in his Tower Notebook. The same knowledge is displayed in 'Henry VIII'. William Shakespeare of Stratford was not in a position to have known this, nor was he a baron of the Cinque Ports, so how could he write 'Were't aught to me, I bore the canopy...' in Sonnet 125? Indeed, royalty had the sole right to have canopies borne above them, and those entitled to bear them were chosen exclusively from the restricted circle of those men allowed – through various links with the Cinque Ports – to assume the title of 'baron'of those towns.

89 – 97 Henry Neville continued as an MP, but his later correspondence shows him in all probability to have been involved in secret diplomatic and/or spying missions. For instance, in his 'letter to a noble Lord' (c.1606) he mentions that some actions of Sir Edwin Sandys in Scotland had been attributed to him. Henry

Neville must therefore have been in Scotland again, at the same time as Sir Edwin, which was sometime between 1593 and 1597.

Henry Neville was afraid of being recognised by certain Spanish gentlemen, as he only agreed to attend Phillip II's memorial service in Paris in disguise, because he knew that Spanish visitors would be present. When Henry Neville became the French Ambassador in 1599, it was obvious he already knew many of the Scottish Lords, who had themselves been in Spain. Henry Neville was also able to give Cecil information on an errant Lord – Ogleby – who was involved, among other things, with spreading misinformation in Spain, regarding King James VI's religious leanings. When James I came to the throne, he quickly suggested that Henry Neville might become our Ambassador in Spain, which he would surely only have done had he known Henry Neville already knew the country and spoke the language. (In fact, however, Henry Neville resisted this post so vigorously that James soon appointed someone else.)

'Two Gentlemen of Verona', which was written in 1594, was in fact based on a Spanish book by Jorge de Montemayor (1521 – 61, and more especially on the Cervantes version of this book)[215]. This book was not published in English until 1598, which argues for its author knowing Spanish, or at least French, as a French translation was available in France in 1578. Neither language was taught to was part of the Grammar School (i.e. primary school) school curriculum, which is the only kind of education Shakespeare could have received.

'A Midsummer Night's Dream' (written in 1596) would most probably have been inspired by the Midsummer Eve festival, which was always more a feature of Scottish and Scandinavian society than English.

1597 – Henry Neville lost his Windsor seat to William Knollys and took his brother in law's Cornish Seat and sat on various Committees, including those to stop 'irksome and outmodish' recruitment of soldiers, on monopolies, on poor relief, on horse stealing and on 'abuses committed by the lewd and licentious soldiery.'

'Henry IV part 2' displays the outmoded mustering of men for a battle. 'Henry V' portrays that King hanging Bardolph for looting in France.

1598 – Henry Neville sells his Sussex properties and most of his interest in the Ironworks. He leaves his friend, George Carleton (future husband of our man's widow, future Bishop of Chichester after Bishop Harsnet, and cousin of Dudley Carleton) as vicar in Mayfield.

Dudley Carleton was a fellow member of the Mitre Club – a club for progressive lawyers and writers, whose members also included John Donne and Inigo Jones. Bishop Harsnet was the man whose work on 'devils' and 'Popish plots' is quoted in 'King Lear.'

ril 1599 – Henry Neville is sent to France as the English Ambassador. He recruits Sir Ralph Winwood as his secretary and Sir Thomas Edmondes – member of the Mermaid Club and friend of the acting community – as his personal assistant. He travels also with Richard Carew (author of a survey of Cornwall and the Cornish Language) and Carew's son, with a commission to help the son learn the French language. Henry Neville actually fought against being appointed ambassador and finally went only at the Earl of Essex's request. The Earl's then 'spy' in France, Naunton, had long requested to return to England, so Henry Neville was his replacement.

At this specific time, the Earl of Essex had just gone off to Ireland, a fact mentioned in 'Henry V'. That same play also reflects much of Henry Neville's own position and knowledge at the time: one of its scenes is written wholly in French; waiting for the wind to change and so being forced to stay in an English port is described both in the play and in Henry Neville's diplomatic letters; the sea journey is described by the 'Chorus' in that play, and it is a journey that Henry Neville experienced at the same time. Henry Neville was sent to recover an English loan given to help Henri of Navarre in fending off the Spanish – the most ever given by one monarch to another by that date; it is mentioned in the play that Henry V has been given more for his wars in France than any monarch ever before, and Henry V himself uses the imagery of '20 French Crowns'one more than one occasion, while it was 20,000l[pounds] that Henry Neville was supposed to recover. Both Henry V and Henry Neville show a concern to be well prepared with their arguments; both Henry V and Henry Neville indulge in a spot of disguising while they are in France. Henry Neville must stay in an inn in Dover while waiting for better sailing weather; Falstaff is killed off in that play – at an inn in Eastcheap. The parallel of Henry Neville seeing that side of his own English life, with its love of food and good drink, dying, and Falstaff, a similarly well-fed man, breathing his last, is particularly graphic.

And Henry Neville chooses Thomas Edmondes as his steward – a man who had a link to the actors and theatres of London.

May 1599 – Henry Neville arrives in France and is embraced by King Henri IV who, as Henri of Navarre, had stayed at one of his father's homes. Henri IV commissions the first translation of Plato into French. Henry Neville gets along with Henri on an intellectual level but is disgusted with his opinion and treatment of women. Henry Neville does not get along with the other French aristocrats, who treat him with disdain because of his 'lack of a noble title.' While in France, his many diplomatic letters show him to be greatly concerned with the lot of the English Merchant Traders.

Shakespeare's later plays show knowledge of 'mystic' Neo-Platonism that would have been difficult for the unlearned to encounter. In addition to Henri sponsoring the translation of Plato into French, however, Henry Neville was already a student of Greek and of Plato as Savile – Henry's friend and Oxford tutor – was a Platonist and called on Neville to help him with the Greek texts he was discovering during their time together in Italy. While in France, Neville would also have been able to read the essays of Montaigne, (whose philosophy and ideas unquestionably find their way into Shakespeare's plays, and are specifically used in 'Hamlet'), plus the poetry of Ronsard, lines from which have long been identified within the Sonnets .

Henry Neville stays in constant touch with Sir Robert Cecil, who tells him not to have too much to do with Paget and also not to use so much diplomatic writing paper! Henry Neville's main original mission is to recover the 20,000l. which Elizabeth loaned Henri IV. He also knows he must eventually negotiate with the French and Spanish in the Treaty of Boulogne.

May 1600 – Henry Neville travels to Boulogne to negotiate the Treaty, but he is constantly snubbed by the Spanish contingent, who refuse to deal with an untitled gentleman.

A dislike of the 'haughty Spanish noblemen' is displayed throughout the plays of Shakespeare, and also in Henry Neville's letters.

June 1600 – Henry Neville writes to Cecil that he will 'return and live hermit in the Forest of Windsor and contemplate my time as a bad ambassador.'

This 'ambassador turned bandit' is the precise background of Jacques in 'As You Like It'. The same play also calls its jester 'Touchstone' which was a mineral used to discern gold from base metals. These were the only two new characters added to the original text (by Thomas Lodge) on which 'Shakespeare' based this play. Henry Neville was metallurgist enough to know all about touchstones, and there is a scene in that play where 'Will of the forest' is told by Touchstone that he is 'not the one' and that he is the empty glass that is only filled by his, Touchstone's, wit.

ly 1600 – Treaty negotiations break down but Henry Neville is refused permission to return to England, even though the other Commissioners return. Henry Neville is incommunicado for five weeks, during which time Sir Ralph Winwood writes five desperate letters of enquiry about his whereabouts and welfare.

d August, 1600 – Henry Neville at last arrives back in England.

ugust 23rd, 1600 is the first time that the name 'Shakespeare' is ever mentioned in the Stationer's Register! It is quite obvious that the clear parallels between Henry Neville and his texts might soon cause his identity to leak out, so it seems Henry Neville took decisive action to put a halt to such burgeoning 'theories' by making sure the name in the Stationer's Register belonged to someone else. And that 'someone else' was an actor from Stratford known to at least two of Henry Neville's friends – Ben Jonson and Thomas Edmondes. William Shakespeare of Stratford may also have been distantly related to Henry Neville's cousin, Edmund Neville of Stratford. (William and Edmund both had Ardens for mothers.) Besides this, the name 'William Spear' appears on a gravestone outside the north door of Waltham St. Lawrence's church. The Spears were a neighbouring family to the Nevilles in the same village. The challenging nature of 'Spear' and 'Shakespeare' would doubtless have appealed to Neville as a name, as well as being connected to his surroundings and his extended family.

th August, 1600 – Henry Neville writes to Sir Ralph at last, giving him news, not of France but the Low Countries! (Paget had a house in Brussels, so it is likely Henry Neville stayed there and in the Ardennes during his period of absence.) Queen Elizabeth now continues to push Henry Neville to return to his commission in France, saying that he will only be expected to finish the remainder of his two years service. Henry Neville writes to Winwood that he does not really trust the Queen's word in this matter.

'As You Like It' is not set in Arden but in the Ardennes, as witnessed by the very French names of the characters, and within the text itself. However, Henry Neville would have seized the

chance of confusion here: by appointing W.S. from Stratford in the forest of Arden to put his name to the works (officially) he could divert suspicion away from his own life and experience to that of the English Arden boy.

October 21st, 1600 – John Chamberlain writes to Dudley Carleton "Sir Henry Neville is urged to return to France, but he makes many excuses and so resolute resistance that he pretends he will not back again unless he be sent 'pieds and poings liez'" [tied hand and foot.]   At the same time, Henry Neville writes to Winwood that he must delay his return because of 'matters concerning his estate.'   He also tells him, sometimes in code, how matters are proceeding between the Queen and the Earl of Essex.

As well as direct and oblique referencess to Essex in the plays, Henry Neville always shows great concern about the progress of this man who, with his uncommon humanity, nobility and humane concern in Cadiz and Ireland, was fast becoming a role model for all that Henry Neville held to be the true flowering of honest Feudalism. Shakespeare's works are full of examples of Kings in crisis and the bad consequences if Feudal Lords stress their privileges rather than their responsibilities. Essex, like Henry V, seemed to stand alone at that moment as a leader who truly cared for people and had very humanistic values and ideals. It must be remembered too that Henry Neville had, in the end, only agreed to go to France as a result of Essex's request, and that he was there partly to send him 'intelligences' as well as the Queen.

October 29th 1600 – Winwood describes the festivities surrounding Maria de Medici's marriage to Henri IV, and also sends Henry Neville the texts of the entertainments, for which Henry Neville sends his thanks, remarking 'such things please here...'

Winwood describes what are in fact the beginnings of opera. In 'The Winter's Tale' Shakespeare stresses music and makes oblique references to a composer who wrote 'Orfeo' (especially for the marriage by proxy of Maria de Medici in Florence – the very 'texts' of which Winwood sent to Henry Neville).

20th November 1600 – Winwood writes to Henry Neville about Don Verginio Orsino's impending visit to London.

Orsino is one of the main characters in 'Twelfth Night'. Only Henry Neville and Winwood had enough forward knowledge of Orsino's coming to England to have been able to include that name in the play. Besides, the story of Orsino's adventures form part of the plot and imagery of the play, yet only Winwood and

Henry Neville knew of these at the time. William Knollys is specifically supposed to be represented by Malvolio – a man who had been one of the commissioners at the Treaty of Boulogne and who was now back in England, blaming Henry Neville for the failure of that Treaty. Who but Henry Neville, then, would have had an interest in raking up some of Knollys' murky past, when he (the fifty year old Knollys) had chased Mal Fitton, the beautiful 17 year old maid in waiting to the Queen? (This neatly accounts for the joke contained within the name Malvolio – or Mal voglio, meaning 'I want Mal!' in Italian.)

February, 1601 – Henry Neville is passively involved in Earl of Essex's uprising.

th February 1601 – Trial of the Earls of Essex and Southampton. Henry Neville is named to Robert Cecil as being a friend of Essex and that Earl's choice for Secretary of State to replace Robert Cecil, should the rebellion have succeeded. Yet Robert Cecil – Henry's friend and cousin to Henry's wife – never makes this evidence public.

'Hamlet' Shakespeare's first really dark play, was written at this time. Essex may well be Hamlet, the man who behaved often so infuriatingly, yet whom everybody loved. Essex's wicked stepfather was none other than the Earl of Leicester, in whose downfall Henry Neville seemed to be so interested. That Earl is therefore probably represented by Claudius – the man who seemed to carry out his office quite well, but who was involved in sinister, secret plots, stopping at nothing to gain ultimate power – exactly as he is portrayed in Henry Neville's annotated copy of 'Leycester's Commonwealth'. Just like Claudius in 'Hamlet', Leicester was accused of using poisoned goblets at a banquet. Indeed, the Earl of Essex sometimes blamed his own irrational outbursts on his accidental sipping of the 'wrong' goblet.

Henry Neville attempts to go to France, accompanied by his family, but is pursued by soldiers, flees from his family, is caught and brought back to London. Henry Neville is placed under house arrest, first with his father-in-law, then with the Lord Admiral Howard, Earl of Effingham, who, though a Catholic, was an old friend of his father, to whom he willed his falcon.

At his 'Hearing', Henry Neville denies having any special connection with the Earl of Essex, and says that he had not seen the Earl of Southampton 'since he was a boy at my old Lord of Burghley's house.' Privately, however, Southampton refers to

Henry Neville as his 'best friend', and the Earl of Northampton was later to refer to Sir Henry Neville as Southampton's 'Dear Damon'. (Damon was, historically, a poet. This poet was also written up as a character from a play about two friends – Damon and Pythias – who swear undying friendship to each other.

1601 – On May 1st Henry Neville is committed to the Tower.

1602 Henry Neville pays a researcher to research Tower of London records for a) the history of Coronation Ceremonies, and b) old manorial records pertaining to King John and King Richard II. *Henry Neville's annotations in the notebook contain justification from historical records for what was written in the History Plays, and also notes relating to the Coronation Scene in Henry VIII. All this was, however, done before Elizabeth had died, and thus when it was treasonable to talk of the next monarch or their coronation. Neville, already under suspicion of (as yet) unproven treason, would not have risked carrying out this research unless he could prove that it was for purposes of 'pastime', such as he declares – on the opening page of his booklet – is his purpose here. This raises several questions: Why did a politician, like Sir Henry, want material which he could use in a mere 'pastime'? Why did he especially choose to write about the Coronation Procession of Anne Boleyn in such detail? Why was that detail so close to the action portrayed, and specifically commented upon, in Shakespeare's play? [Taken together with the other evidence of continual overlapping circumstances between Neville and Shakespeare's works, this seems to constitute a very strong pointer to Neville's authorship of the play, and thus to the other works too.]*

April 1603 Death of Queen Elizabeth I.
It was remarked upon by contemporaries that William Shakespeare of Stratford never wrote any tribute on the passing of the Queen. This fact still remains unexplained today, until we recognise Henry Neville as the true writer, for Henry Neville was languishing in the Tower of London at the time and could never have forgiven the Queen for killing the Earl of Essex, his 'ideal Lord.'

April 1603 – Henry Neville and Southampton leave the Tower together, on the order of King James I.
Shakespeare's sonnet 107 celebrates an unexpected release from what he supposed was 'a confined doom.'

03 – Henry Neville is resigned to taking a back seat in politics " ... But I am out of my proper Orb when I enter into State Matters; I will therefore leave these Considerations to those to whom they appertain, and think of my husbandry in the Country, which puts me often in mind of that Beatitude which Horace so much commends...." The 'beatitude' Horace 'so much commends' is writing in the countryside!

04 to1606 – Henry Neville sits on various committees looking into various matters, including punishment for the parents of bastard children, raising finances for Grammar Schools in the North of England, and the 'New River' project, bringing a water supply to North London.

The issue of punishment for the parents of bastard children appears at this time in 'Measure for Measure'. Henry Neville had also encountered a discussion of this topic while in Vienna, in which country that play is set.

William Shakespeare of Stratford was said at this time to be lodging with Christopher Mountjoy in Silver Street, Cripplegate. This is strange, since Mountjoy was a French Huguenot, and most of his family spoke little or no English. Henry Neville's step mother-in-law, Jael de Peigne, was a French Huguenot. She was now a widow, and Henry Neville and his family were no longer able to lodge in the Killigrew House in Lothbury, London. This had been a convenient house right next to the printers' and publishers' area. It seems therefore possible that Jael could have found Henry Neville and/or William Shakespeare the Mountjoy house through her Huguenot connections. The Mountjoys were also wig and hat makers who sometimes supplied the Globe Theatre, so even this could have been a contact made through Henry Neville's extended family. No other contender, nor indeed William Shakespeare himself, has any such connections.

08 – the Virginia Company receives its royal charter. It is formed to promote the colonisation of Virginia in America. Henry Neville's name is the first one below that of the Earls – he becomes its chief officer for a time. (The Earl of Southampton had already financed previous expeditions to Virginia while in the Tower with Henry Neville.)

15 July 1610 Sir Thomas Gates leaves Virginia to return to England. He brings with him an extremely long letter of over 20,000 words (more a long pamphlet or short book) from Sir William Strachey to an unnamed 'Lady', which may well have

been a code name for the officers of the Virginia Company itself, 'Virginia' being a 'Lady'. The letter deals with the tempest, the wreck, life in Bermuda and the Virginia colony. C.M. Gayley in his Shakespeare and the Founders of Liberty in America (1917), p. 50, writes of the letter: "It was confidential and from June 2 1609 up to the time of its despatch, describes with vivid fidelity and unvarnished detail all the happenings of the intervening period – discouragements, mutinies and murders, factions, misgovernment, wanton sloth and waste, misery and penury, fraud and treason, death by starvation and disease and cruel encounter with the savages". *Henry Neville was a chief officer on the Council of the Virginia Company and would certainly have read the letter. William Shakespeare of Stratford could not have done so, and perhaps not even Sir Francis Bacon would have been allowed to see it, as he was not in the first Virginia Company.*

Scholars have long agree that much in The Tempest is based on the Strachey letter. For instance, the letter in describing the tempest, says:

"Here the glut of water (as if throttling the wind erewhile) was no sooner a little emptied and qualified but instantly the winds (as having gotten their mouths now free and at liberty) spake more loud and grew more tumultuous and malignant".

The play at 1.1.57-8 says:

"Though every drop of water . . . gape at widest to glut him".

The word "glut" as a transitive verb is not used by Shakespeare elsewhere, so what but the Strachey letter could have suggested it here?.

Strachey's letter also describes a strange light appearing around the mast of the wrecked ship. We now believe this to have been St. Elmo's fire, but the phenomenon would not have been generally known then. Henry Neville would have read about the letter and so heard of the phenomenon, which is thought to be the origin of Ariel, the spirit-assistant of Prospero.

Between 1601 and 1612 (representing Henry Neville's 'retirement', firstly in the Tower, then partaking of Horace's beatitude in the countryside) the following plays were written: Hamlet, Henry VIII, Timon of Athens, All's Well that Ends Well, Macbeth, Troilus and Cressida, Measure for Measure, Othello, King Lear, Cymbeline, Pericles, Coriolanus, The Tempest, The Winter's Tale, The Two Noble Kinsmen. Shakespeare was last seen on the stage in 1604, and therefore was said to have 'retired' at exactly the same time as Henry Neville. The most sombre of the plays also coincide with the most sombre, Tower-period, of Henry Neville's life, only beginning to 'lift' in tone after the Virginia Company began to flourish. No other Shakespeare contender displays such parallels between the themes of the plays and the mood and circumstances of the writer. This had in fact been the case, right from the earliest plays themselves.

Shakespeare's 'Sonnets' were published in 1609. This was just after the Virginia Company (founded by the Earl of Southampton) had received its royal charter, and just before the marriage of Sir Henry's eldest son. The first 17 sonnets are trying to persuade a young man to marry and had been first circulated in 1598. The impending marriage of Henry's son was therefore an opportunity for Neville to disguise the true origin of the poems, should the Code within the Dedication to the Sonnets be cracked and his name discovered.

Henry Neville had a strange relationship with James I at the time, one minute appreciating his more liberal approach to the Court, and always sharing his love of literature and the arts, even entertaining him at Billingbear and helping him with his writing, while the next minute absolutely opposing his autocratic rule of the country. Sir Henry Neville always found it difficult to flatter the King, probably mainly because of James' bisexuality, and consequently he did not receive the favours granted to others. It is possible that the 'homoerotic hints' within some of the sonnets (when read out of their true context) may have addressed this King's preferences. Also, the publication of the Sonnets comes immediately before Henry Neville's eldest son's wedding (to a relative of the Sidneys – the friends who were all so fond of poetry) - so they may have served a dual purpose. Certainly, there followed a close link between the subsequent Stuarts and some of Neville's descendants, with Charles II holding his Restoration Party at Billingbear.

ecember 1610 – Henry Neville challenges the King with a list of grievances. He especially complains that the King has been granted a larger proportion of the national wealth than ever any monarch before. (A notebook found among Henry Neville's Worsley descendants' possession in Lincoln Record Office demonstrates his historical background research in this regard. This book was in the same bundle as the Tower Notebook, described above.)

1611 – Ben Jonson writes a cryptic epigram on Sir Henry Neville. This appeared at the same time as the King James Bible, which Savile had envisaged since 1598:

> Who now calls on thee, NEVIL, is a Muse,
>   That serves nor fame, nor titles; but doth chuse
> Where vertue makes them both, and that's in thee:
>   Where all is faire, beside thy pedigree.
> Thou art not one, seek'st miseries with hope,
>   Wrestlest with dignities, or fain'st a scope
> Of seruice to the publique, when the end
>   Is priuate gaine, which hath long guilt to friend.
> Thou rather striv'st the matter to possesse,
>   And elements of honor, the[a]n the dresse;
> To make thy lent life, good against the Fates:
>   And first to know thine owne state, then the States.
> To be the same in roote, thou art in height;
>   And that thy soule should give thy flesh her weight.
> Goe on, and doubt not, what posteritie,
>   Now I haue sung thee thus, shall iudge of thee.
> Thy deedes, vnto thy name, will prove new wombes,
>   Whil'st others toyle for titles to their tombes.

1612 – the death of Robert Cecil. Henry Neville (quietly) lets it be known he may be interested in becoming Secretary of State. Henry Neville, already a friend of William Herbert, Earl of Pembroke (subsequently Patron of the First Folio of Shakespeare's plays) makes friends with one of the King's Scottish favourites, Robert Carr. Carr, however, becomes embroiled with Lady Frances Howard and the Thomas Overbury murder, and is replaced in the King's affections by the Duke of Buckingham. This business seems to be the beginning of Henry Neville's 'sea of troubles' with James I.

While Sir Francis Bacon supported James in his autocratic stance, Henry Neville spent his time writing to the King advising him on how to rule with the assent of Parliament!

1612 - Henry Neville devises an overland trade route from India to the UK.

1613 – The Office of Secretary of State is granted to Sir Ralph Winwood, Henry Neville's one time secretary in France, but it is widely rumoured that his policies were really devised by Henry Neville. Henry Neville refuses the office of Treasurer, offered by Carr as compensation.

15 death (although two reports in 1616 and 1617 speak of him as if he is still alive), and the 'Stationer's Note' to 'A King and No King' by Beaumont and Fletcher, published in 1619 but written in 1611, again leaves the impression that he might still be living. No one wrote of his death in 1615, despite the great affection in which he was held. The funeral was very private, and the inscription said to have been given to his son to place on his tomb was never put there. The blank space for this inscription remains to this day.

THE SONNET in which NEVILLE NAMES HIMSELF
Sonnet 121

'Tis better to be vile than vile esteemed,
When not to be, receives reproach of being,
And the just pleasure lost, which is so deemed,
Not by our feeling, but by others' seeing.
For why should others' false adulterate eyes
Give salutation to my sportive blood?
Or on my frailties why are frailer spies,
Which in their wills count bad what I think good?
No, I am that I am, and they that **level**
At my abuses, reckon up their ow**n**,
I may be straight though they themselves be **bevel**;
By their rank thoughts, my deeds must not be shown
Unless this general **evil** they maintain,
All men are bad a**n**d in their badness reign.

Neville's family motto was Ne vile velis. This sonnet begins with seeming, yet not being, vile. The word 'nevel' (as emboldened above) can also be prominently seen, and this is the spelling of the name used in the first setting of the Dedication Code. Then there is another reading of the name on lines 13 & 14.

Katherine Duncan-Jones, among other scholars, remarks how strange is the choice of the words 'level' and 'bevel' in this sonnet. In fact, it is the one single time that 'Shakespeare' uses the word 'bevel' in all his works, yet here it conveniently re-inforces 'nevel'.

The sentiment in this sonnet is also very much in keeping with Neville's feelings – his 'frailties' are being spied upon by 'frailer' spies; and he does not wish 'false, adulterate eyes' to salute his 'sportive' (play-writing?) 'blood'.

Diagrams

DIAGRAM 1: Tracing the ancestry of Sir Henry Neville

Showing that Richard Neville, Earl of Warwick, the Kingmaker, was a first cousin of Neville's great grandfather. (It is also noticeable from all the family trees that Sir Henry's relatives usually appear prominently in the 'Shakespeare' plays. The names of those in the plays are shown in bold lettering.)

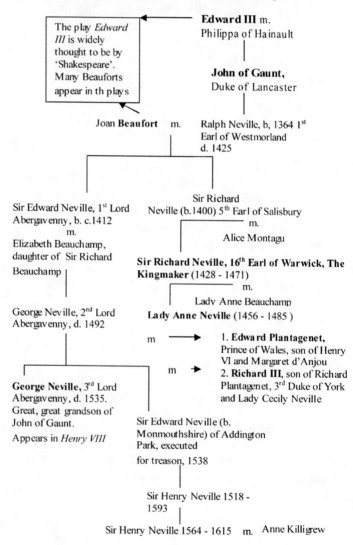

The play *Edward III* is widely thought to be by 'Shakespeare'. Many Beauforts appear in th plays

Edward III m.
Philippa of Hainault

John of Gaunt,
Duke of Lancaster

Joan **Beaufort**   m.   Ralph Neville, b, 1364 1st
Earl of Westmorland
d. 1425

Sir Edward Neville, 1st Lord Abergavenny, b. c.1412
m.
Elizabeth Beauchamp, daughter of Sir Richard Beauchamp

Sir Richard Neville (b.1400) 5th Earl of Salisbury
m.
Alice Montagu

Sir Richard Neville, 16th Earl of Warwick, The Kingmaker (1428 - 1471)
m.
Lady Anne Beauchamp

George Neville, 2nd Lord Abergavenny, d. 1492

Lady Anne Neville (1456 - 1485)

m → 1. **Edward Plantagenet,** Prince of Wales, son of Henry VI and Margaret d'Anjou

m → 2. **Richard III,** son of Richard Plantagenet, 3rd Duke of York and Lady Cecily Neville

George Neville, 3rd Lord Abergavenny, d. 1535. Great, great grandson of John of Gaunt.
Appears in *Henry VIII*

Sir Edward Neville (b. Monmouthshire) of Addington Park, executed for treason, 1538

Sir Henry Neville 1518 - 1593

Sir Henry Neville 1564 - 1615   m.   Anne Killigrew

352

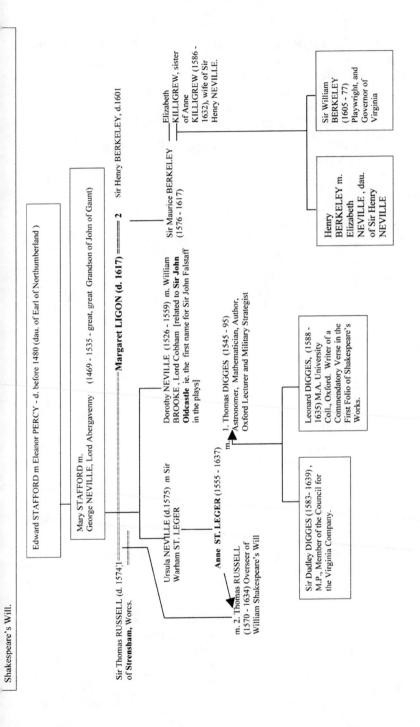

Shakespeare's Will.

Edward STAFFORD m Eleanor PERCY - d. before 1480 (dau. of Earl of Northumberland)

Mary STAFFORD m.
George NEVILLE, Lord Abergavenny   (1469 - 1535 - great, great Grandson of John of Gaunt)

Margaret LIGON (d. 1617) ======== **2**   Sir Henry BERKELEY, d.1601

Sir Thomas RUSSELL (d. 1574) |
of **Strensham**, Worcs.

Ursula NEVILLE (d.1575) m Sir
Warham ST. LEGER

Anne ST. LEGER (1555 - 1637)

m. 2. Thomas RUSSELL
(1570 - 1634) Overseer of
William Shakespeare's Will

Dorothy NEVILLE (1526 - 1559) m. William
BROOKE , Lord Cobham [related to **Sir John
Oldcastle** ie. the first name for Sir John Falstaff
in the plays]

m   1. Thomas DIGGES (1545 - 95)
Astronomer, Mathematician, Author,
Oxford Lecturer and Military Strategist

Sir Maurice BERKELEY
(1576 - 1617)

Elizabeth
KILLIGREW, sister
of Anne
KILLIGREW (1586 -
1632), wife of Sir
Henry NEVILLE.

Sir Dudley DIGGES (1583-1639) ,
M.P., Member of the Council for
the Virginia Company.

Leonard DIGGES, (1588 -
1635) M.A. University
Coll, Oxford. Writer of a
Commendatory Verse in the
First Folio of Shakespeare's
Works.

Henry
BERKELEY m.
Elizabeth
NEVILLE, dau.
of Sir Henry
NEVILLE

Sir William
BERKELEY
(1605 - 77)
Playwright, and
Governor of
Virginia

353

<u>DIAGRAM 3</u> THE NEVILLES AND THE BULMERS

Jonson's Play, *The Staple of News* gives clues to
Neville's authorship of the Shakespeare Works,
and also talks of a character whom Jonson names
as 'Sir Beavis Bullion' whom everyone at the
time would have recognised as Bevis Bulmer

Bertram de Bulmer of Brancepath
d. 1166

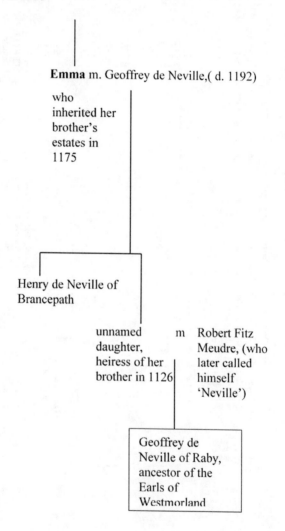

Emma m. Geoffrey de Neville,(d. 1192)

who
inherited her
brother's
estates in
1175

Henry de Neville of
Brancepath

unnamed   m   Robert Fitz
daughter,   Meudre, (who
heiress of her   later called
brother in 1126   himself
                  'Neville')

Geoffrey de
Neville of Raby,
ancestor of the
Earls of
Westmorland

Endnotes

[1] Lambros de Calimahos eventually gained much experience and prestige as a code-breaker. Starting off as a musician, cryptology was just a hoby for him, until his talents were finally recognised and he trained and worked with professionals.

[2] p.249 *Winwood's Memorials*, vol.1

[33] p.52 G.B. Harrison *Elizabethan Plays and Players*, London, 1940

[4] Robert Greene, *Greene's Groatsworth of Wit bought with a Million of Repentance*, 1592 (Quoted p. 247, F.E. Halliday, *A Shakespeare Companion*, London, 1955)

[5] p. 585, F.E. Halliday, ibid.

[6] See p. 204, Phillips, G and Keatman, M. *The Shakespeare Conspiracy*, London, 1994, The writers quote 1596 Joseph Hall, in his *Hall's Satires* Book IV, where Hall suggests that Bacon is the author of Shakespeare's poems.

[7] *Pigmalion's Image* by John Marston published in 1598

[8] Anon. *The Returne from Parnasus: or the Scourge of Simony: Publiquely acted by the Students in St. John's Colledge Cambridge.* (c. 1602)

[9] See '*Shakespeare, Neville and the Iron Men of the Theatre*' by Brenda James, *The Journal of Neville Studies, Vol.1 no1.*, April, 2007

[10] pp.77- 78 Charles Mills Gayley *Beaumont the Dramatist*, re-issued by Athenium Publishers, 1969 (first published 1914)

[11] See the Stationer's note, prefacing Beaumont and Fletcher's *A King and No King*, in which the Stationer says he is **returning** the play to Sir Henry Neville's hands, and that the writers are most grateful for the encouragement they have received from Sir Henry.

[12] Francis Bacon owed much of his promotion to the patronage of Robert Devereux, Earl of Essex; yet he readily and publicly condemned him and joined in the prosecution of his old 'friend' after the Essex uprising. Moreover, when Robert Cecil died, Bacon wrote a very nasty essay about how physically-deformed or disabled people were usually thoroughly bad - clearly hinting at Cecil himself, who had been crook-backed.

[13] p.396 *The Politics of Shakespeare's History Plays* (1874) by Richard Simpson [New Shakespeare Society trans.]

[14] Wiliam Speare's grave is in the churchyard of St. Lawrence Church in Waltham St. Lawrence. The group of Speare family tombs stood just outside the church door, so Neville would have seen these whenever he went to that church.

[15] The proposition that Sir Henry senior did not actually wed Elizabeth Gresham is examined in Chapter 11. However, he certainly lived with her and had children by her.

[16] *Winwood's Memorials*, Vol. 2, p.35, Letter from Sir Henry Neville, London, 1st November, 1604.

[17] See entry for Henry Neville in The Victoria County History for Berkshire

[18] See p.37, 'The Elizabethan Secret Services' by Alan Haynes, Sutton Publishing, 1992

[19]Dr. Leslie Hotson in his book, *I, William Shakespeare*, London, 1937 p. 102 implies that he has seen a document naming Sir Henry Neville of Billingbear, Berkshire as being knighted along with others after the Cadiz campaign.

[20] Essex Record Office 'Commonplace Book kept by Richard Aldworth Neville' ref. D/DBy/Z75

[21] See Neville's many letters, concerning his estate, among the Neville Papers in the Berkshire Record Office.

[22] See an account of Arthur Throckmorton's travel diary in *Ralegh and the Throckmortons* by A.L. Rowse, London, 1962, p.81

See also Neville's 'letter to a noble Lord' (written c. 1604) now in the Berkshire Record Office. Neville says he spent £4,000 of his own money while he was in France (and this was on top of his and his family's travelling expenses.)

[23] See notes for Sir Henry Neville in – HASLAR, HISTORY OF PARLIAMENT – THE COMMONS, hmso 1981, which quotes this letter (kept at Hatfield House) from HN to Sir Robert Cecil

[24] *Winwood's Memorials*, op.cit., Vol.1. p.325

[25] William Camden, the historian and antiquarian, rarely speaks of Sir Henry Neville without calling him noble: "He appeached also Sir Henry Nevill, a most Noble Knight, as being not ignorant of the conspiracy, who was now ready to returne Embassador Legier into France about the ratifying of the treaty of Bloys and restrayning of depredations on both sides, whereupon he was called backe from his journey and committed to the Lord Admirals custody." Camden also reports Henry Cuffe's speach from the scaffold: "...But whereas I have brought that Noble Knight Sir Henry Nevill into danger, I am hartily sory for it, and I earnestly intreat him to forgive mee. ..." (from William Camden's account of the Earl of Essex's rebellion in Part two of his *Annales*, comprising its fourth book, published posthumously in Latin at Leiden in 1625, appearing in London in 1627, available at http://www.philological.bham.ac.uk/camden/1601e.html)

[26] See J Spedding's extensive biography on Sir Francis Bacon (written 1857-74) especially the sections where Spedding unjustifiably runs down Sir Henry's political abilities in comparison with those of Bacon. Owen Lowe Duncan, in his doctoral dissertation, *The Political Career of Sir Henry Neville*, Ohio State University, 1974, also takes issue with Spedding's assessment.

[27] See various references to this in Neville's letters in R. Winwood *Memorials of the affairs of state in the reigns of Queen Elizabeth and King James I*, ed. E. Sawyer (1725), vol.1]

[28] *Pepys' Diary*, edited by Richard Neville, Lord Braybrooke, 1825

[29] HISTORICAL MANUSCRIPTS COMMISSION, Duke of Rutland's documents

[30] [Sir Henry's involvement with the Essex faction also explains the precipitous nature of the Essex uprising itself. As I argued in *The Truth Will Out*, Sir Henry was being forced to return to France, but Essex wanted him to take the reins of government under the new regime. Thus was Essex forced to take a more hasty action than any of the rebels would have wished.]

[31] *Winwood*, op.cit, Vol.2. p.33 Letter from Sir Henry Neville, London, 1st November, 1604 "Though in much paine of the Gout (which with shame I do now acknowledge) I could not dismiss this messenger, without a line or two of Salutations...."

[32] For a description of this book see *The Annotator* by Alan Keen and Roger Lubbock, London 1954. Keen, though he demonstrated his copy of 'Halle's Chronicles' had once belonged to a Worsley (and been annotated by 'Shakespeare') traced the 'wrong' branch of the Worsleys and so did not discover Sir Henry Neville. (I detail all this in *The Truth Will Out*.)

[33] p. 65 *A Companion to Shakespeare's Works, Vol. II*, ed. Jean E. Howard, Blackwell, 2003. [From the Paper *Censorship and the Problems with History in Shakespeare's England*, by Cyndia Susan Clegg.

[34] Even when Neville was carrying on his ironworking business at Mayfield, correspondents knew he was still often at Lothbury, because they generally addressed their letters to that London base, e.g.
" *to the right worshipful his very good master Mr Henry Nevill esquire give these, leave this at Sir Henry Kyllegrewes house in Lothbury to be conveyed Abraham a James letter in November 1595*" (copy of letter provided by Tim Cornish)

[35] See accounts of the various inhabitants of the former Blackfriars Monastery, in 'Shakespeare's Blackfriars Playhouse' by Irwin Smith, New York, 1964]

[36] For further information on this topic, see *Neville, Shakespeare, and the Iron Men of the Theatre*, Brenda James, op.cit

[37] Quoted from a letter written by Sir Henry Neville senior in 'My Ladye Nevell Revealed' by John Harley and Christopher Foley, <u>Music and Letters</u> 86.1 (2005)

[38] See *The Truth Will Out*, op. cit. See also notes on Henry Neville and Billingbear in *The Victoria County Histories, Berkshire*

[39] David Nash Ford, *Royal Berkshire History*, which can be accessed at <u>www.berkshirehistory.com</u>

[40] See, for example, notes on Thomas Posthumous Hoby in *Who's Who in Shakespeare's England,* by Alan and Veronica Palmer, Methuen, 2000.

[41] See details of Wessex Archaelogy Project exploring the shipwreck in the Thames at
http://www.wessexarch.co.uk/projects/marine/thameswreck/gresham.html:
"The outbreak of war in the Low Countries compelled Gresham to leave Antwerp in 1567. His interest in the Weald iron industry is noted in 1570 when he was using the Mayfield Furnace, Sussex. He is named as the owner of the Mayfield furnace in 1574, the same year in which he was granted a licence to export guns to Denmark. Gresham leased a second furnace near Frant, Wadhurst, in 1574 and he was given a second licence to export armaments in 1578."

[42] Adam Mosley, [notes for] 'Chamber, John (1546–1604)', Oxford Dictionary of National Biography, Oxford University Press, Sept 2004;

[43] See draft of HN's will in the Neville Papers at Berkshire Record Office

[44] 'My Ladye Nevell Revealed' by John Harley and Christopher Foley, Music and Letters 86.1 (2005)

[45] See THE TANGLED WORLD OF ELIZABETHAN ESPIONAGE: SIR HENRY NEVILLE AND CHARLES PAGET, DOUBLE AGENT by Brenda James, *The Journal of Neville Studies,* vol.1, issue 1, April, 2007. See also John Bossy, *Under the Molehill, An Elizabethan Spy Story,* Yale, 2001

[46] See, for instance, Lansdowne MSS 65 no 22, f 82, in which Neville describes the 'irregular' process involved in obtaining an export licence for his ordnance from Ambrose Dudley, Earl of Warwick: ...*he* [Warwick] *referred me for the despatching of it to one Pistor that then was his deputy, Mr Pistor plainly told me that I should have no licence unless I would give (my Lord as he said) forty shillings upon every ton, which I then refused, and I hope may do still.*

[47] See notes for the Neville family in *Burke's Peerage*

[48] Winston Graham *The Spanish Armadas* Fontana, 1976.

[49] See Essex Record Office 'Commonplace Book kept by Richard Aldworth Neville' ref. D/DBy/Z75

[50] Neville's reputation in this respect spread so far that a 'ballad' eventually included him remarking that he trusted the rights of Parliament and the people would not be infringed. HN is here referred to as 'Henry the hardy', though some versions of the ballad omit mention of him. One version of it is *The Parliament Fart* (1607) MS Malone 23, in the Bodleian Library.

[51] See *The Tangled World of Elizabethan Espionage: Sir Henry Neville and Charles Paget, Double Agent,* by Brenda James, The Journal of Neville Studies, op. cit.

[52] See, for instance, Mordechai Feingold's mention of these facts in his book, *The Mathematician's Apprenticeship,* 1984, published by CUP in 1987

[53] *Winwood's Memorials,* vol. 1 op.cit. p.17

[54] This is 1599 - and we know it's date from the fact that the Earl of Essex's expected triumphant return from Ireland is spoken of by the narrator in the play. Essex left for Ireland in March of that year, and did not return until September. This covers the dates Neville travelled to and became resident in France.

[55] See Brenda James, ibid. See also, *Under the Molehill, An Elizabethan Spy Story* by John Bossy, Yale, 2001

[56] See Hatfield House papers, quoted in HISTORY OF PARLIAMENT – THE COMMONS – HASLAR, hmso 1981, notes for Sir Henry Neville.

[57] Neville wrote this letter on the occasion of his being asked to attend a Memorial Service for the King of Spain. He protested that he did not wish to go because the Spanish Ambassador (Neville's enemy) would be there, so that his presence would 'but spoil the feast.' However, he confessed to Cecil that he went secretly, in disguise, though wished he hadn't as (he remarks) 'I never saw a poorer thing.' *Winwood, op.cit.,* vol. 1.

[58] See pp. 229-230 *The Third Earl of Southampton* by Charlotte Carmichael Stopes, Cambridge, 1922. Stopes copies out the Confession of the Earl of Southampton, from the Salisbury Papers, vol 11, p.72, which is dated as 'after February 19th, 1600-01' . The Earl states, "There bee two thinges which I have forgotten to sett in their right places,... One is, that not longe before the day of our misfortune My Lord of Essex towld mee that Sir Henry Nevill, that was to goe embassador into Fraunce, was a man wholy att his devotion, and desired to runn the same fortune with him, and therfore hee towld mee that hee would appoint him to come to my loginge in Drury House, and I should make him acquainted with his purpose of goinge to the Courte, which I did ackordingly,... I understood that he [Neville] had devoted him selfe to my Lord of Essex ...Hee answered me that what Mr. Cuffe had sayed hee would performe, therefore desired me to say on. ,,,[Neville] concluded that when he should be appointed hee would be at the Courte before, to give him [Essex] furtherance with himself and his people. ..."

[59] Camden, op.cit.

[60] p. 479, Norman Egbert McClure, **Chamberlain Letters** 1, The American Philosophical Society, 1939

[61] Owen Lowe Duncan, doctoral dissertation, *The Political Career of Sir Henry Neville,* Ohio State University, 1974

[62] p.203, Charlotte Carmichael Stopes, op.cit

[63] James and Rubinstein, 2005, op.cit.

[64] See note 7

[65] See Richard Eedes' *Iter Boreale* 1583,. available at http://www.philological.bham.ac.uk/eedes/ Translated by Dana F. Sutton, The University of California, Irvine

The work consists of Eedes' description of his journey from Oxford to Durham via York. Eedes and his party meet Neville and his companions on the way back from their mission to James VI in Scotland:

> Accedunt istis, queis purpura fulget et aurum
> Mildmaius, doctusque **libros tractare Nevillus**
> Et generosa satis pubes Aquilonica, Lowther,
> Widdrington, Barnston, doctique equitare caballos,
> Musgravii, spoliisque Scoti Fenwickus opimis,
> Flammeus ipse satis natura, sed magis illi
> Flammam auget, patris ut mortem ulciscatur in illos
> Illo qui puero patrem trucidasse feruntur.

[66] See *The Elizabethan Secret Services* by Alan Haynes, Sutton Publishing, 2004

[67] See Haynes, ibid.

[68] *Hamlet*, act 1, scene 5.

[69] Sir Thomas Gresham, Neville's great uncle, was the founder of the Royal Exchange, which establishment was the forerunner of the Bank of England. It was from him that Neville had inherited his ironworks and therefore his early introduction to the world of Business and Finance.

[70] p. 68, *Elizabethan People,* by Joel Hurstfield and Alan G.R. Smith, Old Woking, 1978

[71] Winwood Vol. 2, p.35, op.cit.

[72] See Professor Jim Goding and Bruce Leyland, the Higher Education Supplement of *The Australian,* July 19th, 2006

[73] See, for example, several references in the Neville Papers at the Berkshire Record Office:

> Letter from Sir Henry Neville [of Billingbear, Waltham St Lawrence] (signs **Henri Nevell**) to his "very Friend" Richard Staverton (spelt Stafforton) of Warfield, transferring an order by the Earl of Sussex, [Chief Justice of Royal Forests south of River Trent], for two bucks to be allocated for hunting by two unnamed gentlemen (apparently staying at the house of [Thomas] Dabridgecourt [MP], one of the bucks to be provided by Richard Staverton's under Humfrey. Also notes Earl of Leicester's similar orders in Windsor [Great] Park. [Dated 4 September, year missing where document is torn [1567-1583, probably 1570s. Probably relates to deer in Windsor Forest.] - ref. D/EZ 138/1 - date: nd [c.1570s]

and also references among the Thynne Papers at Longleat House:

> Frances, widow of Sir John Gresham, jun. to Sir J. Thynne proposing a match for his daughter [Elizabeth] and a son of Sir Ralph Sadler: Pillings [i.e. Billingbear], 21 Aug. 1576. f.270: (b) on the desire of "Mr Nevell" [Henry Neville, of Billingbeare co. Berks, her son in law] to Mary "Lady Doyle my Lord keppers dafter", and his intention to break the promise he made to her and her deceased daughter in order to provide a jointure: Pillingbeare, 18 Nov. 1577. In the hand of, and with a postscript by, Elizabeth Thynne. f.272

[74] See entry for Henry Neville in *The Victoria County History* for Berkshire

[75] See Notes for John Napier in the Oxford Dictionary of National Biography, op.cit

[76] See Mordecai Feingold, *The Mathematician's Apprenticeship*, Cambridge, 1984

[77] Robert Lomas, *The Invisible College*, London, 2002

[78] p.203, Charlotte Carmichael Stopes, op.cit.

[79] See 'Sir Henry Neville's case' - *Winwood. vol.1*, op.cit.

[80] William Camden, *Annales*, op.cit.

[81] *Winwood's Memorials*, vol 2, p. 216

[82] See p.64, 'Ungentle Shakespeare' by Katherine Duncan-Jones, London 2001

[83] See Brenda James, *Journal of Neville Studies*, vol.1 issue 1, op.cit.

[84] If correct, Camden's allegation explains the 'Arthur Dudley' story (see *Historical Manuscripts Commission* State Papers, Spanish, 1895) Dudley claimed to be the illegitimate son of the Earl of Leicester and Queen Elizabeth I.

[85] A contemporary writer wrote: "A house is kept at Essex House for the Lord and Lady Southampton and the family", see p. 173 Mary Carmichael Stopes, op.cit.

[86] Even from a purely psychological point of view, it seems that Neville may have been at least subconsciously following in the footsteps of his ancestors. Richard Neville had constantly indulged in Kingship conspiracies, and HN's own grandfather - Edward Neville - had been executed for being involved in an alleged dynastic conspiracy. Even Neville's own father had promoted the interests of Lady Jane Grey, to such an extent that he felt it necessary to flee abroad when Queen Mary came to the throne. Anne Ancelin Schützenberger, in her excellent book, *The Ancestor Syndrome*, Routledge, 1998, investigates this phenomenon of inheritance.

[87] Camden Series, 82. D.S.S.P.

[88] *Idea*, Michael Drayton, 1594

[89] William Saunders' autograph letter to Richard Bagot, 1585: '...by the losse of my good father, my onlie frende and best staie...' *Elizabethan Handwriting 1500 - 1650* by Giles E. Dawson and Laetitia Kennedy-Skipton, Chichester, 1981

[90] This fact is yet another piece of evidence that Wriothesley, not William Herbert, Earl of Pembroke, was the intended dedicatee of the Sonnets. Herbert never had any known history of refusing a relationship with girls!

[91] Clapham wrote a Latin poem, 'Narcissus', in 1591 - see p.164, *Ungentle Shakespeare* by Katherine Duncan-Jones, London, 2001

[92] See Neville's own deposition regarding the Earl of Southampton 'as a boy' in Burghley's house - quoted p.203 Stopes, op. cit. For a general background to Burghley as a guardian, see Stopes, and also *The Queen's Wards*, Joel Hurstfield, London, 1957

[93] p. 102, Leslie Hotson, *I, William Shakespeare*, op.cit.

[94] p.19, R.K Gilkes *The Tudor Parliament* London, 1969

[95] Gilkes ibid, p.56, where Gilkes quotes from a letter of the Earl of Essex concerning the contrived reason for sending him to Ireland

[96] Sonnet 37, '...So I, made lame by Fortune's dearest spite /Take all my comfort of thy worth and truth... So then I am not lame, poor, nor despised,' Sonnet 89 'Speak of my lameness, and I straight will halt: / Against thy reasons making no defence.' Neville was lame from gout. This must have troubled him greatly, as he writes of this to Ralph Winwood. His sister in law wrote a letter to him commisserating with his problem and hoping that his visit to the 'bath' would help. (This letter can be seen among the Neville Papers in Berkshire Record Office.) John Chamberlain and other of his friends worry about Neville's increasing inability to get around the Court and Parliament because of this problem.

[97] p. 305, Lawrence Stone, *The Family, Sex and Marriage in England, 1500-1800,* Pelican Books, 1979

[98] Tony Robinson, in *Britain's Real Monarch* - an historical documentary shown on Channel 4 on January 3, 2004 - quoted the research of Dr Michael Jones. He had found previously overlooked evidence from Rouen Cathedral, leading to the conclusion that Cecily Neville's husband had actually been away in the wars at the time when one of her sons would have been conceived. This was rare, restricted information, yet the writer of *Richard III* appears to have been aware of this probable illegitimacy in the line which ultimately became monarchs of England [As a Neville, however, Sir Henry would have had access to this information]:

> GLOUCESTER. Go, after, after, cousin Buckingham.
> The Mayor towards Guildhall hies him in an post.
> There, at your meet'st advantage of the time,
> Infer the bastardy of Edward's children.
> Tell them how Edward put to death a citizen
> Only for saying he would make his son
> Heir to the crown - meaning indeed his house,
> Which by the sign thereof was termed so.
> Moreover, urge his hateful luxury
> And bestial appetite in change of lust,
> Which stretch'd unto their servants, daughters, wives,
> Even where his raging eye or savage heart
> Without control lusted to make a prey.
> Nay, for a need, thus far come near my person:
> Tell them, when that my mother went with child
> Of that insatiate Edward, noble York
> My princely father then had wars in France
> And, by true computation of the time,
> Found that the issue was not his begot;
> Which well appeared in his lineaments,
> Being nothing like the noble Duke my father.
> Yet touch this sparingly, as 'twere far off;
> Because, my lord, you know my mother lives.
>
> ACT3|SC5

[99] Frank Kermode, *Shakespeare's Language,* Penguin Books, 2000

[100] p. 245 *Mr. WH,* Leslie Hotson, London, 1964

[101] Ben Jonson often uses the same device of suggesting a homely parallel to a classical or literary theme – see examples in *Volpone,* where the classical river becomes the Humber or the Thames, etc.

[102] Aldermen's CourtRepertories No. 25, p.24, quoted by Hotson, *Mr.W.H.,* op.cit. - p. 254

[103] MONTAGU HOUSE PAPERS {HIST MSS COM}1899 edition 'Report on the Manuscripts of the Duke of Buccleuch and Queensberry, preserved at Montagu House, Whitehall, vol.1 [Eyre and Spottiswoode Her Majesty's Stationery Office.Historical Manuscripts commission, p.31

[104] *Winwood's Memorials,* vol. 1 p.271

[105] p.482, F.E. Halliday, *A Shakespeare Companion,*op.cit., quoting the title page of the 1601 edition of *The Phoenix and the Turtle.*

[106] Neville Papers, Berkshire Record Office. ref. D/EN F6 2/3

[107] Draft of Neville's Will, Neville Papers, Berkshire Record Office

[108] Halliday, *Shakespeare Companion,* op.cit., p. 154

[109] For more connections between Sir Henry Neville and the First Folio, see Brenda James and William Rubinstein, *The Truth Will Out,* Longman, 2005

[110] See the Beasley letters in the Neville Papers in Berkshire Record Office.

[111] p. 239, Amos C. Miller *Sir Henry Killigrew,* Leicester, 1963

[112] Halliday, op.cit. p.586

[113] Historical Manuscript Commission's report, 1899. published by Eyre and Spottiswoode, (under Her Majesty's Stationery Office), as 'Report on the Manuscipts of the Duke of Buccleuch and Queensberry, preserved at Montagu House, Whitehall, vol.1'

[114] See entry for Richard Martin in the Oxford Dictionary of National Biography (elsewhere cited as ODNB) , Edited by H. C. G. Matthew and Brian Harrison, Oxford

[115] See list given in Fulke Greville's notes by John Gouws in the ODNB, ibid

[116] p. 267, *Winwood's Memorials,* Vol.1., op.cit. Ralph Winwood to Sir Henry Neville - "The entertainments ... are very smal, but what they are your Lordship by this inclosed shall understand. Here are neither Excercises of Honor to entertaine the Princes and Gentlemen, nor any Comedies or Tragedies, or publick Feasts to give Contentment to the Ladies; whereof at *Florence* there was Variety, full of many witty and worthy Conceits, whereof the Dialoge will give your Honor some kind of tast." [This strongly suggests that Winwood knew of Neville's interest in the stage and had sent him the 'Dialogue' of one of the operas performed for Maria de Medici in Florence. There is also a hint of this Opera in *The Winter's Tale,* which will be the subject of a future Paper in *The Journal of Neville Studies* - see www.henryneville.com

[117] *The Shakespeare Companion* op.cit. p.427

[118] Owen Lowe Duncan, doctoral dissertation, *The Political Career of Sir Henry Neville,* Ohio State University, 1974, p. 275 (quoting Judge James

Whitelock, "...he [Neville] was the most sufficient man for understanding of state business that was in this kingdom..., and a very good scholar and a stout man, but was as ignobly and unworthily handled as ever gentleman was..." from Whitelock's *Liber Familicus*, ed. John Bruce for the Camden Society, London, 1858

[119] ODNB, op.cit. – Davenant biographical entry by Mary Edmond

[120] Ref. Pl F2/1/24 10.4.1703 Portland (London) Collection: Catalogue of Family and Financial Papers of the Dukes of Portland, 1583-1940)

[121] See *Shakespeare-Neville, Cervantes and The Treaty of Boulogne* by Brenda James, Journal of Neville Studies, February, 2008

[122] See Winwood's Memorials, Vol. 2

[123] William Drummond, *Conversations at Hawthornden*, 1619

[124] p. 45, Winwood's Memorials, Vol 2

[125] Neville's friend and scribe, John Packer, also writes about the same masque in a letter to Ralph Winwood, dated 12th December, 1604 - p.39 *Winwood, vol.2, op.cit.*:

"Now Sir for Women's News. Wee have here great Preparation for the Queen's Mask; wherein besedes her Majesty will be eleven Ladies, Bedford, Suffolk, Susan Vere, Lady Dorothy Rich, a Daughter of my Lord Chamberlaines, Lady Walsingham, Lady Bevill, and some other which I have forgotten for haste. ..."

[126] See Anne Somerset, *Unnatural Murder, Poison at the Court of James I,* Phoenix Books, 1997

[127] "The king was there (Billingbear) lately and solemnly entertained, but was not so busy with the young wenches as the time before, having his head much troubled about an answer of his book..." p.105, *Dudley Carleton to John Chamberlain 1603 - 1624, Jacobean Letters,* ed. Maurice Lee Jr. University of New Jersey, 1972

[128] p. 140 *Winwood,* op.cit. Vol. 2

[129] notes for Matthew Gwinne by Iain Wrigh, ODNB, 2004 - 7 op.cit.

[130] p. 109. *Dudley Carleton to John Chamberlain, 1603 -1624* Jacobean letters, Ed. Maurice Lee, New Jersey, 1972

[131] ref. Reference: D/EN/L4
Case relating to Peter Gandon a Frenchman who brought it into Star Chamber and accused Henry Neville of piracy. (The Neville Papers, Berkshire Record Office.)

[132] p.141 Winwood, op. cit, Vol 2

[133] For further evidence, see also John Casson with Brenda James, Journal of Neville Studies, April 2007, op. cit.

[134] On 16th September, 1600, for instance, Neville asks Cecil if the Queen might be willing to finance a lapsed French priest, now married, on a spying mission into Spain. Neville seems delighted to explain the plan to Cecil:

...He will take upon him the Habit [i.e. disguise as a monk] and, for need, the function of a Priest, which will also give him credit and trust there, and means thereby to do better service. He hath been sundry times employed by this King, first at Bruxells ... and afterwards twice into Calais, while the Spaniards held it. Language he hath none perfect but the French. Spanish and Italian he understands, but speaketh not; but makes account within three months to speak Spanish sufficiently for his purpose.. *p. 104, Winwood, vol. 1op.cit*

[135] HISTORY OF PARLIAMENT – THE COMMONS – HASLAR, hmso 1981 – entry for Sir Henry Neville (c.1520 – 1593)

[136] Hasler, ibid

[137] Mormon genealogy database, founded on records now kept in the Guildhall Library.

[138] Reference: TH/VOL/II
Creation dates: 1542-1557 The Thynne Papers, Longleat House
Sir John Mason; 25 Feb. 1558. f.14: (c) on the match between his son and "Besse Gresham"

[139] Irwin Smith – *Shakespeare's Blackfriars Playhouse*, New York, 1964

[140] http://shakespeare.folger.edu/other/html/dfoloseley.html -
Guide to the Loseley Collection, 1489-1682 (bulk 1538-1630),L.b.1-712, Folger Shakespeare Library, ms. ref. L.b.348 More, Sir William. 1520-1600. Lease of a "house ... conteyninge ffour Romes" in the Blackfriars, to Sir Henr Neville. June 10, 1560

[141] Mormon database

[142] W.R. Stretberger *Court Revels 1485 – 1559* University of Toronto Press, 1994.

[143] Irwin Smith, op.cit. p.135

[144] This may have been an Italian fencing master, about whom there had been some complaints. Sir Henry Neville had clearly re-let part of the property at an even earlier date, probably once he had married Elizabeth Gresham and was thus able to return to Billingbear.

[145] Irwin Smith, op.cit. p.135

[146] p. 102, Irwin Smith, op.cit.

[147] The Losely House documents, Folger Library, op.cit. L.b.402 Cawarden, Sir Thomas. d. 1559. A survey of the buildings of Blackfriars. ca. 1555. - The inhabitants of Blackfriars in a petition had complained that Sir Thomas Cawarden had defaced their parish church, St. Anne's, Blackfriars, and had pulled down the roof. This document was probably prepared to be submitted to the Privy Council. It surveys the estate, points out which tenements had been bought from the king and which were included in the residue granted to Cawarden. It then presents an argument that the greater part of the maintenance and rebuilding of the church should fall upon the purchasers of tenements and not upon Cawarden. Printed in Feuillerat, 1913, pp. 1-6.
L.b.467 More, Sir William. 1520-1600. Notes regarding Blackfriars. ca. 1585. - Rough jottings concerning the title to gardens formerly part of the churchyard of St. Anne's Church. The gardens are claimed by Thomas Butcher, who claim, More asserts, is false. Entirely in More's autograph. The date is implied internally.

[148] Neville's 'Letter to a noble Lord', Neville Papers, Berkshire Record Office

[149] See notes for Sir Henry Neville (c.1520 - 1593) in HISTORY OF PARLIAMENT – THE COMMONS – HASLAR, hmso 1981

[150] MR. W. D'OYLY BAYLE is mistaken in supposing that Sir Henry Nevill, the first settler of his race at Billingbear, was thrice married. ... [there] is a fine ancient pedigree certified by Brooke in 1666, and corrected by Charles Nevill, Vice-Provost of Kings college, Cambridge, who was esteemed a learned herald in his day; and it seems impossible that he should have omitted all mention of his own grandfather's first wife. Your correspondent may consult, in Ashmole's Berkshire, vol. ii. p. 432, the account of the Nevill monument still extant in the church of Laurence Waltham, upon which are **the effigies of Sir Henry Nevill, his two wives, and his eldest son.** I do not trouble you with the inscription, as it has been frequently printed; but it removes all doubt on the subject. It is equally clear that all Sir Henry Nevill's children were the issue of his first lady, Elizabeth, daughter and sole heir of Sir John Gresham, including his eldest son and successor, who was sent in 1599 ambassador to France, and Catharine, who married Edmund D'Oyly, of Shottisham, Norfolk. With respect to the right of quartering the royal arms, I have always understood that Frances Lady Gresham, the mother of Lady Nevill, was ultimately sole heir of her parents, Sir Henry Thwaytes, of Lounds, and Anne Saville, who descended from the Pastons. Unquestionably the Lounds estates devolved upon the second Sir Henry Nevill, and were alienated by him, or his son and successor, the third knight of the same names, seated at Bilhlngbear.

Yours, &c. - BRAYBROOKE

[151] David Hume (1711-1776)
The History of England in Three Volumes, Vol.I., Part D - From Elizabeth to James I. 'Nevil was thrown into prison, and underwent a severe persecution...' Hume held Neville's writing to be a main example of the best from the times: "...and there want not productions of that age, which, being written by men who were not authors by profession, retain a very natural manner, and may give us some idea of the language which prevailed among men of the world. I shall particularly mention Sir John Davis's Discovery, and Throgmorton's, Essex's, and Nevil's letters. ..."

[152] F.E. Halliday, *The Shakespeare Companion* London, 1955, p.201

[153] F.E. Halliday, ibid

[154] Frank Kermode, *Shakespeare's Language*, op.cit.

[155] Harold Bloom, *Shakespeare - the Invention of the Human*, Fourth Estate, 1999

[156] See

http://www.wessexarch.co.uk/projects/marine/thameswreck/index.html
which is the Wessex Archaeology's report of its work with the Port of London Authority in recovering the lost ship and its cargo.

[157] M. Greengrass, 'Neville, Sir Henry (1561/2–1615)', Oxford Dictionary of National Biography, Oxford University Press, Sept 2004.

[158] See endnote 156

[159] See endnote 156

[160] Tim Cornish's research

[161] See Lansdown papers researched by Tim Cornish.

[162] For my fuller discussion of the significance of this sonnet and Neville's bearing of the 'canopy' mentioned therein, see *The Truth Will Out*, op.cit.

[163] *Henry IV, part 1, ACT4|SC4:*

> WARWICK (a 'Nevil') My gracious lord, you look beyond him quite.
> The Prince but studies his companions
> Like a strange tongue, wherein, to gain the language,
> 'Tis needful that the most immodest word
> Be look'd upon and learnt; which once attain'd,
> Your Highness knows, comes to no further use
> But to be known and hated. So, like gross terms,
> The Prince will, in the perfectness of time,
> Cast off his followers; and their memory
> Shall as a pattern or a measure live
> By which his Grace must mete the lives of other,
> Turning past evils to advantages.

[164] G.B. Harrison, *Elizabethan Plays and Players,* op.cit., and F.E. Halliday, op.cit.,(entry on 'Censorship of Plays')

[165] Brenda JamesVolume 1, issue 1, The Journal of Neville Studies

[166] L. Hicks, *An Elizabethan Problem,* London

[167] *Winwood's Memorials,* Vol. 2, op.cit., p.217

[168] *Contemporary Review,* Dec, 1998

[169] See Naunton's remarks that Neville was helping Savile with this at Eton and was trying to promote the book with Lord Hay, MONTAGU HOUSE PAPERS {HIST MSS COM}1899 edition 'Report on the Manuscipts of the Duke of Buccleuch and Queensberry, preserved at Montagu House, Whitehall, vol.1 [Eyre and Spottiswoode Her Majesty's Stationery Office.Historical Manuscripts commisssion : p.112 Sep 15 1612 Sir Robert Naunton to Winwood from Holeborne:

> Your letters of the 24th of August I received by Mr. Sa. Calvert about the 5th September. The same day, hearing that his Majesty was determiuned for Windesore, I went thither, and the next morning delivered your enclosed to Sir. H. Nevil at Sir H. Savill's in Eaton,... Sir Henry sought me out, as requesting me to show his Lordship [Lord Hay] the great work of his Chrysostome then under press,

[170] Ref. D/EN F6 2/1 - Neville Papers, Berkshire Record Office, letter from Sir Henry Killigrew.

[171] Historical Mss. Commission, op.cit., p.33 Sir Henry Savile to Mr. Winwood 1601 2Feb Westminster. ...Must know from the Vatican and the Library of Vienna whether there is any commentary by Chrysostom on any more Psalms than can be had here and in Paris. Names several foreigners from whom the information may be obtained. Giorgi, keeper of the library at Venice, is a great

acquaintance of the writer's brother, Thomas. Refers to a catalogue of Constantinople. Sends catalogures of "our books here."

[172] *Hamlet,* **Ham**. O, horrible! O, horrible! most horrible! {ACT1|SC5

[173] Ben Jonson epigram to Sir Henry Neville, 1610

[174] In Sir Henry's case, we know the identity of one of his scribes – John Packer – whom he often employed because he suffered from gout which affected his hands. – see letters from Packer himself in *Winwood,* Vol.2, op.cit. John Packer was also the scribe of Richard Martin's Treatise on the Royal Mint, now in the Worsley Collection at the Lincolnshire Archives. (This is just one of the factors which add weight to my contention that a whole section of that collection originally belonged to Sir Henry Neville.)

[175] See notes for Aurelian Townsend by Peter Beal in the ODNB, op.cit.

[176] See *Elements of Statistics* - an Open University Publication of 1995 by Daley, Hand, Jones, Lunn and McConway, pp.502 - 505

[177] See esp. *Winwood* , Vol. 2, p.35, op.cit.

[178] See Neville's Diplomatic Notebook, at the National Archives in Kew. See a transcription of this in R. Winwood,vol 1, op.cit. p.45

[179] Winwood, Vol 2, p.216

[180] See Haslar, History of Parliament, op.cit. Notes for Sir Henry Neville (1562 - 1615)

[181] Ted Warren, author

[182] Winwood vol 1 p.81, letter from Neville to Cecil, 28th July, 1599

[183] p.127 *Shakespeare's Language* by Frank Kermode, London 2000

[184] Winwood, vol.1 op.cit. pp.303-304

[185] It may be relevant that Neville was made a member of the Brotherhood of the Guildhall in Windsor - see Haslar, op.cit.

[186] British Library, Sloane Manuscript 1792

[187] 'Sir Henry Killigrew, Elizabethan Soldier and Diplomat' by Amos C. Miller, Leicester, 1963. Also see various letters of Neville's, mentioning William Killigrew, in Winwood, vol.1 op.cit. For Neville's friendship with Robert Killigrew, see Anne Somerset, op.cit. 'Shakespeare' is also said to have given Robert Killigrew a handwritten version of Sonnet no. 2.

[188] See my description of the documentary evidence in *The Truth Will Out,* James and Rubinstein, op.cit.

[189] The Paper was originally published in 1931, then reprinted in 1972 by Haskell House Publishers, New York

[190] Richard Topcliffe (1532 - 1604), who maintained a private torture chamber - see Alan and Veronica Palmer, 2000, op.cit.

[191] See A.L. Rowse on this subject - p.4, *The Elizabethan Renaissance - the cultural achievement,* A.L. Rowse, Edinburgh, 1972

[192] Probably a satirical reference to the 'Master-Mistress' in Sonnet 20.

[193] See notes for William Herbert, Third Earl of Pembroke, by Victor Stater in the ODNB. Also, Robert Lomas, *The Invisible College,* op.cit. , p.186

[194] See Lomas, *The Invisible College,* ibid

[195] Lomas, ibid.

[196] See Lomas, ibid.

[197] See my article on *The Coast of Bohemia* in <u>www.henryneville.com</u>

[198] See notes for Beavis Bulmer in the ODNB, op.cit.

[199] *Winwood, Vol 2*, p. 78

[200] See notes for Phillip Herbert by David L. Smith in the ODNB, op. cit

[201] See the correspondence from Elizabeth Bacon-D'Oyly-Neville in the Neville Papers at the Berks. Record Office.

[202] Lambeth Palace Library FILE - Bacon papers - ref. MS 936 - date: 1594-1624, 249 Speech in the Privy Council against James Whitelock, [12 June 1613]. Draft in Bacon's hand. Works, XI, 353-6. 2 ff.

[203] See Simons' letters to Sir Henry Neville, (Neville Papers, Berkshire Record Office.)

[204] ref. D/EN F6 3/3 Berkshire Record Office - Letter from Simons to Sir Henry Neville: "...The use of his [Neville's son's] time and moderation of his expense I would he had such care of, that he might satisfie you. My miserie is, that I am interested in both, and cannot, according to my desire, helpe either. As you have given me order to send for money, soe I beseech you, give him charge to have care of the employinge of it, ..."

[205] John Chamberlain's letters, op.cit. In one of them, written in 1616, Chamberlain tells how 'Sir Henry Neville' dined with them all at a large banquet. It is strange that neither he nor Dudley Carleton ever mentioned Neville's death in their letters (though they were friends of Neville and constantly writing of him when he was alive) and that Chamberlain here is talking as if this is still the same Sir Henry at the banquet, even though Neville is reported to have died in July, 1615. There is also a strange letter in one of the Worsley Collection's HN notebooks, which suggests Neville *may* still have been alive in 1617, so my investigations are necessarily ongoing!

[206] See Dr. John Casson with Brenda James: EVIDENCE FOR THE AUTHORSHIP OF SHAKESPEARE-NEVILLE IN DOUBLE FALSHOOD: THE 'LOST' PLAY OF CARDENIO in *The Journal of Neville Studies, Vol.1.issue 1, April, 2007*

[207] See Ben Jonson, 'To my beloved, the author, Mr. William Shakespeare' in the Dedicatory Verses to the First Folio, 1623

[208] See Robert Lomas, *The Invisible College,* op.cit. p.186

[209] See *Winwood* op.cit. Vol 3, p. 235 - letter from Mr. More to Ralph Winwood, 1st Dec., 1610: "... Thereupon Sir Henry Neville did directly answer to the first, that he thought indeed his Majesty was in want, ... 'Then', said the King, 'Tell me whether it belongeth to you that are my subjects to relieve me or not'. To this, quoth Sir Harry, I must answer with a distinction: Where your Majesty's expense groweth by the Commonwealth, we are bound to maintain it; otherwise not.

[210] *Plato Redivivus* by Sir Henry Neville, 1683. This is written by Sir Henry's grandson, in the form of a dialogue between a Venetian visitor and an English Gentleman, who is trying to explain the reasons behind the English Civil War (1640 - 1649.) The 'Gentleman' begins by putting forward possible reasons why both political philosophers and monarchs have heretofore not wanted to discuss the nature of a new type of Constitution, based on a true partnership between a monarch and Parliament. In doing so, Neville relates the experience of his own grandfather, our Sir Henry:

ENG. GENT. ...possibly, such a reformation might not consist with the merchandize they make of the prince's favour; nor with such bribes, gratuities and fees as they usually take for the dispatch of all matters before them. And therefore our counsellors have been so far from suggesting any such thing to their master, that they have opposed and quashed all attempts of that kind: as they did the worthy proposals made by certain members of that parliament in the beginning of king James's reign, which is yet called the undertaking parliament. These gentlemen considering what we have been discoursing of, viz. that our old government is at an end; had framed certain heads, which, if they had been proposed by that parliament to the king, and by him consented to, would, in their opinion, have healed the breach: and that if the king would perform his part, that house of commons would undertake for the obedience of the people. They did believe that if this should have been moved in parliament before the king was acquainted with it, it would prove abortive; and therefore sent three of their number to his majesty: sir James Croft, grandfather or father to the present bishop of Hereford; Thomas Harley, who was ancestor to the honourable family of that name in Herefordshire; and sir Henry Neville, who had been ambassador from queen Elizabeth to the French king. These were to open the matter at large to the king, and to procure his leave that it might be proposed in parliament: which, after a very long audience and debate, that wise prince consented to; with a promise of secrecy in the meantime, which they humbly begged of his majesty. However, this took vent; and the earl of Northampton, of the house of Howard, (who ruled the roost in that time) having knowledge of it, engaged sir R. Weston, afterwards lord treasurer and earl of Portland, to impeach these undertakers in parliament, before they could move their matters: which he did the very same day; accompanying his charge (which was endeavouring to alter the established government of England) with so eloquent an invective, that if one of them had not risen, and made the house acquainted with the whole series of the affair, they must have been in danger of being impeached by the commons, but however it broke their design, which was all that Northampton and Weston desired; and prevented posterity from knowing any of the particulars of this reformation: for nothing being moved, nothing could remain upon the journal.

So that, you see, our predecessors were not ignorant altogether of our condition; though the troubles which have befallen this poor kingdom since, have made it much more apparent; ...

[211] p. 22, *Ben Jonson and the First Folio,* by Lansdown Goldsworth, reprinted 1972 by Haskell House Publishers Ltd., New York

[212] W. Lansdown Goldsworthy 'Ben Jonson and the First Folio', reprinted by Haskell House, New York, 1972

[213] Jonson's introduction to his Epigrams, which were published in 1611 makes a specific statement that he does not need a code to introduce his poems, which has strongly suggested to scholars that he knew Shakespeare's Sonnets (published two years earlier) had been introduced by one.

[214] See Chapters 1 - 6

[215] See *Shakespeare-Neville, Cervantes and The Treaty of Boulogne* by Brenda James, Journal of Neville Studies, February, 2008.

Index

LaVergne, TN USA
05 August 2010
192250LV00007B/31/P